14. 50

Decoding the Past

Decoding the Past

The Psychohistorical Approach

Peter Loewenberg

ALFRED A. KNOPF · NEW YORK · 1983

Copyright© 1969, 1971, 1974, 1975, 1982 by Peter Loewenberg.
All rights reserved under International and Pan-American Copyright Conventions. Published in
the United States by Alfred A. Knopf, Inc., New York, and simultaneously in Canada by
Random House of Canada Limited, Toronto. Distributed by Random House, Inc., New York.

Some of the essays in this volume previously appeared in slightly altered form in *The Center
Magazine, The American Historical Review,* and the *Psychohistory Review.*

Grateful acknowledgment is made to the following for permission to reprint previously
published material:

The Journal of Higher Education: "Emotional Problems of Graduate Education," by Peter
Loewenberg, *The Journal of Higher Education,* 40, no. 8 (Nov. 1969): 610–23. Reprinted by
permission. Copyright © 1969 by the Ohio State University Press.

Cornell University Press: From Peter Loewenberg, "Psychohistory," in *The Past Before Us:
Contemporary Historical Writing in the United States,* edited for the American Historical
Association by Michael Kammen, pp. 408–32. Copyright © 1980 by Cornell University. Used
by permission of the publisher, Cornell University Press.

Library of Congress Cataloging in Publication Data
Loewenberg, Peter.
  Decoding the past.
  1. Psychohistory. I. Title.
D16.16.L68 1983   901'.9   82-47796
ISBN 0-394-48152-6

Manufactured in the United States of America
First Edition

For two Sams,
Anna Sophie, and Gracie

It might be described as the *"decoding"* method, since it treats dreams as a kind of cryptography. . . . The essence of the decoding procedure, however, lies in the fact that the work of interpretation is not brought to bear on the dream as a whole but on each portion of the dream's content independently, as though the dream were a geological conglomerate in which each fragment of rock required a separate assessment.

—Freud, The Interpretation of Dreams

Du gleichst dem Geist,
den Du begreifst.

You resemble the spirit which you comprehend.

—Goethe, Faust, Part I

The true history of the human race is the history of human affection. In comparison with it all other histories—including economic history—are false.
—E. M. Forster, "De Senectute"

Contents

Acknowledgments *xi*

On Psychohistory: *A Statement on Method* *3*

PART I
Psychoanalysis and History: *The Scope of the Problem* *9*
  Psychohistory: An Overview of the Field *14*

PART II
The Education of a Psychohistorian *43*
  Emotional Problems of Graduate Education *48*
  The Graduate Years: What Kind of Passage? *59*
  Love and Hate in the Academy *67*
  The Psychobiographical Background to Psychohistory:
  The Langer Family and the Dynamics of Shame and Success *81*

PART III

Austrian Portraits: *Identity, Murder, and Vacillation*   97

  Theodor Herzl: Nationalism and Politics   101

  Victor and Friedrich Adler: Revolutionary Politics and Generational Conflict in Austro-Marxism   136

  Austro-Marxism and Revolution: Otto Bauer, Freud's "Dora" Case, and the Crises of the First Austrian Republic   161

PART IV

The German Case: *Leaders, Followers, and Group Process*   205

  The Unsuccessful Adolescence of Heinrich Himmler   209

  The Psychohistorical Origins of the Nazi Youth Cohort   240

Index   285

Acknowledgments

To give recognition to those who have taught and stimulated me, listened to and criticized me, shared with and supported me, is highly satisfying. I wish to acknowledge my teachers: Wilbur R. Jacobs, from whom I first learned the pleasures of history; the late Raymond J. Sontag, who taught me the disciplines of political and diplomatic history and archival research; Werner T. Amgress, who taught me German history; Nicholas V. Riasanovsky, who was sympathetic to a psychohistorical approach when it counted; and Carl E. Schorske, who imparted his appreciation of social and cultural history. His delight in intellectual history and his acute sensibility to the psychological nuances of culture are lasting ideals.

I am deeply indebted to my teachers in the theory and clinical practice of psychoanalysis, Sigmund Gabe, and John A. Lindon, who taught me that there are more ways of understanding human behavior than were admitted to in history departments in my student days. To the members of the Southern California Psychoanalytic Institute and above all to Samuel Eisenstein, who from 1969 to 1977 was chairman of its Education Committee and director of its Training School, I acknowledge the invaluable opportunity to learn psychoanalysis from within on both sides of the couch, as an analy-

sand, as a clinician, and as a teacher. Dr. Eisenstein's energy and enthusiasm
are largely responsible for the sustained support of the research training
program of the Southern California Psychoanalytic Institute, and his vision
of the mutual enrichment of both academia and psychoanalysis through
intensive personal knowledge is a continued inspiration.

In a profession such as history, which is often resistant to change and
wary of new approaches to old problems, the editor of its leading scholarly
journal is frequently an orthodox influence who fears to travel new paths,
preferring to stay within the secure boundaries and well-trodden routes of
traditional scholarship. By contrast, from 1968 to 1975, our profession was
fortunate in having R. K. Webb as editor of *The American Historical Review*.
He and his competent managing editor, Nancy Lane, were, at an early and
critical time, open to new enterprises in psychohistorical scholarship. Their
discernment fostered the maturation of the field of psychohistory and moved
the scholarly understanding of our collective past a decisive step forward.
Those who had the courage and wisdom to risk sponsoring psychohistory
before it was fashionable to do so deserve a special acknowledgment and it
is a privilege to record it.

I often learn best by trying out my ideas on others. Among the real
gratifications of a life in academia is the emotional and intellectual intercourse with colleagues who are generous with their talents, time, and themselves. For the tactful balance of counsel and criticism that the following
friends gave me, there is no substitute. For my errors I, of course, am alone
responsible. My work is better to the extent I was able to assimilate the
insights shared by my past and present colleagues at UCLA: Robert Dallek,
Richard Weiss, the late Fawn Brodie, Isser Woloch, Arthur J. Slavin,
Temma Kaplan, Amos Funkenstein, Hans Rogger, Frank Otto Gatell, Daniel W. Howe, David O. Sears, Franklin Mendels, Albert Hutter, and Erhard
Bahr.

Those who work in new fields such as psychocultural studies often share
manuscripts, thoughts, and problems. I have benefited from the good minds
and hearts of scholars in many fields whose work has been informed by
psychodynamic perspectives and has immeasurably enriched my own. These
include the late Margarete Ruben, Miriam Williams, Heiman van Dam,
Jerald Simon, Rudolf Ekstein, Martin Grotjahn, Alfred Goldberg, Los Angeles; John Hassler and Robert Nemiroff, San Diego; Norman Reider, San
Francisco; William Niederland, Jules Glenn, Martin Wangh, Jacob Arlow,
and Oscar Sachs, New York; Pietro Castelnuovo-Tedesco, Nashville;
Charles Kligerman, George H. Pollock, Chicago; oncologist David Plotkin
and forensic dentist Reidar F. Sognnaes, Los Angeles.

I am the beneficiary of expertise and kindness, correction and criticism,
freely given by Frank E. Manuel, Brandeis University; John Fitzpatrick, the

Menninger Foundation; George Kren, Kansas State University; Andrew Rolle, Occidental College; Eberhard Jäckel, University of Stuttgart; Geoffrey C. Cocks, Albion College; Judith and Stuart Hughes, U.C., San Diego; William McGrath, University of Rochester; Robert G. L. Waite, Williams College; Fred Weinstein, SUNY Stony Brook; Herbert Moller, Boston University; the late Eric Kollman, Cornell College; the late Robert Kann, Rutgers University; Nathan Leites, RAND Corporation, and Elizabeth W. Marvick, Claremont Colleges. I also profited from participation in the Los Angeles Interdisciplinary Psychoanalytic Study Group, whose members, Drs. Ernst Lewy, Alfred Goldberg, Robert Dorn, Ira Carson, Gerald Aronson, Herbert Kupper, and Professors Alexander George, E. V. Wolfenstein, Fawn Brodie, and Arthur Slavin, met regularly from 1966 to 1970.

Research in recent history offers the prospect of using living sources—the oral history of recollections held by those who participated in events and were themselves, or personally knew, the central people involved. Among those who graciously consented to interviews were the late Paul Lazarsfeld, New York; Marie Jahoda, Sussex, England; Hans Zeisel, Chicago; Carl Schorske, Princeton; Rowena Morse Langer, Cambridge, Mass.; Joseph Buttinger and Muriel Gardiner, New York; Kurt Herbert Adler, San Francisco; Mendel Singer, Haifa; Ella Lingens, Chancellor Bruno Kreisky, Manfred Ackerman, Josef Pleyl, the late Jacques Hannak and Hilda Hannak, Wanda Lanzer, Ernst Winkler, Anton Pick, Vienna; and J. W. Breugel, London. Peter Merkl and Ronald Inglehart shared their research with me prior to publication; Douglas D. Alder generously gave me copies of the court psychiatric reports on Friedrich Adler in his possession.

Timely material support of my training and research was given by the following institutions: the Austrian Cultural Institute and Ministry of Education, German Fulbright Commission, National Foundation for Jewish Culture, Ford Foundation, Social Science Research Council, American Council of Learned Societies, Rockefeller Foundation, Memorial Foundation for Jewish Culture, National Endowment for the Humanities, John Simon Guggenheim Memorial Foundation, Academic Senate Research Committee of UCLA, and the University of California Humanities Fellowships. To all these I am thankful for facilitating my researches.

A historian is helpless without the aid and goodwill of archivists, who can guide or frustrate him, who may be giving or withholding. The best of guides is Michael Heymann, director of the Central Zionist Archives, Jerusalem. I am also indebted to archivists Sven Bodin, Archive of the Swedish Worker's Movement, Stockholm; Absalom Hodik, Jewish Historical General Archive, Jerusalem; Esther Sadan, Archives of the Hashomir Hatzair in Kibbutz Merhavia; the staffs of the Israel Labor Party Archive, Beit Berl, and the Histadrut Archive, Tel Aviv; Götz Lenkau and Daisy

Devrees, International Institute for Social History in Amsterdam; Herbert Steiner and Peter Neugebauer, Dokumentationsarchiv des Österreichischen Widerstandes, Vienna; Rudolf Neck, Haus-, Hof- und Staatsarchiv, Vienna; Ernst K. Herlitzka, Archiv für Geschichte der Arbeiterbewegung, Vienna; Irene Wagner, Labour Party Archives, Transport House, London; Robert Wistrich Jerusalem and Walter Laqueur, Wiener Library and Institute of Contemporary History, London; Fred Grubel and Sybil Milton, Archives of the Leo Baeck Institute, New York. Other archives and depositories that contributed to my work were the Institut für Zeitgeschichte, Munich; Political Archive of the Foreign Ministry, Bonn; National Archives, Washington, D.C.; Centre de Documentation Juive Contemporaine, Paris; Archives Romain Rolland, Paris.

While I was away from home I particularly appreciated the hospitality and generosity of Harald and Arlette Leupold-Löwenthal, Heinz and Margit Fischer, Otto and Siguna Hartmann, Thomas and Dalia Smolka, Vienna; Arthur Mitzman and Marleen Wessel, Amsterdam; Shlomo and Miriam Giwati, Kibbutz Matsuva; Kurt and Kati Spillmann and Ferdinand and Joanna Meyer, Zürich.

From my psychiatrist father I learned the value of systematic psychological understanding of political affairs; my mother demonstrated to me the importance of engagement in the cause of social justice. My students and my patients taught me precious private lessons about men, women, history, and self. Angus Cameron and Barbara Bristol of Alfred A. Knopf did all of the things editors should do and more. To all of them I am grateful.

Decoding the Past

On Psychohistory

A Statement on Method

Psychohistory is currently crystallizing as a vital method of historical research and conceptualization. This volume is conceived as a contribution to
an emerging synthesis between the disciplines of history and psychoanalysis.
The papers it contains represent over a decade and a half of exploration of
the frontier between the humanistic, social, political, analytic, and narrative
crafts of history and the clinical art of psychoanalysis. I believe psychohistory to be the most powerful of interpretive approaches to history because
(1) it is the only model of research that includes in its method the countertransference phenomenon—the emotional and subjective sensibility of the
observer—and (2) it enriches the historical account of political, social, and
cultural-intellectual events with a perception of latent or unconscious
themes, of style, content, and conflict, that integrate apparently discordant
data from a specific historical locus.

Both history and psychoanalysis rely on the arts of interpretation and
communication. Psychoanalysis clinically, and history by "immersion" in
the vestiges of the past—thought, documents, artifacts, and physical ambiance—share the quality of placing the observer in the midst of the field he
analyzes and requiring of him a special mixture of identification and detach-

ment as a prerequisite to interpretation. The subjective aspect of both clinical and historical experience is an integral part of psychoanalysis as well as
history. Whereas in psychoanalysis it is a canon of method, in history it is
often denied or unrecognized. It is high time that historians take from
psychoanalysis its scientific approach to human subjectivity. This means
recognizing, taking seriously, and utilizing the cardinal discoveries of the
transference and countertransference: the bringing of unconscious patterns
of feelings, attitudes, behaviors, fantasies, loves, and hates, from other persons and periods of one's life into the present. The transference is always
ambivalent, and usually rooted in experiences with significant others, such
as parents, siblings, grandparents, servants, and teachers from earlier periods of life. Transference is the terrain on which the battle against the
neurosis is fought; its resolution defines the psychoanalytic cure.

The analysand's unconscious is perceived by the analyst in his own
countertransference responses. As Freud put it: "Everyone possesses in his
own unconscious an instrument with which he can interpret the utterances
of the unconscious in other people." He further said: "It is a very remarkable
thing that the *unconscious* of one human being can react upon that of
another, without passing through the *conscious.*" This is empathy achieved
by the analyst at a preverbal, non-linguistic level. Freud called for the
analyst to "turn his own unconscious like a receptive organ towards the
transmitting unconscious of the patient. He must adjust himself to the
patient as a telephone receiver is adjusted to the transmitting microphone."
Thus the countertransference need not bar communication; indeed, it may
facilitate transmission and a profound depth of perception, both clinically
and in historical research. The analyst's constant scrutiny and use of his
countertransference feelings guides him in perceiving communications from
the analysand's unconscious and in interpreting the meanings of his behavior, feelings, and thoughts. The psychoanalyst's task is to become an integral
part of the psychic field of the analysand and to experience it as fully as
possible without either being damaged by its tensions or resisting its power.
The result is the establishment of a new field of work known as the psychoanalytic situation. The object of research, the analysand, and the researcher, in his subjectivity, fuse and mutually influence each other while
also maintaining autonomy in large areas of life. Transference and resistance, says Hans Loewald, "are basic phenomena, interactional phenomena,
of psychic life, and . . . no psychoanalytic investigation is possible without
their making their appearance and being taken into account."[1]

When historians immerse themselves in the documents, data, and literature of a period, when they visit the locale of events and interview the
principal actors, they strive to achieve an empathic understanding of a
period and to establish the clearest possible direct communication with it.

Historians are as susceptible to transference and countertransference in their work as are other humans. They are as subject to anxiety emanating from their data and to defensive reactions that distort perceptions and interpretations and give rise to resistances in understanding. Yet good historical method should not empty the data of their anxiety-arousing content. Anxiety-inducing material must be taken in, assimilated, and dealt with in a cognitive manner. The anthropologist George Devereux conceptualized the value of countertransference in research:

> The disturbance occurs "within" the observer and it is this disturbance which is then experienced as the real stimulus and treated as the relevant datum. It is logically permissible to say that it is this— and only this—disturbance to which the observer reacts by saying: "And this I perceive."[2]

Much historical narrative and explanation, especially that concerned with surface description, obsessive detail, rational order, and "common sense" explanations, reflects the historian's defense against unconsciously disturbing material. Of course, history does not involve a direct personal interchange with the subject, as does a clinical interview. But historical data of all kinds do have an intrapsychic dimension, albeit a unidirectional one. History is communication with the past, usually but not exclusively, through the medium of language. There is a basic intellectual-emotional bond between the historian and his material from the past, be it personal documents, geography, papers of state, or cultural artifacts such as buildings, paintings, and music. There is, as R. G. Collingwood maintained, a necessary communication between past historical creators and present historian perceivers.[3] The historian should be capable of some kind of genuine contact with the cognitive and emotional communications from the past.

The process of historical perception may be analogized to the psychoanalyst's relation to the analysand's productions. Freud called for the analyst to listen with "evenly suspended attention." "We will suspend our judgement and give our impartial attention to everything that there is to observe."[4] This injunction defines a special kind of perceptive objectivity that is of value to historians. It means the perceiver should give no special, a priori significance to any aspect of the communication. He must allow his unconscious to scan the material as freely as possible, and suspend for the moment the models of his intellectual armamentarium that will later direct his attention. The researcher must be able to tolerate the lack of control of the experience. Thus the historian and the analyst discover the unconscious connections in a communication.

For Freud this demand upon the analyst was the counterpart to his "fundamental rule of psychoanalysis" for the analysand: "that he should communicate everything that occurs to him without criticism or selection." "The rule for the doctor," said Freud, "may be expressed: 'He should withhold all conscious influences from his capacity to attend, and give himself over completely to his 'unconscious memory.' "

> Just as the patient must relate everything that his self-observation can detect, and keep back all the logical and affective objections that seek to induce him to make a selection from among them, so the doctor must put himself in a position to make use of everything he is told for the purposes of interpretation and of recognizing the concealed unconscious material without substituting a censorship of his own for the selection that the patient has foregone.

The ideal historian, as the ideal analyst, in Freud's words, "may not tolerate any resistances in himself which hold back from his consciousness what has been perceived by his unconscious. . . . there can be no reasonable doubt about the disqualifying effect of such defects in the doctor; every unresolved repression in him constitutes what has been aptly described by Stekel as a 'blind spot' in his analytic perception."[5] How many historical "blind spots" do we know of in ourselves and can we see in the work of others? This, indeed, constitutes the stuff of historiography—tracing and analyzing the unconscious scotomata of past historians. Any such exercise ought to teach humility to the present rather than self-righteousness toward the past.

How is anxiety-inducing material dealt with in analysis? How are we to cope with the "blind spots" resulting from unconscious selection and distortion that interferes with our ability to grasp historical meanings? Freud was insistent that a knowledge of unconscious processes "will be sought in vain from studying books and attending lectures." There is no substitute for thorough psychoanalytic training, including an experience as an analysand, for the historian who would become sensitive to psychological data. Perhaps an adequate conversance with economics or statistics can be acquired by reading and study alone. But psychodynamic insight is qualitatively of a different order, as are linguistics and cultural anthropology, which demand field work of their practitioners, because the total personality is engaged in the research. That conscious and unconscious perception of what Theodor Reik called "the third ear," with which the psychoanalyst listens for unconscious communications,[6] cannot be developed by the intellectual enterprise of reading the corpus of psychoanalytic works. What is required is an analysis of the defenses of the ego—the inhibitory and selective functions of cognition, an emphasis on what is felt and feared to be felt, rather than what is reasoned. The psychoanalyst analyzes his countertransference by focusing and pursuing to their unconscious source feelings of anxiety. Self-analysis is the way that historians can eliminate in themselves defenses against understanding portions of their materials of research.

What Freud demanded as a psychoanalytic ideal and what historians may derive from him in method is an unconscious scanning of the mass of analytic material to discern the themes and conflicts that reveal the inner life of a person. Historian Frank Manuel estimates that every classical psychoanalysis produces about ten million words of clinical data.[7] This is analogous to the flood of data that confronts any modern historian. It is not logically ordered or easily accessible to conceptual analysis and rational apprehension. We must listen to the chaotic disorder of raw data for the dialectical flow of relationships and connections out of which we create coherence. To do this we must listen with the suspended motives and free-floating attention of psychoanalysts.

Programmatic statements on psychohistory, however valuable they once were in opening the field, are now not enough. It is time for psychohistorians to demonstrate how they work and to practice their craft in concrete historical research. Whether the method makes a permanent contribution to historical method will, in the last analysis, be tested in the empirical task of doing history.

In these pages, I have explored the training of a psychohistorian and examined the method of psychohistory applied to studies of personality and leadership, cultures, groups, and mass movements. The issues are raised, not settled; the debate is continuing, not closed. I have chosen as my forum the half century from 1895 to 1945 in Europe. The two decades from 1895 to 1914 mark the rise and theoretical development of Marxian socialism, which made the Social Democratic parties the largest in Central Europe on the eve of World War I. Culturally they witnessed the Secession in Vienna and Berlin, the birth of expressionism in art and theater, and the development of a new architecture. A novel twentieth-century nationalism emerged which was to create new states in Europe, the Near East, and the Third World, and great discoveries transformed man's view of himself, his culture and creativity, and, not the least, his view of his past. The years 1914 to 1945 were a revolutionary period that can only be compared with 1517–1525, 1618–1648, and 1798–1815 as times of such decisive change in institutions and relationships, and in man's view of himself, that the world would never be the same again. Here are the two generations molded by two world wars, the Russian Revolution, fascism and Nazism: the generations that saw the power of psychotic fantasy to turn words into nightmares lived, and the power of words to turn fantasy into political actuality.

I hope these investigations on the interface of history and psychoanalysis may contribute to a necessary discussion and reexamination of method, data, and self in the places where history is practiced and enjoyed. History is not the collective memory of mankind. It is the reformation and reinterpretation of that memory by each historian according to his time, social circumstance, method, and subjective past. We desperately need new canons of validity, methods of analysis, and techniques of research, applied to the historian's traditional areas of political, social, and economic research. We also need to open new vistas of exploration into emotional areas of man's experience of the past—the qualities of feeling, passion, and temperament that are transmitted by records and artifacts. In studying man's past, we are also, inevitably, studying ourselves. In doing so, our empathic capacity is our most valuable, and most humane, tool of understanding.

Notes

1. Sigmund Freud, "The Disposition to Obsessional Neurosis: A Contribution to the Problem of Choice of Neurosis" (1913), *Standard Edition of the Complete Psychological Works,* trans. and ed. James Strachey et al. (London, 1953–1974), 12: 320; "The Unconscious" (1915), *ibid.,* 14: 194; "Recommendations to Physicians Practising Psycho-Analysis" (1912), *ibid.,* 12: 115–16; Hans W. Loewald, "Psychoanalytic Theory and the Psychoanalytic Process," *Psychoanalytic Study of the Child* (New York, 1970), 25: 55.

2. George Devereux, *From Anxiety to Method in the Behavioral Sciences* (The Hague and Paris, 1967), pp. 301–2.

3. R. G. Collingwood, *The Idea of History* (New York, 1946, 1956), pp. 215–93.

4. Freud, "Recommendations to Physicians Practising Psycho-Analysis," p. III; "Analysis of a Phobia in a Five-Year-Old Boy" (1909), *Standard Edition,* 10: 23.

5. Freud, "Recommendations to Physicians Practising Psycho-Analysis," pp. 112, 115, 116.

6. *Ibid.,* p. 117; Theodor Reik, *Listening with the Third Ear: The Inner Experience of a Psycho-Analyst* (New York, 1948).

7. Frank E. Manuel, "The Use and Abuse of Psychology in History," *Dædalus,* 100 (1971): 197.

PART I

Psychoanalysis and History

The Scope of the Problem

History is both what happened in the past and the historian's account of it. Today, we have a proliferation of organizing principles, or models of understanding, and an explosion of new kinds of evidence about the past. We need new canons of validity, methods of analysis, and techniques of research applied to the historian's traditional subject matter—change in time.

The notion of change is a primary epistemological principle for the historian. Every action connotes a change of some kind or quality and this implies continuity through time. Each event is the culmination of preparations, and it is also the inception of further developments. All human actions realize implicit trends within past situations and generate new situations for future evolution. This time axis permits the historian to conceive of every fact in terms of a covering model and of every generalization in terms of unique events. The historian poses to the humanist the question of the temporal dependency and conditioning of a discrete event or artifact of culture. On the other hand, of the behavioral and social scientist who seeks abstract typologies, the historian asks: "Why now? Why did these events occur at *this* particular time?" The historian studies the relationship of events in a specific time series. He has a multifaceted, pluralistic, and infinite notion of change. He relates the dynamic of human activity across many structures—for example, from the realm of ideology to economic and social activity *and vice versa.* He also treats time relatively—by moving backward retrospectively from a consummation, as does Marc Bloch; by freezing the moving process at a given point and looking at a cross-section of society, as does Jacob Burckhardt; or by considering the immanent, developing trends of a situation from a beginning toward a point of completion in time, as do most historians.

I take my position firmly in the camp of the historical relativists who stress the import of both the conscious and unconscious interactions between historian observer and historical subject. I question both the knowability of the past and the autonomy of the historian's organizing faculties. The anxious clinging to "hard" facts and the refusal to view "facts" in any but what is interpreted as the "obvious" way—i.e., in the manner which a given researcher can tolerate and therefore "see"—is the scholarly analogue to the psychoanalyst's countertransference. Freud introduced the therapist's unconscious feelings into the essence of the therapeutic situation; Einstein and Heisenberg placed the physicist as an integral part of scientific experiment; but the historian as a person is yet to be placed as a subjective consciousness in the historical enterprise. No phenomenon has an inherent meaning. It becomes a datum by being assigned a frame of reference which confers meaning. The observation, recording, and interpretation of historical phenomena are related, and responsive, to the historian's personal psychodynamics. The historian's personality accounts, not only for the historical material and themes selected, but also for the conscious and unconscious conceptual schemata imposed upon it. Distortion arises from the failure to account for the observer in each act of knowledge. It is particularly marked where the historical material mobilizes unconscious anxiety which is then defended against by unconscious denial, obviation, misunderstanding, ambiguity, reversal, or even neglect of material.

My solution to this problem of cognition, and it is an imperfect and always a partial solution, is to bring the countertransference feelings into consciousness and to *use them as a tool of perception.* All research is unconsciously self-relevant, regardless of how distant it appears to be from the self on a detached scholarly level. All research represents indirect, and often circumlocutory, introspection. This indirect self-examination should be especially obvious to those in the historical and humanistic disciplines. The development and enlargement of the realm of healthy observing ego—the capacity to simultaneously be both subject and observer—will foster a creative awareness and empathy with the object of study. The identification of subject with object calls, not for denial and defensive maneuvers, but for a conscious policy of rational management and exploitation in the service of objectivity.

Psychohistory

An Overview of the Field

"Love has to be reinvented," said Rimbaud. History too needs to be reinvented by every historian and each generation. The task of this generation has been to dilate the traditional meanings and definitions of historical research to include the behavioral and human sciences. Psychohistory, one of the newest methods of historical research, combines historical analysis with social science models, humanistic sensibility, and psychodynamic theory and clinical insights to create a fuller, more rounded view of life in the past. The psychohistorian is aware of the dynamic interaction of character, society, and human thought and action. This is consonant with the historian's traditional commitment to the unity of man and culture, of life and ideas, in past and present. For historians have always recognized the existence of the non-rational and the irrational in history, but their categories of explanation have too often been limited to the utilitarian, materialistic, or intellectual rationality of motives. Now we have enlarged and refined concepts of explanation of human conduct to include the emotional and unconscious basis of historical thought and action.

Historians now recognize more clearly than ever before the integral subjective relationship between the researcher and his work. We also acknowledge that there is no external criterion of what is admissible, relevant, or excludable and unimportant in history. Each historian and each age redefines categories of evidence in the light of its needs, sensibilities, and perceptions. Among the new recognitions is that both "external" social and political events and more personal life and family settings predispose historians to given kinds of materials, values, research problems, and interpretations.[1]

The forces of passion and irrationality which are all about us, as well as in us, are so overwhelming in history that only by the utmost stretching of all plausibility can they be denied. There are many phenomena which a conventional political-social history cannot adequately account for with utilitarian and material categories of explanation. Historians are scrupulous and painstaking in ascertaining whether an event has taken place and when it occurred. Yet in explaining the event they have too often been content with the amateur maxims of common sense and the explanation of historical "accident" to cover blunders, coincidence of events, or subjective feelings in the historian that are too uncomfortable to face. Historians must be determinists. The attribution of historical events to "accidents" is usually the historian's way of saying: "I do not know or cannot look any further."

Historians see in their materials only what they are prepared to perceive. Thus the value of any conceptual framework is what new combinations of data or inferences from the data it may contribute to the historian's ability to interpret documents and the other raw material of history. A knowledge of psychodynamics sensitizes the historical researcher to nuances of shifting relationships in the documentary material that he might not otherwise notice and respond to. Psychohistorians treat the same sources as other historians: government documents, diaries, journals, and memoirs, cultural and literary artifacts, account books and fiscal data. However, they observe them with new lenses.

A psychological contribution to history consists of three essentials: (1) It seeks the function of the unconscious in human behavior as evidenced by life styles, adaptations, creativity and sublimations, character, slips of speech, hearing, and writing, errors, accidents, dreams, neuroses and psychoses, and human action or inhibition. (2) Psychohistory is a genetic approach in the sense that it is *historical.* It emphasizes the importance of origins, antecedents, and patterns of repetition. Thus it is developmental—stressing the longitudinal growth and adaptation of the person, including events and learned behaviors from infancy, childhood, adolescence, and young adulthood. Psychohistory is oriented to dynamic psychology in which the present reality interacts at all times with and is related to the personal and social past of the person in the unconscious. (3) Psychohistory gives due place to the aggression, sexuality, passions, fantasy, and emotional states of the inner world of its subjects. It rejects the myth of the asexuality and innocence of child or adult, man or woman. Psychohistory recognizes that the fantasies of the subject, rather than meaning externally ascribed, constitute the relevant determinant of the emotional meaning of an event, symbol, or image.

Psychohistorians seek patterns, repetitions, deviant cases, and their meanings in the private and often unconscious world of their subjects and of themselves. They pursue visible traces of the unconscious and its defenses. Psychohistory is, to paraphrase what Freud said of psychoanalysis, a general history. His view of his work was that "the main value of my synthesis lies in its linking together the neurotic and normal processes." The human personality is indivisible. The processes we know clinically are just as relevant to this morning's newspaper or yesteryear's diary or legislative conflict as to a patient's neurotic symptom. It was Marc Bloch who said: "Historical facts are, in essence, psychological facts. Normally, therefore, they find their antecedents in other psychological facts." While historians have always recognized the role of emotions and irrationality in human action, they now have begun to account for a proportion of previously inexplicable behavior by seeking patterns of explanation using the insights that the science of psychodynamics has developed in this century.[2]

Historians study past human actions, thoughts, and motives. This is also what the psychoanalyst studies in his patients. When dealing with issues of motivation, both disciplines are committed to the theory of overdetermination. It would be a poor historian who would maintain that a major historical event had only one cause. We must necessarily look to many levels of causation and appraise the significance of each. Freud too insisted upon the overdetermined nature of the affects, dreams, and symptoms of psychic life. Thus both disciplines seek multiple explanations for single phenomena; both disciplines follow the law of the conservancy of evidence. No detail is so minor that it can be ignored, no deviant case is so trivial that it may be overlooked. This distinguishes history and psychoanalysis from the social and the natural sciences that seek to fit or subsume individual events under general covering laws of behavior. The epistemological problem is identical for the historian and the psychoanalyst. They must both reconstruct, or re-create in their minds, the life of their subjects.[3]

The formal call to the historical profession to engage seriously with psychoanalysis and apply it to historical research and conceptualization was issued by William L. Langer in his Presidential Address to the American Historical Association in December 1957. Langer was conditioned to the use of psychoanalysis in historical research by the distress of his personal symptom and his experience in psychoanalysis, which he found "a most effective method for learning about oneself," as well as his role as chief of the

Research and Analysis Division of the Office of Strategic Services (OSS) and the organizer of the Board of National Estimates for the Central Intelligence Agency. Psychodynamic studies of foreign leaders, texts, and propaganda by American intelligence services contributed to intelligence gathering and evaluation and strengthened his belief in the value of psychodynamics for the historian's armamentarium.[4]

The necessity of professional training in two disciplines has been reflected in criticism by mental health specialists of the crudeness of method of historians who write psychological history.[5] Conversely, historians criticize clinicians who are not historians yet offer interpretations of history. The model of interdisciplinary teams and collaboration by specialists at the interface of the disciplines has not been a generally successful solution. The ultimate synthesis must take place in the mind of a psychohistorian professionally trained in both disciplines if the research and conceptualizations are to have integrity as both historical and psychological accounts.

A new development in America within the past two decades has been the return to the traditional model, as it evolved on the European continent and in Great Britain, of the professional training of non-medical researchers in psychoanalysis. Systematic postdoctoral training of social scientists, historians, and humanists, including didactic analysis, seminars, and the supervision of clinical control cases, now takes place in psychoanalytic institutes. In 1977 the state of California recognized by law the importance of psychoanalytic clinical training and practice "as an adjunct to teaching, training or research." A new professional identity and a new historical discipline are emerging. Rather than historians and critics who do amateur "armchair" psychoanalysis, or clinicians who dabble as dilettantes in history and the humanities, there are now academically trained professional historians who conduct programs of research, teaching, and administration in their respective fields in universities and also practice as clinicians, keeping in daily contact with the unconscious processes and defenses of both themselves and their patients. The new academic historian–psychoanalysts are products of a merger in methods and perspectives at an early stage of career development, usually shortly after the completion of graduate training. Instead of the previous collaboration between specialists at the interface of two fields, these hybrid scholars with dual training have created a personal fusion of style, discipline, and method within their own minds. The dual training is especially important in psychohistory because, unlike other methods of history, it is precisely repressed emotional material which is the substance of study. Painful, frightening, anxiety-inducing, disgusting, or shameful feelings are too easy for the historian to obviate and avoid in his research and writing. Historians will be less likely to run away from these feelings, or to not see them at all, if they have faced them personally. The interchange must be constant, unconscious, instantaneous, spontaneous, and intrapsychic rather than interpersonal. "In this connection," said Freud, "the psychoanalytic mode of thought acts like a new instrument of research." Thus Freud's famous vision of 1926 has been realized:

> If—which may sound fantastic today—one had to establish a university of psychoanalysis, . . . analytic instruction would include disciplines which are remote from the physician and which he does not come across in his work: cultural history, mythology, the psychology of religion, and literary criticism. Without a good orientation in these fields, the analyst stands helpless before a great part of his material.[6]

A new historical subdiscipline now exists whose practitioners are not psychoanalysts doing history or historians utilizing psychoanalysis, but psychohistorians. The feedback to the historical field as a whole and to the vigor of psychoanalysis is already evident, as well as the solid contributions to academic research and training.

Several of America's leading scholarly journals, such as *The American Historical Review,* the *Journal of Modern History, The Journal of Interdisciplinary History,* and *The Historian,* have published special issues on psychohistory. *The Journal of Psychohistory* (formerly known as *The History of Childhood Quarterly*), which is devoted to the history of childhood and the family, the psychohistory of individuals and groups, and the proposition that the long-neglected history of childhood is the basis for psychohistory, was founded in 1973. The Group for the Use of Psychology in History, an affiliate of the American Historical Association, publishes *The Psychohistory Review,* which contains articles, reviews, bibliographies, and discussions of teaching methods. According to a recent survey, courses in psychohistory are currently offered at approximately thirty major American colleges and universities.[7] Psychohistory has been offered as a field of doctoral study in history at UCLA, Yale, Kansas State University, SUNY–Stony Brook, Princeton, MIT, and Boston University.

The historical profession has, on the whole, been wary of, if not antagonistic to, the use of psychoanalytic perceptions in historical research and interpretation.[8] The most serious objection to psychohistory by its critics is that too often psychobiographers make inferential leaps from adult to infantile behavior, ignoring intervening developments and variables. This charge, frequently well founded, raises an issue over the kind of psychohistory being written rather than the purpose or potential value of the enterprise itself. Some writers have used psychological categories as weapons with which to attack and discredit political figures. These expositions tend to make leaps directly from infantile traumas to public political life. But much of the hostility has been defensive, because psychohistory, unlike other historical methods, deeply involves the subjectivity of the researcher. Often one of the unconscious motives of the study of history is to displace conflict to the past. Therefore attempts to confront and deal with conflict in the immediacy of current research are met with hostility.

Some recent commentators have issued calls for historians to utilize non-psychoanalytic psychological models in their research. Many of the conceptual differences between schools of psychodynamics turn out to be fictive when they are applied in actual cases. There are many common aspects in all psychodynamic therapies; only the nomenclature changes. This can be seen in the way what psychoanalysis terms "insight" based on "interpretation" is called "cognition" by the learning theorist. What the psychoanalyst calls "catharsis" is "a release of tension in a setting of hope" to a humanistic psychologist; what the late authority on psychoanalytic technique Ralph Greenson defined as the "therapeutic alliance" and the "real relationship" between analyst and analysand is a "constructive relationship" to a transactional therapist.[9] Elements of suggestion and persuasion, overt and covert, exist in all therapies. What the psychoanalyst sees as the patient's identification with the analyst in which the patient incorporates some of the analyst's values and behavior patterns, such as a more tolerant superego, the behaviorist sees as operant conditioning in which the therapist's approval moves the "client" in the direction of "mental health." What the learning psychologists call the practice and rehearsal of new adaptive techniques is called "reality testing" and "working through" by psychoanalysts.

The problem of theory choice for historians is in many ways simpler than for clinicians. Historians may be eclectic and choose explanatory models to elucidate their material from whatever theories appear to be most useful. Historians require of a theory of behavior only that it be historical, that it be sufficiently rich and complex to explain the manifold problems of human behavior encountered by the historian, and that it be consistent and structurally coherent. Most psychohistorians reject non-psychoanalytic psychologies for use in historical research because of their ahistorical non-developmental character and because they are either so simplistic that they explain only elementary traits or so lacking in structural coherence as to be unusable by historians. "In the last analysis," says Saul Friedländer, "only the psychoanalytic (or psychoanalytically influenced) theories can furnish psychohistory with an adequate general framework, for these theories are the only ones that satisfy the criteria which *for the historian* are fundamental."[10]

The reciprocal relationship of history and psychoanalysis dates from Freud's works on culture and history in the early years of this century. He wrote widely on aesthetics and freely used literary, artistic, and anthropological examples to demonstrate his ideas, including discourses on the beginnings of social contract, religion, group leadership, poetic creativity, and biography.*

Further developments have taken place in the ego-psychological and object-relational areas both from the psychoanalytical side and from historical contributions as psychoanalysis has become assimilated as a research tool and interpretive modality among historians and social scientists. Ego psychology and character analysis are particularly important and welcome to historians because they are based on the evidence of adult behavior. They do not require reconstruction of infantile experience or reductions to origins —the behavior and patterns of accommodating to the world exist in adulthood and the evidence is historical. Clinically all aspects of personality are related—work, creativity, sexuality, social intercourse, attitudes toward money, intellectual style, fantasies, modes of conflict, and transferences. It is on these levels of ego functioning that interpretations are made to the patient. The historian has many of these kinds of data of personality and ego functioning at his disposal. If he looks at them with an eye toward the psychological relationship of different kinds of evidence, many connections that were not previously apparent will appear, for human beings are integral in many more ways than they consciously realize. The historian may now seek psychologically informed structures of behavior that make relationships and connections out of hitherto discrete or incomprehensible pieces of behavior.

Schmidl proposed that the methodological tie between psychoanalysis and history is the use of psychological configurations or "gestalten," where the entire context of observable behavior is indicative of particular uncon-

---

*These writings were based on clinical insights derived from Freud's self-analysis and the fantasy material of his patients. He assumed the similarity of neurotic and primitive behavior and that the development of the individual recapitulates the development of culture. His Lamarckianism implied that each child recapitulates the history of the race. Freud offered his bold cultural hypotheses as inventions and in 1934 planned to subtitle his book on Moses "a historical novel." Freud to Arnold Zweig, Sept. 30, 1934, in *The Letters of Sigmund Freud and Arnold Zweig,* ed. Ernst L. Freud, trans. E. and W. Robson-Scott (New York, 1970), p. 91. Freud's ventures in applied psychoanalysis are particularly welcome to the historian and humanist because they provide accessible material from our cultural heritage rather than from the private realm of the consulting room where no independent observation or replication is possible. But they have also stimulated criticism for his lack of expertise in the areas of literature and anthropology. Renaissance art historians point out inaccuracies in the translations Freud used, Russian literary critics show that he knew no Russian, Egyptologists claim he used outdated and partial sources. We ought not to read Freud's essays on Moses, da Vinci, Michelangelo, Shakespeare, Ibsen, and Dostoevsky as scholarly tracts in ancient, Renaissance, or modern cultural history. "Moses and Monotheism" is an essay on the psychodynamics of anti-Semitism, the da Vinci on the psychodynamics of a kind of homosexuality, the Michelangelo on the dynamics of rage and control. His use of Shakespeare's Lady Macbeth and Ibsen's Rebecca West of *Rosmersholm* is to illustrate an important insight into the dynamics of success and guilt. Likewise, the Dostoevsky essay deals with an insight into gambling, guilt, and masturbation. For these didactic purposes, the essays are valid and the use of cultural evidence is appealing in its universality.

scious content. The millions of messages from the patient in a psychoanalytic communication are organized into a configuration by the psychoanalyst. This is the synthetic psychoanalytic work which goes on while the analyst is listening with what Freud called "evenly suspended attention [*gleichschwebende Aufmerksamkeit*]."[11] The historian too is confronted in his research with innumerable facts, ideas, and communications from which he must synthesize a coherent story.

Psychoanalysis, which has developed certain formulations derived from extensive clinical experience, may supply the latent content behind manifest fantasies and meanings that the historian notes. Thus repetition of a maladaptive pattern in varied life situations is one of the indicators that unconscious processes are at work. Such repeated patterns of provocation and deadlocked conflict in adult life provided a key to the interpretation of Woodrow Wilson by the Georges.[12]

One of the most useful of all psychodynamic clinical categories for the historian is the idea of the character. This was first conceptualized by Freud in a brilliant three-page paper in 1908 in which he presented the famous triad of character traits—orderliness, parsimony, and obstinacy—which are psychodynamically related to each other and which make up the anal erotic syndrome. This triad is the result of reaction formation of conflicts stemming from the anal phase of growth, approximately between ages one and three, when issues of control and autonomy are paramount in the child's development. In two later essays Freud associated the anal erotic reaction formations of cleanliness, reliability, and conscientiousness with sadism. Ferenczi was to make the critical link to the acquisitive mercantile social culture of modern Europe in his 1914 paper "The Ontogenesis of the Interest in Money." Wilhelm Reich delineated the exterior characterological attributes of the "compulsive character" in terms of character "armor"—that is, a focus on the actual behavior and ideas of the person—such as living his life by a program, thoroughness, pedantry, evenness of attention and feeling which in some cases amounts to an affect block.[13]

A feature of Reich's conceptualization and clinical technique that has not yet been exploited by historians is its significance for intellectual artifacts such as literature, philosophy, and history itself. Reich demonstrated that *modes of thought,* such as circumstantial, ruminative thinking, or emphasis on restraint and control, or indecision, doubt, and distrust, are all indicative of character structure. The reliance on what is observable and easily identifiable, in contrast to what is inner, makes Reich's approach appealing and especially useful to the historian. The external features that would denote a compulsive character structure include a character armor of flat, affectless tone and an attempt to avoid emotional engagement by intellectualization or denial.

An important and neglected aspect of the historical and social application of psychoanalytic concepts, particularly the obsessive-compulsive syndrome, is the positive and adaptive role of these character defenses. Too often the psychoanalytic method is used to deprecate and disparage a subject. If compulsivity is a defense against anal aggressive and sadistic drives, and this was utilized in Nazism, we may not discount the culturally productive variations of the same defenses which result in control and discipline, precision and accuracy, dedicated performance and order, which have given us science, industry, and economic achievement. In this psychological sense both scholarship and economic activity may be culturally adaptive variations of the compulsive drive to dominate and manipulate which comes to pathological expression in sadistic perversions.

This, from the psychohistorical side, is a psychogenetic complement to Max Weber's essentially psychological characterization of the behavioral norms of Protestant capitalist culture. The "Protestant" archetype of Weber is controlled in emotion and pocketbook, hard-working, guilt-ridden, and aggressive. Regardless of the controversies that have raged among economic historians concerning the accuracy of the Weber thesis, it cannot be gainsaid that Weber forged a profound psychological insight into the emotional nexus of northern and western European civilization which demands the repression of instinctual and drive gratification in the service of socially normative performance values.

One of the most trenchant of the historian's objections to the use of psychoanalysis is its apparently timeless, and to this extent, ahistorical, quality. The diversity between the assumptions of the two disciplines comes into precise focus, and the difference between libido psychology and ego psychology is made manifest on this issue. Freud said that "unconscious mental processes are in themselves 'timeless.' This means in the first place that they are not ordered temporally, that time does not change them in any way and that the idea of time cannot be applied to them."[14] For the historian, on the other hand, the essence of history is change in time, the very process of temporaneity itself. The historian wishes to know: a leader of what period and cultural milieu, for what kind of political or military crisis, and of what type of following, at what precise point in time?

Otto Fenichel, a psychoanalyst who studied anti-Semitism, was keenly aware of the inadequacy of a purely timeless unconscious approach and the centrality of the historical dimension:

The instinctual structure of the average man in Germany was no different in 1935 from what it was in 1925. The psychological mass basis for anti-Semitism was not a political force then. If an understanding of its origin and development in that ten-year period in

Germany is sought, then the investigation must be focused on what happened there in those years, and not on the comparatively unaltered unconscious.[15]

Some current psychohistorians write with pre-1930's models of psychodynamics, as though ego psychology had never been developed, as though Freud as early as World War I had not already conceptualized and dealt with the problems of the individual's adaptation to reality, work that was extended by Anna Freud, Heinz Hartmann, Ernst Kris, and Rudolph Loewenstein.[16]

In 1916 Freud wrote a short paper crucial for the understanding of ego psychology and highly relevant to historians; it is his section "Those Wrecked by Success" in "Some Character-Types Met With in Psycho-Analytic Work." In his introduction to these essays Freud says that while the psychoanalyst would like to know "what instinctual impulses are concealed behind [the symptoms] and are satisfied by them, and what course was followed by the mysterious path that has led from the instinctual wishes to the symptoms," he is obliged by psychoanalytic technique to follow another course. Demanding "first claim" on his interest are the resistances that "are often brought to light in surprisingly increased intensity by the psychoanalytical investigation."[17] Freud offers examples drawn from literature so that his readers may share his data base (methodological charges against clinical case material of "having no controls" and "non-replicability" cannot lie here). To make the point Freud shows how the characters of Lady Macbeth and Rebecca West in Henrik Ibsen's *Rosmersholm* functioned well in achieving their ruthless aims. They trod over other human beings, planned, plotted, and executed, until they reached their goals. Then they were unable to enjoy the fruits of their labor, and their triumph turned to ashes in their mouths. In the end they destroyed themselves. What Freud told us is that in their history these two characters persevered to meet demonstrable challenges and difficult obstacles, to overcome all impediments, until they reached their goal. Then these same ego qualities of reality testing, insight, judgment, acumen, timing, frustration tolerance—all the necessary arts and talents of adaptation to the world—failed them. Suddenly at a specific juncture these ego assets which had formerly been available were absent; they were no longer functioning in the personalities under study—they were in suspension and superseded by other, conflictual attributes. Freud goes on to ask why these characters no longer functioned well at given points in their lives and suggests that it is *timing* which is the essential clue to the mystery of the change in behavior. He points out that it was precisely at the moment of success that the characters spoiled things for themselves and their cause by their own ac-

tion or inaction. Freud relates this pattern to a common clinical observation of persons in psychoanalysis who cannot allow themselves to enjoy
the fruits of their hard work and earned success but destroy their favorable
situation out of unconscious guilt.

With this, Freud built one half of the bridge that the psychohistorian
must complete, for the dimension of time is also cardinal to the historian's
discipline. In both historical studies and psychoanalysis there is no more
productive or crucial question than "Why now?" The elaboration of plans
coupled with an inability to bring them to consummation in the life of the
British general Sir Henry Clinton led Wyatt and Willcox to seek a psychoanalytic interpretation on the model of Freud's "Those Wrecked by
Success."[18]

The leading modern ego psychologist is Erik H. Erikson, who has
integrated personal, psychosocial, and historical experience in his concept
of identity. Erikson conceptualized eight epigenetic stages, or "ages of
man," in which phase-specific biological developments meet psychosocial
crises of growth. Thus the progressive development of the individual from
birth through infancy, childhood, youth, adolescence, adulthood, maturity,
to death, is of importance to historians because in addition to infancy it
emphasizes later stages of life, especially adolescence, as critical periods for
reworking earlier problems and integrating new solutions. Erikson defines
personal identity as "the accrued confidence that the inner sameness and
continuity prepared in the past are matched by the sameness and continuity
of one's meaning for others." A psychosocial identity is the sense of continuity between one's personal, family, ethnic, and national past and one's
current role and interaction with the present. It means that one may say:
"The way you see me now is the way I really am, and it is the way of my
forefathers." Identity as a historical tool

> is the sum of all images, ideas, and forces which—roughly speaking
> —make a person (and a people) feel more "like themselves" and act
> more "like themselves"—which means in historical terms: like what
> they have come to consider their historical selves. . . . Every infantile
> or pre-rational item thus recognized and named must be studied in
> its double nature of being a property of each individual life cycle,
> *and* of being a property of a communality, and for this reason subject
> to the fate of institutions. Psychohistorical actuality would therefore
> have two components: The relevance of historical changes for the
> identity formation of the individual, and the relevance for further
> historical change of the kinds of identity formation which have be-
> come dominant in a given society in a given period of history.[19]

Erikson's contribution to history is to use the lives of creative individuals such as Martin Luther and Mahatma Gandhi to elaborate on the psycho-social identity crises of a specific historical movement.[20] Thus Erikson treats Luther not in psychogenetic terms alone but also as the expression of a social and economic class in movement, a northern European consciousness, and a crisis in faith of the early sixteenth century. While he gives due credit to the theme of Luther's anality, he finds this characterological trait in the adult modes of stubborn sticking to principle, of an uncompromising certainty in his own rectitude. The excremental experiences, language, and imagery of Luther are invoked by Erikson, but not with a pejorative intent. The admiration and respect of the biographer for his subject as a persona and for Luther's historical role are evident throughout.

The concepts of psychosocial and historical identity present an opening for the discussion of national groups in terms of the kinds of identities they cultivate in their young. Erikson did this in three brilliant concluding sections of *Childhood and Society*. There he portrays German, American, and Russian identity formation as the young adolescent experiences it. The descriptions are clinical and literary in the style of a psychologically sophisticated anthropologist. Instead of employing survey techniques and statistical modes, Erikson uses cultural artifacts such as folk songs, folk myths, films, and pseudo-autobiography such as *Mein Kampf*. His clinically and personally (Erikson grew up in Baden) informed account of how a young German of the first third of this century experienced his home, his mother and father, school, youth groups, *Wanderjahre,* the military, and national belonging is highly convincing.[21] In each case Erikson uses a personality, either mythical as in the case of "John Henry," the idealized subject of an American folk song, or a cultural artifact such as Maxim Gorky's *Mother,* or the life of Adolf Hitler as he portrayed himself. This essay, which is a classic of its kind, views Hitler's *Mein Kampf* as a skillful projection of the image of an adolescent who never gave in, who refused to surrender to the domineering father, and who insisted on protecting the loving mother—an image designed to appeal to the unconscious fantasies engendered by German family patterns. It is less an essay about Hitler than about those who followed him.

Until recently Erikson's work was criticized only on historical grounds, but a new social and theoretical critique of his model has developed. Yet his ego-psychological model has understandably had great influence on and appeal to historians. The special power of the psychobiographer's use of ego psychology is the attention to the adaptation by the historical actor of the forces of his upbringing to the needs of the reality situation, rather than a focus on clinical pathology. Thus Richard Bushman, for example, examines how Benjamin Franklin became a superb diplomat and conciliator from learning to cope with his demanding father and brothers. Cushing Strout likewise deals with William James's work inhibitions in the ego-psychological terms of his father identification, and David Musto relates John Quincy Adams's identity formation to strong family pressures internalized since childhood. Robert Tucker's biography of Josef Stalin is Eriksonian in its smooth integration of emotional life themes and politics. For example, he relates the violent beatings Stalin's father administered to his mother and the boy's futile efforts to protect her to the way in which Stalin used the imagery of "lashing across their mugs, good and hard, and without letup" in political discourse, and literally when instructing investigative judges.[22]

The pioneer of the important field of personality and politics was Harold Lasswell, whose famous formula: $p) d) r = P$, means that private motives are displaced onto a public object and rationalized in terms of the public interest; this equals the political man. The encounter of psychoanalysts and social scientists with fascism and Nazism in the 1930's and 1940's brought forth many works that have become classics of conceptualization in the field of political personality. Erich Fromm interpreted the frightened person seduced by fascism who could not tolerate the responsibility or the ambiguity of freedom. This theme was fully developed with a broad clinical sample, quantitative methods, and projective tests (including the widely used "F" or "Fascism" scale) by Adorno et al. in *The Authoritarian Personality.* The Adorno group relied heavily on the psychoanalytic model of the obsessive-compulsive and the sadomasochistic personality in explaining the relationship of personality to political ideology. They sought the crucial variables determining democratic and non-democratic political views. The authoritarian is oriented toward power on a dominance-submission dimension. He is both totally obsequious and servile toward those viewed as superiors or arrogant and condescending toward his inferiors. This has been described as the stance of the bicycle rider—bend to those above and tread on those below. He is intolerant of ambiguity and tends to polarize all issues into stark black and white. There are no gray or uncertain areas in the authoritarian's world. While it has been possible to define an "authoritarian personality," it is much more difficult to delineate a "democratic" personality. Among the criticisms mounted against *The Authoritarian Personality* has been the neglect of left-wing authoritarian behavior, as though rigidity and dogmatism are monopolies of the political right.[23]

The psychological aspect of the history of racism is so important that it cannot be overlooked in any study of the subject. Studies of the psychodynamics of anti-Semitism have provided models for the integration of historical, social, and psychological variables in research.[24] Racial prejudice may be seen as a cultural Rorschach test because it serves as a projection of all those forces and fantasies with which a culture is ill at ease and that it needs to repress. By these defense mechanisms all the attributes which are most repressed or conflictual in a culture are ascribed to the ethnic outgroups. These may concern libidinal or aggressive drives such as being dirty, sexual, lazy, and irresponsible, or such idealized stereotypes as ambition, intelligence, and shrewdness. In the case of Nazi propaganda images of Jews, for example, the contradictions were blatant. The Jews were portrayed as being both lazy and striving, inept and brilliant, Bolsheviks and capitalists.

The historiography of the relations between the white, black, red, and yellow ethnic groups in American history has necessarily engaged with the theories and clinical findings of psychoanalysis as well as ethnography and cultural anthropology. A nation built with a moving frontier, which in three centuries displaced the native population, necessarily had complex and ambivalent feelings toward the American Indians. From their arrival, European settlers in North America had to deal with natives who already occupied the continent. The often violent displacement of the American Indians had its psychological concomitants in rationalizations of civilizing missions, religious justifications, projections of sexual and aggressive impulses onto the Indians, and paternalism. The recent biography of Andrew Jackson by Michael Rogin views his life in the context of early-nineteenth-century America's struggle with the problem of Indian "removal," paternalism, violence, and war.[25]

No problem in American social and political life has been greater, nor received more psychohistorical attention, than the human saga of domination, adaptation, and resistance which began in Negro slavery and is yet to be resolved in American life. Stanley Elkins's famous psychological conceptualization of the midpassage and slave experience using the analogy of the Nazi concentration camp has stimulated a considerable historiography of its own. White majority relations with minority populations in various regions of the United States followed the national patterns of discrimination with a psychology of phobia, paranoid projections, and displacement in the case of Oriental minorities in the Far West and Mexican-Americans in the Southwest.[26]

The psychohistorian must strive to comprehend not only primitive aggressive and libidinal drive behavior and universal infantile fantasies, but also their varied expression at given times and places in history by men and institutions. The methodological link between universal models of the unconscious and the particular social setting must be made. Historians need studies on groups of leaders and activists of how the life experiences, political constellations, critical personal traumas (such as expulsion from home, death of a parent, or early illness) and social traumas (such as war, famine, and depression) have differed and how this has conditioned the style of

leadership and the nature of group functioning. A group that has experienced such a common historical situation constitutes a cohort and may
possess common features or patterns of response that can be identified
decades later. Some traumas, such as the atomic bombing of Hiroshima,
which Lifton studied, are so overwhelming that all age groups are hit with
the blow at once.[27] Other, prolonged traumas, such as the blockade and
starvation of Germany in World War I, affected some groups, such as young
children, more intensely. This requires that psychoanalytic concepts of
phase specificity be used by the historian to examine what was the impact
of a particular kind of deprivation on a given age group at a certain historical
time.

The generation before the U.S. Civil War, typified by Abraham Lincoln,
is treated in psychoanalytic terms by George Forgie as a cohort born early
in the history of the Republic that forged its identity against the legacy of
a powerful generation of founding fathers who were all heroes and could
never be equaled without a crisis and struggle that was even greater than
that of the immortal fathers. Forgie interestingly applies the common childhood experience of the family romance in which children fantasize that they
are in fact the children, not of ordinary mundane parents, but of heroes.
Thus, with Forgie, the political and ideological issues of slavery and union
are cast in a new mold of emotions and fantasies based on the psychodynamics of generational oedipal combat.[28]

When dealing with small groups, as, for example, the leadership level of
a political party or a financial power elite, historians have relied on quantitative economic and social data that produce external evidence such as income, education, membership in associations and clubs, or comparative
intellectual development. This kind of evidence, while it may be statistically
broad, is necessarily collected without emotional depth. It is thin in the
perception of common dynamic development and phase-specific emotional
experiences that the members of a group have had. One of the major problems historians confront is bridging the gap between personalities and institutions—finding the juncture between the individuals and the organization
or power structure which they shaped or to which they belonged.

The problem now in the forefront of conceptual synthesis is to conceptually and empirically connect the singular personal experience which lends
itself to psychoanalytic explanation and the larger social matrix of historical
movements. Bion has applied Kleinian theory to the functioning of groups
in what has come to be known as the Tavistock model of group dynamics.[29]
The aim of a Tavistock "work group" is to study the emotional "work" of
a group independent of any reality task that groups conventionally have to
perform. This enables the members to see and observe in their behavior and
emotions how the psychological processes of group function occur.

The relevance to history and politics of these group fantasies is readily apparent. This is also the way such groups as a cabinet or a parliament, a general staff, or a governing committee operate. Brown and Ellithorp applied Bion's categories in their study of Senator Eugene McCarthy's 1968 campaign for the U.S. presidency. An exciting innovation in the training of historians occurred at Yale University in 1967 when Musto and Astrachan gave a group of history graduate students a Bion Tavistock group experience with the intention that they should apply what they had learned through the emotional experience to the study of groups functioning in history.[30]

Historians of the future will explore and capture the common emotional dimensions of the lives of a generation which may cut across traditional definitions of elites or class lines. What psychohistory offers the historian is a new and subtler category of inner emotional evidence with which to complement the "surface" or external statistical data by which he usually defines a temporal era or a social or leadership subgroup. Historians could examine and compare the emotional experiences and maturational development of an entire leadership caste, such as the top echelon of National Socialism. In-depth longitudinal studies of the ego development, object relations, gender identity, and character structure of such elite groups as various "kitchen cabinets," parliamentary factions, the Committee of Public Safety in the French Revolution, the early Bolsheviks, or of small groups such as the Anabaptists in the Reformation, may bring forth emotional common denominators which would be all the more decisive for being only partly conscious. It is only in the realm of feelings that the individual can be fully understood. The unique person can best be comprehended in his full cultural context, meaning in relation to the lives of others with whom he has deeply rooted emotional affinities. In both cases, the group and the individual, the explanation of motive, of deep-seated fears and aspirations, runs from the single person to his peers and then back to the unique psyche as the dialectic of feeling and thought, leader and group, stasis and action, is played out in history.[31]

Biography, which studies the individual in depth and intensity, has been the classic forum where the blending of history and psychoanalysis, which is also an individual clinical method par excellence, takes place. As Donald Meyer stated, "psychoanalytic biography constitutes a perspective, or a focus, from which history can organize all its narratives, no matter how vast a range of social data these may comprehend." Biographies have been enriched by psychoanalytic understanding in the areas of political leadership from classic to modern times, arts and letters, explorers and adventurers, and philosophers and scientists. We also have contemporary leadership studies of such recent political figures as John F. Kennedy, Lyndon Johnson, Henry Kissinger, Richard Nixon, Jimmy Carter, and Jerry Brown, with differential results. Many of these studies have crossed the line where biography becomes journalism and sometimes pop journalism.[32]

There is a growing application of psychoanalytic object relations theory to historical problems. Object relations theory is derived from the first year of life when the child is learning to distinguish self from non-self or subject from object. To the infant all sources of pleasure, such as the mother's breast, are viewed as a part of the self and as "good." Sources of discomfort, such as a pressure in the colon or a pain in the stomach, are believed to be outside of the self and "bad." This primitive "splitting" serves as a model for the defense mechanism of projection in later life. Projection is the tendency to take feelings or qualities that belong to the subject and to attribute them to persons or objects in the external world. The assumption of object relations theory is that adult functioning and relations to the persons and problems of the outer world are patterned on the first relations of the infant to its primary mothering figure.[33]

Object relations theory is attractive to social scientists because it does not require an instinctual theory of love and aggression as libido theory does. It merely postulates that individuals relate as they have learned to, or were programmed to, according to the unconscious fantasies of infancy. Thus, such questions may best be answered in object-relational terms, as for example: What is the subject's image of himself? Does he achieve intimacy? How and by what means? If not with people, then with animals, plants, or nature? Further problems that present themselves in historical research and which would be illuminated by questions stemming from the object-relational as well as the oedipal level of analysis are: How does the subject relate to masculine and feminine authority? Does he perceive it as helpful and friendly, as exploitative and demanding, as cruel and domineering, or as distant and disinterested? Does he respond to authority by submission, rebellion, compliance, passive aggression, or identification? What are the individual's emotional relations with men, women, equals, superiors, subordinates? How does he handle feelings of tenderness, rage, love, hate, frustration, rejection?

Three psychohistorical studies of Bismarck provide examples of how varied psychodynamic models may illuminate even one of the most carefully studied historical subjects and complement each other conceptually. Charlotte Sempell demonstrates Bismarck's bad relationship with his mother. Otto Pflanze, using a Reichian psychodynamic model, treats Bismarck's arrogant character as an external defense against underlying passive-dependent needs. Judith Hughes relies on a Fairbairnian object-relational model of his relations with his mother to explain Bismarck's adult mode of exploiting and misusing other people, including his son Herbert, his allies, and his political opponents, or counter-players.[34]

In the realm of applied psychohistorical research, Paul Kecskemeti and Nathan Leites, in studies for the Office of War Information, demonstrated the relevance of psycholinguistic analysis for understanding the emotional configurations of a culture. They subjected World War II German press and radio broadcasts to semantic analysis to draw characterological conclusions. Gregory Bateson analyzed the psychodynamics of the Nazi film *Hitlerjunge Quex* (1933) and explained why it was such effective propaganda.[35]

Among psychohistorical techniques utilized by the U.S. Office of Strategic Services in World War II was a personality study of Adolf Hitler. The particular value of this study for historians is that it used Hitler's own texts as the primary source for interpretation, and this is a kind of evidence that historians have in abundance and interpret in the regular course of their work. This wartime intelligence psychobiography of Hitler was of value to R. G. L. Waite in his psychohistory of Hitler and the Third Reich, which also uses more recently discovered documents and data such as the Soviet autopsy report indicating the absence of one of Hitler's testicles.[36] The significance of such data is not trivial or incidental. The integral nature of human psychodynamics—the fact that all elements of the person, even the most apparently disparate aspects of fantasy or behavior, are related to each other—means that politics cannot be separated from the person. In the case of Hitler, if he had a genital malformation and the fantasies to which this gave rise, this undoubtedly affected his ideas, images, and actions concerning masculinity and femininity, brutality and compassion, hardness and softness, strength and weakness, perfection and mutilation. The personal data, as Waite demonstrates, illuminates and explicates the public record.

Rudolf Binion pursues actual traumas he demonstrates or infers in Hitler's life, such as in infancy, when he was presumably overindulged by a mother made anxious by the loss of earlier children, to presumed fantasies at age eighteen when his mother died from breast cancer, to his being gassed in World War I, to the Final Solution.[37]

A definitive biography of Hitler must give close attention to his successes and adaptations, and they were numerous, such as the party crisis of 1925/26 or his diplomacy of the 1930's. A balanced psychohistorical view must also look with detailed care to those points in Hitler's life and politics where he failed to see reality and adjust to it, as for example in the Dunkirk and Russian campaigns. This is an ego-psychological approach in that it focuses on and evaluates historically when the ego functions of reality testing, perception, and tolerance of stress, frustration, ambiguity, and ambivalence are intact and when they are vitiated or overwhelmed by forces of the unconscious.

A major area of psychoanalytic insight applied to historical processes is colonial and revolutionary America. Among group phenomena to which psychoanalytic perceptions have been applied are Puritan childhood, the Salem witch trials, and the American Revolution. David Horowitz has reinterpreted the colonial resentment of England and the politics of the American Revolution by synthesizing these economic and political events with the psychology of the virtually perpetual Indian wars of early American history. Peter N. Carroll places the biography of Samuel Johnson of New England in the context of his personal life as well as generational and religious developments. Philip Greven offers a model that relates political attitudes toward England and revolution to child raising and the moral severity of particular styles or "temperaments" of Protestantism practiced in colonial and revolutionary America. He distinguishes three varieties of Protestant belief and behavioral systems: the evangelical, the moderate, the genteel, each with its own child-rearing standards, morality, and attitude toward authority which was expressed in politics as well as personal conduct and theology. The psychohistorical interpretation of emotional themes in American culture has been highly developed, including interpretations of frontier violence, love, and politics.[38]

Among the most creative applications of psychoanalytic insight to cultural and intellectual history is research on the fecund culture of *fin de siècle* Vienna, a milieu which spawned much that is the essence of modern art, literature, theater, music, philosophy, statecraft, and psychology. Carl E. Schorske has integrated politics, art, and literature with psychological dimensions of Viennese culture in a sweeping and superbly sensitive study. William McGrath has developed the political and psychological implications of the aesthetic commitments of a generation of middle-class Viennese intellectuals who shaped the rich political, literary, musical, and psychological milieu of Vienna in the 1890's.[39]

Because a psychological history is based on a developmental model, researchers have explored the history of childhood and the family, and historians of the family have naturally looked at intergenerational relationships in the family. The classic study which has influenced the development of the field was Philippe Ariès, *L'Enfant et la vie familiale sous l'ancien régime* (Paris, 1960). Ariès proposed that "childhood" as a category of life developed among the aristocracy and bourgeoisie of western Europe in the sixteenth and seventeenth centuries. Most of the subsequent American work has also focused on early modern France and on the upper and middle classes. A notable exception, because of his emphasis on the ordinary people, is Edward Shorter, *The Making of the Modern Family.*[40]

Changes in the concept of childhood in America have been related to the development of adolescence as a phase of life between childhood and adulthood. Historians of childhood in America have also studied the history of changes in public policies between state and non-state roles in strengthening the family. David Potter developed an interpretation of American national character and history based on a neo-Freudian model of viewing culture and personality "in an integral sense, as a totality." Potter pointed out that "these things were not understood prior to the work of Sigmund Freud. Freud recognized that the workings of the personality could be understood only by piercing through the superficial zones of intellect and reason to the vasty, irrational deeps of the id and ego beneath."[41]

It is difficult to extrapolate a clinical schema to a national polity without an intervening level of sociocultural concepts and operationalized studies of processes to make the linkage between a mode of parenting and a pattern of national or group behavior. Until this intermediate link is available, the historian will have microcosmic studies of mother-child interaction on the one hand and action in history on the other, but he will be unable to functionally relate the two poles to each other in a given case. What is needed is a solid series of studies of mothering, family patterns, childhood and adolescent socialization, and adaptive processes for each historical period and geographical and cultural area. Historians of the family have begun to fill in some of the gaping areas of ignorance and provide answers to these questions.

The history of childhood and of the family, collective biography and prosopography, are now moving to the forefront of historical interest. The family and the collectivity of a small group are seen as the mediating agency between social class and the individual. Both the economic and the national consciousness of individuals are established at the crucial periods of life when psychic patterns are imparted unconsciously—in the family. Thus a psychological history of the family, childhood, and generations may provide the crucial psychohistorical link between Freud and Marx, between the micro-individual level and the macro-social economic scene, in each epoch of history.

As a research and explanatory model, psychohistory is value-neutral. It has been used in the service of both radical and conservative cultural positions. Freud, who was a skeptic, saw an immortal combat between man's biological drives and the demands of historical culture. He believed that human culture is in unalterable conflict with the demands of man's instinctual life, and that "the price of progress in civilization is paid in forfeiting happiness through the heightening of a sense of guilt." This heritage, which recognizes the fundamentally ambiguous nature of history, is very much alive among humanists.[42]

Psychohistory is also a powerful mode for expressing culture critiques of the Western world, its family and work ethos, patterns of aggression, and interpersonal relations. In some cases the critics, writing what may be termed a "meta-psychohistory," include a postulated utopian future. Other interpretations have stressed adaptation to change, internalization of social norms, and integration of personality in a historical setting. The chief synthesizer of social analysis with psychoanalytic ego psychology and object relations theory was Talcott Parsons. Fred Weinstein and Gerald Platt have successfully applied Parsons's psychoanalytic object relations model of social internalization to psychohistory.[43]

Psychohistory provides a new tool for historians with which to analyze their data and interpret the complex configurations of human behavior in the past. Historians have applied it both crudely and well, both daringly and conservatively. To the historians of the next decades falls the task of moving beyond these beginnings to explain mankind's past and current behavior with greater sophistication and certainty.

Notes

1. George Devereux, *From Anxiety to Method in the Behavioral Sciences* (The Hague and Paris, 1967).

2. Sigmund Freud to Wilhelm Fliess, Nov. 14, 1897, in *The Origins of Psychoanalysis: Letters to Wilhelm Fliess, Drafts and Notes, 1887–1902,* eds. Marie Bonaparte, Anna Freud, Ernst Kris, trans. Eric Mosbacher and James Strachey (New York, 1954), Letter No. 75, p. 234; Marc Bloch, *The Historian's Craft,* trans. Peter Putnam (New York, 1953), p. 194. Peter Gay makes a persuasive case for psychoanalysis as the general psychology particularly suited to historical explanation—"all history must be in significant measure psychohistory"— in the Introduction to *Art and Act: On Causes in History: Manet, Gropius, Mondrian* (New York, 1976), pp. 1–32. The quotation is on p. 19. See also the excellent introduction by Peter N. Carroll, "Some Theoretical Assumptions and Implications of Psychohistory," *The Other Samuel Johnson: A Psychohistory of Early New England* (Rutherford, N.J., 1978), pp. 17–30. The most complete bibliographical survey of psychohistory is Faye Sinofsky, John J. Fitzpatrick, Louis W. Potts, and Lloyd de Mause, "A Bibliography of Psychohistory," *History of Childhood Quarterly,* 2 (1974): 517–62. An impressive survey of the literature from ancient to modern is Thomas W. Africa, "Psychohistory, Ancient History, and Freud: The Descent into Avernus," *Arethusa,* 12 (1979): 5–33. See also George M. Kren and Leon Rappoport, "Clio and Psyche," *History of Childhood Quarterly,* 1 (1973): 151–63; Dirk Blasius, "Psychohistorie und Sozialgeschichte," *Archiv für Sozialgeschichte,* 17 (1977): 383–403, and "Psychoanalyse— eine 'historische' Wissenschaft?" *Neue Politische Literatur,* 18 (1973): 453–68; Peter Loewenberg, "History and Psychoanalysis," in *The International Encyclopaedia of Psychiatry, Psychology, Psychoanalysis, and Neurology* (New York, 1977), 5: 363–74; "Psychohistory," in *The Past Before Us: Contemporary Historical Writing in the United States,* ed. Michael Kammen (Ithaca, N.Y., 1980), pp. 408–32.

3. For a discussion of the similarities of clinical and historical methods, see Hans Meyerhoff, "On Psychoanalysis and History," *Psychoanalysis and the Psychoanalytical Review,* 49 (1962): 3–20. See also Michael T. McGuire, *Reconstructions in Psychoanalysis* (New York, 1971); Samuel Novey, *The Second Look: The Reconstruction of Personal History in Psychiatry and Psychoanalysis* (Baltimore, 1968); Paul Ricoeur, "The Question

of Proof in Freud's Psychoanalytic writings," *Journal of the American Psychoanalytic Association,* 25 (1977): 835–71.

4. William L. Langer, "The Next Assignment," *American Historical Review,* 63 (1958): 283–304; *In and Out of the Ivory Tower* (New York, 1977), pp. 168–72, 180–93, 218–23, 247–50. For the earliest uses of psychoanalysis by historians, see Preserved Smith, "Luther's Early Development in the Light of Psychoanalysis," *American Journal of Psychology,* 24 (1913): 360–77; Harry Elmer Barnes, *Psychology and History* (New York, 1925). Langer's famous Chapter 3, "The Triumph of Imperialism," in *The Diplomacy of Imperialism* (New York, 1935), pp. 67–100, is a sensitive psychological treatment of popular fantasies. For examples of psychoanalytical studies of Axis propaganda and leaders in World War II, see Peter Loewenberg, "Psychohistorical Perspectives on Modern German History," *Journal of Modern History,* 47 (1975): 229–79, esp. 253–74.

5. Harald Leupold-Löwenthal, "Psychoanalyse und Geschichtswissenschaft," *Zeit Geschichte,* 2 (1975): 83–91, esp. 86–7; *The Psychiatrist as Psychohistorian,* Report of the Task Force on Psychohistory of the American Psychiatric Association (Washington, D.C., 1976).

6. California Business and Professions Code, Division 2, Chapter 5.1, Sections 2529–30, "Research Psychoanalysts"; Freud, "The Claims of Psycho-Analysis to Scientific Interest" (1913), *Standard Edition of the Complete Psychological Works,* trans. and ed. James Strachey et al. (London, 1953–1974), 13: 185; "The Question of Lay Analysis" (1926), *ibid.,* 20: 246. The translation is mine.

7. Survey by John Fitzpatrick as cited in George M. Kren and Leon H. Rappoport, eds., *Varieties of Psychohistory* (New York, 1976), pp. 2, 14 n. 3. The most sophisticated engagement with the problems of psychohistory is Saul Friedländer, *History and Psychoanalysis: An Inquiry into the Possibilities and Limits of Psychohistory,* trans. Susan Suleiman (New York and London, 1978).

8. David E. Stannard, *Shrinking History: On Freud and the Failure of Psychohistory* (New York, 1980); E. J. Hundert, "History, Psychology, and the Study of Deviant Behavior," *Journal of Interdisciplinary History,* 2 (1972): 453–72; Philip Pomper, "Problems of a Naturalistic Psychohistory," *History and Theory,* 12 (1973): 367–88; Hans-Ulrich Wehler, "Geschichtswissenschaft und 'Psychohistorie,' " *Innsbrucker Historische Studien,* 1 (1978), 201–13; Jacques Barzun, *Clio and the Doctors: Psycho-History, Quanto-History, and History* (Chicago, 1974); and reviews by Fred Weinstein in *Journal of Modern History,* 48 (1976): 117–18, and Peter Loewenberg in *Clio,* 5 (1975): 123–7. See also Robert Coles, "Shrinking History," *New York Review of Books,* 20 (Feb. 23 and March 8, 1973): 15–21, 25–9; Gertrude Himmelfarb, "The New History," *Commentary,* 59 (1975): 72–8; Geoffrey Barraclough, "Psycho-History Is Bunk," *Guardian* (Manchester and London, March 3, 1973); Gerald Izenberg, "Psychohistory and Intellectual History," *History and Theory,* 14 (1975): 139–55.

9. Ralph R. Greenson, "The Problem of Working Through" (1965), in *Explorations in Psychoanalysis* (New York, 1978), p. 261.

10. Friedländer, *History and Psychoanalysis,* p. 11.

11. Fritz Schmidl, "Psychoanalysis and History," *Psychoanalytic Quarterly,* 31 (1962): 539–43; "Problems of Method in Applied Psychoanalysis," *Psychoanalytic Quarterly,* 41 (1972): 402–19; S. Freud, "Recommendations to Physicians Practising Psycho-Analysis" (1912), *Standard Edition,* 12: 111.

12. Alexander L. and Juliette L. George, *Woodrow Wilson and Colonel House: A Personality Study* (New York, 1956, 1964). See also Edwin A. Weinstein, James William

Anderson, and Arthur S. Link, "Woodrow Wilson's Political Personality: A Reappraisal," *Political Science Quarterly,* 93 (Winter 1978/79), and the convincing reply by Juliette L. and Alexander L. George, "Woodrow Wilson and Colonel House: A Reply to Weinstein, Anderson, and Link," *Political Science Quarterly,* 96: 4 (Winter 1981/82).

13. Freud, "Character and Anal Erotism" (1908), *Standard Edition,* 9: 167–75; "The Disposition to Obsessional Neurosis: A Contribution to the Problem of Choice of Neurosis" (1913), *ibid.,* 12: 311–26; and "On Transformations of Instinct as Exemplified in Anal Erotism" (1917), *ibid.,* 12: 125–33; Sandor Ferenczi, "The Ontogenesis of the Interest in Money" (1914), in *Sex in Psycho-Analysis,* trans. Ernest Jones (New York, 1956), pp. 269–79; Wilhelm Reich, *Character Analysis* (New York, 1949), pp. 193–200.

14. Freud, "Beyond the Pleasure Principle" (1920), *Standard Edition,* 18: p. 28.

15. Otto Fenichel, "Elements of a Psychoanalytic Theory of Anti-Semitism" (1940), in *Anti-Semitism: A Social Disease,* ed. Ernst Simmel (New York, 1946), p. 12.

16. For an example of how psychohistory should *not* be written, both because it lacks all sensitivity to ego psychology and adaptation and because here psychodiagnostics are used as a weapon for political purposes, see Dana Ward, "Kissinger: A Psychohistory," *History of Childhood Quarterly,* 2 (1975): 287–349. Whatever one may think of Henry Kissinger's diplomacy, he certainly had a great capacity to adapt creatively to new personal, social, and political situations. See Peter Loewenberg, *Walther Rathenau and Henry Kissinger: The Jew as a Modern Statesman in Two Political Cultures,* Leo Baeck Memorial Lecture (New York, 1980).

17. Freud, "Some Character Types Met With in Psycho-Analytic Work" (1916), *Standard Edition,* 14: 311.

18. Frederick Wyatt and William B. Willcox, "Sir Henry Clinton: A Psychological Exploration in History," *William and Mary Quarterly,* 3rd Ser., 16 (1959): 3–26; Willcox, *Portrait of a General: Sir Henry Clinton in the War of Independence* (New York, 1964).

19. Erik H. Erikson, *Childhood and Society,* rev. 2nd ed. (New York, 1963), pp. 129, 261; *Insight and Responsibility: Lectures on the Ethical Implications of Psychoanalytic Insight* (New York, 1964), pp. 203–4, 207. See also *Identity and the Life Cycle: Selected Papers* (New York, 1959); *Identity: Youth and Crisis* (New York, 1968); *Dimensions of a New Identity* (New York, 1974); *Life History and the Historical Moment* (New York, 1975). For an appreciation, see Robert Coles, *Erik H. Erikson: The Growth of His Work* (Boston, 1970); for a sometimes savage critique, see Paul Roazen, *Erik H. Erikson: The Power and Limits of a Vision* (New York, 1976); for a balanced discussion by a psychoanalytically trained historian, see John J. Fitzpatrick, "Erik H. Erikson and Psychohistory," *Bulletin of the Menninger Clinic,* 40 (1976): 295–314. See also "Special Issue on Erik H. Erikson," *Psychohistory Review,* 5 (1976).

20. Erikson, *Young Man Luther: A Study in Psychoanalysis and History* (New York, 1958, 1962); *Gandhi's Truth: On the Origins of Militant Nonviolence* (New York, 1969).

21. Erikson, " 'Identity Crisis' in Autobiographic Perspective," in *Life History and the Historical Moment,* pp. 17–47.

22. On Erikson see John J. Fitzpatrick, "Erik H. Erikson and Psychohistory," *Bulletin of the Menninger Clinic,* 40 (1976): 295–314; Howard I. Kushner, "Pathology and Adjustment in Psychohistory: A Critique of the Erikson Model," *Psychocultural Review,* 1 (1977): 493–506, and "Americanization of the Ego," *Canadian Review of American Studies,* 10 (1979): 95–101; Richard L. Bushman, "On the Use of Psychology: Conflict and Conciliation in Benjamin Franklin," *History and Theory* 5 (1968): 225–40; Cushing Strout, "William James and the Twice-Born Sick Soul," *Dædalus,* 97 (1968): 1062-82,

and "Ego Psychology and the Historian," *History and Theory,* 7 (1968): 281–97; David F. Musto, "The Youth of John Quincy Adams," *Proceedings of the American Philosophical Society,* 113 (1969): 269–82; Robert C. Tucker, *Stalin as Revolutionary, 1879–1929: A Study in History and Personality* (New York, 1973), p. 74.

23. Harold D. Lasswell, *Psychopathology and Politics* (Chicago, 1930; New York, 1960), pp. 75–6; Erich Fromm, *Escape from Freedom* (New York, 1941). T. W. Adorno, Else Frenkel-Brunswik, Daniel J. Levinson, R. Nevitt Sanford, et al., *The Authoritarian Personality* (New York, 1950); Richard Christie and Marie Jahoda, eds. *Studies in the Scope and Method of "The Authoritarian Personality"* (New York, 1954).

24. Gordon W. Allport, *The Nature of Prejudice* (Cambridge, Mass., 1954); Bruno Bettelheim and Morris Janowitz, *Social Change and Prejudice Including Dynamics of Prejudice* (New York, 1964); Nathan W. Ackerman and Marie Jahoda, *Anti-Semitism and Emotional Disorder: A Psychoanalytic Interpretation* (New York, 1950); Ernst Simmel, ed., *Anti-Semitism: A Social Disease* (New York, 1946); Peter Loewenberg, "Die Psychodynamik des Antijudentums," in *Jahrbuch des Instituts für Deutsche Geschichte,* ed. Walter Grab (Tel Aviv, 1972), 1: 145–58.

25. Winthrop Jordan, *White over Black: American Attitudes Toward the Negro, 1550–1812* (Chapel Hill, N.C., 1968); Joel Kovel, *White Racism: A Psychohistory* (New York, 1970); Peter Loewenberg, "The Psychology of Racism," in *The Great Fear: Race in the Mind of America,* ed. Gary B. Nash and Richard Weiss (New York, 1970), pp. 186–201; "Racism and Tolerance in Historical Perspective," in *Race, Change, and Urban Society,* ed. Peter Orleans and William Russell Ellis, Jr. (Beverly Hills, Calif., 1971), pp. 561–76; Gary B. Nash, *Red, White, and Black: The Peoples of Early America* (Englewood Cliffs, N.J., 1974); "The Image of the Indian in the Southern Colonial Mind," *William and Mary Quarterly,* 3rd Ser., 29 (1972): 197–230; Wilbur R. Jacobs, "The Fatal Confrontation: Early Native-White Relations on the Frontiers of Australia, New Guinea, and America—A Comparative Study," *Pacific Historical Review,* 60 (1971): 293–309; *Dispossessing the American Indian: Indians and Whites on the Colonial Frontier* (New York, 1972); Roy Harvey Pearce, *The Savages of America: A Study of the Indian and the Idea of Civilization* (Baltimore, 1953); Michael Paul Rogin, *Fathers and Children: Andrew Jackson and the Subjugation of the American Indian* (New York, 1975).

26. Stanley M. Elkins, *Slavery: A Problem in American Institutional and Intellectual Life* (Chicago, 1959); Ann J. Lane, ed., *The Debate over "Slavery": Stanley Elkins and His Critics* (Urbana, Ill., 1971); Kenneth Stampp, "Rebels and Sambos: The Search for the Negro's Personality in Slavery," *Journal of Southern History,* 37 (1971): 367–92; David Brion Davis, *The Slave Power Conspiracy and the Paranoid Style* (Baton Rouge, La., 1969). Eugene Genovese attacks a psychological approach to slaveholding in *The World the Slaveholders Made* (New York, 1969), pp. 143–4, but five years later he finds that guilt played an important role among slave owners, *Roll, Jordan, Roll* (New York, 1974), pp. 120–3, 453. Gunther Barth, *Bitter Strength: A History of the Chinese in the United States, 1850–1870* (Cambridge, Mass., 1964); Stuart C. Miller, *The Unwelcome Immigrant: The American Image of the Chinese, 1785–1882* (Berkeley and Los Angeles, 1969); Roger Daniels, *The Politics of Prejudice: The Anti-Japanese Movement in California and the Struggle for Japanese Exclusion* (Berkeley and Los Angeles, 1962); Alexander Saxton, *The Indispensable Enemy: Labor and the Anti-Chinese Movement in California* (Berkeley and Los Angeles, 1971); Jacobius ten Broek, Edward N. Barnhart, and Floyd W. Matson, *Prejudice, War, and the Constitution* (Berkeley and Los Angeles, 1954); Robert Coles, *Eskimos, Chicanos, Indians,* vol. 4 of *Children of Crises* (Boston, 1977); Mauricio Mazon, "Illegal Alien Surrogates: A Psychohistorical Interpretation of Group

Stereotyping in Time of Economic Stress," *Aztlan,* 6 (1975): 305–24; Rodolfo Alvarez, "The Psycho-historical and Socioeconomic Development of the Chicano Community in the United States," *Social Science Quarterly,* 54 (1973): 920–42; "The Unique Psycho-historical Experience of the Mexican American People," *Social Science Quarterly,* 52 (1971): 15–29. A pioneering work was Carey McWilliams, *North from Mexico: The Spanish Speaking People of the United States* (Philadelphia, 1949).

    27. Robert Jay Lifton, *Death in Life: Survivors of Hiroshima* (New York, 1967); *History and Human Survival: Essays on the Young and Old, Survivors and the Dead, Peace and War, and on Contemporary Psychohistory* (New York, 1971).

    28. George B. Forgie, *Patricide in the House Divided: A Psychological Interpretation of Lincoln and His Age* (New York, 1979). For a Kohutian approach, see Charles B. Strocier, *Lincoln's Quest for Union: Public and Private Meanings* (New York, 1982).

    29. W. R. Bion, *Experiences in Groups and Other Papers* (New York, 1959).

    30. Steven R. Brown and John D. Ellithorp, "Emotional Experiences in Political Groups: The Case of the McCarthy Phenomenon," *American Political Science Review,* 64 (1970): 349–66. For an application of psychodynamics to leadership groups, see Irving L. Janis, *Victims of Groupthink: A Psychological Study of Foreign-Policy Decisions and Fiascos* (Boston, 1972). David F. Musto and Boris M. Astrachan, "Strange Encounter: The Use of Study Groups with Graduate Students in History," *Psychiatry,* 31 (1968): 264–76.

    31. H. Stuart Hughes, "History and Psychoanalysis: The Explanation of Motive," in *History as Art and as Science: Twin Vistas on the Past* (New York, 1964), pp. 42–67.

    32. Donald Meyer, "A Review of *Young Man Luther,*" in Bruce Mazlish, ed., *Psychoanalysis and History* (Englewood Cliffs, N.J., 1963, 1977), p. 179; Thomas W. Africa, "The Mask of an Assassin: A Psychohistorical Study of M. Junius Brutus," *Journal of Interdisciplinary History,* 8 (1978): 599–626; Fawn M. Brodie, *Thaddeus Stevens: Scourge of the South* (New York, 1959); *Thomas Jefferson: An Intimate History* (New York, 1973); Elizabeth W. Marvick, "Childhood History and Decisions of State: The Case of Louis XIII," *History of Childhood Quarterly,* 2 (1974): 135–200; E. Victor Wolfenstein, *The Revolutionary Personality: Lenin, Trotsky, Gandhi* (Princeton, N.J., 1967); *Personality and Politics* (Belmont, Calif., 1969); Bruce Mazlish, *The Revolutionary Ascetic: Evolution of a Political Type* (New York, 1976); David H. Donald, *Charles Sumner and the Coming of the Civil War* (New York, 1960); Maynard Solomon, *Beethoven* (New York, 1977). Editha and Richard Sterba, *Beethoven and His Nephew: A Psychoanalytic Study of Their Relationship* (New York, 1954, 1971), is particularly interesting in making use, more than a century after Beethoven's death, of oral tradition in Heiligenstadt, the suburb of Vienna where he lived (this is an application of Marc Bloch's research technique of "understanding the past by the present," *Historian's Craft,* pp. 43–7). Bernard C. Meyer, *Joseph Conrad: A Psychoanalytic Biography* (Princeton, N.J., 1967); Phyllis Greenacre, *Swift and Carroll: A Psychological Study of Two Lives* (New York, 1955); Humberto Nagera, *Vincent van Gogh: A Psychological Study* (New York, 1967); Frederick Crews, *The Sins of the Fathers: Hawthorne's Psychological Themes* (New York, 1966), and Crews, ed., *Psychoanalysis and Literary Process* (Cambridge, Mass., 1970); Kurt R. Eissler, *Goethe: A Psychoanalytic Study, 1775–1786,* 2 vols. (Detroit, 1963); Martha Wolfenstein, "Goya's Dining Room," *Psychoanalytic Quarterly,* 35 (1966): 47–83. The most creative psychoanalytic approach to literary texts, and of great value for historical texts as well, is Norman N. Holland's "reader's response" method, which utilizes "countertransference" or the subjective feelings of the researcher as a tool of cognition, *The Dynamics of Literary Response* (New York, 1968). For a Lacanian view,

see Shoshana Feldman, ed., "Literature and Psychoanalysis: The Question of Reading: Otherwise," *Yale French Studies,* vols. 55–6 (1977). Fawn M. Brodie, *The Devil Drives: A Life of Sir Richard Burton* (New York, 1967); John E. Mack, *A Prince of Our Disorder: The Life of T. E. Lawrence* (Boston, 1976); William G. Niederland, "An Analytic Inquiry into the Life and Work of Heinrich Schliemann," in *Drives, Affects, Behavior,* ed. Max Schur (New York, 1965), 2: 369–96; Jerrold Seigel, *Marx's Fate: The Shape of a Life* (Princeton, N.J., 1978); Arthur Mitzman, *The Iron Cage: An Historical Interpretation of Max Weber* (New York, 1969); Bruce Mazlish, *James and John Stuart Mill: Father and Son in the Nineteenth Century* (New York, 1975); Frank E. Manuel, *A Portrait of Isaac Newton* (Cambridge, Mass., 1968); William Blanchard, *Rousseau and the Spirit of Revolt: A Psychological Study* (Ann Arbor, Mich., 1967); Bennett and Nancy Simon, "The Pacifist Turn: An Episode of Mystic Illumination in the Autobiography of Bertrand Russell," *Journal of The American Psychoanalytic Association,* 20 (1972): 109–21; Nielsen H. Minnich and W. W. Meissner, "The Character of Erasmus," *American Historical Review,* 83 (1978): 598–634; Nancy Clinch, *The Kennedy Neurosis* (New York, 1973); Doris Kearns, *Lyndon Johnson and the American Dream* (New York, 1976); Bruce Mazlish, *Kissinger: The European Mind in American Policy* (New York, 1976); *In Search of Nixon: A Psychohistorical Inquiry* (New York, 1972). The "Special Carter Issue," *Journal of Psychohistory,* vol. 5, no. 2 (1977), is a further unfortunate counterexample of what psychohistory should not be; in his article "Jimmy Carter and American Fantasy," editor Lloyd de Mause irresponsibly predicts that Carter "is very likely to lead us into a new war by 1979," p. 151. See by contrast the highly responsible and cautious interpretations of John J. Fitzpatrick, "Jerry Brown: The Man Behind the Mask: A Psychological Portrait," *New West,* 3 (1978): 34–43.

33. For theoretical and clinical exposition of object relations, also sometimes called the "English School," see W. Ronald D. Fairbairn, *An Object-Relations Theory of the Personality* (London, 1952); Harry Guntrip, *Schizoid Phenomena, Object-Relations and the Self* (New York, 1968); *Personality Structure and Human Interaction: The Developing Synthesis of Psychodynamic Theory* (New York, 1961); Donald W. Winnicott, *The Child and the Outside World: Studies in Developing Relationships* (New York, 1957); *The Maturational Processes and the Facilitating Environment: Studies in the Theory of Emotional Development* (New York, 1965); *Playing and Reality* (London, 1971). For the theories of Melanie Klein, see Hanna Segal, *Introduction to the Work of Melanie Klein* (London, 1964); Melanie Klein, *Contributions to Psycho-Analysis, 1921–1945* (London, 1948); *Envy and Gratitude and Other Works, 1946–1963* (London, 1975). Among contemporary preoedipal theorists with a clinical emphasis, see the work of Heinz Kohut, "Thoughts on Narcissism and Narcissistic Rage," *Psychoanalytic Study of the Child,* 27 (1972): 360–400; "Forms and Transformations of Narcissism," *Journal of the American Psychoanalytic Association,* 14 (1966): 243–62; *The Analysis of the Self: A Systematic Approach to the Psychoanalytic Treatment of Narcissistic Personality Disorders* (New York, 1971); Otto Kernberg, *Borderline Conditions and Pathological Narcissism* (New York, 1975). The work of Margaret Mahler and associates is especially important: *On Human Symbiosis and the Vicissitudes of Individuation: Infantile Psychosis* (New York, 1968); *The Psychological Birth of the Human Infant: Symbiosis and Individuation,* with Fred Pine and Anni Bergman (New York, 1975).

34. Charlotte Sempell, "Bismarck's Childhood: A Psychohistorical Study," *History of Childhood Quarterly,* 2 (1974): 107–24; Otto Pflanze, "Toward a Psychoanalytic Interpretation of Bismarck," *American Historical Review,* 76 (1972): 419–44; Judith M. Hughes, "Toward the Psychological Drama of High Politics: The Case of Bismarck,"

Central European History, 10 (1978): 271–85; *Emotions and High Politics: Political Cohesion in Late Nineteenth Century Britain and Germany* (Berkeley and Los Angeles, 1982).

35. Paul Kecskemeti and Nathan Leites, "Some Psychological Hypotheses on Nazi Germany," *Journal of Social Psychology,* 26 (1947): 141–83; *ibid.,* 27 (1948): 91–117; *ibid.,* 27 (1948): 240–70; *ibid.,* 28 (1948): 141–64; Gregory Bateson, "Cultural and Thematic Analysis of Fictional Films," *Transactions of the New York Academy of Sciences,* 2nd Ser., 5 (1943): 72–8. See also Elizabeth Wirth Marvick, ed., *Psychopolitical Analysis: Selected Writings of Nathan Leites* (New York, 1977), which includes brilliant psychological treatments of Soviet, American, German, and French political behavior based on language analysis.

36. Walter C. Langer, Ernst Kris, and Bertram D. Lewin, "A Psychological Analysis of Adolph [*sic*] Hitler" (Washington, D.C.: Office of Strategic Services, 1943); Robert G. L. Waite, *The Psychopathic God* (New York, 1977); Lev Bezymenski, *The Death of Adolf Hitler: Unknown Documents from Soviet Archives* (New York, 1968); Walter C. Langer, *The Mind of Adolf Hitler: The Secret Wartime Report* (New York, 1972); Peter Loewenberg, "Hitler's Psychodynamics Examined," *Contemporary Psychology,* 19 (1974): 89–91; review in *Central European History,* 7 (1974): 262–75. For a recent interpretation of the latent emotional content of Hitler's writings and speeches, see Richard A. Koenigsberg, *Hitler's Ideology: A Study in Psychoanalytic Sociology* (New York, 1975).

37. Rudolf Binion, *Hitler Among the Germans* (New York, 1976); see Loewenberg, "Psychohistorical Perspectives," pp. 241–4; Geoffrey Cocks, "The Hitler Controversy," *Political Psychology,* 1 (1979): 67–81.

38. Philip J. Greven, Jr., *Four Generations: Population, Land, and Family in Colonial Andover, Massachusetts* (Ithaca, N.Y., 1970); *The Protestant Temperament: Patterns of Child-Rearing, Religious Experience and the Self in Early America* (New York, 1977); John Demos, *A Little Commonwealth: Family Life in Plymouth Colony* (New York, 1970); "Underlying Themes in the Witchcraft of Seventeenth Century New England," *American Historical Review,* 75 (1970): 1311–26; Emery J. Battis, *Saints and Secretaries: Anne Hutchinson and the Antinomian Controversy in Massachusetts Bay Colony* (Chapel Hill, N.C., 1962); Edwin G. Burrows and Michael Wallace, "The American Revolution: The Ideology and Psychology of National Liberation," *Perspectives in American History,* 6 (1972): 167–306; Winthrop Jordan, "Familial Politics: Thomas Paine and the Killing of the King, 1776," *Journal of American History,* 60 (1973): 294–308; David Horowitz, *The First Frontier: The Indian Wars and America's Origins,* 1607–1776 (New York, 1978); Carroll, *The Other Samuel Johnson;* Leslie Fiedler, *Love and Death in the American Novel* (New York, 1960); *Return of the Vanishing American* (New York, 1968); Richard Hofstadter, *The Paranoid Style in American Politics* (New York, 1965); *The American Political Tradition* (New York, 1948). See also the psychological interpretation by Daniel Walker Howe and Peter Elliott Finn, "Richard Hofstadter: The Ironies of an American Historian," *Pacific Historical Review,* 43 (1974): 1–23, in which Freud is called "the greatest of Hofstadter's mentors," p. 15 n. 47; David Brion Davis, ed., *The Fear of Conspiracy: Images of Un-American Subversion from the Revolution to the Present* (Ithaca, N.Y., 1971). For conspiracy fantasies in the American Revolution, see Bernard Bailyn, *The Ideological Origins of the American Revolution* (Cambridge, Mass., 1967), pp. 144–59.

39. Carl E. Schorske, *Fin-de-Siècle Vienna: Politics and Culture* (New York, 1980); William McGrath, *Dionysian Art and Populist Politics in Austria* (New Haven and London, 1974); "Freud as Hannibal: The Politics of the Brother Band," *Central European History,* 7 (1974): 31–57.

40. Philippe Ariès, *Centuries of Childhood: A Social History of Family Life,* trans. Robert Baldick (New York, 1962), p. 28; David Hunt, *Parents and Children in History: The Psychology of Family Life in Early Modern France* (New York, 1970). For an interesting comparative treatment of the interaction of upper-class and working youth in English and German university towns, see John R. Gillis, *Youth and History: Tradition and Change in European Age Relation, 1770–Present* (New York, 1974), the critique by Peter Loewenberg, "A New Tyranny over Youth," *Reviews in European History,* 3 (1977): 39–43. Edward Shorter, *The Making of the Modern Family* (New York, 1975). Shorter criticizes Ariès precisely on this point of ignoring the lower classes, thus presenting skewed results, pp. 170, 192. However, see the critique of Shorter by Christopher Lasch, *Haven in a Heartless World* (New York, 1977), pp. 168, 219 n. 4.

41. David M. Potter, *People of Plenty: Economic Abundance and the American Character* (Chicago, 1954), p. 33; Joseph F. Kett, *Rites of Passage: Adolescence in America, 1790 to the Present* (New York, 1977); John and Virginia Demos, "Adolescence in Historical Perspective," *Journal of Marriage and the Family,* 31 (1969). See also Gillis, *Youth and History.* For contemporary American adolescence, see Kenneth Keniston, *The Uncommitted: Alienated Youth in American Society* (New York, 1960); *Young Radicals: Notes on Committed Youth* (New York, 1968); Stanley Rothman and S. Robert Lichter, "The Case of the Student Left," *Social Research,* 45 (1978): 535–609; Robert Schnitzer, Phillip Isenberg, and Stanley Rothman, "Faces in the Crowd: Portraits of Radical Youth," in *Adolescent Psychiatry,* Vol. 6, ed. Sherman C. Feinstein and Peter L. Giovacchini (Chicago, 1978), pp. 195–223. Robert Bremner et al., eds., *Children and Youth in America: A Documentary History,* 3 vols. (Cambridge, Mass., 1970–74). See also Bernard Wishy, *The Child and the Republic: The Dawn of Modern American Child Nurture* (Philadelphia, 1968). For the most useful synthesis of the field of culture and personality and psychodynamics, see Robert A. LeVine, *Culture, Behavior and Personality* (Chicago, 1973).

42. Freud, "Civilization and Its Discontents" (1930), *Standard Edition,* 21: 134; Hans Meyerhoff, "Freud and the Ambiguity of Culture," *Partisan Review,* 24 (1957): 117–30; Philip Rieff, *Freud: The Mind of the Moralist* (New York, 1959); *The Triumph of the Therapeutic: Uses of Faith after Freud* (New York, 1966); Lionel Trilling, *Freud and the Crisis of Our Culture* (Boston, 1955); *Sincerity and Authenticity* (Cambridge, Mass., 1972); Robert Waelder, *Progress and Revolution: A Study of the Issues of Our Age* (New York, 1967).

43. Talcott Parsons, *Social Structure and Personality* (Glencoe, Ill., 1964); *Family Socialization and Interaction Process,* with Robert F. Bales (Glencoe, Ill., 1955); Fred Weinstein and Gerald M. Platt, *The Wish to Be Free: Society, Psyche, and Value Change* (Berkeley and Los Angeles, 1969); *Psychoanalytic Sociology;* "The Coming Crisis of Psychohistory," *Journal of Modern History,* 47 (1975): 202–28.

PART II

The Education of
a Psychohistorian

The education of a psychohistorian is decisively different from that of any other historian because his education deeply involves his inner self. Through personal analysis and later self-analysis, the psychohistorian learns about himself and his relation to the subject of research. He learns to know and trust his unconscious as a perceptive guide to further exploration.

The psychohistorian has relativized modern categories of historical explanation, so that while there may be issues of fact over data, no interpretation of data is entirely "right" or "wrong." The historian deals with degrees of complexity, relevance, and appositeness in interpretation. The issue is never whether an interpretation is 100 percent correct, but whether it is more inclusive than prior explanations, whether it can subsume more and apparently disparate data, and whether it elucidates new facts or dimensions of previously accepted truth.

My first writing on doctoral training was "Emotional Problems of Graduate Education." Its observations were based on the psychoanalysis of patients, both student and faculty, in academic life and on my own experience of over two decades as a student and teacher. Some women colleagues correctly pointed out that both the oedipal psychodynamics and the language of the article were posed from a masculine viewpoint. They said that although they recognized much of emotional validity, surely the emotional dynamics must be otherwise with women students and women faculty. Issues such as sexual exploitation, mother transferences by and from women faculty, and defenses of incompetency ("I am a little girl, please take care of me") by graduate students do exist and deserve careful description and study by a woman psychohistorian who has experienced them clinically. Such an essay would be a valuable contribution to the sparse literature on emotional forces in academic institutions.

"Love and Hate in the Academy" moves from an oedipal understanding to an object relations theoretical framework for analyzing academia. An object relations approach means that parts of the self that are projected and internalized become the unconsciously operative elements in feelings and decisionmaking. The two pieces, one written in the immediate years after graduate study, the second after an apprenticeship that consolidated my identity as an academic, also provide an excellent basis for the comparison of and demonstration of the difference between libido and object relations theory.

My desire to make these theories vivid with specific illustrative cases taken from modern historiography led to the paper "Graduate Years: What Kind of Passage?" and "The Psychobiographical Background to Psychohistory." Concepts and theories are best comprehended when they are presented in functional settings that show their application to life situations. When we have an eloquent and insightful historian-witness such as Pieter Geyl or William L. Langer to demonstrate a point out of his own academic and life experience, we should call on him.

The problem of integrating two disciplines is that usually one of them is held static while the other is considered the variable. Thus most historians consider consciousness and rationality as givens while they turn their expertise to analyzing and explaining the political, social, and economic variables of the world in the dimension of change over time. By the same token, psychoanalysts regard the external world as, in Heinz Hartmann's phrase, an "average expectable environment," while they meticulously monitor the internal life of their subjects. What clearly is needed—and this is the case for the demanding and difficult task of dual training in two disciplines—is the integration on any problem of a model of two independent variables, the inner and outer worlds over time. The project of psychohistory is to work with both psychology and history as complex variables, a process of mutual interaction, modification, and informing between disciplines that are committed to understanding the present by reconstructing the past.

The enterprise begins with the subjectivity of the investigator, the inner world and outer setting of the psychohistorian. His locus is academia, and the struggles for maturity and insight into historical reality occur in that habitat with its initiation rituals and ordeals. One of my aims is to conceptualize these rites as a process in psychoanalytical terms while dealing with the actual life situation of an important historian, Professor William L. Langer, who was also a seminal figure in the initiation of the psychoanalytic approach to history.

Emotional Problems
of Graduate Education

Conventionally we tend to conceive of graduate education as a linear development from uncouth ignorance to knowledge and grace. This straight, or possibly diagonal, or staggered, ascent to maturity may be an accurate representation of the intellectual processes during the graduate years. However, learning is much more than an intellectual process. In the graduate school it is a series of emotional involvements which are themselves a vital communication between students and teachers and which may constitute a resistance against the intellectual process. In discussing the pattern of graduate school, I would like to treat it as an emotional rather than an intellectual experience. The substantive content of graduate education has been dealt with extensively; however, the essence of any learning experience is an intrapsychic process.*

I wish to suggest that a more fruitful conceptualization of the graduate

*Some will feel that in the ensuing discussion I am painting too gloomy a picture of the graduate school, making it appear as a seething cauldron of unbridled unconscious passions. This, however, is inevitable when one seeks to direct attention to what behavioral scientists term the "latent functions" of an institutionalized relationship. This analysis is devoted to that aim and should therefore not be considered a normative description of the graduate school.

process is one of transference regression to earlier situations and fantasies of childhood, particularly in respect to authority.* If the course of study is satisfactorily concluded, a reversal of this regression and its resolution to a new level of maturity will be achieved. Frequent failure to accomplish this is due to the unconscious nature of the processes involved on the part of the active partners in the working alliance of graduate study, the students and faculty. Rather than fostering growth, together they too often work to counter it and perpetuate a psychology of domination and infantilization.

If one has been in the ambiance of higher education for any length of time, one cannot help but be struck by the very intensity of feelings toward faculty by students. The idealization of some professors is coupled with the most violent hatred of others. I am reminded of the postdoctoral student who keeps a photograph of his professor on his desk and the graduate student's wife who dreams of her husband's professor every night. Often the same people who adore one of their teachers respond to the name of another professor with a torrent of abuse in which the hated man is portrayed in the blackest diabolical colors. During the free speech demonstrations on the Berkeley campus one often heard the "deanocracy" referred to in transparent imagos of the "bad father" who betrayed his trust, was callous and neglectful of his children, and did not hesitate to use physical violence against them. The most paternal among the faculty felt threatened by the revolt of the sons and called for stern disciplinary measures.

In these cases we are dealing with one of Freud's great discoveries, the phenomenon of transference. It is one of the most potent intrapsychic forces in human interaction, "a universal phenomenon of the human mind" which "dominates the whole of each person's relations to his human environment." Transference is the experiencing of emotions and feelings toward a person in the present which are inappropriate to that person and are a repetition, a displacement, of reactions from some significant persons of earlier life. Said Freud, "A whole series of psychological experiences are revived, not as belonging to the past, but as applying to . . . the present moment."[1]

To deal with the transferences proves "to be by far the hardest part of the whole task" of analysis. It is "the strongest weapon of . . . resistance" and "the best instrument of the analytic treatment. Nevertheless its handling remains the most difficult as well as the most important part of the technique of analysis." In psychoanalysis a careful and systematic use is made of the transference: it is analyzed and brought to consciousness, thus becoming the

---

*Although transferences exist in all relationships, and this is especially true of authority relationships between students and instructors, I am limiting my observations to the graduate level because graduate students are older, their relationship to a single professor is more sustained and intimate, and they are usually materially more dependent on the nature of their transference for both immediate and long-range rewards.

"vehicle of success" in psychoanalytic treatment.[2] It is systematically studied, controlled, and effectively used as a therapeutic tool in psychoanalytic training because it is brought to consciousness.

Those concerned with higher education, on the other hand, appear to be unaware of the existence of transferences, a fact that amplifies their affect. As a psychological characteristic, transferences are especially in evidence in graduate academic settings where they are exacerbated by reality factors which infantilize the student and magnify the omnipotence of the teachers. Their effects are particularly pernicious here because they remain largely unconscious and unanalyzed. They are acted out instead of being made an instrument of learning and intellectual independence.

Great concern is perennially exhibited by graduate deans over the inordinate length of time involved in graduate work and the high rate of attrition among qualified doctoral candidates, leading to numerous surveys of graduate schools and their students. The outcome of these studies has been recommendations for "tightened" doctoral programs, shorter dissertations, more generous student support, and flexible requirements to fit the student's intellectual needs—all measures that are unexceptionable to anyone who has experienced graduate education. However, the feeling is inescapable that these studies, presuming to explain and meliorate student disaffection, miss their mark. No one has yet focused on the emotional conditions of graduate studies. It may be productive to investigate the behavioral aspects of graduate student disenchantment. I suggest that a large portion of student dissatisfaction lies less with the pedagogical content of the curriculum than with the psychological conditions of infantilization to which the student, often a pater- or materfamilias, is subjected.

It is a melancholy truth of the current situation that many of our brightest talents from our best graduate schools are lost to the humanistic disciplines each year for emotional reasons. I believe this is because they cannot tolerate the forced regression of graduate school: while demanding a high level of performance and integration in both the verbal-linguistic and behavioral spheres, it compels them toward an earlier stage of integration marked by deprivation and dependency.

Now, the stark fact is that the faculty-student relationship, particularly on the graduate level, is not that of equals. It is one of domination and submission. Whereas reality factors in other professional relationships such as attorney-client or doctor-patient are limited to a contractual transaction whereby the latter agrees to pay and obey while the former ministers with the promise of relief, in academia the reality gives the professor authority over the student's finances, employment, academic record, references—to say nothing of the emotional rewards—heightened self-esteem, enhanced prestige, and the fantasy of the eventual inheritance of power. The professor combines the transference authority of the parent with the actual power and institutional authority of a director of graduate studies. The student is in the almost totally impotent position of dependent child. For any student who has been an independent adult on his own, a return to graduate school most certainly represents an emotional regression. For his peer who has never left the institutional setting, it represents emotional dependence and stasis at exactly the age when he should be developing toward maturity. There may well be students who are so strong and adaptable that they are impervious to the traumas of a graduate education. With these fortunate souls we need not be concerned. We must be concerned with the high degree of demoralization and attrition among many of our most competent graduate students.

We know that transferences are inevitable in any relationship. All sustained relations between two people become dyadic. The partners form a pair with defined roles for each unit of the dyad. The student will seek a professor whose personality pattern complements his own. Their interaction may become adept and ritualized, with great mutual satisfaction. Identification will take place in any event, especially in the case of the most humane teachers. It is a given of the institutional situation that the student is infantilized by placing him in a position of filial dependence. The compassionate authority will induce in the student guilt for feelings of hatred; an adviser who withdraws will increase frustration. The brutalizing authority will in turn incite fear, hatred, and brutality in his students. The question is, will the transference identification be one that cripples the student or one that liberates him?

Regression takes place in regard to the nature of the things asked for from the teacher. When teacher and student engage in their initial encounter, the expectations appear clear and unambiguous. The student wants knowledge: data, method, and interpretation. The instructor wants to teach: to impart, demonstrate, and expose. Soon both parties realize they want other things as well. They desire all of those signals from each other that human beings want in any relationship: approval, acceptance, praise. The student wants sympathy, interest, and guidance; the instructor wants an audience, narcissistic supplies, and power.

A great many of these expectations will be fulfilled; others will be frustrated. The frustration provokes a reaction of elaboration on the expectation. It is as if the student said: "I want proof of your affection. Give me symbols of it. Do things for me (and with me and to me). Give me more intellect, more power, more money, a job." As he confronts the crises of graduate school, the student regresses to infantile fantasies in which he wishes for expressions of love from his teacher. He wishes to be talked to, reassured, comforted as a child facing anxiety. When these needs are not gratified, frustration is aroused. In many cases good manners and fear of the danger of arousing antagonism, as well as the satisfactions of regression, control and suppress the anger. The anger may be discharged in attempts to tease or embarrass the professor or in feeling schadenfreude at his misfortune. The basic anger that is felt against the authority, the feeling that the authority is disappointing, punishing, or neglecting, the desire to hurt the teacher, does not arise only from the graduate situation. It is anger that has been carried around since childhood against the father who beat him, the mother who shamed him, the brother or sister who mistreated him. The transference potential varies according to the personalities of the student and the teacher. As students make demands on their teachers for gratification, for approval, the instructor becomes "various someones"—a brother, father, husband, grandfather, mother, wife, sister, grandmother—in the unconscious fantasies of the pupil. German academics have incorporated a vital fantasy in the common expression *Doktor-Vater*, which is given to Ph.D.-sponsoring professors. This is what is meant by transference regression.

The graduate student confronts a quintet of crises which, if they are successfully resolved, will issue in an uninjured Ph.D. who has fully identified with the parents and is therefore prepared to subject his doctoral candidates to the same series of traumas.*

The impact on the student in his initial contact with graduate school is a feeling of helplessness, a striving toward closeness often accompanied by submission anxiety and fear of being dominated. The unconscious threat is of temptation to homosexual submission. In return for submission the student may share the parent's power and be assured the older person's protection. The hostility aroused takes the manifest form of wishing to pay the authority back, to irritate and make fun of him, to damage and cheat him, to discourage and exasperate him, to baffle and humiliate him and show him up. However, the student is forced to repress the deeper levels of hostility, to hold in his murderous wishes. He wishes to destroy the master, to take his place and inherit his power. Since this is impossible in immediate reality, the student wishes to partake of the power of the mighty one, to merge with him, to be devoured by him. The position of apprentice is to be passive toward the master, to give him fealty and devotion. In return the apprentice shares in the power and enjoys the advantages of being small: protection and

*The schema I present is merely a tool to think with in order to facilitate comparison and to attempt to structure theoretically the obscure feelings and observations we all have about the graduate experience. The series of crises I outline are not inclusive or mutually exclusive. There are certainly others, and the ones I articulate as discrete may well converge. Thus, it should be needless to say that with this, as with any typology, it can illuminate reality only so far and no further. I leave it to the reader to see what recognition of unconscious fantasies it may bring forth.

a minimal competitive standard of performance. He may in fantasy antici-pate the future when he will be greater than the master, but meanwhile he has "pull," that is, participation in power before he has been formally admitted to the ranks of the rulers.

Relationships with fellow graduate students may be supportive in under-going the initiatory experience. Older students can be advisers in the role of big brother who steers the neophyte past the graduate shoals where he may be wrecked. For the veteran student the role of guide who has weath-ered the dangers of professorial caprice intensifies his identification with authority while his helping the infantilization of the novice enables him to escape the consciousness of his own dependence.

There is the same ambivalence in these friendships among peers as there is among any siblings. The impulse toward competitiveness, to struggle with other graduate students, to win and become the favored child must be paid for by reparation to them. The hatred of rivals is compensated and repaired by reactive friendliness and socializing. Aggressive, jealous, and murderous wishes are defended against and undone by kindness, an attempt to repair harm which has been fantasied or actually done to peers. The sense of guilt is decreased and the rivalry for the professor's love and appreciation may continue. The struggles for approval are accompanied by fears of being rejected and abandoned by the professor which may be made worse by object lessons from those who have been discarded from the graduate fellowship and expelled to the outside world. The graduate candidate yearns to be protected, shielded, defended from external threats such as hostile faculty members or reality testing of his ability.

If the student has negotiated the first two stages of isolation and antag-onism without being psychically crippled or driven out, he proceeds to a position of "identification with the aggressor," in which he incorporates qualities of his professor in his personal demeanor and his views.[3] This identification may be of the feared object but it can also be a beloved object. Authorities are always ambivalently hated and loved. Sooner or later the teacher is introjected and becomes a part of his pupil's psychic reality. All new growth begins as imitative learning. This includes both intellectual structure and personal mannerisms. The hope is that the stu-dent will evolve mature thinking processes independent of his transference identifications. The danger is that of being devoured. Many disciples so closely embrace their mentor's thought that any originality has no chance to develop or disappears. They have become second-imprint surrogates of the powerful one.

Whenever they occur, examinations entail a self-evident graduate trauma. At this critical juncture, anxiety, guilt, and inferiority feelings are enforced. The student's strivings for reassurance and self-esteem are heightened. Now the authority will decide whether the candidate is accepted and allowed to participate in the privileges of the guild.

The doctoral examination is the modern initiation rite par excellence. Initiations have both regressive and progressive features. Striving for mastery at new integrative tasks arouses regressive needs. Puberty ceremonies among primitives, where the teaching of tribal lore is intimately bound with subincision rites or circumcision, point to the bond between learning and the threat of castration. Themes of death and resurrection, mutilation, and the acting out of instinctual tendencies mark initiation rites.

The issue in graduate school is whether the student shall obtain the narcissistic supplies he craves and be admitted to the fellowship of the big brothers, or whether he is to be rejected and sentenced to expulsion and narcissistic hunger. His reaction to this test will depend on his sexual and aggressive relationship to paternal authority and on his narcissistic needs. If the student sexualizes the examination, hoping thereby to overcome his inferiority feelings and castration fear, all the while having to face the danger that his efforts will result in his total annihilation, an anxiety hysteria may result. Any conflicts around passive-feminine longings vis-à-vis the father, exhibitionism, or shame will come to the surface during the emotional stress of the doctoral examinations. Fears of destruction may be defended against by purchasing the examiner's goodwill by submission: "We are not enemies, we are friends." This, of course, implies the readiness to become aggressive against the teacher who does not respond to this mild identificatory love. Then we see the fury with which love can suddenly be converted to destructive hatred. The ambivalence was always there.

Because he has aggressive fantasies against authority, the student expects to be annihilated by authority. The fear of being destroyed grows out of the wish to annihilate. Much of the shame and fear witnessed in oral doctoral examinations is the unconscious fear of retribution by faculty for fantasies of mutilation and destruction harbored by frustrated students according to the formula: "They will now do to me what I have wished to do to them." These fantasies are contemporized reenactments of responses to cruel and hurtful situations from long ago that have been aroused by the infantilizing quality of graduate school relationships.

The student, having traversed the hurdle of the examinations, has before him the prospect of independence. Paradoxically, although this vista is invariably celebrated, it is not uniformly welcomed by the unconscious. To terminate an unresolved regressive relationship to a person and an institution who have protected, enclosed, defended, means growing up. The dangers of autonomy, threats of unknown destruction, await. Fear of being literally "out in the cold," of leaving the protecting parent, give rise to the separation anxiety which, if the terror of aloneness is great enough, may prevent the student from ever emerging into manhood.

For today's graduate students, the five traumas of helplessness, dangerous rivalry, fear of incorporation, examinations, and final separation anxiety, form a modern ordeal of graduate transference regression and—if surmounted—resolution into new autonomy and strength. The favorable emergence is problematic and frequently in doubt because of the almost completely unconscious role played at the controlling end by the faculty. Instead of abetting independence, they all too often act out fantasies of omnipotence and sadism, utilizing and encouraging the willing accomplices to be found in their students because of their unconscious need to be tyrannized.

The unhappy concomitant is that too often the selective variable of the "successful" graduate student is he who can by obsequious behavior best fill the professor's unconscious needs. Faculty tend to fight for the student who is compliant and against the student who threatens them. The student quickly realizes that if he submits and convinces those in authority of his compliance, he will receive a degree and its correlates in money and status. It is relevant to ask, what happens to the student's approach to the subject matter when it is taught under such circumstances? The tyranny of the teacher over his pupil may become lifelong. We have only to look at professional meetings and journals to see the sense of filial obligation dutifully acted out daily. This is a natural consequence of a situation in which dependence on the goodwill of authority has become a character trait. A premium is placed on the ability to conform to current orthodoxy. Fear and competition for favor among students is encouraged. The true measure of excellence becomes faithful discipleship rather than creativity.

The crippling effects of this psychological position should be obvious. The student is frustrated in matters of participation in decisions governing his life. In the most important matters relating to his vocational goals and future he is in a dependent position. The transference, induced by his frustration, is an attempt by regression to overcome the obstacles to autonomy and volition that graduate school embodies. This regression to a passive identification and dependency may be compared to the regression the mature traveler undergoes as an alien in a land whose language and customs are foreign to him. He reverts to the position of the dependent child who is forced to communicate in the primitive language of gestures and signals. While graduate students do not generally suffer a diminution of their verbal-linguistic skills outside of examinations, they do engage in the most primitive symbolic communication. They unconsciously imitate the language, gestures, bearing, mannerisms, and idioms, not to mention the ideas, of the ambivalently loved and hated professor. These are unconscious attempts to identify with the idealized authority, to be loved by him, to incorporate and to become one with him as well as to defend against him and by identification to ward off the threat of being destroyed by him. This, not coincidentally, is also the behavioral model for brainwashing: ego impoverishment by overwhelming anxiety; then love, consisting of a smile, approval by the granting of a trivial position of authority, and signs of favor such as cigarettes. Thereafter the captor becomes a transference object and the prisoner is amenable to any suggestion.

The gratifications of the professor in the teaching relationship are manifold and deep. He is the subject of direct, rapt attention. His function in the seminar room or on the lecture podium is elevated by the student's awe to a position unapproached in his other roles in life. His narcissism is fed by an infantile adoration which those who relate to him as a whole person, such as his family, cannot supply. The "love" relationship, based on the student's idealized omnipotent fantasies, which feeds the instructor's narcissistic fantasies, can lead to a protraction of graduate studies in which the student continues to bask masochistically in the glow of the professor's protection while the teacher sadistically perpetuates the duration of graduate work by being impossible to satisfy.

If transference is inevitable, are there possible correctives? Must we live with the psychic traumas of graduate education forever? A number of panaceas, such as unrevokable and uncontingent four-year fellowships, have been proposed. Certainly, all measures that reduce the student's economic and career dependence on his emotional relationship to his teachers are commendable. Placement, for example, could be by open listing on a national register. The written Ph.D. examination should not be drafted or evaluated by the student's major professor. Student representation on the governing boards of educational institutions would certainly be salutary. However, my aim is not to outline another proposed revision of graduate school format. Before any changes in structure will be effective, instead of merely being reinstitutionalizations of domination, a consciousness of the emotional dimensions of the academic teacher-student relationship must be achieved.

Can transference manifestations be dealt with only by a complete psychoanalysis of all students and instructors? Even a full personal analysis has residuals and leaves blind spots by which regressions to satisfactions of infantile needs in unrealistic ways are still open. But a teacher who is aware of his attitudes and reactions that interfere with his pedagogical aim, which should be the increasing maturity and self-direction of his students, may make proper allowances for his neurotic tendencies in his teaching relationships.

The first step toward mental health is consciousness. Transference is most pernicious when it is ignored. We can all try to recognize those transference phenomena which enter into our research as well as our work with students. We can analyze their meaning in the light of our personal self-knowledge. Any person should be able to ask of himself, "Why am I angered, excited, or irritated? Why am I pleased or aroused? Why does this come up now? What is the student subtly trying to get me to give him? Can I perhaps not see it clearly because I so much want to do it? What does this student mean to me other than his interest in the subject being studied?"

The task of the instructor who would deal rationally with his transference feelings is a difficult but essential one: He must become conscious of the fantasies within himself, recognize their source, separate the student's fantasies from his own, and so restore an objective situation where learning can once again take place instead of the acting out of neurotic fantasies.

Good teachers from the time of Socrates have been aware of the transference phenomenon and have pedagogically used it. We see it all about us daily. Identification is one of our most valuable tools. Students eagerly learn to please teachers they love and admire. Such transference love may supply the necessary motive to persist in an unpleasant task such as mastering a dull subject where intrinsic intellectual curiosity could not sustain learning incentive. The teacher's concern for the student stems unconsciously from two normal basic constructive drives: the reparative and the parental. The desire to repair counteracts the latent destructiveness in us all. The student stands for the damaged parts of himself in the teacher's own unconscious which are still endangered by aggression and still in need of reparation. To the instructor, the student is his early self. His interest and empathy, his feeling of recognition and identification with the student, are the motives for a relationship of humanness, warmth, and freedom.

The values of great teachers, their ideologies and their lives, have inspired and influenced their pupils. Students learn by emulation. The inevitable identification with the master will not be permanent if the teacher is aware of the graduate transference and recognizes it for what it is. Then he can take account of it and guide the student through it. Sometimes this will mean providing the necessary emotional support to help the student up and out of his dependency. The most inhumane and inexcusable course of all is to induce the graduate regression and then sadistically abandon the student because of his irrational emotional demands.

The very spirit of education is to help a student to realize his own potentialities, to let him discover what he really can do, not as imitation, not in response to command, nor because it has been charted for him, but because he has acquired a new view of himself and his capacity.

We dare not allow ourselves the gratification of our own or our student's infantile and neurotic wishes. Compassion, concern, and pedagogical intent toward the student are essential to an emotionally healthy graduate setting. The student must be respected as an individual. We cannot demean the student by imposing irrational rules and regulations upon him without explanation and then expect him to develop the capacity to work seriously with us as an adult.

Social scientists who are aware of modern psychology no longer accept the existence of a dichotomy between subjectivity and objectivity. All perceptions of the world are refracted through the prism of our inner life, resolving it into components that produce a significant pattern. The scholar's task is to exercise intellectual integrity and avoid sentimentality in his treatment of sources; but his responsibility demands that he say what reality means to him in his human uniqueness. All experience is interpreted in terms of its subjective implications. The creative act of a scholar is to achieve insight into the data of observation, to subject this insight to empirical discipline, and to impart to this experience of the particular event a meaning of human validity.

To achieve this high order requires of graduate students self-definition through the clarification of experience and the establishment of self-esteem. The goal of graduate study should be a person capable of subjective intensity, disciplined but not repressed. The graduate years are a quest for creativity and maturity that faculty can aid rather than hinder by themselves experiencing the emotions of transference with integrity.

Notes

    1. Sigmund Freud, *Standard Edition of the Complete Psychological Works,* trans. and ed. James Strachey et al. (London, 1953–1974), 20: 42; 7: 16.

    2. *Ibid.,* 7: 16; 20: 43; 12: 105.

    3. Anna Freud, *The Ego and the Mechanisms of Defense,* trans. Cecil Baines (New York, 1946), pp. 117–31.

The Graduate Years

What Kind of Passage?

The usual picture of the years of graduate study is one of blissful learning at the feet of scholars and of congenial companionship with peers. While both of these exist and are essential to morale, I wish to suggest another and more creative model for what actually takes place—a conflict model in which the graduate student learns the skills and acquires the tools by which he revises and overthrows his teachers, just as he in turn will be superseded by his own students.

The graduate years are a passage toward growth, maturation, and intellectual acquisition. What kind of journey will it be? Emotionally it will exist somewhere on a continuum between two extremes. A journey fraught with fear and anxiety, one stifling to creativity, a passage that serves to block and disrupt the attainment of original purposes, ending at best in bitterness, cynicism, and disillusionment? Or, a journey of growth, self-realization, intellectual independence, and autonomy? In pursuing this question, let us look at the major emotional experiences of graduate training, which are essential to its course and success, but which can become impediments to reaching personal and professional goals if the parties to the experience so permit.

The difficult emotional struggles of the graduate journey are centered on:
(1) the faculty's evaluative and institutional functions, (2) rivalries and competitive pressures, (3) overestimation of the major instructor and a tendency
to identify excessively with him, and (4) the nature of the structured demands of the educational process which tend to stifle the fresh, new, and
innovative insight.

Evaluative and reporting roles are inseparable parts of the instructor's
relationship with his students. Students are aware that at all stages of their
graduate careers they are being critically appraised as human beings, as
intellectuals, and as potential colleagues. Is he or she an acceptable professional product? Will they represent their teacher, their department, and
their institution positively?

Unfortunately, it is today increasingly true that there are only limited
fellowships, grants, research funds, and academic positions, for which there
are a virtually undiminished number of seekers. This is in the realm of real
faculty power and student fear. The material and social rewards of degree,
prestige, money, and the eventual inheritance of power are the explicit
promise of the teachers and the motivations of the student. These awards
and prizes become the affirmations of intellectual and professional worth.
They tend to be seen as ultimate verdicts rather than as the tentative symbols
which they are. The evidence of this is the anger, jealousy, and depression
that arise during the graduate years within those who perceive themselves
as outsiders as against the others whom they fantasy as belonging.

The greatest emotional investment of the doctoral candidate is his desire
to become a doctor. Students will idealize their graduate teachers in seeking
to emulate them, just as children identify with, and wish to become like,
their parents. This is a necessary psychodynamic of any educational process.
But it may, if the idealized distortions are not corrected, result in intellectual
and emotional dependency and crippled creativity. Some faculty play into
the dependency longings of their students because of their own need for
narcissistic validation through the creation of models in their own image.
The clear message is: "If you want to be successful, be like me." The
academic's ego ideals demand of him that he do a good job and the proof
lies in his students, their preparation, success in competition, and achievement. Some faculty are avid proselytizers who compete with colleagues and
who need to feel they have succeeded where others have failed.

The classic means by which subordinates handle conflict with superiors
is passive aggression. Those who are conversant with the current revisionist
historiography of antebellum slavery in the United States will recognize that
the arguments about malingering, absenteeism, incompetence, and accidents
on the job are also discussions about the modes of passive aggression.

Sociologists of industry like Harvey Swados point to the destruction of automobiles by workers on assembly lines and the obstruction and sabotage of "rational" factory procedures among laborers.[1]

There may also be a tendency to more overt aggression: defying the "old man" and tearing down his point of view. As one friend of mine, who happens to be a Marxist, put it: "You have to kill your *Doktor-Vater* in order to be your own man." There is an important element of truth in this. Virtually all scholarship is written in support of or against an existing point of view, and innumerably more pieces begin as acts of intellectual destruction than as contributions to the buttressing of old concepts. A number of academic careers have been made by attacking, for example, the Weber, Pirenne, Becker, Turner, or Beard theses. These acts of intellectual aggression are overdetermined in motive.

Admixtures of displaced attacks on the father, identifications with or displacements from the *Doktor-Vater,* and sometimes cultural, ethnic, or generational battles are fought out in scholarship as well. The sociology of knowledge is an infinitely rich mine to work and, as Mannheim was aware, its subtlety is increased when it is fused with the psychology of knowledge. As Freud put it in 1909:

> The liberation of an individual, as he grows up, from the authority of his parents is one of the most necessary though one of the most painful results brought about by the course of his development. It is quite essential that that liberation should occur and it may be presumed that it has been to some extent achieved by everyone who has reached a normal state. Indeed, the whole progress of society rests upon the opposition between successive generations.[2]

Sometimes a point is best made by moving to a neutral time and place. The example I would like to draw is from one of my favorite historians, the great Dutch scholar Pieter Geyl (1887–1966). He is unusual in spelling out for us his acute awareness of the unique blend of personal, nationalistic, and generational motives and conflicts that infused his scholarship and career. His self-consciousness was not harmful; indeed, it was a positive aid in providing him with direction, balance, and impetus.

Geyl was responsible in his career of research and writing for an entire reversal in interpretation of the origins of the Dutch nation. He pointed to new and hitherto neglected historical forces of conquest and geography that had determined the survival of the Dutch State. His views are now well established and widely accepted. What is relevant here is Geyl's awareness that his commitment to a "Great Netherlander" interpretation of Dutch history came years *before* his important historical research. He tells of his enthusiasm at coming into contact with the Flemish student movement while he was still a student himself. In what appears to have been a conversion experience, Geyl describes himself as a student as being

> deeply impressed by the moral fervor that met me there. . . . These men were conscious of a great social task. . . . I felt that we of the North had an active obligation toward them. . . . These impressions were never effaced, and they led me to question the spirit in which the history of our common past was generally written. . . . To question the Little Netherlands, or Dutch State, view . . . seemed to me . . . our own duty. . . .
>
>   I got immersed in the counsels of the newborn Flemish Nationalist movement as intimately as if I had been a Fleming.[3]

Geyl also had a professional enemy and target. His bête noire was the much older, well-established historian, the esteemed Professor Henri Pirenne (1862–1935), historian of Belgium and the leading medievalist of his time. Pirenne was a Walloon, a French-speaking Belgian, teaching in French at the University of Ghent in the Flemish-speaking part of the country. He was, to the quarter-of-a-century-younger Pieter Geyl, the Dutch student who was at that time visiting a Flemish student congress at Ghent, a man who

> occupied an advanced outpost in the movement of penetration and conquest which French civilization, under the auspices of the centralized Belgian State, was carrying on in Flanders. . . . Pirenne contributed to the struggle by offering [his] historical conception. . . . It is no more than a smokescreen behind which is hidden the stark and incontrovertible truth.[4]

These conflicts with prevailing views and personalities played a major role in Geyl's professional life. A professorship at a Dutch university was withheld from him until he was fifty-two. And when he was finally appointed, it was over powerful opposition in a long struggle and against the recommendation of the faculty of the University of Utrecht. The contest shifted to The Hague in a fight that Geyl described as "vehement . . . and to me painful." Personal distaste was disguised in the language of the academy while his work was called "Nothing but politics! Unscholarly!" by his adversaries. His final struggle, a matter of having "to wait another painful three months," was due to the opposition of the Queen, who refused to sign his decree of appointment, presumably because Geyl had criticized her eighteenth-century ancestor, William IV. Geyl was regarded as anti-Orange.[5] There was a follow-up to this official antagonism when, in 1945 upon his return from German internment in Buchenwald, Geyl was made to wait four months for the royal decree reinstating him as a professor.

Geyl was keenly aware that, as he put it, "history cannot be conceived, and it cannot be written or communicated, except from a point of view conditioned by the circumstances of the historian." This may be asserted, as it was by Geyl, without succumbing to that variant of the genetic fallacy which reflects on the adequacy of a historical view because the emotional sources of that view have been exposed. Indeed, the opposite position is more often accurate. The intensity of emotional commitment of the researcher motivates him to secure data and work on it in a way that less involved scholars would not. The lesson of Professor Geyl to us is to use our life experience and feelings, all of them, with the greatest intensity and to the greatest depths possible, in our professional work. Geyl used his concentration camp experience to refract and reinterpret the role of an earlier dictator who had conquered Europe and had had limitless ambitions for power. The book that came out of this dialogue, *Napoleon: For and Against,* related present to past in Geyl's mind. An unexcelled study in French historiography, it is infused with Geyl's own values as a western European liberal, which are not hidden, but are explicit, and do not detract from, but rather add to, the value of the work.[6]

One way of approaching the problems of the graduate student is to look at the various coping devices that one may develop to deal with, circumvent, or aggravate the situation confronting the student. The metaphor I wish to employ is the one Professor Carl Bridenbaugh used in his notorious Presidential Address to the American Historical Association to say that "urban-bred scholars of today" do not "show any real, perceptive comprehension of the workings of human nature" and therefore cannot understand American history. He said they lacked empathy with the American experience because they did not know how to teach a calf to drink out of a milk pail, a skill which Professor Bridenbaugh asserted he possessed. He went on to say, "Many of the younger practitioners of our craft, and those who are still apprentices, are products of lower-middle-class or foreign origins, and their emotions not infrequently get in the way of historical reconstructions."[7]

Of course we can dismiss this "milk-pail" line of argument as an example of just how foolish scholars can be, for we all know that it takes at least as much "human understanding" for a child to make his way through a city neighborhood as it does to live on a farm. But the main point I wish to make is that emotions do not get in the way of intellectual cognition, they are the means to understanding. The emotional defenses of intellectualization and isolation of affect (removing what we study from our feelings) lead to a rigid and constricted view of reality that interferes with the capacity to understand human phenomena. To categorize and conceptualize, to isolate and intellectualize, are among the most valuable of mental tools. Experience and data must be structured and ordered to be useful in any discipline. But this is too often done at the expense of emotional cognition. Preferably the fullest possible openness to experience should come first, for this is the source of creativity. As one who has on occasion engaged in the feeding and milking enterprise, by both hand and machine, I wish to suggest that graduate education is like milking the cow. You may get no sustenance, a little, or a lot, depending on how you approach the beast. You may even antagonize her and get kicked so that your bucket of accumulated milk spills and is wasted. Which is to say that there are many personality types in academia and how you best exploit what the faculty has to offer is an idiosyncratic matter which requires adjustment from case to case. The various coping mechanisms are poles on a continuum which may be positively adaptive on one end and self-defeatingly maladaptive on the other. A moderate variation, like the slight turn of a kaleidoscope, often throws a whole new perspective on a situation.

　　The best psychoanalytic works on the nature of creativity stress three elements in the creative process, beginning with a period of intensive preparatory work which may entail the acquisition of scholarly techniques and disciplines. This period is filled with effort and often marked by feelings of defeat and frustration, inferiority and depression. There follows a recourse to dissociated states, similar to free association in psychoanalysis, or the state immediately prior to falling asleep. The sources of creativity are from some not readily accessible areas of the mind, called preconscious, unconscious, or subconscious. To come into touch with these areas requires a freshness, a special quality of spontaneity and freedom from mental rigidity and stereotyped conventional thinking. This openness to encounter with hitherto inaccessible parts of the self is called "regression in the service of the ego" in psychoanalytical parlance. The final element is the fitting together of the newly accessible intuitions, perceptions, and feelings into a coherent schema. This is the moment of insight, and is accompanied by euphoria and exhilaration. The ideas click, they fit into each other, forming a new pattern, configuration, or whole. The integrative linking results in novel combinations of data or syntheses which are then scrutinized and tested.[8]

　　Concrete thinking, literalness, conscious repression, and self-control are the enemies of creativity. To tie symbolic processes to nit-picking definitions or to false precision robs us of the openness to experience that is necessary to see new connections. The mind must be free to leave traditional thoroughfares, to go unhampered by the restrictions of received signposts to the neglected backwaters, the quiet by-ways, to gather seemingly unrelated impressions and sensations, and to allow them to fall into varied combinations until new relationships and patterns emerge.

If this view of the creative process is correct, and I believe that it is, if it approximates reality, you will recognize elements of it in your own experience of the quiet hours of the night and the unofficial working hours of rest and play, when the real mental work still goes on. You will also recognize that this view is entirely syntonic with Thomas Kuhn's "paradigm shift" theory of scientific revolutions and Paul Feyerabend's relativism about "truth"[9] and "reality."[9] But there is more—this view of creativity implies the most radical critique of education as we know it. Dependence on rote learning of data, drill, repetition, and imitation of our teachers, examination systems that place a premium on the memorization and delivery of data— all tend to produce creative paralysis, unimaginative conformity, and intellectual submissiveness to our teachers long after they should have ceased being our teachers. That education is best which allows the student to accept, reject, or modify the authority of his past and his teachers.

The dangers cited may result in the graduate training's being a success and the experience's being a failure. Instead of a teacher's lifelong unconscious tyranny over a pupil, the goal of a successful educational experience is to provide the student with tools, techniques, knowledge, and the setting, so he can be a person himself.

We should always remember that conceptual leaps in knowledge and theory were initially unofficial, uninstitutionalized, and, by definition, antiorthodox. All truths began as heresies, usually propagated by amateurs or outsiders who challenged the authority of prescribed belief. The creative minds we admire most—Copernicus and Darwin, Marx and Freud—did not have it easy. Their insights were ridiculed and their lives made difficult by isolation, contempt, and prejudice.

The collaborative task of establishing and maintaining an internal and institutional atmosphere of creativity and intellectual collaboration requires ever continuing effort and internal vigilance.

Notes

1. Harvey Swados, *On the Line* (Boston, 1957), pp. 191–4.

2. Sigmund Freud, "Family Romances" (1909), *Standard Edition of the Complete Psychological Works,* trans. and ed. James Strachey et. al. (London, 1953–1974), 9:237.

3. Pieter Geyl, *The Netherlands in the Seventeenth Century:* Vol. I, 1609–1648, Vol. II, 1648–1715 (London, 1961–1964); "The National State and the Writers of Netherlands History," *Debates with Historians* (Cleveland, Ohio, 1958), pp. 219–20; "Looking Back," *Encounters in History* (Cleveland, Ohio, 1961), p. 358.

4. Geyl, *Debates with Historians,* pp. 216–17.

5. Geyl, *Encounters in History,* pp. 364, 401.

6. Geyl, *Debates with Historians,* p. 221; *Napoleon: For and Against* (New Haven, 1949).

7. Carl Bridenbaugh, "The Great Mutation," *American Historical Review,* 68 (January 1963): 319, 328, 322–3.

8. My views on the psychodynamics of creativity have been shaped by: Ernst Kris, *Psychoanalytic Explorations in Art* (New York, 1952); Lawrence S. Kubie, *Neurotic Distortions of the Creative Process* (Lawrence, Kans., 1958); Elliott Jaques, "Disturbances in the Capacity to Work," *International Journal of Psycho-Analysis,* 41 (1960): 357–67; "Death and the Mid-Life Crisis," *ibid.,* 46 (1965): 502–14; Eliot Dole Hutchinson, "Varieties of Insight in Humans"; "The Period of Frustration in Creative Endeavor"; "The Nature of Insight," in *A Study of Interpersonal Relations: New Contributions to Psychiatry,* ed. Patrick Mullahy (New York, 1949), pp. 386–445; Rose Spiegel, "Creative Process in the Arts," *Science and Psychoanalysis,* Vol. 3 (New York, 1965), pp. 107–32.

9. Thomas S. Kuhn, *The Structure of Scientific Revolutions* (Chicago, 1970); Paul K. Feyerabend, "Explanation, Reduction, and Empiricism," in *Minnesota Studies in the Philosophy of Science,* 3 (1962); 28–97, and "Against Method," in *ibid,* 4 (1970).

Love and Hate
in the Academy

Each of us in the course of his personal development has worked out a set of devices that offers some protection against fear and uncertainty. The externalization of unknown distortions in our inner world brings about most of the distortions in our outer world. Warped evaluations, misassessments of fact, and personal vituperation have a foundation in the emotions of the individual. One sees and fears in others what one is trying to control in oneself.

The university furnishes an excellent illustration of this. Academic rivalry, professional envy, and defamation represent attempts to gain a sense of personal security and safety by making the outer world safe against fantasied internal dangers. In this sense a great deal of professional behavior is irrational.

Of all the defense mechanisms that shield us from insight into ourselves and others, projection is the most pervasive. Everyone uses this mechanism to a greater or lesser degree. We perceive our own vices in others, whether they are there or not. The purpose of projection is to get rid of the depressed parts of the self: the sense of worthlessness and inferiority, of being despised.

Projection is often a form of manipulation which is a defense against anxiety, that is, against the fantasied dangers of the inner world.

The idea that what we select to persecute in others reflects something in ourselves may seem implausible. But one cannot imagine any sentiment or affect in someone else unless one has known it in some degree oneself, either consciously or unconsciously. The emotions and passions we fantasize in others are only a selection from the wide range of feelings that we might infer from their behavior. We are rarely dispassionate observers. Usually we are interested in seeing only those aspects of others that concern their relation to ourselves. Surprisingly large elements of the omnipotent and projective belief systems of infancy and childhood survive in the unconscious. Here they disturb the thought, feeling, and conduct of the most sane, brilliant, and accomplished persons in our world, as any honest autobiography or journal will demonstrate.

Projection onto others of something in ourselves results in failure to understand others. We deprive them of their good qualities and endow them with bad qualities which they do not have, thereby projecting our own worthless, envious, hostile, and murderous selves. We may also project onto others good qualities which they do not have, making them into idealized external figures who will defend us against inner evil and emptiness.

Such splitting and projection, while present in all normal people, can assume massive and highly pathological shapes.

The founder of psychoanalysis gave us, from his own self-analysis, some lucid examples. Freud was aware of how such mechanisms governed his own interpersonal relations:

> My emotional life has always insisted that I should have an intimate friend and a hated enemy. I have always been able to provide myself afresh with both, and it has not infrequently happened that the ideal situation of childhood has been so completely reproduced that friend and enemy have come together in a single individual—though not, of course, both at once or with constant oscillations, as may have been the case in my early childhood.[1]

Ordinary people also experience projection. We may see it in the dreams and nightmares which reveal our inner world. A frequent theme of these is the destruction of one tormenting pursuer followed by his reincarnation and multiplication, so that the "good" self is never secure from the projected bad parts of the self. The uses of projection have been most fully investigated in the works of Melanie Klein, R. E. Money-Kyrle, Elliott Jaques, and W. R. Bion.[2]

These processes also permeate the life of organizations. Often, in order to preserve its existence or its threatened values, a group will exclude one of its members. It will choose a victim to be isolated who can serve as the impotent outsider. Destroying him solidifies and raises group morale. The selected victim is often subjected to a third degree intended to force him to believe that he is guilty of all the flaws with which he is charged. Group manipulation is often used not merely to falsify the ideas of another person but also to force some role upon him.

The accuser who persecutes the selected "outsider" is so frightened of his own shortcomings that he must force someone else to display these vices. This can often be managed by pressuring the victim to behave in a paranoid fashion. When manipulation has this intent, the targeted person will experience it as a pressure to which he may or may not give way, or against which he will be aware of having to use great force and tenacity to preserve his own identity. He will find his own picture of himself assaulted, disparaged, and denigrated. In some cases he may feel like the victim of a secret police investigation and be in danger of believing himself guilty of anything he is accused of.

The pathological nature of such a projection is betrayed by the inordinate degree of anger, anxiety, and depression aroused in the manipulators if the target proves recalcitrant. Incipient feelings of inadequacy may be warded off if others can be found who, by being treated as failures, can be made to feel they are empty and have little or no value.

Of course, it is only to the degree that the targets have their own latent feelings of inadequacy and worthlessness to be aroused that such techniques can be successful. But since everyone harbors these feelings in some measure, no one is altogether immune. It is a psychological fact of group life, demonstrable in family and group psychotherapy, that to arouse depressed feelings in one person can cause them to subside in another.[3] Families may mark one member as the "bad" child, or the "sick" one, or the perpetual "mess-up." Groups also handle stress and avoid tension by making one of their members the butt, the "cause" of all their difficulties, and the target for hostility. The victim feels as if he has not only become worthless and shameful, but also that he has lost the qualities and abilities he thought he had.

Good parts of the self may also be projected in this way. For example, the desire of teachers to have disciples is in part an expression of the urge to transcend mortality and the fear of extinction. Many of the most supportive relationships between professors and their students are grounded in the need to repair damaged objects in the teacher's self-representation. Parts of his self which were damaged in the past and are still endangered by aggresssion are projected to the still uninjured student. In him these parts may be nourished, cared for, and will thrive as the older scholar identifies with the struggles of the novice.

To the teacher the student is his early uninjured self through whom he may repair the wounds and scars of his own development. But the teacher who tries compulsively to force his students or younger colleagues to be exact replicas of his ideal self is under the influence of something more than normal separation and identification. He is trying to project onto others the good parts of himself which he cannot defend against his own aggressiveness. His unconscious picture of the self is that of an arena in which the good parts are locked in a losing struggle with the evil components. Therefore there is a desperate effort to save something good from impending destruction by forcing it on another faculty member or student.

The unconscious survival of depressed parts of the personality, maintained in some degree in everyone, are certain to compromise the rationality of our evaluations and behavior. The academic world counts as ideals impeccable scholarship, lucid writing, and stimulating, effective teaching. Since no man or woman can attain these ideals all the time, and all have known painful failure, there are in all faculty members parts that fall short of the best possible performance at all times. It is these unacceptable qualities which distort our assessments and evaluations when they are projected onto others.

When there is an unfused internal mixture of idealization and denigration, one of the incompatible self-images will be projected. If one projects his idealized self, only the bad self will remain. The idealized figure can do no wrong. But when one projects his disparaged self, he feels contempt for others and arrogant conceit about himself.

Contempt combined with hatred conceals the fear which underlies them both. Contempt for the inferiority projected onto others also covers a denial of the envy of their desired qualities. Envy is the desire to possess the attributes of another person. The kinder the other person is, the more gifted, brilliant, and generous, the more he may be envied for his very goodness. This creates a fear that the destructive rage of envy will annihilate what has been projected from the self, but is at the same time most valued, as the envy of it proves.

Motives of spite and vengeance often dominate academic controversy and decision making. As in other cases where the unconscious provides the controlling motive, the spiteful aim is concealed behind conscious good intentions. Actions are elaborately justified as being in the service of "academic excellence," "for the good of the department," or because of the "quality of mind" of the people involved.

That individuals can be hated for their admired qualities is rarely admitted. The contempt that intellectuals often have for each other covers a great deal of mutual envy. The main reason for crushing and frustrating a rival in academic life is often not that he has too little value, but that he is unconsciously envied too much. We destroy as worthless that which we strongly desire and are unable to possess. The most authoritarian personalities, for example, cannot tolerate those of their younger colleagues who do not capitulate to authority, not merely because of the manifest challenge but also because they are filled with envy for the virility they do not share. Their own authoritarianism is the product of having cowered before authority in their past. Now they find that those among their colleagues who are freer than they were and are not obsequious to authority are not only the most threatening but the most envied. These younger men cannot be tolerated because they possess a quality that was treasured and lost—autonomy. Now it cannot be regained and the envied ones who have it must be punished for it just as those who have lost it were once punished for it. Whenever arrogance and contempt cover envy there can be little chance for mutual understanding leading to a solution of common institutional problems.

Neither envy nor the competition it feeds can ever be abolished. What is pathological is not the existence of envy but the denial of it, which serves to heighten it far beyond the level it would otherwise attain. The guilt feelings it gives rise to are what maintain and foster the denial of envy. The intensity of guilt aroused by envy is what holds it at a level over what it would otherwise be.

The forcible projection of bad qualities is often combined with the greedy introjection of virtuous ones. A group seeks candidates for membership who possess the desirable qualities the group idealizes. When such a person is targeted, he becomes superhuman in the eyes of the group. The most idealized fantasies of intellectual quality are projected onto him. Having created this paragon of consummate scholarship and pedagogy, members of the department then claim his presumed strengths and virtues as their own. Each member feels improved and validated.

But when the idealized figure has become one of the group, disillusionment soon sets in. Not only is he now seen as fallible, he becomes the target for the ambivalent splitting and projections of his colleagues. Almost every university department has had some experience with this cycle from idealization to disparagement in the tenure of its chairman or dean. When he takes office he is the beneficiary of good projections, the negative feelings have been projected to his outgoing predecessor. In due time, he in his turn becomes the target of the bad projections of his constituency.[4]

A healthy emotional atmosphere in an academic department depends above all on clear and unambivalent communication, which is not to be confused with information. While selectivity in transmitting information is often necessary and is not always a symptom of trouble, barriers to the free flow of communication are a genuine cause for concern.

Communication connotes much more than the explicit transmission of verbal messages. Communication includes all those processes by which people influence one another. It includes both verbal and non-verbal behavioral messages. It is the sum total of transmitted feelings, attitudes, and wishes. It conveys literal content and is also a comment on the relationships among the people involved.

Communication always occurs within a context. When does it take place? Where? How is it carried out? By whom? Under what circumstances? When viewed this way, communication also includes all those symbols and cues used by persons in giving and receiving meaning. Taken in this sense, the techniques people use to communicate can be reliable indicators of department morale.

People who do not know themselves will be ignorant of other people and they will be unable to communicate effectively. Ignorance about people will lead to unsuitable goals and inappropriate methods to achieve them. Ignorance about other people is the result of ignorance of self. Those who do not know themselves cannot identify with others in important respects; they find other people's feelings and motives enigmatic and incomprehensible. Persons who are not in touch with their feelings cannot communicate. Their affect is so restricted by being tied up in concealing parts of themselves that they are insensitive to large areas of experience. They have blind spots. They are so concerned with channeling communication into "safe" areas and away from painful or suppressed feelings that they deny themselves the spontaneity essential to interpersonal communication.

In the case of love, when a man relates to a woman, and a woman relates to a man, each identifies with an idealized part of the self which he or she has projected onto the other. "The object," says Freud, "serves as a substitute for some unattained ego ideal of our own. We love it on account of the perfections which we have striven to reach for our own ego."[5]

Persons who isolate their affects may become excellent scholars but they are not equipped to deal with people. People who intellectualize send to others messages that are mixed, one part saying "yes," the other part saying "no." Because the message is ambivalent it creates anxiety in the listener who will "know" the sender is unreliable in terms of feelings. Individuals who give a message which they do not feel will unconsciously act to "undo" the content of that message. A man who suffers from an incongruence between his thought and his feelings will say, "I want to read what you have to say," and then will proceed to lose the letter or memorandum when he receives it. A man who is out of touch with himself will say, "I want to hear you," and will forget the appointment.

People can be talked to, at, and around, but if the overt message is not accompanied by integrity of emotions, they will not trust the message. In psychotherapy this is known as the "double bind."[6] When small children live amidst such double-bind messages they may become schizophrenic. Among faculty members, trust breaks down, morale is depressed, and a mood of crisis sets in.

The end result could not survive examination by a critical intelligence were it not for the capacity of the intellect to reinforce rationalizations that it has constructed and perhaps even make them come true. It is easy to find flaws and weaknesses in anyone or anything. These can then be criticized with an irrationality which enables the critic to conceal from himself his own hatred and envy. Moreover, by treating others unjustly he may succeed in turning them against himself, thus making his own anger legitimate.

Intellectuals have an insatiable desire to argue about abstract subjects. Many of the friendships of academics are based on and maintained by the desire to talk about metaphysical propositions ad infinitum. We soon discover, however, that this fine intellectual performance makes little or no difference in actual behavior. The intellectual's comprehension of idea systems does not prevent him from being blind to what is going on inside himself and inside others. While he has eroticized thought—deriving gratification from the mere process of thinking, criticizing, and debating—his behavior is determined by other factors and is not even slightly influenced by his mental gymnastics.

Invariably an analysis of the intellectual processes of academics shows that the subjects to which they professionally commit themselves—political power and authority, elites, dominance, deference and submission, revolution, slavery, conquest and control, to name only a few—are the displacements to abstractions of the very problems that cause conflict in their psychic life. For many scholars the conflicts of the present are displaced in time and space to the remote past or to the symbolic world of abstraction in order to isolate immediate emotions.

Intellectualization and isolation are necessary and adaptive tools of the mind. Data must be structured and conceptualized to be used. However, intellectualization may also be a defense against experience. Preferably the ordering and abstract intellectualization should occur after the emotional cognition. The abstract discussions in which academic intellectuals delight are often not genuine attempts at solving real problems. Their intellectualization is rather an indication of an alertness for the breakthrough of the emotional problems underneath, and their unconscious defense is to transpose into abstract thought what they do not wish to feel.

Inner conflicts will always obtrude upon our functioning in the outer world. This is often apparent in academic departments and in faculty relations with students. Men who are otherwise above normal in intelligence will suddenly develop a blind spot for the problem of authoritarianism in the classroom when their authority is at stake. Men who are generally in command of ordinary English usage will break forth with an obsessional defense of definition ad infinitum in criticizing a student proposal.

If people want to understand, they can understand. But if people do not want to understand, they do not hear, they misconstrue and misapprehend, they pervert and distort, and play with words. In short, they don't get it; communication with them is impossible.

These patterns of obtuseness are not limited to student-faculty relations. They also exist in faculty interactions with each other. One of the chief areas of built-in tension in the faculty is the dividing line between junior and senior members of a department. The boundary between the two is marked by the possession of tenure, a coveted status which confers security of employment and a decisively larger voice in department decision making and in some cases a significantly larger salary. It is in these relations that stresses in a faculty come most easily under observation, for it is here that latent tensions are exposed in crises.[7]

The structure of all institutions of higher learning is status oriented and hierarchical. This need not impede the flow of information and communication. The effectiveness of communication depends on the quality of the relationships among the people involved. For communications to operate effectively in hierarchical channels, there must be relative freedom from anxiety at the top, and a willingness not only to receive upward communications but also to exert a continuous pull to ensure that subordinates bring crucial problems forward. This they will do only when they know that they will get help and support, or even fair criticism.

Of course, it is impossible to avoid communicating feelings and attitudes to others on some level of consciousness. A failure to communicate is itself a communication. The meaning of behavior intended to isolate or bypass is not missed. A closed door, a missed appointment, or "forgetting" to notify a member of a committee meeting, whether he is the youngest faculty member or the most senior man in the department, means rejection; and rejection fosters resentment.

The lack of personal insight and empathy for the emotions of others often obstructs the functioning of leaders of institutions such as universities. Assistant professors who have recently left the graduate school are particularly sensitive to any move that threatens their intellectual autonomy by reducing them to being someone else's man rather than their own. Where suspicion, fear of exposure, and rejection are the mood, a positive commitment to the department or the institution cannot develop. As long as the motives of a chairman are suspect, there can be no trust or sense of stability. Once a mood of mistrust and suspicion exists, it is fed by the projective fantasies of the junior members and fanned by the sadistic manipulativeness of the senior members of a department into whose pathology it plays. It cannot be easily dispelled.

Most desired changes can be instituted with the full cooperation of the junior staff when there have been prior consultation, explanation, and adequate safeguards against surprise, potential embarrassment, and suspicion of motives. However, when a chairman by his tone or by the manner of his proposals conveys his love of power, his ambition, and the desire to dominate, something else will happen. The department will respond to the calculated spreading of anxiety and the drive to control rather than to the merits of a proposal. When tact and empathy for the people with whom he is dealing are present, a leader can obtain a virtually limitless measure of devoted support and cooperation. When these are lacking, even the most meritorious proposals will be met with destructive hostility.

Any group of academic persons includes a wide range of differences in backgrounds, temperaments, styles, methods, and talents. G. B. Harrison, the Shakespearean scholar, has said: "A good department of English should include a diversity of creatures, like a good zoo, which is incomplete without its lion, giraffe, hippopotamus, and giant sloth, not omitting the indigenous fauna such as the viper and the skunk, who usually are also unbidden specimens in the collection. Personality is far more important for a teacher than an assortment of degrees and diplomas."[8]

Differentness can be used either destructively as a source of conflict or as an opportunity for enrichment. If people are low in self-esteem, differences which lead to disagreement will be seen as evidence of being disliked. Legitimate conflicts of interest will seem to threaten autonomy and identity. The scholar with self-esteem, who knows what he has to offer, can use the differentness of another as an opportunity for growth. He has learned how to assert his knowledge, thoughts, wishes, and feelings without destroying, invading, or obliterating those with whom he disagrees or fearing that they will destroy him.

The test of reality—that is, the ability to accept what is perceived, including what can probably be inferred, whether it is agreeable or not—should be the basic tool for overcoming the feelings of fear and depreciation which confound effective academic functioning. Tasks of scholarship, teaching, and administration allow faculty members to test their personal anxieties against the realities of the academic world. A piece of work well done has the reassuring effect of proving anxiety unnecessary; the control of disturbing feelings becomes more secure; and the expression of both critical and complimentary attitudes becomes freer.

One may ask, what if there are differences in evaluations of "good" work? Any evaluation is both an intellectual and an emotional response. An evaluation is not the kind of judgment that is absolutely true or false. If this is so, may we then say that one evaluation is "better" than another? We may and we should make such distinctions. Differences in evaluations result from differences in the perception and the internal criteria of the evaluators.

The capacity to see external things as they are is a function of intelligence, information, and most importantly, of internal integration. The degree of integration of the personality is a measure of its capacity to form a true and complete picture of itself and to face the world as an integrated ego. Integration of personality is a sense of inner continuity between one's past —personal, ethnic, and social—and one's present interaction with the world. It is what Erik Erikson has defined as ego identity: "the accrued confidence that the inner sameness and continuity prepared in the past are matched by the sameness and continuity of one's meaning for others." The ideal identity is that of the all too rare person who can say with assurance: "The way you see me now is the way I really am, and it is the way of my forefathers."[9]

Few of us can, or would wish to, live "the way of our forefathers" in any spatial, technological, vocational, or social sense. Yet many men would deny, or cut off and isolate, aspects of their past. Their inner and outer life has many barriers blocking connections with what preceded; it lacks continuity. Academic life in America has many pseudo-Englishmen, crypto-Frenchmen, and quasi-Italians. The desire to disassociate oneself from one's own personal and collective past will have as a correlate an inability to tolerate a depth experience in the present.[10] Any profound encounter, any basic confrontation, must dynamically call forth the resources of the forgotten past.

The person who has not integrated all the aspects of his past into his ego will move from one superficial personal interaction to another. Sometimes such individuals make good administrators; their skill in superficial encounters meets the needs of modern corporate structured universities. But such thin surface encounters will not yield an understanding of what is going on among faculty and students.

The evaluations of an integrated person who knows himself and knows what the whole of him is and likes will be more rational than those of a fragmented person who knows only a part of himself. To the degree that a person is integrated, he will be less apt than the unintegrated either to overidealize or denigrate others. His splitting and projective defenses will be diminished. His capacity to discover the actual character of other persons will be enhanced over that of the partial or façade person because he is in touch with his own and other people's affective responses.

Differences in evaluations are attributable to differences in the degree of self-knowledge and self-acceptance or personality integration of the evaluators, and to differences in the completeness of their pictures of the world. The second factor is dependent on the first because the precondition for being able to form a "true" picture of the world and of people is the possession of a true picture of one's inner world. An individual who has a true picture of his inner world—that is, one who is integrated in his identity —will also be likely to have a true picture of the outer one.

The fact that academics are intellectuals complicates the problem. They use elegant rationalizations to block real communication. They develop the most complex arguments to reinforce what they want to believe and to stave off inner anxieties. Intellectuals have been trained to work with and to respect ideas; they are specialists in pursuing the convolutions of a line of logic; this is their virtue and their raison d'être. But it also becomes a resistance that enables them to repress emotional facts. The academic's intellect often stands between him and what he is feeling and doing—and the words to avoid genuineness spin on.

Such strategies are self-defeating and, in the long run, they do not assuage inner anxiety. How can these distortions be removed and rectified? Direct attack has no chance of permanent success. We may succeed for a time in reasoning ourselves out of one or another irrational suspicion or dislike which plagues us, but as long as the cause remains untouched, we will construct, sooner or later, an equally irrational alternative.

There is only one way permanently to reduce distortions caused by projective defense, and that is by bringing their cause to light. When falsities in the prerational world of infancy and childhood are psychodynamically exposed and corrected by conscious perception and inference, their irrational consequences will subside.

William Inge, the playwright, put the solution of personal insight in its most favorable light:

Psychoanalysis seems to me to be the great learning experience that the twentieth century can provide. Once one has worked through this experience, he cannot help but have a more basic understanding of human life and of all Western culture. . . . Any analysand today can distinguish between those people prominent in our society and culture who have had experience "on the couch" from those who have not, and the former do appear to us more humane, more deeply aware of human needs, and more able to face the complexity of life today.[11]

We need to introduce psychoanalytic education in our graduate curriculum in the social sciences. The resistance to the use of psychoanalytic theory and clinical insight among social scientists is not due to a lack of agreement among schools of depth psychology or to the difficulty of the concepts. It can be attributed to the fact that psychodynamics threatens people where they are most vulnerable. No other discipline is so immediately personal.

Psychoanalysis would not only illuminate research materials; it would also have an impact on the scholar's own thoughts and feelings. It would reach to his motivations and relationships. This, of course, is highly threatening to many academics, who like nothing better than remote detachment between their work and their emotions and who will cling to this cleavage with ferocity.

Christopher Jencks and David Riesman are acutely aware of the necessity of integrating subjective experience with graduate education. They say:

> The critical problem of graduate instruction in the social sciences and the humanities is to narrow the gap between individual students' personal lives and their work. The graduate school must somehow put the student in closer touch with himself, instead of making him believe that the way to get ahead is to repress himself and become a passive instrument "used" by his methods and his disciplinary colleagues. This is no mean task. The difficulty of the job is not, however, an excuse for the present situation, where the student's subjectivity is not even regarded as a problem.[12]

The answer to this problem is, I suggest, to integrate psychodynamics into graduate education by offering seminars in theory, a personal therapeutic experience which need not necessarily be a complete psychoanalysis, and some clinical exposure to case material.[13]

If there are still gaps between our inner and outer views of the world, if there are aspects of our internal model that do not correspond to perception and experience, these should result from insufficient and misleading data, and should be correctable by new data inputs. If this is not so, we may assume we are in the presence of an emotional flight from the truth.

Regular opportunities for all members of an academic department to contribute to crucial decisions that affect their lives and work are essential for sound policy making. Conflicts should be argued and clarified. Disruptive feelings must be matched against the realities of relationships as actually experienced. The mechanisms of reality testing with each other can assist in the resolution of the unconscious anxieties aroused in departmental relationships. The resulting emotional climate will permit the day-to-day work of the department to proceed more smoothly.

Once a group has developed insight and skill in recognizing forces of envy, status, security, authority, suspicion, "territory," hostility, and the memories of past events, these forces can no longer be as powerful in distorting discussion and impeding decisions.

Notes

1. Sigmund Freud, "The Interpretation of Dreams" (1900), *Standard Edition of the Complete Psychological Works,* trans. and ed. James Strachey et al. (London, 1953–1974), 5: 483.

2. See Melanie Klein, *Contributions to Psycho-Analysis, 1921–1945* (London, 1948); Hanna Segal, *Introduction to the Work of Melanie Klein* (London, 1964); Melanie Klein, "Love, Guilt and Reparation," in *Love, Hate and Reparation,* with Joan Riviere (New York, 1964); R. E. Money-Kyrle, *Psychoanalysis and Politics: A Contribution to the Psychology of Politics and Morals* (London, 1951); *Man's Picture of His World: A Psychoanalytic Study* (New York, 1961); Elliott Jaques, *Work, Creativity, and Social Justice* (New York, 1970); W. R. Bion, *Experiences in Groups and Other Papers* (New York, 1959).

3. Virginia Satir, *Conjoint Family Therapy: A Guide to Theory and Techniques* (Palo Alto, Calif., 1967); William J. Lederer and Don D. Jackson, *The Mirages of Marriage* (New York, 1968); Jay Haley, *Strategies of Psychotherapy* (New York, 1963); Paul Watzlawick, Janet Helmick Beavin, and Don D. Jackson, *Pragmatics of Human Communication: A Study of Interactional Patterns, Pathologies, and Paradoxes* (New York, 1967).

4. See Pandarus, "One's Own Primer of Academic Politics," *American Scholar,* 42 (1973): 569–92; Anonymous, "Confessions of an Academic Administrator," *New Republic,* 171 (1974): 18–19.

5. Freud, "Group Psychology and the Analysis of the Ego" (1921), *Standard Edition,* 18: 112–13.

6. G. Bateson, D. Jackson, J. Haley, and J. Weakland, "Towards a Theory of Schizophrenia," *Behavioral Science,* 1 (1956): 251.

7. F. M. Cornford, *Microcosmographia Academica: Being a Guide for the Young Academic Politician* (London, 1908).

8. G. B. Harrison, *The Profession of English* (Garden City, N.J., 1967), p. 119.

9. Erik H. Erikson, *Childhood and Society* (rev. 2nd ed.; New York, 1963), pp. 129, 261.

10. Martin Duberman, "On Becoming an Historian," *Evergreen Review,* 13, no. 65 (1969), and *The Uncompleted Past* (New York, 1969), pp. 335–56.

11. William Inge, "A Statement," in *Celebrities on the Couch: Personal Adventures of Famous People in Psychoanalysis,* ed. Lucy Freeman (New York, 1971), p. 137.

12. Christopher Jencks and David Riesman, *The Academic Revolution* (New York, 1969), p. 518.

13. Musto and Astrachan have conducted Bion Tavistock Model group experiences with graduate students at Yale University: David F. Musto and Boris M. Astrachan, "Strange Encounter: The Use of Study Groups with Graduate Students in History," *Psychiatry,* 31 (1968): 264–76.

The Psychobiographical
Background to Psychohistory

The Langer Family and the Dynamics of Shame and Success

In December 1957, Professor William L. Langer (1896–1977), America's most distinguished historian of Europe, delivered his famous Presidential Address to the American Historical Association, advocating the use of psychoanalysis in history. The historian's "Next Assignment," said Langer, is "the urgently needed deepening of our historical understanding through exploitation of the concepts and findings of modern psychology," by which he explicitly meant psychoanalysis and "dynamic" or "depth" psychology. The question I wish to pose is: why, of all people, was this conservative scholar of diplomatic history, "the most established branch of the historian's craft," the one to champion a radical new method of historical research to his peers? The social climate and politics of the historical community in general in the late 1950's were not hospitable to behavioral science innovations. Robert Wohl recalls the reactions to Langer's "Next Assignment": "I can remember very well the snide remarks about the address that were being made in the Princeton History Department in the first few months of 1958; many of my professors regarded Langer as a strange man lacking in common sense."[1] Where did "the next assignment" come from in Langer's life?

Even more perplexing, if Langer wished to demonstrate the value of psychoanalysis for history, why did he not choose a case in his own field, modern history, the area with which he was most familiar? There are obviously many issues of irrationality in modern European history to which he could appropriately have turned his attention. Among others, there is the mass-psychological underpinning of nineteenth-century imperialism, to which Langer devoted his masterful Chapter 3 of *The Diplomacy of Imperialism*. Here Langer explores the social psychology of British imperialism, including high and popular culture, literature, and the emotional dimensions of misapplied Darwinism. To cite other examples that come to mind as obvious subjects of psychological analysis, there is the personality of Chancellor Otto von Bismarck, his relation to his son Herbert and Holstein, the Eulenburg affair, or any of the mass phenomena of National Socialism. But Langer did not choose a lesson from the modern period to demonstrate his point. Instead he turned for his case study to the Middle Ages—to the Black Death and its terrible psychological impact on survivors who felt "unconscious guilt and a fear of retribution, which apparently go back to the curbing and repression of sexual and aggressive drives in childhood and the emergence of death wishes directed against the parents." He takes special note of how the anxiety of parents is passed on to "children [who], having experienced the terror of their parents and the panic of the community, will react to succeeding crises in a similar but even more intense manner. In other words, the anxiety and fear are transmitted from one generation to another, constantly aggravated."[2]

We are confronted then with two puzzling questions: Why, of all historians, was William Langer the champion of psychoanalysis to his profession, and why did he choose the particular historical example of the Black Death and its effects to make his case? He did maintain an interest in "the repercussions—economic, social, spiritual—of so massive an experience of dying" in subsequent studies,[3] but we may discover better answers than we have yet had, by examining two new historical sources, William Langer's memoir published shortly before his death and his brother's autobiographical essay.

The resolution to the second question—why was Langer so interested in the traumatic aftereffects of mass death, and the impact of such a "shattering experience" on survivors?—comes to us immediately on reading his autobiography. Born in 1896, he wrote: "I naturally have no memories before the turn of the century." There follows "a vague childhood recollection of hearing about the assassination of President McKinley in 1901, and of the prolonged artillery salute on March 17, 1901, celebrating the 125th anniversary of the evacuation of Boston by the British." This is but scant preparation for what follows in the next line: "But of the great tragedy in our family —my father's death—I could not, when two years old, have any recollection." The dual childhood memories of the killing of the President and the liberation of the home from an occupying tyranny could not have been more poetically chosen as screen memories of the early death of a father. This is the catastrophe—the personal Black Death—that shattered Langer's early emotional and material existence. His mother was left penniless with three small boys to raise. She became a home dressmaker and took in boarders to make ends meet. This early and irreparable father loss, with its lifelong mourning, was what Langer appears to have been still working through with his choice of the effects of the plague as a research subject. This was his individual version of "the worst catastrophe ever to have befallen the human race, [which] struck Europe suddenly as a new phenomenon about which nothing was known," which shook "European society to its very founda-tions" and "deeply affected . . . mankind . . . in many ways." Although Langer tells us, "I have no personal memory of my father," his unconscious had early memory traces of the intense grief, anxiety, and panic of his childhood home. He dealt with this dark and terrible disaster all his life and particularly in his Presidential Address.[4]

We come now closer to the solution of the problem—why did this conservative diplomatic historian advocate psychoanalytic research among historians? One may suppose, as I do, that Langer's work in wartime intelli-gence, where he was head of the Research and Analysis Division of the Office of Strategic Services, or his later position as chairman of the Board of National Estimates of the Central Intelligence Agency, both of which used psychodynamic policy studies, may have forcefully persuaded him of their value for the historian's armamentarium. Also, his younger brother, Dr. Walter C. Langer, a psychoanalyst whose work on Hitler was solicited by the OSS, certainly influenced William. Indeed, this brother receives generous acknowledgment in the first note of "The Next Assignment." Yet these explanations, while real and contributory, are superficial. They do not tell us the full story from the depths of William Langer's past and his character. Access to these levels is now possible by an informed reading of his autobiography.

Professor Langer's memoir, written in 1975 and published in 1977, is remarkable in its innocence and naïveté. It is not the kind of autobiography that a person of the current generation could write. The discordant note which immediately strikes the reader is his candid, if unconscious, need for praise. The past president of the American Historical Association, a profes-sor at Harvard University, editor of the major series of the history of modern Europe, and the doyen of American historians, reprints extensive excerpts of the reviews of his work, not merely of his early fledgling efforts but also of his late writings of the 1950's and 1960's. The reviews of *The Challenge to Isolation* (1952) and *The Undeclared War* (1953) he chose to cite to prove that "leading experts stamped it a monumental contribution to scholarship" are embarrassing to read.[5]

The reader wonders: Why such a need to reprint all these encomiums? It might be noted that at this late point in his distinguished career, Langer had many friends, allies, and admirers. The politics of academia suggests that his work would not be lightly scourged by his peers. Thus, we may also ask: How much praise and honor is enough? Would any quantity from whatever source truly satisfy the author?

The autobiography provides the answer in Langer's account of his mother, who withheld all praise and approval from her boys regardless of their achievements. "She always took the attitude that we were only meeting the requirements of an impoverished family." On one or two occasions he "overheard her talking to friends and was almost stunned" to hear her commend her sons.[6]

Shame at failure emerges as a salient theme of Langer's boyhood. When at age twelve he failed the entrance examination to the Boston Latin School, he "felt so humiliated that for a week or ten days I could not bring myself to break the news of my failure to my mother. I did not go to the old school, but killed the time knocking around here and there and wondering how I might face the music." The experience he describes—a fear of contempt and intense anxiety aroused by failure to live up to internalized maternal ideals—refracts the deepest and earliest fear known to man, one with which Langer was tragically familiar: abandonment and the threat of death by emotional starvation.[7]

Langer's memoir gives us a clear answer as to why it was he who presented the study of psychoanalysis as the "next assignment" for historians. The answer is not, as we might suppose, that it was family influence from his brother, or his exposure to the uses of psychodynamics in intelligence work in the OSS and CIA. It was a more immediate and truer reason grounded in personal experience. Langer recalls in 1938 he was "sitting with my brother Walter in his automobile listening to Hitler's impassioned speeches. I confess I was never so frightened for the future of the world. The Fuehrer's speeches, two hours of constant crescendo, struck me as the ravings of a madman who was dangerous."[8]

The next paragraph in Langer's text gives his association to himself as a speaker at that time:

I hardly knew, then, what hit me in February 1938, when, in the middle of a discussion on the condition of the Italian peasantry, I was suddenly overcome by a wave of emotion so severe that for a few moments I was unable to speak and became so dizzy that I had to hold on to the podium for support. . . . It was naturally greatly distressing to find that the same thing, akin to stage fright, happened in each lecture, usually within the first ten or fifteen minutes. . . .

Lecturing now became a chronic ordeal, and I found myself becoming panicky even before entering the classroom. . . . I sometimes felt that I was facing a hostile group, ready to attack me at any moment.

Carl E. Schorske, who was a graduate student and Langer's teaching assistant at the time, recalls watching "in terror as he faltered in that lecture, very nearly fainting, and having to be helped from the room." This was the most anguishing symptom possible for a teacher. It was public, not restricted to the bedroom; nor was it a symptom that invited easy avoidance, such as a driving phobia or a cat phobia. Langer could undoubtedly have accommodated to almost any symptom that was private and did not strike so directly at his professional identity. This was a symptom about which he wrote: "Its effect on me was devastating."[9]

When a trip to Bermuda "in the hope that a short rest might help" failed to give relief, Langer had a few sessions with the psychoanalyst Dr. Hanns Sachs, who had been the first Training Analyst at the Berlin Institute and was then in Boston. He later entered psychoanalysis with Dr. Jenny Waelder. This is the same Jenny Waelder Hall who was later to be a consultant for Walter Langer on his wartime psychological study of Hitler, to which William also associates on the same page. Of his psychoanalysis, Langer said that it was "highly instructive" and "a most effective method for learning about oneself." However, he tells us his "affliction proved absolutely recalcitrant." During the next twenty years "every occasion for public speech was a certain ordeal."[10] Yet those who heard him lecture in later decades were surprised to learn of his suffering when they read his autobiography. Although Langer tells us that he was not cured of his symptom, it appears that, as psychoanalysts say in such cases, "the voice of the symptom grew distant." Langer managed to adapt to it and to function well. His stage fright was never resolved and his exhibitionism was also never adequately analyzed.

Langer confronted three emotional crises in 1938, a personal, a political, and a career crisis. His personal crisis was the breakup of his marriage to the philosopher Susanne K. Langer, to whom he had been married since 1921 and who had borne him two sons. As he wrote: "In the early part of the war my wife and I were divorced after having drifted apart for some time." His second marriage, in 1943, was to Rowena Morse Nelson, the divorced wife of a professor of history at Duke University who was to have been a contributor to the series on European history which Langer edited. Langer and Mrs. Nelson first met at the American Historical Association meetings in Providence, Rhode Island, in December 1936.[11]

Langer's political crisis was related to his work in diplomatic history. His historical interpretations glorified the sagacity of Germany's "Iron Chancellor," Otto von Bismarck. Langer regarded Bismarck "as a master diplomat and an almost unique example of the successful statesman who knew when to stop; who recognized the interests of others and the need to respect such interests."[12] His intention was to take his diplomatic history down to the peace settlements of 1919 and 1920. With the triumph of Nazism after 1933, historical analysis that sought the sources of German political immaturity focused on the authoritarian domestic legacy of Bismarck. Langer's emphasis on foreign policy and praise of the Iron Chancellor was becoming increasingly questionable.

Langer's position on the threat of Hitler to the West was appeasement oriented. On a trip to Europe in 1933 he visited an S.A. headquarters in North Berlin and Oranienburg concentration camp, where the son of former President Ebert was pointed out to him. He also sought an interview with Adolf Hitler. As late as February 1938 he was writing in the columns of the New York *Herald Tribune:*

> The hope of the future, so far as international affairs are concerned, lies in the growth of influence of the military men. Hitler has always liked the army and revels in military demonstrations. . . . It may be, therefore, that he will gradually veer in that direction, and that Germany will, over a period of time, be recast till it resembles the Old Germany. . . . Things have come to such a pass that the need for some concession has become evident to many thoughtful people. Whether the fanatics of the Nazi party are in control or whether the more circumspect army men hold the reins, the fact remains that Germany's economic situation is a desperate one. People, when they are desperate, become dangerous, and when they number 65,000,000 and are well trained and brainy, the menace is a real one.[13]

His Harvard lectures of 1940 still held that "appeasement should have come sooner and gone farther." He presents appeasement as "the policy of sense . . . which might have achieved much under normal circumstances." Of Hitler, he said: "At first no one could recognize him for what he was any more than they could recognize Napoleon."[14] For Langer that recognition began with the radio broadcast of February 1938.

It is not surprising that suddenly psychoanalysis took an important place in Langer's history lectures of 1938: "Science has relieved us of the terrors of our world, but psychoanalysis has shown us that instead we are breaking down under the burden of artificiality." He asked, "Is there not room for a greater human sympathy, even if our whole civilization is on the way to a break-up?" He had all of the high overestimation of psychoanalysis that one may anticipate of a new analysand: "The mystery has gone out of life and and [sic] psychoanalysis has shown us even our most hidden motives."[15]

What we see in William Langer is a classic configuration of shame as a defense against exhibitionistic impulses. The exhibitionism is evident until the end of his life in the need to republish the laudatory reviews of his books. His intense and painful stage fright was a defense against the desire to display, to show off, to say, "See, Ma! Look how good I am!" The onset of his symptom is described as an association coming immediately after listening to Hitler's fearsome oratory. Hitler was an exhibitionist who successfully used the mode of speaking to control, dominate, intimidate, and bend people to his will.

Stage fright as a symptom means: "I am so ambitious and competitive, so eager for glory and adoration, and I am so guilty about this craving because it is vain and selfish and forbidden, that I must erect a defense of shame against it." Shame means to hide one's face, to say, "I do not want to be seen." It may also mean hiding the body or parts of it. In 1919 Langer wrote an account of his military unit on the Western Front in World War I in which he describes bodily shame before his mother over a wound on his buttocks. He was lighting another man's cigarette:

> I leaned forward just far enough to touch my rear on the stove. To this very day I remember the sticking sensation and my mad leap to safety. Next morning, when I reported for sick call, the doctor exclaimed: "Why, Sarge, you have a burn as large as a pie plate." For a time I was quite immobilized, never stirring from my pillow, but spiritually free and deeper than ever immersed in my narrative. Only one mistake I made in this connection. I wrote my mother that I had had a rather painful mishap and should probably not have been surprised when, on my return home, she greeted me with the question: "Now where were you wounded?" "Wounded? Me? Nowhere." "Well, you certainly wrote me of a mishap and of course I knew what you meant." Demonstration was hardly feasible, so I had to rely on argument to put her mind at rest.[16]

Here we see Langer's shame dynamics confirmed. Neither in a letter nor by "demonstration" could he deal with his buttocks when relating to his mother who had diapered and cleaned him as a baby. The fear is of being ostracized and punished, of being mortally criticized, pilloried, and abandoned instead of loved. Langer's anxiety was that his audience was going to know his exhibitionism as false posturing, and that they would expose and humiliate him dreadfully. His underlying insecurity and low self-esteem, which was manifested by a doubt of the worth of what he had to offer, was expressed in the fear of being attacked and disgraced as a fool, as one who knew not whereof he spoke, of being destroyed as a person.

Otto Fenichel wrote in 1946 that he could "not remember any published case of the psychoanalysis of stage fright." My own current search of the leading psychoanalytic indices also disclosed no cases of stage fright in the clinical psychoanalytic literature. However, the best and richest psychoanalytic material is that of self-analysis, particularly when the analyst is also a gifted writer such as Sigmund Freud or George Engel.[17]

Psychoanalyst Allen Wheelis has described his own agonizing bout with stage fright and his analysis of it. He calls the experience of his performance anxiety "steel fingers."

> Steel fingers seize my heart. My chest constricts as if in a giant hand. I struggle to breathe, to continue talking. My sentences break down.

Wheelis's self-analysis is:

> The trigger for anxiety is the giving of an account upon which I may be judged. . . . I felt like a student psychiatrist presenting a case to a senior colleague. . . . I felt like a student writer who is called upon to read his work before a class. . . . The occasion for anxiety . . . is any situation which has somewhat the form of my giving an account of myself. I must infer within me a hidden conviction that my accounting will be inadequate, that the judgment will be adverse and beyond appeal.

To Wheelis, judgment is danger. The fear is the same as with William Langer, that the audience will turn against him, expose and humiliate him, and thus become the representative of the stern forbidding inner power which was an outer sanction from his past. Stage fright in William Langer was the defense against primitive destructive impulses stimulated by listening to Adolf Hitler speak. The unconscious temptation was to obtain gratification of his narcissistic demands. The anxiety of stage fright arose from the dread of being exposed as a sham, of being seen as a fraud, and publicly shamed.[18]

Heinz Kohut, in his work on the narcissistic line of development, points to "the tensions produced by the damming up of primitive forms of narcissistic-exhibitionistic libido (the heightened tendency to hypochondriacal preoccupation, self-consciousness, shame, and embarrassment)" when the child's early exhibitionistic behavior is crushed rather than met with an empathic response. In psychoanalysis these primitive grandiose fantasies are recovered, allowed to be experienced, elaborated, and worked through. The analyst empathically understands the anxiety and shame which the analysand suffers. "Shame, because the revelation is at times still accompanied by the discharge of crude, unneutralized exhibitionistic libido; and anxiety because the grandiosity isolates the analysand and threatens him with permanent object loss." Narcissistic personalities predominantly tend to be "overwhelmed by shame, i.e., they react to the breakthrough of the archaic aspects of the grandiose self, especially to its unneutralized exhibitionism," and are subject to the temporary paralysis of psychic functions.[19]

Kohut's research explains the genesis of the narcissistic personality in the painful childhood experience with a mother who narcissistically used the child's performance for her own validation but who lacked empathy for the child's independent need to be acclaimed and to exhibit. The child's need for attention and importance was "belittled and ridiculed at the very moment when he most proudly had wanted to display himself."[20] These needs were rebuffed and were therefore repressed to be manifested in low self-esteem, shame reactions, and hypochondria.

Freud called the family "the germ cell of civilization [*die Keimzelle der Kultur*]."[21] In the family, the basic patterns of behavior and character defenses are shaped. The family is the conduit which transmits the many messages of approved conduct that constitute the norms and values of a society. If the above hypothesis about Professor Langer's psychodynamics being focused on exhibitionism and shame reactions is correct, we could expect confirmation from other family members who had the same mother, upbringing, and childhood socialization.

We are fortunate in having a companion memoir from the Langer family to place next to William's autobiography. In 1975, the same year that William wrote his life story, his younger brother Walter (1899–1979) put his recollections in writing for the Committee on History and Archives of the American Psychoanalytic Association. This brief memoir tells of his experiences in Europe, where he acquired psychoanalytic training in the late 1930's. He began his training analysis with Anna Freud in Vienna in 1936 and continued it as he traveled to London with the Freuds and the psychoanalytic movement in 1938. It is relevant to the Langer family constellation to see how Walter presented himself to Anna Freud as a prospective analysand: "I dangled a little bait which I thought might be appealing to her. This consisted of the fact that I was not born until four months after my father's death. Furthermore, my mother had never remarried, and since there were no close uncles or other father surrogates, I had never known anything, as a child, except a mother who was compelled to play all roles at all times for three developing boys."[22]

After a description of life in Vienna among the psychoanalytic group under the Nazis as viewed by an American Protestant, and a moving account of his successful efforts to help anti-Nazis and Jews escape from Austria, Dr. Langer's recollections come to their climax. While in London in 1938, he received word that one of his oldest friends in Vienna, an ardent anti-Nazi to whom he had denied help earlier because there appeared to be more urgent cases, had now been arrested by the Gestapo. As soon as he could, Langer flew from London to Vienna. In the air, the stewardess spilled a cup of coffee in his lap. "This," said Langer,

> was unfortunate. Not only was it scalding hot but since I only expected to be gone two or three days, and it was the middle of summer, I was wearing a very light beige tropical worsted suit and had not bothered to pack another. The strong black coffee over my shirt and trousers made an ungodly mess which all of her apologies could not eradicate. In spite of all her efforts I arrived in Vienna in soaking wet, heavily stained clothes. It was not what one would call a gala entry. I took a taxi to the hotel where the clerk was shocked at the strange apparition that asked to register.

It is valuable to have Dr. Langer's account in his own words before us. For he relates the experience of shame that comes from a shattered self-ideal and the expectation of response violated. He went to Vienna with a fantasy of rescue. He trusted himself to a situation that was not there. He opened himself in anticipation of a response that was not forthcoming. He became a child again, unsure of himself in a hostile world.

> I explained [to the hotel clerk] what had happened and asked where I could get the suit cleaned in the shortest possible time. In those days they did not have a "Three Hour" dry cleaning service in Vienna. In fact, according to the clerk, it would take at least a week. The only other thing he could suggest was that I send it to a tailor who had a shop nearby and let him try to get the stain out and press it so that it would not be so conspicuous. Of course it was now Saturday evening and nothing could be done until Monday morning. And so I hung the clothes up to dry and spent Sunday sitting in the hotel room in my pajamas. The first thing on Monday morning I sent the bell-boy out to the tailor with my clothes and sat down to await their return. While still waiting in my pajamas two Gestapo officials

arrived with my passport. After a lengthy interrogation of my relationship with my friend and my purpose in returning at the present
time along with innumerable other questions concerning people I
had never known, I finally managed to explain to them that the
friend had written to me in London a while back and said that he
would like to emigrate to the United States if it could be arranged.
I had come to Vienna for no other reason than to see if the American
Embassy could make such arrangements for him under my sponsor-
ship. They then informed me that this would be impossible. My
friend had been arrested, tried and found guilty of crimes against the
Third Reich and that he was no longer in Vienna. They also recom-
mended that I leave Vienna as quickly as possible since I was no
longer welcome there. I pointed out that my attire was such that I
could not leave in any great hurry and that I had taken measures to
rectify my predicament. They informed me that there was a plane
leaving for London the following morning and that they expected me
to be on it. Since there obviously was nothing that I could do in my
friend's behalf I assured them that I would be on it. . . . The bell-boy
returned with my suit late in the afternoon. The coffee stain was still
very obvious but not quite as vivid as it had been. The tailor had told
the bell-boy to explain to me that coffee stains were extremely difficult to eradicate but that he had done his best. This came as no great
surprise and I was happy to have some means of getting out of that
hotel room. I walked the streets I had known so well but the farther
I walked the more depressed I became. Somehow or other they
seemed lifeless with apparent automatons carrying on the usual business. I went to one of my favorite restaurants for dinner but found
that it had changed hands and I was now a stranger there. The
monotony of the "Heil Hitler" greetings that one encountered in
every turn pounded in my ears like a death knell. I retreated to my
hotel room and packed my things. The next morning I was on the
plane for London never to see Vienna again.[23]

The coffee stain on his suit was a seemingly trivial item that carried the
weight of almost unbearably painful emotion, a threat to his identity, the loss
of trust in expectations of himself and other persons. It was his symbol for
disappointment and rebuff, the failure to obtain a favorable outcome from
a morally right action. Rather than being a daring and successful rescuer,
Dr. Langer had to "retreat" in anguish and defeat. His trip was in vain.
There was nothing he could do, even without a coffee stain.
    When he returned to London, "Vienna seemed like a dream and I had

no desire to talk about what had transpired there and nobody questioned me about it. Like good analysts they sensed that I had undergone a personal trauma which, at the time, I could not share with them."[24]

The language and affect is of a shameful experience that was best forgotten and repressed. Why, we may ask, should he have felt shame for doing his best in a noble humanitarian cause? He may have felt guilt over having rejected his friend's plea for help earlier when he had blank U.S. affidavits to give. But the central emotional experience of his rescue attempt is also shaming. The shame he felt for his failure was displaced to an overconcern with a coffee stain on his suit. His feeling of vulnerability and exposure, which is the essence of shame, was pronounced when he had to face the Gestapo in his pajamas in his hotel room. He came as a rescuer with fantasies of glory; he left in defeat and impotence, confounded and in humiliation. Shame is associated with exposure of the body and covering the face. His self-ideal was wounded. He felt exposed and uncovered. He was literally almost naked. He was faced with, and relates to us, the experience of a violation of expectation, of incongruity between anticipation and outcome. Dr. Langer's trust in his capacity, even in his bodily appearance, his competence and skill, even in his identity, was in question, and it was not until his return to London that his intermeshed trust in himself and the outer world was restored. He was now no longer a stranger in a world where he thought he was at home:

> What a relief it was to get back to London where nothing had changed. The following morning I reported for my analysis at the usual hour and in the evening our little group . . . got together and discussed some analytical problems.[25]

He could again trust his immediate world and trust other people in a relation of mutuality.

Returning to the career crisis of William Langer as a college teacher in the late 1930's, we must examine him as a teacher. All teachers and scholars are more or less vain. They strive for an audience, applause and approval from their auditors. They seek and need the approbation of an audience. Teachers are performers. They derive direct narcissistic satisfaction from the rapt attention of their class. Their success in lecturing increases self-esteem from an outward source—the audience. The teacher's authority, superiority, and power soothe his anxiety—the anxiety of being small and insignificant, unimportant and trivial.

In 1936, William Langer was appointed the first occupant of a chair named after his teacher, Archibald Cary Coolidge, an appointment which gave him "the greatest possible pleasure." The onset of his symptom, which interfered critically with his teaching, shortly thereafter suggests that his triumph was not unambivalent. He had conflictual feelings about his success. To displace the father and hold his "chair," to sit at the head of his table and conduct his seminar, is certain to arouse powerful emotions over what is permitted and what is forbidden. Behind the desire to "participate" in his power and authority lurks the original intention of robbing and destroying him. To have taken the father's place, to possess the trophy of his chair and sit in it in triumph, demands a price. To have conquered the father's throne unleashes anxiety, passive love and submission, and remorse. The attempt to enjoy his power may fail, and the revenge of the father takes place through the guilt of the son who has displaced him. One common neurotic compromise is to develop a symptom that will interfere with the task and make teaching an ordeal as Langer did, thus punishing himself for his victory. Freud termed this a character "wrecked by success," a syndrome which applies to persons who cannot permit themselves to enjoy the fruits of their hard work and earned success but instead destroy their achievements and favorable situation out of unconscious guilt.[26]

To this it must finally be said that none of the three Langer boys were in any important sense "wrecked."* They grew up to be highly productive and successful men who obviously got the love and care they needed from their widowed mother. They also received adequate, if conflicted, supplies of self-esteem and inner worth. Each did exceptionally well in his chosen profession. William Langer excelled as a historian. He had an unusually close and long-lasting relationship with his mother. He supported her financially and took her along with his family on his tours of Europe. When she lived alone the professor did chores and heavy work around her house, such as "mowing the lawn, trimming the edges, setting up bean poles," and constructing a ten-foot trench for an asparagus bed in the New England granite. Later, she lived with him and his family. William is an example of Freud's observation:

> I have found that people who know that they are preferred or favoured by their mother give evidence in their lives of a peculiar

---

*The oldest brother, Rudolph Ernst (1894–1968), got a late start in his education via correspondence school, moved to Harvard College and graduate school in mathematics, followed by postdoctoral study at the University of Göttingen. He became professor and chairman of the Department of Mathematics at the University of Wisconsin and founder and director of the U.S. Army Mathematics Research Center. It would be most interesting to know whether he shared the defensive character structure of his brothers that I have addressed in this paper. He certainly shared their ego strengths, which William termed "the well-known Protestant ethic stressing integrity and hard work." W. L. Langer, *In and Out of the Ivory Tower* (New York, 1977), p. 261. All three brothers identified with the "power" of the government-military security establishment.

self-reliance and an unshakable optimism which often seem like heroic attributes and bring actual success to their possessors.

Mother Langer did not get along well with her other two sons and was a chronic complainer who felt her sons had left her and resented their wives, feeling they "had made no contribution to our success and, indeed, were reaping the benefits of her sacrifices and efforts." William "wondered why my mother could not derive joy rather than sorrow from the success of her three sons."[27] He dedicated his autobiography to his "devoted mother."

It as particularly poignant that at the end of his exceptionally productive life Langer felt he was only two-thirds as good as he should have been. He said of his neurosis: "This affliction reduced my capability by at least a third and . . . for the rest of my life my effectiveness was substantially impaired."[28] We may respond with Abraham Lincoln, who, when he was told by a group of ladies that General Grant drank too much whiskey, replied, "Please tell me his brand of whiskey—I need it for my other generals." In the case of Langer we could rejoin: The historical profession needs more such impairments! His immediate adaptation to his symptom was a constructive shift in career to government service in the intelligence community, where he applied his analytic and synthetic talents as a historian.

Indeed, Langer did much more than merely adjust to a painful neurotic symptom. He turned it to brilliant effect in a singular way by breaking new trails for his profession. Most historians tell us the same thing over and over, rehearsing old scholarly battles along lines drawn in early professional combat. Most presidential addresses are research presentations of interest only to professional specialists. Not so William Langer! In his maturity he reached far beyond the limitations of diplomatic history to historical demography, nutrition, disease, urban revolutions, and psychoanalysis. We who profess psychohistory as a method should take Langer's initiative and youthful "Explorations in New Terrain" during his established years as a model. Would that we may have the freshness of mind and the personal insight to apply creatively our neuroses and personal misfortune to new perspectives and innovations in research method as he did.

Notes

1. William L. Langer, "The Next Assignment," *American Historical Review,* 63 (1958): 284–5. Carl E. Schorske, "Introduction," *Explorations in Crisis: Papers on International History by William L. Langer,* ed. Carl E. and Elizabeth Schorske (Cambridge, Mass., 1969), p. xxxvi; Robert Wohl to Peter Loewenberg, May 11, 1980.

2. Langer, "The Triumph of Imperialism," *The Diplomacy of Imperialism* (New York, 1935), pp. 67–98; "The Next Assignment," pp. 299–300.

3. Langer, "Population in the Perspective of History," *Harvard Public Health*

Bulletin, 22 (1965), Supplement: 6; "The Black Death," *Scientific American,* 210 (1964): 114–21.

4. Langer, *In and Out of the Ivory Tower: The Autobiography of William L. Langer* (New York, 1977), pp. 4, 5–6, 249.

5. *Ibid.,* p. 223.

6. *Ibid.,* p. 32.

7. *Ibid.,* p. 25; Gerhart Piers and Milton B. Singer, *Shame and Guilt: A Psychoanalytic and a Cultural Study* (Springfield, Ill., 1953), p. 16.

8. *Ivory Tower,* pp. 170–2.

9. *Ibid.;* Schorske to Loewenberg, June 8, 1980.

10. *Ivory Tower,* pp. 170–2.

11. *Ibid.,* p. 192; Rowena Langer to Loewenberg, November 12, 1980.

12. *Ivory Tower,* p. 139.

13. *Ibid,* pp. 159–160; Langer, "A People Who Prefer Uniforms to Votes," *New York Herald Tribune Books* (February 20, 1938), IX: 3.

14. Langer, 1938 Lecture II, pp. 6, 8, and concluding lecture, 1940, p. 8, William Leonard Langer Papers, Harvard University Archives, Cambridge, Mass.

15. 1938 Lecture II, pp. 3, 5, *Ibid.*

16. Langer, *Gas and Flame in World War I* (New York, 1965), pp. xvi–xvii.

17. Otto Fenichel, "On Acting" (1946), reprinted in *Collected Papers: Second Series* (New York, 1954), p. 360 n. 19. See the outstanding article by George L. Engel, "The Death of a Twin: Mourning and Anniversary Reactions. Fragments of 10 Years of Self-Analysis," *International Journal of Psycho-Analysis,* 56 (1975): 23–40.

18. Allen Wheelis, *How People Change* (New York, 1974), pp. 39, 42. I am influenced in my formulations by the sensitive work of Helen Merrell Lynd, *On Shame and the Search for Identity* (New York, 1958).

19. Heinz Kohut, *The Analysis of the Self: A Systematic Approach to the Psychoanalytic Treatment of Narcissistic Personality Disorders* (New York, 1971), pp. 144, 149, 232.

20. *Ibid.,* p. 232.

21. Sigmund Freud, "Das Unbehagen in der Kultur," *Studienaugabe,* ed. Alexander Mitscherlich, Angela Richards, James Strachey (Frankfurt am Main, 1969–75), 9: 242.

22. Walter Langer to Sanford Gifford, November 11, 1975; "An American Analyst in Vienna during the *Anschluss,* 1936–1938," *Journal of the History of the Behavioral Sciences,* 14 (1978): 50.

23. *Ibid.* pp. 45–6.

24. *Ibid.,* p. 46.

25. *Ibid.*

26. *Ivory Tower,* p. 165; Freud, "Some Character-Types Met With in Psycho-Analytic Work" (1916), *Standard Edition of the Complete Psychological Works,* trans. and ed. James Strachey et al. (London, 1953–1974), 14: 306–31.

27. Freud, "The Interpretation of Dreams" (1900), *ibid.,* 5: 398 n; Langer, *Ivory Tower,* p. 167.

28. *Ibid.,* p. 172.

PART III

Austrian Portraits

Identity, Murder, and Vacillation

The final years of the Austro-Hungarian Empire were the setting for a development of new nationalistic movements, an intellectual and artistic flowering unequaled in modern cultural history, and the flourishing of a school of Marxist democratic socialism that was markedly original in dealing with the problems of nationalism and culture.

There are relationships between the issue of Jewish identity in twentieth-century Europe and the socialist quest for a better world—in the case of the Austro-Marxists, a world that would include space for national differences. I have explored these relationships in the following essays on the founders and leaders of these two movements: Theodor Herzl of Zionism and Victor and Friedrich Adler and Otto Bauer of Social Democracy.

These are studies of founders and leaders as well as of the emotional disposition of movements. Leadership studies are my method of choice for exploring historical movements because through personality studies over time we have the opportunity to trace the minutiae of decision making with the precision of clinical psychoanalysis. Only by studying individuals and their adaptations over time as they interact with ideology, and the political and social situations that constitute history, can we discover the nuances that expose the dynamics conditioning historical choices.

The reader will find variations in approach to psychoanalytic theory and conceptualization in the following portraits of Austrian personalities. These differences reflect and correlate to my theoretical and clinical sophistication over the past decade and a half. "Theodor Herzl" was the earliest of these attempts. It bears the imprint of the classical psychoanalytic theory, with both the mechanistic quality and the deep-cutting rigor of that model. As someone has said of classical analysis, it is like the Model T Ford: not very elegant, but reliable as hell. In the Herzl essay adult symptoms are reduced to their origins in specific phases of childhood. An apt archaeological metaphor, such as Freud loved to use, is that the Herzl essay is excavating with a steam shovel, which takes one immediately to the earliest layers laid down, rather than working with a spade, which leaves the exterior shell intact.

The Marxist alternative was a major response of Jewish intellectuals to the shedding of their religious faith and the traumas of the experience of assimilation. Other important historical responses were the nationalism of Herzl and the cultural universalism of Freud. These are vital historical options whose assessment and reevaluation are a central concern of contemporary historical writing, including the current work of Carl Schorske, Fritz Stern, Peter Gay, Ismar Schorch, Robert Wistrich, Uriel Tal, William McGrath, Jehuda Reinharz, W. T. Angress, and others.

The problems of the nature of political leadership, the ever-present issues of morality and effectiveness, of the uses of power which cannot preclude destructiveness and aggression, the poignant dialectic between theory and action that is the dilemma of all movements for social change, are probed in the Adler and Bauer essays. While the response of Friedrich Adler to these dilemmas was that of impulsiveness and immediate action of the most radical kind, Otto Bauer's mode of handling crisis was cautious to the point of being dilatory. Both these leaders were in a true sense children of Victor Adler, whose balance of theory and tactics, of mass mobilization and parliamentary successes, was the training ground and inspiration of each of them though in different ways. Yet both the young Adler and Bauer also reacted against the founder's principles and style of leadership, as children and successors must. This is the emotional familial dialectic that binds the generations to each other and moves the political struggle forward in syncretism with economic and social developments that together make history.

Theodor Herzl

Nationalism and Politics

The visitor or immigrant to Israel, on entering the customs shed in the port of Haifa, is confronted with a towering portrait of Theodor Herzl. A tourist or pilgrim to Jerusalem will see his visage staring down upon the Knesset chamber and may visit his tomb and museum on Mount Herzl among Jerusalem's western hills. Herzl is the founder of modern political Zionism and the father of the State of Israel. He was a consummate diplomat and politician who, with no base of power, created the permanent institutions of the Zionist movement, such as its international congresses, its bank, its newspaper, and its sympathetic political affiliations in England that were to come to fruition in the following generation. However, all the attention to his political achievement overlooks the other Herzl, the dreamer who lived in private fantasies that he committed only to his diaries, the man who gained moral strength for his struggles with internal depression and loss, and derision and disbelief from others.

In this essay, I felt it important to focus on the nature and quality of the fantasies in Herzl's life as he developed his Zionist vision. During his creative period he was in a detached dream world, quite unable and unwilling to relate to his surroundings. Had he been a "realist," he could not have worked with the driving sense of inner conviction which carried him over diplomatic and political hurdles in creating his movement, and which caused his early death. This essay examines the sources of Herzl's sense of inner mission.

Herzl's vision included not only a Jewish state as a political solution to anti-Semitism but one inhabited by a new kind of Jew whose life would be governed by a code of behavior patterned on the ethos of honor, courage, and nobility of the European aristocracy, yet who would be living in an environment reflecting all of the late-nineteenth-century bourgeois faith in the illimitable potential and beauty of technology. Herzl completely rejected both the isolation of the ghetto and the wish for assimilation, not merely as insecure domiciles but primarily in terms of character type. He fantasied a new Jewish personality: direct, stalwart, unafraid of its own aggression, because the new Jews in their own land would live in harmony with their Arab neighbors and at peace with all other peoples. This is the ultimate irony of Herzl's saga.

If Herzl had a serious flaw as a politician, it is that although he somberly foresaw that Jews had no future in Europe, he regarded Palestine as a social-political vacuum, as though it were uninhabited by natives who would exercise claims to the land. It is as though here his sense of reality failed him; he had a blind spot for the indigenous Arab population. Perhaps he had to be myopic, for if he had foreseen this complex barrier to his plans as well as the many impediments that he did see, and if he had tried to cope with it, he could not have acted at all—he would have remained an idle dreamer or *Luftmensch*. And to have taken no initiative would have been an even greater tragedy than to have acted with partial and imperfect vision, but with a hope that changed history, as he in fact did.

The founder of modern political Zionism, Theodor Herzl, presents an excellent case of the charismatic personality whose psychopolitical fantasies influenced history and were acted out in reality. The true subject matter of history is human consciousness. As a man who has left a startling record of his consciousness at work in all its levels, Herzl is a particularly attractive subject for a psychoanalytical historical case study. In him we confront many problems rarely found together in one historical figure. We trace the entire unfolding of a program of political action from the painful regression to narcissism out of which fantasy brought a frustrated man. We may derive insight into the nature of the charismatic political mass leader and the dynamics of ideology formation as we see personal fantasies as a prelude to action, these fantasies then being acted out in the social world. Herzl is one of the rare political leaders who was a *littérateur*. He has left us a rich body of creative writings from both his non-political and his Zionist periods. By correlating his plays, stories, essays, and novels with his political fantasies, we may observe the interaction of the literary creativity with the psyche of the author. Herzl also gives the historian a fascinating demonstration of the value of perceiving the psychic response of historical figures to organic disease. Biographical and medical data are often abundant in the case of famous figures. The unconscious fantasies induced by disease, whether infectious or degenerative, are of value to historical interpretation.

A further fact that makes Herzl exceptional as a historical subject is the rare quality of total candor in his *Diaries*.[1] He confessed his private feelings and his most grandiose fantasies to his notebooks because no one in his world took him seriously. Even his best friend thought him mad.

Herzl was born in Budapest in 1860, the second child of a highly as-similated Jewish middle-class family. His father was a bank director and timber merchant. Theodor was almost exclusively raised by his mother, his father being involved in business affairs and often away from home. The boy worshipped his mother and sought her counsel; the man remained very close to her until the end of his life. Herzl's father had a "managing nature," which he tried to exercise on his son. The Herzl home was noted for its formality and its attention to externals. Theodor was always elegantly clothed and well mannered.

His paternal grandfather, an orthodox Jew who died when Theodor was twenty, was a follower of the Sephardic rabbi Alkalai of Semlin (1792–1878), who preached the ideal of the return of the Jews to Palestine. It is doubtful whether the young Herzl could have avoided hearing his grandfather talk of Alkalai and his dream of returning to the homeland. It is a matter of speculation as to what impact this may have had on him.

In 1878, following the death of Theodor's elder sister, Pauline, the family moved to Vienna. There is now an emerging body of scholarship on the social, political, and aesthetic culture of late-nineteenth-century Vienna.[2] Bearing in mind the social and cultural milieu that is Herzl's scene of action, we will focus on the depth interpretation of his biography.

Zionist hagiography would have it that Herzl came to his Jewish nation-alism by firsthand observation of the Dreyfus case as a correspondent in Paris. I suggest that Herzl's Zionist calling was determined by a personal need to be a messiah–savior–political leader.

At about age twelve, the period when a Jewish boy is thinking of his forthcoming bar mitzvah, Herzl had a dream, which he later recounted as an adult. In the dreamer's own words:

The King-Messiah came, a glorious and majestic old man, took me in his arms, and swept off with me on the wings of the wind. On one of the iridescent clouds we encountered the figure of Moses. The features were those familiar to me out of my childhood in the statue by Michelangelo. The Messiah called to Moses: It is for this child that I have prayed. But to me he said: Go, declare to the Jews that I shall come soon and perform great wonders and great deeds for my people and for the whole world.[3]

The fact that this youthful dream was remembered all his life is an indication of its profound unconscious significance. We note in this dream Herzl's passivity. He was carried up by a man. Twenty-four years later he experienced his great Zionist conception in the same passive manner, writing: "Am I working it out? No, it is working through me!"[4] This is the passivity experienced when the unconscious is in control of mental activity, and this close contact with the unconscious is the wellspring of all mental creativity.

Herzl's mental associations of himself with the messiah and with Moses are already in evidence in this dream. He has a mission to become a powerful charismatic leader and, like Freud, he has chosen to identify with the greatest leader of his people.

As Herzl grows up, it becomes evident that his emotional life is split into two currents of feeling. The tender, affectionate feelings springing from the earliest years of childhood and attached to the members of his family and the sensual erotic elements that became powerful at the age of puberty were never fused, as is essential for a mature attitude in love. Thus Herzl's tender feelings remained attached to unconscious fantasies of his mother and sister, whereas his sensual feelings were aroused by a "lower" type of sexual object, the woman of the street, toward whom he had no tender romantic feelings but with whom he could find physical gratification.

From documentary evidence it appears that Herzl had an infection (possibly gonorrhea) when he was twenty. The evidence appears in a letter to his closest youthful friend and confidant, Heinrich Kana. Kana, who shot himself in 1891, is the man whom Herzl later wished to make the central figure of his novel. The letter was written in the friendly spirit of camaraderie of young single men in late-nineteenth-century Vienna. Herzl tells his friend that he has laid his syringe aside, that he hopes that his next attack of "xxx" will be cured by zinc sulphate. He has commissioned a custom-made linen sheath for his penis in a prominent ladies' fashion shop. He notes that fortunately the seamstress was a young girl of seventeen years who therefore would not yet know what consequences unhappy love (unplatonic, of course) could have. Though she tried her best to please him, the sheath was too narrow for his penis, but how was she to know this with her mere seventeen years? The penis is placed in its sheath only when he behaves himself quietly as a peaceful dweller in trousers. A second sheath commissioned at the same shop had the shortcoming that either his "young candidate for knighthood" felt cramped or he slipped out. Herzl complains of being plagued by an erection dilemma. Perhaps, he asks, he should take off the hair shirt? But much dripping water flows down into the valley; and what would his laundress think? She might despise him. Dare he risk it?[5]

The significance of the disease for the historian is less in its pathology than in the impact it had on Herzl. How did he respond to the knowledge that he had contracted venereal disease? What were his psychological defenses and accommodations, and what may we learn from them? We see in this letter an attempt to cover a depression with frivolity. The surface tone of the letter is gay and joking. But beneath the lightheartedness are the indications of worry over the unhappy consequences of "unplatonic love." Herzl must have been full of anxiety over his penis drip and threatened loss of potency. Social disapproval of the disease, indicated by Herzl's concern over the possible reaction of his washerwoman, compounded his fear of injury. We also find a boastfulness on the subject of his manly prowess. Herzl makes a point of recounting to his friend the size of his organ, its erective power, the wide experience of his "young knight" in the pursuit of women.

The other side of the emotional split between sensuality and tenderness apparent in Herzl in his twenties was a penchant for deep infatuations with young pubescent girls. When he was twenty-one he fell passionately in love with his sixteen-year-old cousin. "She is a beautiful girl such as one only sees in a dream," he wrote Kana. If he were four years older, he would marry her immediately. "I tell you, my dear friend, I am in ecstasy [*Schwärme*] for this sweet child, as in the time of my full-blown versifying and lovemaking. . . . she is a lyric poem, and I could conceive of no finer life task than to read this prize forever." He visits her parents as often as possible without arousing their suspicion and then he feasts on the sight of her. Herzl thought of asking for her hand. His heart pounded when he suddenly met her on the street. "If I ever do marry," he says, "my wife must be like my lovely cousin."[6]

Four years later Herzl confides to his diary that he is in love—with a thirteen-year-old child. He sought her out at a children's ball.

> I wished to kiss her. She merely turned her blond little head away. I did not kiss her. Then she climbed up onto my arm, like a little queen. . . . I could not see enough of this proud fine little person. . . . she ruled me from the first moment. I was sad when she withdrew from me, the premature coquette; I was jealous of the boys with whom she danced. . . . A true princess? I looked at nothing but her,

> the sweet, sweet, sweet! The little dress was still short, the darling
> body undeveloped . . . but the fine, aristocratic, lovely face! . . . Later,
> as she was frazzled [*zerzaust*] and stood in front of a lamp, I saw a
> halo around that sweet little head.

When Herzl danced with her and she winked at him slyly, he was beside
himself. He had to restrain himself from professing his love to her as to an
adult. He tried to rouse her jealousy by flirting with the most beautiful of
the "big" ladies. "In short," he says, "I behaved madly." He would rather
let himself be torn to pieces than not have a dance with her. He thought
of her in the night and dreamed of her. It was all he could do to avoid
going down to the ice-skating rink where she would be. "Dear God, dear
God!" he moans as he closes the diary entry of his passion for a little girl
half his age.[7]

Throughout these two infatuations of his twenties Herzl's emotions are
highly romanticized projections. His objects are virginal maids, pure and
sentimentalized. They are women to be adored and worshipped, not to
whom he could relate sensually or from whom he would catch a disease.
From such a split between the sensual and tender emotions toward women
we expect to find an inadequate or differential potency and a strengthening
of homoerotic currents in the personality. Because a mature level of genitality has not been reached, libidinal satisfaction must be derived from a
source other than women. In the case of a charismatic leader, this source
is the adoration given him by the masses. Herzl, already having established
the pattern of his great creative phase of the mid-1890's, succeeds in defending against his underlying depression with megalomanic fantasies.

Moods of melancholy alternating with periods of elation pervaded Herzl's
personal life. At age nineteen, shortly after a serious illness of his mother,
he wrote: "I have much to complain about the changes in my moods: to exult
to heaven, to be deathly depressed [*Himmelhoch jauchzend, zu Tode betrübt*]
—soon to delude myself with hope, expansive like the billowing sea, again
to die, to be dejected unto death [*zu Tode, zum Sterben versagt*]." In contrast
with the countless hopes and plans with which he had commenced his trip
two months previously, he has brought home nothing real and positive, "and
this arouses a sneering rage against myself in me," he says. His pessimism
of the moment is expressed in an aphorism, undoubtedly inspired by Scho-
penhauer: "Pain is the substance of life and joy consists only of the temporary absence of pain."[8]

At the beginning of his twenty-third year, Herzl chastises himself because he has to date achieved nothing in life. He is filled with doubts about

his capacity; he has no great achievement in him. He derogates his journal notes as literary onanism. His dreams, hopes, and desires are unachieved. His inability to fulfill them is an impediment to matrimony with the muse of creativity. "But this is an impotence that one hopes may be healed, even if in fact it cannot be; one always hopes for means to lift this sterile failure."[9] The etiology of Herzl's melancholia is suggested by his closely related imagery of masturbation, inability to marry, and creative impotence.

The year 1883 brought many crises for Herzl. Two years earlier he had joined the Burschenschaft Albia, a dueling fraternity, where he dueled for four hours each day. In March 1883 he resigned from Albia because its members had participated in an anti-Semitic commemoration of the death of Richard Wagner. Herzl's decision was made on a point of honor. It was a move that caused deep feelings of isolation and rejection. People do not know how much "pain, suffering, and disappointment" he carried with him hidden beneath his vest, he confided to his diary. This was a decisive encounter with social anti-Semitism which was to leave a lasting impression on him. He referred to his depressions as "an evil guest who calls himself Mr. Uncertainty [*Herr von Zweifel*]" and who was related to the devil. His mood of happiness or misery depended on whether he was potent or impotent in his work.[10]

Further defeats that year were experienced in Herzl's quest for love and in the rejection of his literary efforts. He had a mild flirtation with a young girl and was slapped for it. His diary notes of the same week are desperate and inconsolable. "Powerless, inactive, luckless time!" he dejectedly writes. "Death and pestilence, will this never cease?" he asks. "Success refused to come. And I need success, I thrive only on it," he cries. His finished work containing his aspirations, hopes, the blood and striving of the years of his youth lies in the drawer. He has no desire to submit it, certain that it will be sent back with a printed rejection note. "No love in the heart, no longing in the soul, no hope, no joy . . ." is the refrain with which Herzl closes this melancholy entry.[11]

Some of Herzl's most depressed entries were on the New Year's Eves of his early twenties. He usually spent them alone, writing his diary and retiring early without waiting for midnight, thus closing what he felt was an empty day in an empty life. "All is empty! The heart is empty of hope, the head is empty of ideas, the pocket is empty of money, and life is empty of poetry." He is unable to study for his forthcoming examination in Roman law. He doubts his fitness for love. He is already useless, even for that! He has a piece of work in his desk that embodies his best efforts, but it is not fit for success.[12]

When he was completing his studies at the university, Herzl journeyed at his parents' expense to southwest Germany. In a letter dated "The Month of Distress," Herzl terms himself an "old gambler" who cannot restrain himself from risking his money at the green table.[13] Herzl's episode of unrestrained gambling is psychodynamically related to his later political career and thus deserves our notice. The gambler dares fate, forcing it to decide for or against him. He believes it his right to ask for special favor from fate. Good luck is the delivery of protection and the promise of continued blessings for future acts. Gambling is an attempt to force fate to do right by the gambler. In any casino gambling the odds of losing are slightly larger than the chance of winning. The gambler dares the gods to make a decision about him, hoping for their beneficence. If winning means the getting of needed supplies, loss is interpreted as ingratiation with the gods for the same purpose.

Gambling begins as play. The omnipotent god is asked how he would decide in an actual situation. The earnest cycle of anxiety, need for reassurance, and heightened anxiety over the violent need for comfort overwhelms the ego, and the playful character of "gaming" is lost. It has become a serious matter in which the gambler must in the end be ruined.

For Herzl in Baden, at age twenty-three, gambling was what politics was to become for him later—a trial with fate to prove his destiny. Herzl fought fate at the casino and as a Zionist. He rebelled against her and sought to compel her to let him win.

There is also a deeper psychoanalytical meaning to gambling: its appeal to the infantile, magical, ritualistic, and superstitious part of the self, the paleolithic grandiose part of the person which believes that his wishes will alone bring the satisfaction of needs, that all desires will be fulfilled merely by being wished. This was the megalomanic and omnipotent part of Herzl that denied the need for effort, logic, and intelligence for achievement. Of course, this was not the part of Herzl that came to the fore when he was a political leader. What is most fascinating about Herzl is the subtle blending of the empirical skills of interpersonal relations and plain hard work, to the point of exhaustion, with the omnipotent fantasy of the gambler which was an essential ingredient of his appeal.

Herzl idealized his parents all his life. To him they were the "best" parents in the world, to be honored and adored. According to his biographer Alex Bein, the bond with his father "had never been strained."[14] The oedipal struggle with his father was repressed. It never was externalized in conflict between father and son. The processes of love and hate were separated, affording relief from the guilt of hostility. Only the "good" father was admitted to consciousness. The feelings of rivalry and hatred for his father undoubtedly caused the punishment Herzl experienced in his depressive periods.

Herzl on one occasion relished posing as a nobleman, "Baron Rittershausen," in a social setting. If he ever should become something more than a talentless scribbler, which his doubting self, "Mr. Uncertainty," convinced him was decidedly unlikely, then he would do as the *Arabian Nights* hero, Harun al-Rashid, the caliph of Baghdad, who went among his people in disguise to hear what they were truly thinking. Herzl enjoyed the role of the Prussian nobleman at home in the world of letters. He easily pictured himself the romantic *Arabian Nights* ruler who puts on the mask of a new identity to help his people. At a later date he was to say: "if there is one thing I should like to be, it is a member of the old Prussian nobility."[15]

Herzl fell in love with Julie Naschauer, the daughter of a wealthy business-man, in the spring of 1886. His diaries show a powerful, highly romanticized infatuation. He records his first kiss from her as they stood on a balcony at a party. Three weeks later he received two more kisses. The romance had its vacillations until the couple were married on June 25, 1889.[16] On March 29, 1890, their first child, a daughter named after Herzl's dead sister Pauline, was born. On June 10, 1891, their only son, Hans, was born. He was neither circumcised nor given a Hebrew name, a significant indication of how assimilated the Herzls were in the early 1890's. Finally, their last child, a daughter named Margaret Trude, was born in Paris on May 20, 1893.

Herzl was faced with frustration and rejection personally, professionally, and socially in the period 1891–1895. His marriage was marked by discord "almost from the start." His biographers attribute the breakup of Herzl's marriage to "a mother-in-law problem" and his wife's lack of sympathy as a helpmeet to the struggling journalist-playwright.[17]

Herzl remained attached to his powerful and possessive mother. He would often have dinner with his parents to escape domestic scenes. Julie was spoiled and immature. Plans for a divorce did not materialize, appar-ently for the sake of the children. In 1891 the family separated, with Herzl settling in Paris after he was appointed correspondent for the prestigious *Neue Freie Presse.* In 1892 his wife and children came to Paris, but the attempted reconciliation was to no avail. Herzl was not to have a lasting relationship with a woman, other than his mother, for the rest of his life. She remained the primary "spiritual" love object in his life, to be re-created in the mother figures of his stories and his novel *Altneuland.* As far as we know, another sexual relationship was not a factor in his life between the time of his separation from his wife and his death in 1904.

The significant emotional fact for us is that in August 1891 Herzl sepa-rated from his wife and children. From this time on his emotions were detached from close libidinal ties to others. He was a loner—masterful, narcissistic, independent. Max Weber suggests that the holders of charisma often live in celibacy or at least renounce family life and in fact are single as stated in the call to asceticism of Jesus: "If any man come to me and hates not his father, and mother, and wife, and children, and brethren, and sisters, yea, and his own life also, he cannot be my disciple." According to W. W. Tarn, Alexander the Great "apparently never cared for any woman; he apparently never had a mistress, and his two marriages were mere affairs of policy." Hitler has been considered asexual by Trevor-Roper.[18] Herzl's case would confirm Weber's ideal typology in that the breakup of his marriage coincided with his emergence as a prophet. Weber does not explain the dynamics of such libidinal displacement by charismatic leaders. He recognizes, defines, and evaluates the phenomenon of charisma itself without offering any personality theory to explain it. Psychoanalysis, though confirming Weber's observations on charisma, also presents a dynamic personality theory that interprets it. We may see the depth dynamics of charisma operate in their full manifestations in Herzl's evolution to celibacy, isolation, and charismatic political leadership.

A record of Herzl's unhappy marriage and of his melancholia exists in memoirs of his friends and colleagues. It is apparent that Julie Herzl had little insight into her husband. There is no indication of empathy with his fantasies, understanding of his emotional needs, or interest in his political ideas on the part of his wife. A striking characterization is that of Mrs. Herzl's reaction to the Zionist writer Israel Zangwill, one of her husband's most vital English supporters, when he was a guest in her home. His small unaristocratic stature "visibly disappointed" Julie. Zangwill relaxed after a long journey; he let his hair down. He did not know how to properly eat the crab she served. His natural folksy demeanor was all that she could see. She interpreted it as vulgarity and retired from the table as soon as she could, "distressed by his peculiarities."[19]

The author Maria E. delle Grazie records the change perceivable in Herzl when he was with his wife. From a man gripped by the obsession of a personal mission who tells the writer, "I have staked all my life and all my will on a single hope. Palestine! . . . I too can no longer help myself; for the vision burns in the night when my eyes are closed and I cannot hide from it," he changes in the presence of his wife to nothing more than a suave Viennese wit. The author recalls:

> I saw him once again, once only, in his home, beside his beautiful blond wife, who—it became clear to me in a moment—found only torment in that which was life and fate to him. For that one hour, in her presence, he was . . . the witty feuilletonist—that and nothing more. It was only then that I understood the full tragedy of his life.[20]

Herzl's first attempts at a solution to the Jewish problem were romantic dreams with himself in the role of fantasy hero. To combat anti-Semitism he would use the classic aristocratic mode of dealing with opposition—the duel. He wrote: "Half a dozen duels will do a great deal to improve the position of the Jews in society." He contemplated challenging the leading Austrian anti-Semites, Prince Alois Liechtenstein, George von Schönerer, and Karl Lueger, to duels. If he were killed, a posthumous letter would announce to the world that he had been a victim of "the most unjust movement in the world." He continued:

> If, however, it had been my lot to kill my opponent and be brought to trial, then I would have delivered a brilliant speech which would have begun with my regrets for the death of a man of honor. . . . Then I would have turned to the Jewish question and delivered an oration worthy of Lassalle. I would have sent a shudder of admiration through the jury. I would have compelled the respect of the judges, and the case against me would have been dismissed. Thereupon the Jews would have made me one of their representatives and I would have declined because I would refuse to achieve such a position by the killing of a man.[21]

His next fantasy has moved from a personal to a social solution—he will lead the Jews of Austria in a mass conversion to Catholicism: "We must submerge in the people." But, again, the solution is one embodying Herzl's strictest conceptions of chivalric honor. The baptism would be for the children and the masses only;

> the leaders of this movement—above all myself—would remain Jews and as Jews would propagate conversion to the religion of the majority. In broad daylight, at noon on Sunday, the conversion should take place at St. Stefan's Cathedral in solemn procession with the pealing of bells. Not in shame, as individuals have done it up to now, but with a proud gesture. And because the leaders would remain Jewish, escorting the people only to the threshold of the church and themselves staying outside, the whole procedure would have a feature of great genuineness . . . [W]e would have made Christians of our young sons before they came into the age of independent decision, after which conversion looks like cowardice or social climbing.[22]

Herzl's last non-political attempt to overcome anti-Semitism was through culture. He would persuade by writing a drama of such force that it would forge a new mutual understanding between Jews and Gentiles. Herzl wrote *The New Ghetto* in seventeen days in the fall of 1894. Its hero, a young Jewish lawyer, Dr. Jacob Samuel, is transparently Herzl himself.

He is married to the spoiled and willful daughter of a rich businessman, thus a replica of his wife Julie. The Jewish hero of the play has learned gentlemanly conduct and bearing from his Christian friend, to whom he says: "I have learned from you how to honor a man without crawling at his feet, how to be proud without being arrogant." He professes to have "taken a number of steps out of the Jewish street." Having learned honor, Dr. Samuel is killed in a duel, but not before he can make a dying statement to the Jews: "my brothers, there will come a time when they will let you live again—when you know how to die." It was in vain that Arthur Schnitzler pointed out to Herzl that Jews had known how to die for centuries and had done so by the thousands; this, said Schnitzler, is why they were not permitted to live.[23] Herzl has presented here a solution embodying his future formula—the "new" Jew, the man who has a sense of aristocratic honor and virtue, and knows how to die like a cavalier; but he has done so in the idiom of the old Herzl, the frustrated playwright and author. He is not yet Herzl the political man, the charismatic leader; he is still the bourgeois writer using the aesthetic culture to persuade.

At this time of personal desperation, Herzl tried to gain the friendship of Schnitzler, a man whom he admired, by taking the well-known playwright into a compact of secrecy in trying to get his play *The New Ghetto* produced. Schnitzler faithfully carried out his commitment to act as broker for the anonymous Herzl, but the latter wished a greater degree of intimacy:

> Why don't you send me your play? Have I not come close enough to you in our secret conspiracy of the last months? I have a great need for a good friendship. I almost feel like advertising in the newspapers: "Man in prime of life seeks friend to whom he can confide without fear all his weaknesses and foolishness." . . . I really don't know, am I too shy, or am I seeing too well: I don't find any such friend among my acquaintances here.[24]

Rather than growing closer, the two men grew apart with Herzl's dedication to Zionism.

Herzl was already writing *The New Ghetto* when the Dreyfus case broke in Paris. While the reaction of the mob screaming "Down with the Jews!" at the degradation of Captain Dreyfus left a lasting impression on Herzl, it was his antecedent fantasies that provided the primary impulse for his political development.

In Herzl's *Diaries* we have one of the most candid and historically unique sources available in the literature for the investigation of charismatic leadership formation. To them he disclosed his most intimate thoughts and undisguised doubts. We may trace his day-by-day regression to narcissism, his increasing feelings of estrangement and depersonalization. For him everything has changed. He has the ecstatic experience of a grand and pleasant inflation of the self and a withdrawal of interest in the external world of people and things.

The *Diaries* open in the spring of 1895 with the modest statement: "I have been laboring for some time on a work of infinite magnitude." The line between illusion and reality is blurred: "Even now I don't know whether I will be able to carry it through. It appears like a mighty dream." But it is so powerful he cannot resist—it is an obsession: "For days and weeks it has possessed me to the limits of my consciousness; it accompanies me wherever I go; hangs suspended over my everyday conversations; looks over my shoulder at my comically little journalistic work, disturbs me and intoxicates me." We note the self-depreciation concerning his vocational role in life. Herzl's narcissistic ego ideal is not satisfied with being a prominent journalist, he must be much more—a world shaper and leader of men. His description of the ever-present idea that hovers over his conversation and daily affairs indicates a perception of his narcissistic regression and his libidinal displacement, though he is perplexed by it: "How I move from the ideas for a novel to a practical program is already a puzzle to me, although it occurred in the last weeks. That lies in the Unconscious."[25]

Herzl now compensates for the loss of love in the external world by increased self-love. There is a marked eroticization of his inner world of ideas. He describes his feelings toward his fantasy in the only suitable metaphor—that of a lover to his beloved: "This now so fills me that I relate everything to this cause, like a lover to his beloved."[26]

This self-absorbed proposition is the psychological equivalent of the proposition: "I love only myself." It is the narcissistic expression of the overestimation of the self. Heinz Kohut writes of "the narcissistic nature of the creative act (the fact that the object of the creative interest is invested with narcissistic libido). . . . The sense of isolation of the creative mind is both exhilarating and frightening, the latter because the experience repeats traumatically an early childhood fear of being alone, abandoned, and unsupported."[27] This is an apt description of Herzl in his most creative period of idea formation. The love of external objects was replaced by self-love, and the overestimation usually directed to a loved person was now directed to his own ego and its fantasies.

Herzl's megalomania is visible in the ego ideals he has formed of conspicuous leaders. He draws comparisons between himself and Moses, Bismarck, Napoleon, and Moltke. When he walks in the Tuileries and views the statue of Gambetta, he says: "I hope the Jews put up a more artistic one to me."[28]

Herzl tells us that he is a passive agent of his inspiration. His mission to redeem the Jews is an inspiration from God: "Am I working it out? No! It is working me. It would be a compulsion if it were not so rational from beginning to end. This is what was formerly called 'inspiration.' . . . But if it comes about, what a gift of God to the Jews!"[29] He describes his sensation as like a volcanic eruption shooting up within him. It promises to be a process of internal purification. His work will consist of a life full of manly acts that will dissolve and lift up everything base, barren, and confused within him and reconcile him with all, just as he has reconciled himself to all through his labor.

Herzl was in a hypermanic period which was a defense against depression. He found release from tension through living in the world of his ideas. Writing them down became a relief for him. He was in the grip of unconscious creative forces not of his own volition. His expression is consistently passive, that of natural forces: "I am writing myself free of ideas which rise like bubbles in a retort and which would burst it to pieces if they found no outlet." Or the imagery may be of labor and delivery: "For three hours I have been tramping about the Bois to dispel the pangs of new trains of thought." He is overexcited by his fantasies. He goes to the gardens of the Tuileries and recovers by looking at the statues. He lives in his own world, an inner realm apart from his friends: "Today I dined at a brasserie near the Châtelet. I avoid all my acquaintances. They hurt me because they fail to realize the world I come from; this makes everyday life terribly wounding." Herzl felt an identity with artists and poets because he lived in the realm of his fantasies:

> Much in these notes will seem laughable, exaggerated, crazy. But if I had exercised self-criticism, as I do in my literary work, my ideas would have been stunted. What is colossal serves the purpose better than what is dwarfed, for anyone can do the trimming easily enough.
>
> Artists will understand why I, who otherwise reason clearly, have allowed extravagances and dreams to grow wildly among my practical, political, and legislative ideas—as green grass sprouts between the paving stones. I could not permit myself to be tied down purely to sober fact. This light intoxication was necessary.
>
> Yes, artists will understand this fully. But there are so few artists.[30]

At times Herzl feared that he was going insane. His ego carefully observed his actions and commented: "According to these frank notes, some people will think me a megalomaniac. Others will say or believe that I want to do some business or engage in self-advertisement. But my peers, the artists and philosophers, will understand how genuine all this is, and they will defend me." Or: "Lombroso will perhaps think me mad. And my good friend Nordau will muffle in silence the anxiety I cause him. But they are wrong: I know that two and two is four."[31]

At other times he was unsure of his ability to discriminate between reality and fantasy:

> During these days I have often been afraid of going insane. So shatteringly did the streams of thought race through my soul. A lifetime will not suffice to realize all of it.
>
> But I am leaving behind a spiritual legacy. To whom? To all men.
>
> I believe I shall be named among the greatest benefactors of mankind.
>
> Or is this belief already megalomania?[32]

There were occasions when Herzl sounded like a man who is undergoing a psychotic break: "I believe that for me life has ended and world history has begun." He saw himself as a savior and messiah: "They will pray for me in the synagogues. But also in the churches." He believed in his own total omnipotence: "If I point with my finger at a spot: Here shall be a city, then a city shall rise there."[33]

In early June 1895 Herzl was in a high state of excitation while writing *Der Judenstaat.* He compared his sensation to Heine's description of eagle's wings above his head when he was poetically inspired. Herzl writes:

> I worked at it daily, until I was completely exhausted. My one recreation was on the evenings when I could go to hear Wagner's music, and particularly *Tannhäuser,* an opera which I go to hear as often as it is produced. And only on those evenings when there was no opera did I have any doubts as to the truth of my ideas.

He sought relief from his excitement by attending Wagnerian opera and fantasized incorporating the opulent staging of medieval chivalric opera into his political program:

> In the evening, *Tannhäuser* at the Opera.
>
> We too shall have such splendid lobbies, the men in formal dress, the women as luxurious as possible. Yes, I will exploit the Jewish love of luxury, as everything else.
>
> Again, I think of the phenomenon of the crowd.
>
> There they sat for hours, tightly packed, motionless, in bodily torture! and for what? For an imponderable, which Hirsch does not comprehend: for sounds! for music, and pictures!
>
> I shall also encourage stately processional marches for great occasions.[34]

Herzl tells us that he understands what the old style of philanthropic leaders such as the Barons Rothschild and Hirsch do not, that the modern mass crowds demand operatic spectacle and a politics of emotional manipulation.

He carefully notes the theatrical decor of the setting of the First Zionist Congress in the concert hall in Basel. He compliments Wolffsohn's cleverness in making the new Zionist banner on the format of the talit, the traditional Jewish prayer shawl—a white field with two blue stripes and the star of David. Herzl, the playwright, was always supremely conscious of his political costumes and staging. A visitor to the congress recorded his impression of the leader as stage manager:

> The first time I saw Herzl was in Basle in 1897 when, dressed in evening clothes at ten o'clock in the morning, he appeared on the tribune and opened the First Zionist Congress. The evening dress was characteristic of the man. He had given strict orders that all delegates were to appear at this First Congress in festive attire.

At the opening of the congress Herzl made an issue of dress with Nordau, who refused flatly to go home and change to a full-dress suit.

> I drew him aside and begged him to do it as a special favor to me. I told him: Today, the presidium of the Zionist Congress is as yet nothing, we must establish everything. People must grow accustomed to seeing only the finest and most elegant at this Congress. He allowed himself to be persuaded, for which I embraced him in gratitude. In a quarter of an hour he returned in formal dress.

When Herzl prepared to meet the German Kaiser in Istanbul, he noted: "Careful *toilette*. The color of my gloves was an especial success: a delicate gray." In Jerusalem he inspected the clothes, linen, ties, gloves, shoes, and hats of his entourage to see that all was in order. He gave his party instructions for the reception, the order in which they were to stand and their deportment. In the last minute the cuffs of one of his party did not pass inspection and had to be replaced.[35]

Herzl was a man of the theater who brought the theater into politics, making drama of politics. He had the capacity to pass from the unreal to the real, to mix the spheres of dream and politics, to transfer the enchantment of make-believe staging to the world of diplomacy and political power.

Viennese politics during the 1890's witnessed the decline of rational moralistic bourgeois liberalism and the ascendancy of a new style of politics marked by the demagogic manipulation of masses in an emotional movement dedicated to the personality of a leader. The anti-Semitic lower-middle-class Christian Social party of small tradesmen and independent craftsmen had as its popular and effective leader Karl Lueger. Lueger was to perfect the new style of charismatic Wagnerian mass politics. He was an important politician from 1885 on. In the two years from May 1895 to the end of April 1897 Lueger was elected to the mayoralty of Vienna on five different occasions. The government refused to confirm his election four times. By 1897 the Christian Social tide could not be stopped, and Lueger was proclaimed the lord mayor of Vienna. He served until his death in 1910.

It was against this background of political events that Herzl conceived his style. He observed Lueger's electoral campaigns and the response of the crowd to the public image the anti-Semitic leader projected. He describes an election evening in Vienna's third district, a partly proletarian quarter: "Before the polling place, a silent tense crowd. Suddenly Dr. Lueger came out to the square. Wild cheering; women waved white handkerchiefs from the windows. The police held the crowd back. A man next to me said with tender warmth but in a quiet tone: "That is our Leader [*Führer*].' "[36] A year later Herzl noted that Lueger's wishes were the same as his own: fostering Jewish colonization. He firmly believed that the failure to confirm Lueger was a mistake, for it would only stimulate mass anti-Semitism.

Herzl viewed politics as the craft of effectively creating an uproar: "Yes, noise is everything . . . in truth noise is a great deal. A sustained noise is in itself a noteworthy fact. All of world history is nothing but noise. Noise of arms, noise of progressing ideas. One must put noise to one's service— and still despise it." "With nations," he said, "one must speak in a childish language: a house, a flag, a song are the symbols of communication." Recently "much of the form and political style" of Herzl's Zionism has been attributed to "his direct experience with the German nationalist student movement in Vienna."[37] An examination of the influence of Herzl's thespian experience and the personality needs it failed to fulfill, which were the same narcissistic needs that charismatic politics succeeded in supplying for him, may be an additional relevant explanation of Herzl's "aesthetic symbolic" politics.

Herzl, who failed in the theater, turned politics into theater. He became the director, stage manager, and reserved for himself the leading role. The play was the poignant salvation of a people, the plot was one man's vision and sacrifice, which would overcome all odds, the supporting cast were the rulers of the world's nations, and the backdrop was the grim tale of anti-Semitism and racial persecution in European history. Herzl's genius was that he was simultaneously a man of the theater and a man of action. His familiarity with the theater, where magic and make-believe create stage reality, enabled him to write a scenario for politics that also shaped reality.

Herzl had a "constructive" personality, that of a builder rather than a destroyer. As a boy Herzl's hero was Ferdinand de Lesseps. He would become an engineer and duplicate Lesseps's work. He was going to cut a canal through the Isthmus of Panama. His parents enrolled him in the Pester Technical School, where he took an engineering course. Though Theodor was academically unsuccessful as a technician, he was captivated by technology all his life. He wished to erect a Jewish house in Basel in a "neo-Jewish style." He wrote: "The art which is now most meaningful to me is architecture. Unhappily I have not mastered its techniques of expression. If I had learned anything, I would now be an architect."[38]

When he visited Palestine in 1898, Herzl was filled with visions for the rebuilding of cities, the draining of swamps, and remodeling the countryside. As he first saw Jerusalem he invoked the converse of an ancient Jewish prayer: "When I remember thee in days to come, O Jerusalem, it will not be with pleasure. The musty deposits of two thousand years of inhumanity, intolerance, and filth be in your foul-smelling alleys." But he was going to rebuild it:

> If Jerusalem becomes ours, and I can still do something at that time, the first thing I would do is clean it up.
>
> I would remove everything that was not holy, set up workers' housing outside the city, clear out the filth nests, and tear them down, burn the non-holy rubble, and move the bazaars elsewhere. Then, while keeping the old style of architecture where possible, build a comfortable, airy, sewered, new city around the holy places.[39]

It was typical of Herzl that he was much more impressed by the Suez Canal than by the Acropolis. To him the modern engineering feat represented the triumph of one man's will over nature. When this will grew senile in the case of Panama, the project could not be carried through. Herzl saw the canal as an example of what sheer vision and strength of will can do to overcome obstacles of man and nature. To be a man whose powerful will would transform reality and transcend adversity was Herzl's ego ideal.

The twentieth century has witnessed a dramatic change in the Jewish character. Such a change is unique in history, and of particular interest to historians because the very concept of national character is a highly controversial one that they handle gingerly and with misgiving. When in one generation in modern times we see such a decisive change, it bears close study.

The Jewish people in this generation have been through two crises whose magnitude is so great as to defy ordinary language. Only a term from the realm of geology, a word that connotes a change in substance itself, such as "metamorphosis," will suffice for the process of psychic transformation with which we are concerned. The two shattering experiences that have altered the Jewish character have been the Holocaust of Nazi Germany that cost them a third of their number and the return of the Jewish people to organic life in the land of their origin. The metamorphosis they have undergone is a transformation of values and behavior in response to aggression. The traditional Jewish values had taught passivity and the internalization of guilt in the face of aggression. It was divine punishment for disobedience to the word of God to be accepted stoically in the hope of living for a better day. This traditional pattern of palliation and accommodation tragically failed the Jews of Europe when they had to deal with psychotics having the modern technology of a police state at their disposal.

A new ethos of militant resistance was adopted out of the Holocaust. This was the value system and set of emotional responses to anti-Semitism first codified in modern times by Theodor Herzl. It is as a maker of new Jewish values that he can be appreciated as a creative shaper of ideology. The idea of the return of the Jews to Jerusalem is as old as the expulsion. Herzl's contribution was a new behavioral ethos that first sprang from the needs of his own social position and psyche and was in the end to determine the character of a new people—the new Jew of his fantasied old-new land. Herzl postulated values in direct conscious contradiction to the ghetto way of life. He intended to, and did, found a new nation peopled by new men. It is Herzl as the formulator and institutionalizer of this psychological change whom we will investigate.

Herzl propagated a noble ideal of a new Jew, a man living by the myth of chivalry. For Herzl, Zionism implied a radical transvaluation of Jewish concepts of honor. The traditional virtues of restraint, passivity, and intellection, of the social isolation of the ghetto community, were no longer adequate in an assimilated nineteenth-century Viennese milieu where social interaction with a dominant Gentile culture demanded new psychic defenses. The courtier and noble gentleman became Herzl's ego ideal, his model of conduct. His behavioral code was that of feudal aristocratic honor. The motive of honor was important to Herzl throughout his life and was to be eventually cast as the emotional foundation of the Jewish state.

As a man, Herzl remembered shifting schools in boyhood because of indignation at a teacher's anti-Semitism. As a university student he belonged to a dueling fraternity. When anti-Semitism was on the rise in the university, he withdrew from his fraternity on grounds of Jewish honor. His pre-Zionist solutions to the Jewish question included a fantasy of challenging the leading Austrian anti-Semites—Prince Alois Liechtenstein, Schönerer, Lueger—to duels. "Half a dozen duels will do much to raise the social position of the Jews," he commented at the time. His plan for the mass conversion of all Austrian Jews in St. Stefan's Cathedral would be a solution of pride and integrity because he and the other leaders would remain outside the church doors, "to insure uprightness, and so that the group baptism does not appear as cowardice or opportunism."[40] In Herzl's play *The New Ghetto,* the ghetto Jew acquires a new knightly chivalric conception of honor, and the hero, a transparent projection of Herzl himself, is killed in a duel defending Jewish honor.

In the early days of his movement, indeed while he was conceiving the movement, Herzl noted in his diary: "Jewish honor begins . . ." "And it will be the beginning of our respect in the eyes of the world." At this time he wrote of some middle-class Viennese Jewish friends with whom he had dined: "They do not suspect it, but they are Ghetto creatures, quiet, good, fearful. Most of our people are like that. Will they understand the call to freedom and manliness?" "If they have not yet emigrated at the time of the next European war, Jews must fight for their present fatherlands, on account of Jewish honor."[41]

In his initial interview of 1895 with Baron de Hirsch, Herzl posed the first task of Zionism as improvement of the race, to promote strength for war (*kriegsstark*), love of labor (*arbeitsfroh*), and virtue (*tugendhaft*). He even proposed that Hirsch offer prizes for *actions d'éclat,* for acts of great moral beauty, courage, self-sacrifice, ethical conduct. He planned to "educate all to be free, strong men . . . by means of patriotic songs, sports clubs, religion, heroic theater, honor, etc."[42] Could anything have been a more complete rejection of traditional Jewish values of the ghetto?

Herzl consciously intended to smash stereotypes. He noted in his diaries: "Everyone who comes in contact with me must receive the opposite of the proverbial opinion of the Jew." The images that dominated Herzl's thought and motivated him appear with full clarity when he and his party saw Jewish horsemen singing Hebrew songs during his visit to Palestine in 1898: "We had tears in our eyes as we saw the agile, courageous riders, into whom our pants-peddling boys can be transformed."[43] He used the derogatory image "pants-peddling boys" (*hosenverkaufenden Jünglinge*) from the vituperative anti-Semitic essay *Ein Wort über unser Judentum* the German historian Heinrich von Treitschke wrote in 1880. Herzl portrayed the virile Jewish horsemen farmers he saw in Rehovot as his counter image and aspiration. He said they reminded him of cowboys of the American West he had seen in a Paris show.

This expressed a deliberate effort to forge a new heroic national character (or to recapture a mythical biblical racial character), create a flag and accessory symbols that would be honored and would win "respect in the eyes of the world." This fantasy of a nation peopled by proud militant "new men" is, in Herzl's case, what Anna Freud has defined as "identification with the aggressor.[44] He shares with anti-Semites a negative stereotype of the Jew. Herzl's contempt for "pants-peddling boys" is an admission of hatred of the

Jews of the ghetto—and of the self. He hates but also identifies with this image that he wishes to alter. He hates it because it fails to live up to the derived standards of honor he imposes on it. He loves it and hates it because it is himself—what he was and is, but does not wish to be. In this sense Herzl was a Jewish anti-Semite. He despised the defenseless subjugated Jew of the Pale. Herzl's idea was the self-reliant pioneer. For the learned, humiliated, sensitive Jew of the ghetto, he would substitute the rigorous, heroic, healthy farmer in his own land. Yiddish, the language of suffering, would be replaced by any cultured language. The exclusive nationalism of Europe which rejects Jews would be replaced by a chauvinistic nationalism of Zion. The values of the dominant majority are internalized and via reaction formation would become the ego ideal of the persecuted minority.

Historians should avail themselves of the tools of modern literary criticism in considering the psychological significance of the language used, the imagery employed, the creation and utilization of symbols by their subjects. Images, symbols, and words were formed in the consciousness of Herzl. In seeking the inner emotional content of a novel or story, we should remember that the work is Herzl's and no one else's. It is not an impersonal thing. The character and nature of these fantasies have issued from his consciousness. Their contents are thus always relevant and not fortuitous. The old and rather naïve notion of artistic inspiration that spontaneously appears in the poet's mind no longer suffices. These contents are tissued out of images from his life and fantasies that have become emotionally charged. The work itself may yield what the state of mind and the emotion of that consciousness was. Henry James wrote of the novelist that he "is present in every page of every book from which he sought to eliminate himself." And Henry David Thoreau told us that poetry "is a piece of very private history, which unostentatiously lets us into the secret of man's life."[45]

Among those who seriously imagine private worlds of their own in which they rearrange actuality and create a new order that suits them better are creative artists and writers. They invest fantasies with a great deal of affect, nevertheless separating their fantasy sharply from reality. By the successful objectification of his private illusion, the writer releases his mental tension and gives us the pleasure of sharing highly charged emotional experiences. But when we leave the artist, we go back from the world of imagination to the firm ground of reality.

In the case of a political leader such as Herzl, the form he gives his fiction, its historical and geographical setting, even the words he uses, his choice of phrase and emotional tone, and above all the characters and their interaction, are all, in the last analysis, biographical self-revelation, signatures of his inner being. The historian is particularly well advised to consider Herzl's creative writings most carefully, subjecting them to every possible analytic technique, for the return will be manifold insights into the fantasies of a great leader as he emerges.

We have three products of Herzl's fantasy from the period of the end of his depression in 1896. There is a short fable that bears the imprint of a broken marriage and thoughts of suicide. But its interest for us is special because it also contains the theme of resolution of despair in affirmative creation. From the discarded and worthless material of life, Herzl will mold a new and valued essence. The story concerns a professor of philosophy who has a nagging wife. In bitterness and desperation he goes to the river determined on suicide. There he sees a man with a pipe sitting on a tree stump who identifies himself as a "fisherman of men" and invites him into his Inn of the Anilin. The inn reeks with the odor of tar from the laboratory in which the innkeeper experiments with making synthetic food for the world's hungering millions. Just as beautiful gay colors are made to bloom from dyes that are mere factory waste, so men can be kneaded and shaped into something constructive out of their deepest despair. So says the innkeeper to his moribund guest:

> For despair is a precious substance, from which the most wonderful things may be generated: courage, self-denial, resolution, sacrifice. . . . To the stubbornest I recommended self-realization in a great task, and they have achieved the most. . . . As I look back at the past, it seems to me that all of the great men of history were once at the river's edge and turned back so that their despair bore fruit. All discoverers, prophets, heroes, statesmen, artists—yes, all philosophers also, for one never philosophizes better than when staring death in the face.[46]

With this coda we have Herzl's affirmation from the extremity of despair and his self-dedication to a world historical role. Having once contemplated death and having decided not to forsake the world, he would remake it. It is noteworthy that in this story the central figure was bound on suicide by drowning, that this urge to self-destruction was brought on by the perfidy of a woman, and that he was saved by a fatherly older man.

In the same year Herzl wrote another story with the themes of marital unhappiness and self-destruction. Here too, the means of suicide is by drowning. This time the subject is a young girl, Sarah Holzmann, and the inciting cause, the marital infidelity of her mother. The third published story of the year 1896, "Das Lenkbare Luftschiff," concerns an inventor with a great idea—a flying machine. People think he is crazy and he is locked up in an insane asylum. Even the woman he loves makes fun of him. He protests: "Men resent him who plans great things."[47] He gives up the flying machine and turns to the invention of functional appliances: a railway brake, an unpuncturable bicycle tire, and a gas lamp. He earns millions of gulden, with which he buys off the woman, who has now become loving and admiring toward him. He tells her to bother him no more. In his own story Herzl becomes the hero and vindicates his dream, and thus he evens the score with his materialistic wife. Once again the woman is a cold, selfish, pleasure-seeking creature, but Herzl wreaks vengeance in fantasy.

Taken together with the fact of his depression during 1891 to 1896, these three stories suggest that he was preoccupied with creative loneliness, carping women, marital disharmony, and suicide in these years. I am not necessarily asserting that he ever seriously considered taking his life, though he may have done so. But we may say that the subject of suicide, women who drive men to it, and men who resolve their conflicts through great historical achievements were in his fantasy life. Otherwise he would not have built them into his plots so consistently.

One of Herzl's most personal and revealing fantasies is his novel of 1902, *Altneuland*. He places himself and persons close to him, both living and dead, in constructed relationships that, because they are creations of psychic reality, deserve to be taken seriously as self-revelation. As literature, it is a poor novel. The figures are wooden, the exposition is labored, and the plot sentimental. But as a re-creation of the real and emotional world of Herzl, it offers rich material to those who would wish to know its author.

Herzl himself is the central figure, the young Viennese Jewish lawyer Friedrich Loewenberg. As the novel opens, he is heartsick with unrequited love for a rich Viennese Jewish girl who, unlike Herzl's wife, married a prosperous merchant instead of the struggling journalist. So he rejects the world of women and turns to that of men. He sails to the South Pacific idyll as the devoted companion of a Prussian ex–cavalry officer with the evocative name Koenigshoff ("king's court"). He is pledged to the Junker aristocrat for life in terms of the Book of Ruth: "I belong to you, and go with you wherever and whenever you choose." The two men spent "twenty beautiful years" alone in the paradise of an island archipelago "hunting, fishing, eating, drinking, sleeping, playing chess. . . ." En route to their island idyll, the two men visited Palestine and found it as did Herzl in his visit of 1898: a malaria-ridden, decadent backwater of the decaying Turkish empire. "The once royal city of Jerusalem could have sunk no lower," muses Friedrich as he and Kingscourt walk through the Holy City arm in arm.[48]

Twenty years later, the year is 1923, the Prussian nobleman and his faithful liege return to a transformed Palestine. The Jewish emigration has transpired and rebuilt ancient cities and constructed new ports, water and power projects, and rail networks. Swamps have been drained, deserts irrigated, and agriculture flourishes in cooperative settlements. Socially the "new society," as he called it, is an equalitarian welfare state with all the accouterments of advanced early-twentieth-century social theory: rights for women, free schools and universities, model penal farms, medical, accident, old age, and life insurance. Jews, Arabs, and European Christians live together in harmony. There is no military service because international relations are governed by world law. Amid this cosmopolitanism, it is clear that the more cultured people, even the Arabs, speak a literary High German, "with a slight northern accent."[49]

When he arrives in Palestine, Herzl-Loewenberg finds the family of a poor beggar boy whom he had saved from starvation in Vienna. They are now prosperous leaders of the new community. The son David is about to be elected president of the new society. The family greets him as "our benefactor, our savior (*unser Wohlthäter, unser Retter*")—a self-accorded accolade for a man who has dreamed of being a messiah.[50]

The women portrayed in Herzl's novel are divided into two types, the coarse, vulgar, and emotionally destructive dangerous woman and the delicate desensualized virginal maiden. In Palestine, Herzl-Loewenberg meets the wealthy girl who had broken his heart in Vienna and sent him on a twenty-year voyage with a man. She has become a gaudy, "faded, would-be-arch coquette (*gefallsüchtige, verblühte Frauenzimmer.*)"[51] Indeed, he stoutly defends a sweet young schoolteacher, Miriam, for her dedication to her vocational duties and social responsibilities against the carping criticism of the bejeweled, overdressed woman. Miriam was serious about her duties, unlike Herzl's wife. Such was his revenge on his wife Julie!

Herzl suddenly lost his only sister, Pauline, in 1878 when he was eighteen. She was a year older than he and "the image of her mother." She had been his "earliest and nearest playmate" to a point where "she made other playmates almost superfluous." After the shock of her death, he "guarded every keepsake of hers like a sacred relic."[52] Pauline was to play a major role in his novel. The book was dedicated to her, and she figures in the plot as Miriam, a shy and devoted schoolteacher whom he, Herzl in the person of Friedrich Loewenberg, marries.

The device by which this courtship is consummated tells us a great deal about Herzl's desensualized view of women. Friedrich and Miriam are scarcely aware that their love is mutual. There was no declaration of intentions. Miriam's mother, a representation of Herzl's own, brings them together on her deathbed. She expires moments after the young couple confirm their engagement to her and to each other. They become engaged *to please the mother.* Only in this way is the fulfillment of an incest fantasy possible for Herzl. Any quality of emotional intensity or passion toward the would-be sexual object is absent.

Herzl's attitude toward men of power is a significant reflection of his relation to father figures and an index of father transferences in his unconscious. His stance toward the great of the world was worshipful. He feared being so overawed that he would be ineffective. His defense against the threat of being overawed was to intellectually reduce great men to small size. When he felt impressed, he reduced potent father figures to manageable dimensions by concentrating on their most mundane features or weaknesses. When he for the first time visits the Grand Duke of Baden, we see him fighting against the effects of awe: "It was my first drive up in front of a princely castle. I tried not to be overimpressed by the soldiers on guard." When he has entered the castle and seen the antechamber, it takes his breath away. His response was "to divert myself from becoming overawed by taking inventory like a reporter."[53] He noted the green furniture, the brown wood of the chair legs, and the photographs of the three German emperors.

The pattern of defense against low self-esteem by focusing on the weakness of the powerful man with whom he was dealing is most striking in Herzl's response to a personal encounter with Kaiser Wilhelm II. He found it was essential to study

> the small side of great people. And this is necessary if one is not to be confused by their flashy exterior glitter and if one wishes to associate with them naturally. That is why, when I saw the German Kaiser so frequently during the past week, I sharply observed his deformity. . . . It brings him closer to me as a human being. It proves that underneath his many uniforms of the regiments he commands, he is only a helpless man. As I saw the display of his might, the brilliance of his court, the warlike prowess of his legions on the parade field, I always merely kept observing his crippled arm, in order not to let my spirit be overwhelmed in case I should speak with him personally.

Whereas Herzl's defense against his awe toward men of power was to reduce their stature so he could cope with them, his attitude toward his subordinates and followers was fatherly. He shows warm affection for "my good Wolffsohn," who stood the test of disappointment "as always and bore with me through thick and thin."[54]

When he felt betrayed or frustrated by members of the Zionist movement Herzl committed his anger to his diaries. He referred to the congress opposition as "rascals" and "bastards." At the second congress he was furious with "the successful dirty trick of the Galician bastards. . . . Landau was the noisiest and stupidest."[55]

We have here a definite character style of leadership that differs from ordinary people primarily in its object relationships. The leader of Herzl's type does not develop object relations to persons. After the death of Heinrich Kana he did not have what one could call an intimate friend. After the estrangement of his marriage Herzl had an object cathexis exclusively with his own ideas. His ability to control his aggression, even when sorely tried and when it would have been fully justified, is an indication of the powerful synthetic function of Herzl's ego. Unlike V. I. Lenin, who drove small differences to a party split, Herzl was inclusive, he made room for everyone in his movement. His object relations were not primarily to people; they were to his idea, his cause. For this goal he was able to subvert all impulses and other personal relations. His object realm was ideational. He demanded and received support from others for his ideas. Opposition was fought in the name of the cause. Aggression was rationalized by the injury that opponents were doing to the movement. Herzl thought nothing of sinking his own and his family's personal fortunes into his movement. He was able to convince others of the grandeur of his idea and to persuade them to serve his vision.

Success did not come quickly or easily to Theodor Herzl. He faced storms of criticism and derision. He was jeered at as the "Jewish Jules Verne." The editors of his newspaper asked him to desist from publication of *Der Judenstaat,* threatening his position as feuilleton editor by telling him he could easily be replaced. The *Neue Freie Presse* was never to mention Zionism during Herzl's lifetime. But surely the most poignant case of his attempt at reality testing is best related by Herzl himself:

> When I had completed the book I asked my oldest and best friend to read the manuscript. In the midst of the reading he suddenly burst into tears. I found this natural enough, since he was a Jew; I too had wept at times during the writing of it. But I was staggered when he gave me an entirely different reason for his tears. He thought that I had gone off my head, and since he was my friend he was touched to tears by my misfortune.[56]

Yet Herzl persevered. He was able to discipline his fantasy and adapt it to the service of the ego. He converts all his hostility into partnerships. He is inclusive. There is a place for everybody in his fantasies. No one is cut out. "Not everyone embarks on the ship at the starting point," he says, "some find it more convenient to travel overland, and join her farther on."

To the Jewish communities he said: "We welcome you. There is room and work for all."[57]

In contrast to Herzl's earlier fury toward anti-Semites, for example Dühring, whom he called "this rascal, who should have his teeth knocked out," he now incorporates all oppositional tendencies into his plan. There is a place for the tsar, the Vatican, liberalism, Turkey, the Rothschilds, both orthodox and reform Jewry, the tiny group of settlers already in Palestine, and even the anti-Semites. He graphically described his difficulties as those of doing a dance on invisible eggs. We may subscribe to his appraisal that this was a "labor of Hercules—without exaggeration," and may sympathize with him when he complains that he has "lost his zest for it."[58]

For Herzl there was no choice—he had to continue being a messiah. He could not have stopped laboring for his cause if his life depended on it—and evidently it did. Within less than a year of commencing his Zionist work the family physician diagnosed a heart injured by excitement and warned him against wearing himself out in the Jewish cause. Two years later he wrote: "I am tired, the heart is not in order."[59]

Meanwhile Herzl had in fact become a messiah. He found his following where he least expected it, not among the assimilated bourgeois Jews of western Europe, but among the impoverished masses of the East. In Sofia he was "hailed as 'Führer,' as the heart of Israel." He was greeted by great crowds and told "you are holier than the Torah."[60]

Herzl derives his libidinal rewards from the crowd; he is loved by them, and receives his emotional fulfillment from his audience, from the mass response to his public utterances. This is sublimated oral gratification. His vital organ is his mouth. Words flow from him like warm milk. And from the group he obtains generous supplies of esteem and affection.

Herzl wished to be a messiah, and messiahs must die as martyrs. Herzl willed it so and he died for his cause. His reply to a warning not to work so hard was: "I *will* work, until I kill myself." By 1904, at age forty-four, he was deathly ill. He frightened his friends by his appearance. His doctors found a disturbingly heavy alteration of the heart muscle. He said, "I have become a tired man in these months."[61] A planned trip to London in April was canceled owing to his poor health. In May, Herzl went to Franzensbad for a heart cure. He had heavy attacks of loss of breath and weakness.

A Zionist emissary to Russia came through in May. Despite his illness Herzl stayed up all night to complete a memorandum for St. Petersburg. When his friend Katzenelsohn reprimanded him, saying, "So this is how you wish to get well? This is supposed to be your cure?" Herzl replied, "Yes, my friend, as you saw yesterday, we have no time to lose. These are the last weeks or days . . . we must hurry!" On July 1 he had a lung inflammation and said to a friend, "Greet Palestine for me, I have given my blood for my people."[62] Herzl died on July 3, 1904.

At the time of his death Herzl had established the institutions that would result in the realization of his fantasy—a Jewish state. He had appealed to a mass following in dire need and had invited them to share his vision. The World Zionist Organization was created as the central organ of Jewish national policy. A bank and the Jewish Colonial Trust had been founded. The newspaper he founded, *Die Welt,* became the mass-media organ of the movement. Herzl's most significant personal contribution was the building of diplomatic affiliations with powers and influential public figures, especially in England, that were to eventuate in the Balfour Declaration of 1917. In 1903, he engaged David Lloyd George, of the law firm of Lloyd George, Roberts and Company, as counsel to draft the charter for a Jewish settlement in East Africa. Arthur James Balfour was then Prime Minister. In 1917 Lloyd George was Prime Minister and Balfour was Foreign Minister of the war cabinet that realized Herzl's dream of a British protectorate over a Jewish homeland.

Fantasy may be defined as patterns of thought about actions or desired objects that are unavailable in existing social reality. Fantasies may be conscious or unconscious. When unconscious, they are usually thoughts that have been repressed because they are morally unsanctionable in the adult world. When conscious, they are unsatisfied wishes that are fulfilled in thought and thus improve on an unsatisfactory reality. Fantasies are the universal property of mankind; we sometimes call them daydreams. They usually consist of erotic wishes or dreams of ambition serving to exalt the dreamer. In either case, "His Majesty the Ego" is the hero of all fantasies.

The initial trigger for a fantasy is some immediate dissatisfaction with present reality, some unsatisfied wish. Fantasy improves on this painful reality by bringing two other time dimensions into play. In the intensity of present desire, the mind calls on its memories of an earlier time when things were ideal, when the wish was fulfilled. This realm, often that of early infancy, is recalled, not as it was, but as transmuted into symbols and images of the world as it appeared to the consciousness of an infant. The fantasy then takes the idyllic satisfaction of the past, and transcending immediate experience by illusion, projects it into the future when the wish will again be fulfilled in reality. Paradise lost is recalled by desire present to merge through fantasy with paradise future. Obviously there are neurotic and non-neurotic fantasies. These fantasies may include the idea of an equalitarian world or schemes for the rebuilding of a city, as well as fairy tales and improbable personal triumphs.

Though fantasy always implies an initial turning away from reality, it can also be a preparation for the alteration of reality. Fantasy can be fruitful, not only in art and creative literary realms, and even in that most rational of spheres, scientific thinking, but also in politics. There is an epistemological fallacy in the common dualism that opposes spiritual and poetic imagination to scientific and empirical rationality. From the technical fantasies of Leonardo to the spatial images of Einstein, the two antagonistic faculties are interdependent and complementary. The imagination plays with technical possibilities and assumes a rational character when it comes to their realization.

The psychic life of "normal" adults is never free of some denial of reality. The denied reality is replaced by fantasy formations. These may fulfill a constructive synthetic function by ideationally connecting the needs and goals of a man faced with mental and spiritual collapse with possibilities of their realization, thus enabling him to emerge from his subjective world of omnipotent illusion to increased mastery of the external world. The positive value of fantasy for Herzl was that it enabled him to retreat from the onslaught of pressures of the immediate setting and search for a new role and environment that would offer him and the people he would lead a more fulfilling and congenial existence.

As a *fin de siècle* Viennese liberal, Herzl was typical of his class in its retreat to an internal world of consciousness. In art, literature, psychology, theater, and philosophy this class turned to inner worlds to discover new realities following their defeat in the social and political realm of Austrian politics. Thus, when Herzl said, "No one has thought of seeking the 'Promised Land' where it truly is—and yet it lies so near. Here it is: within ourselves,"[63] he was expressing in Zionist terms the search of his class for truth within man's mind rather than as an external datum to be discovered. In dreaming of a better world which he then labors to bring about, the late-nineteenth-century Central European utopian intellectual found it in the psyche. For Herzl the promised land had no specific geographical location. It could have been anywhere. It initially found its home in the consciousness of its adherents.

In spring 1895 Herzl was disturbed almost to the point of a psychotic break. He was abandoning reality and withdrawing his libido from object ties to his environment. Personal, vocational, and social frustration released redeemer and passive feminine fantasies in him. He took as his fantasy objects Prussian Junker prototypes such as Kingscourt and Kaiser Wilhelm II. His homoerotic fantasies had their root in a longing for his father, which was intensified by heterosexual frustration and professional disappointment.

He withdrew interest from the external world, substituting fantasy for reality. His overestimation of the power of his own wishes and mental processes, his belief in the omnipotence of thoughts, was close to a faith in the magical power of his words: "If you will it, it is no fantasy."[64] Herzl's libido was withdrawn from external objects and returned to his ego. He substituted for actual human relationships (family, journalism, theater) imaginary objects founded on infantile fantasy. The internalization of libido in the ego aggrandized the ego to the level of megalomania. He regressed to the stage of narcissism in which his only sexual object was his own ego and its fantasies.

Herzl's idea usurped his libido and his aggression. He derived little gratification from relationships to individuals, because of the affect intrinsic in the relationship. The finding of a distant delibidinized object is a defense against internal conflict. Objects that are too close may be dangerous, they are too laden with ambivalence. To select a remote ideal object is a defense of avoidance. Herzl was able to sublimate many of his passive ambivalences toward his father in political work.

Herzl's latent homosexuality was strengthened by his denial of the need for the love of a woman and of sex. This appears in his literary fantasies where he is for twenty years the loyal companion of a Prussian officer and in the values he projected for his "new man."

Herzl's ascetic self-denial strengthened his dedication to his messianic vocation as father to his people. He was committed to his task with the celibate devotion of one who is religiously "called" to his historic role. Without such single-minded self-abnegation, Herzl would have been just another dreamer. Instead he found a new identity. His sexual ambivalences were harnessed in the personal role of charismatic leader of a political mass movement. Now his craving for immortality, his desire for a political role, and most important, his conflict-riven Jewish identifications were resolved in an affirmative and productive program that provided for Herzl personal generativity and integrity.

There is sufficient surface material from Herzl himself to permit specific depth interpretation of his idea structure. Reference here is not to the instincts but to instinctual derivatives that come to the fore during ego regressions in times of emotional stress when the ego defenses are weakened. The libidinal excitement of Herzl's creative period, his state of euphoria during which he relates "to his idea as to a lover," is the state of elation accompanying the trespass over established boundaries into realms that are forbidden and dangerous, areas of megalomanic, incestuous, and homoerotic fantasies. The process of his fantasies becoming conscious is experienced by Herzl as an action on him, thus activity of the unconscious is turned into passivity.

The dreams of being carried by a man and literary fantasies of being saved by men or faithfully serving men suggest a homosexual passivity to the father. A passive attitude toward the father implies a feminine identification. Herzl's imagery of birth and conception when writing of his ideas is the masculine creative analogue to women's capacity for biological creation.

According to Freud's libido model of genetic psychosexual development, when the defenses of the phallic genital phase have been overwhelmed, the subject regresses to the anal phase of tension and relaxation. We note Herzl's imagery of retention and release when speaking of his ideas. They "would burst it [the container] to pieces if they found no outlet." The idiom is of the gratification that accompanies expulsion: "For me these notes are not work, but a relief."[65] Creation itself signifies anal production. When he writes, "Goethe! Goethe!" he is saying, "I produce! I am creating too!"

Behind the imagery of anal activity lies a level of oral activity in talking and verbal manipulation. A further psychogenetic derivative is a deeper oral passivity in which Herzl's activity is experienced as passivity. His experience is: "Something is happening to me!" The driving of his unconscious toward consciousness is encountered as an action upon him rather than by him: "Am I working it out? No! It is working me." Herzl's personal life has ended; world history has taken over.

The absence of normal sexual gratification reinforced regression to forms of oral gratification such as speaking and deriving emotional rewards from the adulation of the crowd. He achieved this love from the masses by fantasizing about the world of the oral mother—a "promised land" bountifully "flowing with milk and honey." We see evidence of ambivalence toward his mother not only in Herzl's portrayal of mother figures in his creative writing, where women consistently drive their children or menfolk to destruction, but also in the reparative fantasies evident in his ideas regarding the promised land.

Deeper than any attitudes toward the father are ambivalent feelings toward the oral mother of early infancy. Together with the receptive position there is oral aggression: there are violent fantasies of devouring a grudging mother, of attacking her breast. The derivatives of such infantile fantasies are dreams of forcibly extracting wealth from the soil, of cutting great canals, rebuilding cities, and transforming the land. Such aggressive and destructive fantasies give rise to strong guilt feelings and the need to make reparation to rebuild fantasy damage. By seeking to return to the mother land, to preserve and restore it, to make it "flow with milk and honey," Herzl is repairing fantasy damage to his infantile mother. These are also rescue fantasies. He will rescue those in a degraded moral and political position. What in infancy and childhood was perceived as the degraded mother is in adulthood redeemed as people and land. He will return mother to Zion and all her children will come to live there in happiness. He is making restitution in his unconscious by re-creating the promised land, making it rich as a productive, fertile haven of peace. The motherland will be cared for and cultivated, will be made to bloom and to bear fruit.

What distinguishes Herzl from an ordinary dreamer is his unique ability to act on his vision. He permitted his unconscious omnipotent fantasies to register on his consciousness in political terms. He adapted his operational plans, but never his dream, to the demands of immediate rational "reality." In truly creative ways he adjusted to the demands of a powerless position in a scornful world. He had the insight to appeal to the self-interest of the powers of Europe. Where possible, as in England, he also appealed to the idealism of leaders. His own Jewish following gave him the greatest measure of distress. It is testimony to Herzl's ego strength that he was able, despite repeated crises when all seemed in dissolution, to hold his following together in a movement that he institutionalized for action toward his fantasy goal.

Herzl escaped the injured feeling of nothingness by molding himself in fantasy into a messianic leader. His psychic reality became a substitute for his undermined self-esteem. By creating a fantasy world of his own in which he was the hero, he consoled himself for not being loved and appreciated. Herzl's inner fantasies were to him far more than substitute satisfactions for rejections in the outer world; they saved him from being crushed entirely. They may have literally, but certainly they spiritually, saved his life.

Herzl's Zionist period may be divided into two phases. The primary experience of inspiration was characterized by ego regression. He took little notice of his environment. His consciousness received id impulses and closer derivatives from his preconscious with relative facility and without censorship. We may see a secondary elaborational phase during which his ego functions of reality testing, formulation, and communication with his public were recathected.

His inspiration was the thoughts produced by his unconscious, which were permitted to reach consciousness in a world-shaping politico-messianic guise. But the regression was only a partial and temporary ego regression, one most of the time under the control of Herzl's ego, which in the last analysis retained the function of communication. Herzl strove to establish contact with an audience. His fantasies were not for himself alone as in the case of a psychotic.

He identified himself with his public in order to invite their participation in his fantasy, a participation postulating their identification with him as leader. This was regression in the service of the ego, a regression that made his inspiration possible and that made him a prophet, a leader, and a man of action. Herzl's instinctual processes were dominated by his ego and put to its own purposes. His fantasies and regressions were sublimated in creative activity that changed history.

Herzl's recovery from his depression took place as his narcissistic ego ideal was fulfilled. His infantile narcissism and omnipotence were confirmed as he appealed to the urgent needs of masses of people and became identified with their ancient messianic dream. Herzl became a secular messiah and functioned effectively in the role that corroborated his omnipotence.

Changes in reality are often achieved by regressive adaptation of the ego as in the case of Herzl. His alterations in reality were made by detours over irrational elements, by regressions to megalomania and narcissism. Such regressive detours were the prerequisites to achievement that created a new reality. By withdrawing to an inner world of self-absorbed fantasy, Herzl was able to emerge with a certainty and strength of conviction that transformed the world.

Herzl underwent a renunciation in his personal life that enabled him to act as a chosen one in carrying the responsibility for a people on the stage of history. His sense of mission was so strong that it carried him through ridicule and isolation, detours and blind alleys, rejection and disillusionment, until he found a responsive public in the poor Jews of eastern Europe and they found a charismatic leader in him. Herzl as a leader, gifted in evoking images from his audience, and motivated by the need to be a modern savior of his people, used the great crisis of a people under social and political pressure to resolve personal ambivalence and conflict by creating a program of action that was to shape history. His people consecrated him as a prophet and validated his historical vision.

Notes

1. The original diaries reside in the Central Zionist Archives. The first edition, *Theodor Herzls Tagebücher,* 3 vols. (Berlin, 1922–1923), edited by a group led by Martin Buber and Leon Kellner, has numerous excisions on grounds of political expedience or what was interpreted as good taste. It will be cited as *Tagebücher.* I have used this basic German edition wherever possible. Unless otherwise indicated, the translations are my own. I have relied on *The Complete Diaries of Theodor Herzl,* ed. Raphael Patai, trans. Harry Zohn, 5 vols. (New York, 1960) to supply the excised material. It is hereafter cited as *Complete Diaries.* The translations, however, are smoother in Marvin Lowenthal's abridged one-volume edition, *The Diaries of Theodor Herzl* (New York, 1962), hereafter cited as *Diaries.* For the reader's benefit I have explicitly indicated where portions deleted from the German edition are used. A complete Hebrew edition of Herzl's works, including the diaries, is now in preparation in Jerusalem.

2. See Carl E. Schorske, *Fin-de-Siècle Vienna: Politics and Culture* (New York, 1980); William J. McGrath, "Student Radicalism in Vienna," *Journal of Contemporary History,* 2 (1967): 183–201; William M. Johnston, *The Austrian Mind: An Intellectual and Social History, 1848–1938* (Berkeley and Los Angeles, 1972); Avner Falk, "Freud and Herzl," *Midstream,* Jan. 1977, pp. 3–24.

3. Alex Bein, *Theodor Herzl: A Biography* (Philadelphia, 1962), pp. 13–14.

4. June 12, 1895, *Tagebücher,* 1: 106.

5. Herzl to Heinrich Kana, June 8, 1880, Herzl-Kana Correspondence, Central Zionist Archives, Jerusalem.

6. Herzl to Kana, March 5, 1882, Herzl-Kana Correspondence.

7. Jan. 10, 1886, "Jugendtagebuch," in *Theodor Herzl Jahrbuch,* ed. Tulo Nussenblatt (Vienna, 1937), p. 47.

8. Herzl to Kana, Sept. 4, 1879, Herzl-Kana Correspondence.

9. May 2, 1882, "Jugendtagebuch," p. 40.

10. April 13, 1883, *ibid.,* p. 42; Herzl to Kana, Nov. 22, 1883, Herzl-Kana Correspondence.

11. Nov. 27, 1883, "Jugendtagebuch," p. 43.

12. New Year's Eve, 1883/84, *ibid.,* pp. 43–4.

13. Herzl to Kana, Month of Distress (Aug.?) 26, 1883, Herzl-Kana Correspondence.

14. Bein, *Theodor Herzl,* p. 385.

15. Herzl to Kana, Aug. 30, 1883, Herzl-Kana Correspondence; July 5, 1895, *Tagebücher,* 1: 223.

16. Feb. 28, 1886, "Jugendtagebuch," p. 49; March 21, 1886, *ibid.* See the authoritative discussion "Herzl's Marriage," in Desmond Stewart, *Theodor Herzl* (New York, 1974), Appendix II, pp. 373–5.

17. Marvin Lowenthal, "Introduction: The Diaries and the Man," *Diaries,* pp. xiv–xv; Bein, *Theodor Herzl,* pp. 68–9.

18. Max Weber, "The Sociology of Charismatic Authority," in *From Max Weber: Essays in Sociology,* ed. and trans. H. H. Gerth and C. Wright Mills (New York, 1958), pp. 245–8; *The Theory of Social and Economic Organization,* trans. A. Henderson and Talcott Parsons (New York, 1964), pp. 358–63; W. W. Tarn, *Alexander the Great* (Boston, 1956), p. 123; Thomas Africa, "Homosexuals in Greek History," *Journal of Psychohistory,* 9 (1982): 401–20; H. R. Trevor-Roper, *The Last Days of Hitler* (New York, 1962), pp. 155–8.

19. Leon Kellner, "Herzl and Zangwill in Vienna: A Contrast in Personalities and Types," in *Theodor Herzl: A Memorial* (1929), pp. 73–4.

20. Maria E. delle Grazie, "Father and King: A Remembrance of Herzl's Views on Jewish Destiny," in *Herzl: A Memorial,* p. 40.

21. Bein, *Theodor Herzl,* pp. 87–8, 89.

22. *Ibid.,* p. 91; *Tagebücher,* 1: 8.

23. Bein, *Theodor Herzl,* pp. 105, 106; Arthur Schnitzler to Herzl, Nov. 17, 1894, in Olga Schnitzler, *Spiegelbild der Freundschaft* (Salzburg, 1962), p. 88.

24. Herzl to Schnitzler, Feb. 15, 1895, *ibid.,* p. 92.

25. *Tagebücher,* 1: 3, 15.

26. June 5, 1895, *ibid.,* 1: 38.

27. Heinz Kohut, *The Analysis of the Self: A Systematic Approach to the Psychoanalytic Treatment of Narcissistic Personality Disorders* (New York, 1971), pp. 315–16.

28. June 3 and July 23, 1895, *Tagebücher,* 1: 32, 240; June 3, 1895, *ibid.,* 1: 33; June 3, 1895, *ibid.,* 1: 32; June 7, 1895, *ibid.,* 1: 42; June 7, 1895, *Diaries,* p. 36 (omitted from *Tagebücher*).

29. June 12, 1895, *Tagebücher,* 1: 106–7.

30. *Ibid.* 1: 104; June 16, 1895, *ibid.,* 1: 117; June 11, 1895, *ibid.,* 1: 82; *ibid.,* 1: 84–5.

31. June 12, 1895, *ibid.,* 1: 105; June 12, 1895, *Diaries,* p. 44 (omitted from *Tagebücher*).

32. June 16, 1895, *Tagebücher,* 1: 115–16.

33. *Ibid.*, 1: 116; June 16, 1895, *Diaries,* p. 49 (omitted from *Tagebücher*); Sept. 30, 1898, *Tagebücher,* 2: 129.

34. Herzl, "Experiences and Moods: An Autobiographic Sketch" (1897), in *Herzl: A Memorial,* p. 184; June 5, 1895, *Tagebücher,* 1: 39.

35. Joseph Cowen, "My Conversion to Zionism: Reminiscences of First Meetings with Herzl in England and Elsewhere," in *Herzl: A Memorial,* p. 104; Sept. 3, 1897, *Tagebücher,* 2: 24–5; Oct. 19, 1898, *ibid.,* 2: 186; Nov. 2, 1898, *ibid.,* 2: 223.

36. Sept. 20, 1895, *Tagebücher,* 1: 279.

37. May 12, 1898, *ibid.,* 2: 81–2; July 10, 1898, *ibid.,* 2: 95; McGrath, "Student Radicalism," pp. 195–201. See the further relationship between Freud, Gustav Mahler, and German Nationalism that McGrath establishes in "Mahler and Freud," *Gustav Mahler Kolloquium, 1979, Beiträge '79–81,* ed. Rudolf Klein (Kassel, Basel, London, 1982).

38. July 10, 1898, *Tagebücher,* 2: 95–6.

39. Oct. 31, 1898, *ibid.,* 2: 212; *ibid.,* 2: 212–13.

40. Bein, *Theodor Herzl,* p. 89; *Tagebücher,* 1: 8.

41. June 5, 1895, *ibid.,* 1: 38; June 8, 1895, *ibid.,* 1: 48; June 5, 1895, *ibid.,* 1: 37; June 8, 1895, *ibid.,* 1: 52; June 10, 1895, *ibid.,* 1: 73; and June 11, 1895, *ibid.,* 1: 81.

42. Spring 1895, *ibid.,* 1: 25, 44.

43. Oct. 8, 1898, *ibid.,* 2: 151; Oct. 29, 1898, *ibid.,* 2: 208.

44. Anna Freud, *The Ego and the Mechanisms of Defense,* trans. Cecil Baines (New York, 1946), pp. 117–31.

45. As quoted by Leon Edel, "The Biographer and Psychoanalysis," *International Journal of Psycho-Analysis,* 42, pts. 4–5 (1961): 462.

46. Herzl, "Das Wirtshaus zum Anilin" (1896), in *Philosophische Erzählungen* (Berlin, 1919), pp. 264–5.

47. Herzl, "Das Lenkbare Luftschiff" (1896), *ibid.,* p. 33.

48. Herzl, *Altneuland* (Leipzig, 1902), pp. 48, 95, 176–7, 207.

49. *Ibid.,* p. 77.

50. *Ibid.,* p. 80.

51. *Ibid.,* p. 206.

52. Bein, *Theodor Herzl,* pp. 8, 22.

53. April 23, 1896, *Tagebücher,* 1: 378–9.

54. Sept. 9, 1896, *ibid.,* 1: 531–2; Nov. 5, 1898, *ibid.,* 2: 231–2.

55. Sept. 3, 1897, *Complete Diaries,* 2: 585 (omitted in *Tagebücher*); Sept. 2, 1898, *ibid.,* 2: 653 (omitted in *Tagebücher*).

56. Herzl, "Experiences and Moods," p. 184.

57. Herzl, *Die Welt* (Vienna, 1900), vol 1, no. 1, as quoted in Leonard Stein, "Arbeit für Alle: Herzl's Views on Capturing the Jewish Communities," in *Herzl: A Memorial,* p. 107.

58. Kellner, *Herzl's Lehrjahre,* p. 133; Aug. 24, 1897, *Tagebücher,* 2: 21–2.

59. March 12, 1898, *ibid.,* 2: 64.

60. June 17, 1896, *ibid.,* 1: 421; June 30, 1896, *ibid.,* 1: 463.

61. G. Sil-Vara, "At Herzl's Grave: The Burial of the Leader—and Other Memories," in *Herzl: A Memorial,* p. 21; May 2, 1904, *Tagebücher,* 3: 578.

62. Adolf Friedemann, *Das Leben Theodor Herzls* (Berlin, 1919), pp. 88–90.

63. June 16, 1895, *Tagebücher,* 1: 116.

64. Herzl, *Altneuland,* frontispiece.

65. June 12, 1895, *Tagebücher,* 1: 104.

Victor and Friedrich Adler

Revolutionary Politics and Generational Conflict in Austro-Marxism

The story of Austrian socialism is at once glorious and pathetic. The Austro-Marxists appealed to their own, and to mankind's, highest aspirations for equality and social justice, human decency, happiness, and peace. Austro-Marxism is a term that subsumes not only the radical theory that claimed a mediating position between Russian Bolshevism and Western revisionist socialism but also the practical measures and social legislation adopted in the 1920's in Austria. The Austro-Marxist forum and social laboratory in the early twentieth century was the city of Vienna. Nowhere in the world was the quest for a social order conducive to decent human life pursued with greater idealism and greater success. Socialist material and institutional achievements—municipal housing, kindergartens, and swimming and sports facilities—made "Red Vienna" in the 1920's a social model for the world and testimony to Austro-Marxist energy and inspired vision. On the national level Social Democratic achievements included the eight-hour day, paid vacations, collective bargaining; regulation of women's, children's, and night labor; health, accident, and disability insurance; state assistance for mothers and children, public health measures; and the creation of Workers Chambers (*Arbeiterkammern*).

As a result of the collapse of the Social Democratic party and its Viennese municipal bastion in the civil war of 1934, Austro-Marxist defenders and critics have espoused passionate and polemical interpretations of its legacy. But the passage of time has now made it possible to take a calmer and clearer measure of the movement and its leaders. We can see that the Austro-Marxists' moral nobility was fraught with illusion, their generous idealism all too often attended by rigidity, folly, and self-deception. Although they meant well for humanity as a whole, the Social Democrats were unable to protect either their small portion of humanity or the social and political gains they had achieved.

The question of why the Social Democrats of Central Europe were ineffectual in dealing with fascism in the 1920's and early 1930's has aroused great scholarly interest and stimulated a number of mutually compatible answers. A classic analysis, whose first formulation by Robert Michels predates fascism, pointed to the organizational structure of the Marxist parties as intrinsically conservative. Carl E. Schorske has focused upon the inherent tensions between gradualist political tactics and revolutionary theory in German Social Democracy. By contrast, Susanne Miller has stressed the rigid organizational discipline of the party as the critical factor leading to its division and inner weakness. Critiques from the left by Herbert Steiner, Käthe Leichter, Felix Kreissler, Ernst Fischer, Anson Rabinbach, and Joseph Buttinger suggest that the Social Democrats were not radical and revolutionary enough; the Socialists should have confronted fascism more militantly. More moderately, the advocates of an integrationist model, Karl Renner, Adam Wandruszka, Eric Kollman, and Norbert Leser, have argued that the Social Democrats should have become meliorist, willing to form opportune alliances and coalitions with bourgeois parties to save the first Austrian democracy.[1] Such coalitions, these reformist critics point out, have been the successful "roads to power" for the Social Democratic parties of Willy Brandt in West Germany and Bruno Kreisky in Austria in post–World War II Europe.

Yet none of these studies has examined the psychodynamics of the leadership of Austrian Socialism as an expression of that movement's ambivalence. The following essay on father and son Adler will show that fantasies and behavior in specific crises tell us much about the personified ambivalence of the group which chose and supported these party leaders.

The Austrian Social Democratic party was torn between two political models—revolutionary non-participation in the state and social integration—in the half century between its founding in 1888 and the *Anschluss* in 1938. The model of revolution was a conflict model, calling for the forcing of differences to a violent resolution. The integrationist model was aimed at over-coming and avoiding conflict. Its premise was the upward social and eco-nomic mobility of the proletariat and their sociopolitical integration into the state.

This tension between alternative tactics in crisis may be seen by studying the lives, politics, and actions of the leading family of Austrian Socialism, that of Victor and Friedrich Adler. The saga of the Adlers is the most loving and deadly story of idealism and tragedy in modern political history. Victor Adler (1852–1918), the father, founded the Austrian Social Democratic Worker's party and was its leader until 1918; his son, Friedrich, was a party secretary who in 1916 committed the only act of individual terror in over a century of the history of western European Social Democracy when he murdered the Austrian Prime Minister, Count Stürgkh, and lived to become the leader of the Second International in the 1920's and 1930's. The Adler family history is of unique historical interest because the role of practicing physician and political leader are merged in the person of the father, Victor, and because among political assassinations of recent times, such as those of Anwar Sadat, Leon Trotsky, John and Robert Kennedy, and Martin Luther King, Jr., we have in this case the story of an assassin who not only lived to tell about it but who emerged as a hero and for four decades afterwards went on to play an important political role in international socialism.

Victor Adler was born in Prague, the eldest of five children of Solomon Marcus Adler (1826–1886) and Johanna Herzl (d. 1910). In 1855 the family moved to Vienna, where the father acquired wealth in real estate speculation and became a prominent member of the stock exchange, including service on its Court of Arbitration. Both parents converted to Roman Catholicism in 1884. Victor later became a Protestant.

The families of Jewish descent, families whose sons shaped Vienna's intellectual life, lived near one another in Vienna's Ninth District on the north of the inner city, called the Alsergrund because the little stream Alser runs through it. The Adler family lived at Liechtensteinstrasse 48. The family of Otto Bauer lived at Liechtensteinstrasse 32. After his marriage to Emma Braun in 1878, the Victor Adlers moved into a house his father owned nearby on the Berggasse, No. 19, which Sigmund Freud later moved into and inhabited for almost half a century. Emma was the sister of Victor's friend Heinrich Braun, who became a Social Democratic member of the Reichstag.

Emma Adler suffered from severe depressive episodes in the early years of her marriage. In December 1891, Victor wrote to Engelbert Pernerstorfer: "She sleeps a bit more, that is all, on the other hand she and I are tortured by her delusional ideas of the most terrible kind, so that sometimes I do not know how I can stand it." Some weeks later he wrote to Pernerstorfer again: "I am at the end. Emma's situation has not improved despite the change of scene. She suffers from the most frightful anxiety-arousing ideas." After Emma took the waters at Sulz bei Wien for a year, Adler reported: "The anxious ideas are still there as before, but the inhibition, the numbed staring, the apathy, is beginning to lift. The picture is still very sad, but at least there begins to be hope."[2]

Victor had a speech impediment, for which his parents sent him at age eighteen to a special school for stutterers in Westphalia. The school cured the worst of his speech defect; nevertheless, for the rest of his life he preferred to speak extemporaneously rather than deliver a prewritten speech so that he could allow long pauses for emphasis.[3]

In the elite Schottengymnasium, Victor Adler joined with Engelbert Pernerstorfer, Heinrich Friedjung, and seven other *Gymnasiasts* to found the Telyn Society, a literary club dedicated to German nationalism, socialism, and their own literary creativity. Father Adler was pleased to have the boys meet in his home and regularly supplied them with high tea and supper. Victor argued with his father over the Paris Commune of 1871, defending the Communards from charges of being "murderers, thieves, and tramps." He wrote Pernerstorfer that of course "the paternal authority must win" and in the end he himself was seen as "a tramp and thief [who] sits there at the table."[4]

As a student at the University of Vienna, Victor joined the Leseverein der deutschen Studenten. The Leseverein was dissolved by the Austrian government in December 1878 on the ground that it represented a danger to the state. A year later members of the group established a political discussion club named the Deutsche Leseverein. Here Adler was admired by Sigmund Freud, who was four years his junior. Freud vividly described in *The Interpretation of Dreams* an incident between them in the Leseverein that almost led to a duel:

> There was a discussion in a *German* students' club on the relation of philosophy to the natural sciences. I was a green youngster, full of materialistic theories, and thrust myself forward to give expression to an extremely one-sided point of view. Thereupon someone who was my senior and my superior, someone who has since then shown his ability as a leader of men and an organizer of large groups (and who also, incidentally, bears a name derived from the Animal Kingdom), stood up and gave us a good talking-to: he too, he told us, had fed swine in his youth and returned repentant to his father's house. *I fired up . . .* and replied boorishly ['*saugrob,*' literally 'swinishly gross'] that since I now knew that he had fed *swine* in his youth I was no longer *surprised* at the tone of his speeches. . . . There was a general uproar and I was called upon from many sides to withdraw

my remarks, but I refused to do so. The man I had insulted was too sensible to look upon the incident as a *challenge,* and let the affair drop.[5]

Adler studied chemistry for two semesters, then medicine. He was attracted to psychiatry and became the assistant of Professor Theodor Meynert, the man who challenged Sigmund Freud's report of male hysteria after his return from studying with Charcot in Paris.* During his mid-twenties Freud was a dinner guest at Victor Adler's home. Freud recalled over four decades later: "I still remember he was at that time a vegetarian and that I saw little Fritz who was one or two years of age. (I find it noteworthy that it was in the same rooms that I have now occupied for thirty-six years.)"[6] He unconsciously chose to live in the apartment of his idealized student friend Victor Adler and stayed there until he was forced to leave Vienna in 1938.

Victor Adler and his father disagreed over current politics and sometimes fought about Victor's radicalism. Victor felt inhibited in his political tactics by his father's opposition. He wrote articles under a pseudonym to keep his political activity from his father. Once Victor angrily told his father that it was only out of consideration for him that he held back in politics. "If I had done as I wished," said Victor, "I would already have been locked up for at least four months." When his father died in 1886 Adler felt a liberation—a new coming into his own as a free man and an independent political agent. He founded the Social Democratic weekly *Die Gleichheit* with his new money and wrote to Karl Kautsky: "I believe I have shared with you the circumstances that have hindered my working openly and with full energy. Due to the death of my father, to whom I owed the sacrifice, I have become the master of my course."[7] Along with supporting his growing family, Victor Adler covered the financial deficits of *Die Gleichheit* and of the party newspaper, the *Arbeiter-Zeitung,* the cost of party handbills and brochures, and the salaries of party functionaries. After he gave up his medical practice in 1885, Victor's only income was as an employee of the Socialist party at a workingman's pay of twenty-five gulden per week. August Bebel offered to confidentially intervene on his behalf to win him a better salary from the Austrian party.

At the turn of the year 1888/89 at the Congress of Hainfeld Victor Adler united the scattered socialists of the Austrian Empire into the Social Democratic Worker's party. Seventy-three delegates of many different persuasions and nationalities including radicals and moderates, Germans, Czechs, and

---

*Meynert "later confessed to Freud on his death bed that he had himself been a classic case of male hysteria, but had always managed to conceal the fact." See Ernest Jones, *The Life and Work of Sigmund Freud,* vol. 1 (New York, 1953), pp. 230–1, n. h.

Poles met in a small village inn to found the new party.[8] Adler opposed the use of terror, a tactic he regarded as merely individualist, and grounded the party firmly on Marxist political principles of class action, rooted in disciplined political organization. He drove the anarchists and nihilists, the spokesmen of "propaganda of the deed," the radicals who preached terror on the principle of "an eye for an eye, a tooth for a tooth," out of the party.[9] Adler held that no individual act can make a revolution or be a substitute for mass action.

After their marriage in 1878, Victor and Emma spent a year-long honeymoon in Italy, ending in 1879 in Paris, where Victor took a course with Jean Martin Charcot. Their first child, Friedrich, was born shortly after their return to Vienna in July 1879. (In 1881 a daughter, Marie, was born, followed by a second son, Karl, in 1885.) After moving into Berggasse 19, Victor opened a general practice that did not flourish. He became known as a poor people's doctor who not only treated without charge those who could not pay but also gave them medications and money.

Adler family documents disclose areas of unconfronted rage and frustration in family relations that sometimes burst out in impulsive blows or deadly violence. They were a family who never argued or met interpersonal problems head on. Theirs was a marriage of quiet sacrifice and keeping conflict hidden until the explosion that eventually came was so full of resentment that it was unconsciously murderous. For example, both Victor and Emma constantly denied their desperate financial plight. Emma tells how Victor excitedly showed her two thousand bank notes, claiming he won them in a lottery. Later she discovered that he had borrowed the money at usurious rates. While this gallant protection of the woman from unpleasant reality was syntonic with the modes of Adler's upper bourgeois Viennese social stratum, it was also infantilizing and Emma resented it in her recollections.

As was true of enlightened middle-class families, the Adler child-rearing practices were humane and specifically non-violent. Emma Adler recalls that "Fritz was always a quiet, good, well-behaved child [*ein stilles, gutes, artiges Kind*], in fact never childlike." She records but a single instance of corporal punishment meted out to Fritz but does not recount its cause. We know only that Victor was apparently unhappier than the boy. The father cleared his desk, laid Fritz on it, and gave him one gentle spank. On one occasion Fritz received fishing tackle from relatives. Victor was indignant when he found the boy at the seashore fishing. The father roughly seized the fishing tackle with no greeting or explanation. Fritz gazed at him in fear and incomprehension. Victor "explained" how gruesomely the fish suffer when they get hooked, this was no toy, one should not torture animals so. Fritz then himself cast his fishing tackle into the sea.

The other side of this sweetness and restraint was a hidden violence that came out in moments of frustration. Emma relates that Victor hit her in the face with his fist during an argument over furniture. Later, full of remorse, Victor talked of taking his life. The level of unconscious murderous rage Victor experienced came to the surface at the time he and the family moved out of Berggasse 19 in 1892. Emma writes:

> As everything was packed, Victor wished to lay his revolver in a box and said he was certain that the revolver was not loaded, so certain that to test it he aimed at me and pulled the trigger— With a great crack the bullet that was still in the chamber flew past me and lodged in the window frame across the street.[10]

Victor Adler had a record of compassion and effective accomplishment on the humanitarian social issues stemming from the brutalities of rampant industrial capitalism that is unequaled among socialist leaders. He applied his knowledge of chemistry and medicine to the hygienic and public health issues of hours of employment, working conditions, pollution, and industrial poisons affecting the health of workers. In 1883, seeking to become a factory inspector, he traveled to Germany, Switzerland, and England to learn about their systems of industrial regulation at first hand. In London Adler met Friedrich Engels, who was enthusiastic about Adler's idea of working within the administrative apparatus of the state. In 1887 he spoke to the Health Section of the Sixth International Congress for Hygiene and Demography on factory hygiene, factory laws, the curbing of night labor, and the eight-hour day. One of his most important commitments was to the brick workers, whose working conditions were particularly bad and whose companies paid their stockholders exceptionally high dividends. Adler climbed over the wall of the brickworks at night to see the living conditions for himself. This is what he told the court at his trial for writing an article that "disturbed the public peace":

> We saw frightful things. Eighty people live in a room a tenth as large as this chamber. Men, women, and children all pressed together on dirty straw. They had taken their shirts off and laid them next to them in order to keep them clean. In one barrack we saw a woman with a newborn baby next to her. I asked her: "Where did you deliver?" The answer was: "Here." Here amidst the men and children, beneath them the heat of the fire, over them the cold of winter.[11]

Victor Adler also was a spokesman for the tramway workers when they struck, calling their condition "slavery." He took up the cause of striking coal miners, and brought his medical expertise to bear on the chemical poisoning by "white phosphorus" of workers in the match industry in a long, eventually successful, battle for regulation.

Victor Adler was frequently arrested and tried for high treason, holding unauthorized meetings, inciting to riot, insulting the government, circulating forbidden printed matter, violating press laws, and disturbing the public peace in the pursuit of his political activities. Between 1887 and 1899 he faced 17 trials and spent a total of 8 months and 29 days in prison. One of the occasions when he was incarcerated was during the first May Day celebrations, which he had organized and inspired in 1890.

Fritz was exposed to these humanitarian works of his father and invited to identify with them. When workers from the brickyard came to the Adler home and described their wretched conditions to Victor, Fritz listened and wept. Victor said to him, "Do not cry, Fritzi. When you grow up, you will help me to improve their lot." "Yes, I will do that, Father," said the boy as he wiped his tears. The boy also identified with his father as a martyr-hero whose heroism consisted of penal convictions and sentences in jail. When he learned that his father had been sentenced to four months in prison, the ten-year-old Fritz delightedly ran out of the house to tell the verdict to the first coachman he met. At age fourteen he calculated to his "greatest satisfaction" that his father could be sentenced to twenty years' imprisonment. He told this to his little sister, who broke out in tears. He could not comprehend why his mother rebuked him for this. One part of Fritz felt "enthusiasm for his father's martyrdom," but another, less conscious part, clearly enjoyed calculating the length of time his father might be spending away from home, if the worst eventuated. This is the ambivalence in Fritz that Julius Braunthal wished to suggest when he stressed what a gentle child Fritz was, "to whom every aggressive impulse was foreign." He quotes Victor as saying Fritz was "the child with the most delicate feelings I have ever encountered, tender to his siblings, the tenderest son."[12]

As a child, Fritz identified with his father's role and political cause. He was six years old when his father took him to his first political demonstration. He said, "The party played a great role in my life from my sixth year." When he was eight years old he ran errands for the editorial offices of his father's weekly *Gleichheit,* the predecessor to the *Arbeiter-Zeitung,* and folded its first issue. At age ten he was taken to see his first theater, the drama *Wilhelm Tell.* "Since that time," he said, "I never doubted that an Austrian [tyrant] Vogt could be killed and that this was morally justified."[13] During his adolescence he felt himself to be a full-fledged party comrade and read both the *Arbeiter-Zeitung* and the *Neue Zeit* daily from cover to cover. He participated in street demonstrations, meetings, and the *Parteitage.*

Fritz's wish to devote his life to the working-class movement was an issue of intense conflict with his father. Victor insisted that his son acquire an autonomous profession so he would be self-supporting and independent. His father sent Fritz to the University of Zürich in October 1897 to study chemistry. Scarcely had Fritz arrived there than he wrote his father of his wish to learn the worker's life from personal experience. He intended to go to work in a mine for three months followed by nine months in a factory. These ambitions to be a laborer were for Fritz a program of late-adolescent testing of his manhood and principles. He chose a realm of testing within his father's ideals, but in violation of his father's intentions for his son. This was to become his characteristic style of acting out—to subscribe to his father's aims, but to confute his method.

The quality of a self-imposed test of his resolution and his contempt for his father's values is evident in his language: "If I see in a short time that I cannot take it, which I do not believe will be the case, I can always go back and probably do something that you would term sensible." Victor urged that if Fritz wished to be of value to the workers, he must be financially independent of the party. Fritz called on his father to be consistent and not deny to his son the same prerogative of service to the proletariat that the father had claimed for himself: "How can you demand of me that I give up taking the same step out of my milieu that you took?"—a telling and irrefutable argument. If Fritz had a late adolescent's uncanny ability to detect the hypocrisy and point out the clichés and the chinks in the moral armor of authority figures, he also had the teenager's insolence and hurtful contempt: "You wish me to keep the prospect of a bourgeois career open, and I say that I don't give a damn [ich darauf pfeife]."[14]

Victor put his paternal foot down with a firm no. Fritz capitulated and did not leave the university. At the end of his second semester Fritz disclosed that he had by no means given up his plan of dedicating his life to the socialist movement. He proposed to his father that he study history, economics, and philosophy. Victor would not hear of it, insisting on a practical vocation. Victor wrote to his sister-in-law Lily Braun: "I have had a three-day debate with Fritz. He is a fine boy, but dumb and young, and intransigent to a fault. I categorically said no. Now he proposes a compromise. He wishes to become a Doctor of Physics because in physics and mathematics he anticipates 'more humanistic education' than in chemistry." In many ways Victor was not only reliving his struggle with his father, he was also telling his son to be like his grandfather—a worldly success rather than a humanist. He told Fritz: "I would rather see you become a Siemens than a Bebel! Am I not peculiar?? . . . and undemanding for my boys?"[15]

A "compromise" was negotiated and Fritz devoted himself to the study of physics. His friends were other students of physics, one of whom was

Albert Einstein. The clear message Victor transmitted to Fritz, with all the authority of a father-physician, was: You are physically and emotionally fragile, you are sickly and in constant danger of collapse. Victor wrote to his son:

> Your last letter caused me the highest degree of concern. You appear to tax your nerves more than they can tolerate. For heaven's sake, do not make it a test of limits; better to move the stupid examinations and rest for a couple of weeks. It is a matter of absolute indifference whether you finish half a year later. BUT YOU MUST STAY HEALTHY [double underlining in letter], for MY [triple underlining] sake—I could not bear to have you ill as well.[16]

Victor also told his son that he was a drudge, a humorless, tight, joyless person, traits inappropriate to his youth and student status. He wrote to Fritz in Zürich:

> I must say one thing which presses on my heart: Why are you so terribly serious, so sad, so tense, so almost gloomy? Why? A young, capable person, who can accomplish much—why don't you laugh, why never a trace of humor, of youthfulness in you?? Why is all with the burden of fate? Why so constrained, like a family man with six young children, why so absolutely unjoyous?? If you laughingly did foolish things, I would be angered, but solaced. But, since you are so melancholic, I am worried about you. . . .[17]

In 1903 Fritz married Katharina Germanischkaja, a Lithuanian Jewish student of chemistry at the University of Zürich. She came from an orthodox Jewish home and wished a ritual wedding, which was held in Lithuania. The couple had three children: Johanna in 1903, Emma in 1905, and Felix in 1911. Victor, an uncle of Kathia's, and her parents supported the new family financially. By 1905 Victor grew impatient with his son's dependency and began urging Fritz to earn his own bread for his family, writing: "The greatest thinkers from Nietzsche to Helmholtz had to earn their living through teaching or some other means."[18]

On the occasion of the twentieth anniversary of the founding of the Social Democratic Worker's party at Hainfeld, Fritz, who was then thirty, addressed a letter of congratulations to his father which is undoubtedly one of the most ambivalent letters of felicitation on record. The latent levels of hostility under the supposed congratulations are scarcely disguised:

> You never wanted to educate, and did not devote anything to me. And yet your influence was the decisive one on my life due to *what you were*. . . . You always had the most important thing in mind, you

knew not the least consideration for the person, and its adjunct, the family. I who am among your dependents, I who have caused you much worry and trouble, today I wish to tell you that, whatever happens to me, I will always be grateful to you that you were a personality and not a father. You would have deprived me of the *highest* that I have known in life, if you had ever been considerate of us.[19]

Fritz is saying to his father: In my eyes you are not and have never been capable of a normal familial father-son relationship. You were always the political person—saintly, abstract, remote, detached, and morally right. Thank you for giving me nothing emotionally.

A great irony of this father-son conflict is that Victor believed that a dedication to political socialism would inhibit Fritz's academic career. But time wrought decisive changes. The very political acceptance and success that Victor's work facilitated meant that Social Democratic political power could be instrumental in advancing Fritz's university career—if he would let it do so.

In 1908 the University of Zürich decided to establish a chair of theoretical physics. The University of Zürich is a cantonal institution governed by the Zürich Board of Education, and they had the final voice in filling the new appointment. In 1908 a majority of the board were Social Democrats, who offered the chair to Fritz Adler.

During this period Fritz's friend Albert Einstein was still working at the Swiss Federal Patent Office in Bern and was applying to the Zürich Cantonal Gymnasium for details about a vacancy for a mathematics teacher. Fritz wrote a letter to the Zürich Board of Education that is surely one of the most modest in the history of academic appointments:

> If it is possible to obtain a man like Einstein for our university, it would be absurd to appoint me. I must quite frankly say that my ability as a research physicist does not bear even the slightest comparison to Einstein's. Such an opportunity to obtain a man who can benefit us so much by raising the general level of the university should not be lost because of political sympathies.[20]

Einstein got the position and moved to Zürich, taking an apartment in the same building as the Adlers. Fritz clearly did not want an academic career. In frustrating his father and his own scholarly future, he performed a truly altruistic service in aiding a friend, who was also the greatest of mathematical geniuses, to gain an academic start. In 1910 Fritz took a position he much preferred by becoming the editor of the Zürich Social Democratic newspaper, the *Volksrecht.*

Einstein's life was again affected by the Adlers. In 1910 he was excited when he received a call to the chair of physics at the German University of Prague. Ernst Mach had been the first rector of the university, Anton Lampa was the current head of the physics faculty, and there was "a fine institute with a magnificent library."

The appointment seemed certain, until a hitch developed over Einstein's atheism. The Emperor Franz Josef would only confirm academic appointments of confessing members of a recognized church. Although Einstein had never officially renounced his Jewish faith, he was an atheist.

The young Adlers decided to intervene with their father in Vienna. Kathia wrote to Victor on June 23, 1910:

> On Sunday, Einstein came and told us that the offer from Prague was not going to materialize. . . . the trouble is not that Einstein is a "foreigner" but that he is an unbeliever. The university found this out and this is the inevitable result. . . . Now, Einstein is as unpractical as a child in cases like this, and [Fritz] finally got out of him the fact that on the application form he put down that he was an unbeliever but did not say that he had not left the Church. As Einstein very much wants the Prague post, and as the first hurdle would be the question of his religion, [Fritz] suggested to him at the time that he should pass the whole thing over to Lampa in Prague so that should the question arise in discussion Lampa would be briefed. Einstein did not do this. . . . Einstein is naturally disappointed that the appointment is rejected since this means that the same thing will happen with any other position for which he applies.[21]

Three months later Einstein's appointment was revived. He received a request to call on the Minister of Education in Vienna. Fritz wrote his father: "The affair is under way again. Perhaps it would be useful for him to see you and discuss things while he is there. . . . In all practical things he is absolutely impractical."[22] This time Imperial doubts were circumvented and Einstein's appointment to Prague was confirmed.

Four years later, at the outbreak of World War I, Victor Adler also intervened on behalf of Leon Trotsky and the Russian émigrés. On the morning of August 3, 1914, a full week after Austria had declared war on Serbia, Adler was able to go with Trotsky in hand to Geyer, the Chief of the Political Police, and in full confidence ask his advice on the best course for the Russians to follow. Geyer at 3:00 p.m. advised immediate departure for Zürich. Trotsky was on the 6:10 p.m. train that day. All Russians and Serbians in Vienna were arrested the next morning.

These episodes are indicative of the high degree of Social Democratic integration into the social and political order. Adler had influence with the ministries and knew his way around government circles in Vienna. He functioned on a basis of trust and was trusted on many levels by the Imperial establishment. The situation was different in Germany and strikingly so in Russia, where the Social Democrats were a totally alienated opposition.

In the spring of 1911 Victor finally permitted Fritz to join the Austrian Social Democratic party. Karl Seitz, the party chairman, issued a unanimous invitation of the Party Executive to Fritz to take a permanent position as Party Secretary as soon as possible because of the forthcoming parliamentary elections. This call to Vienna could not have been issued without Victor Adler's approval.

The agony of the socialist movements of Europe on the eve of World War I is too well known to require detailed description here. Victor Adler, a leader of the Second International, took the "realistic" passive majority position in his report to the International Socialist Bureau in Brussels on July 28, 1914:

> We already have the war. Until now we fought against war as best we could. The working class of Austria did all it could against warmongering. But expect nothing more from us now! We are under war conditions and our press is censored. We have an emergency situation and war powers in the background. I am not here to address mass meetings, but to tell you the truth, that an action now, when hundreds of thousands are on the way to the frontier, and martial law rules at home, is impossible.[23]

Victor Adler was in severe conflict about the war. As a psychiatrist, he observed with apprehension the passions aroused by the mobilization. As they were driving through Vienna on August 3, 1914 he told Trotsky: "It is those who do not have to go to war who show their joy. Besides, all the unbalanced, all the madmen now come out into the streets; it is their day. The murder of Jaurès is only the beginning. War opens the door for all instincts, all forms of madness." On the other hand Adler was a man who had been a German nationalist since his youth and now once again felt those nationalistic emotions stirred by the crisis of the war.[24]

On October 8, 1914, Victor Adler said about the war:

> My view is: I know one must vote for it, I only do not know how to make it pass my lips, but it must be. It is a terrible decision, a terrible conflict, that has been forced not only on us Germans, but in equal measure on all proletarians who are involved. There is no choice, terrible as it is, since the alternative is still worse. Only one thing is worse than war, that is defeat. A man can do no other, even if our victory means the defeat of the other. In addition the mon-

strous fact that Germany is fighting for its existence. . . . Austria is bad enough, but compared to the ultimate of Russia, we do not wish to exchange it.

This speech entitled "On August 4," which he delivered to the party cadres, makes painful reading, for we can feel his torment. Adler's argument is in the purest sense existential. He is in an "extreme" or "limit" situation in which he is discovering that his firmly held principles, rationally arrived at, are undercut by his existential "being" in the historical situation. He said:

There are decisions that are not created out of arguments, rather they automatically come out of Being and not from thought. Existence decides. . . . If someone had asked me three or five years ago, how will you decide if something like this happens?—my first response would have been: I will not answer such an idiotic question. If you insist on an answer, then of course it will be against war. When the question is actually put in the reality of Being, it is quite different. The interest of the German proletariat in Austria and Germany is certainly no different than that of the German people.

Fritz was with his father at the Brussels meeting. He described as his "most painful experience—that my father at this meeting wished to know nothing of mobilizing the proletariat against the war." He claimed that the Brussels meeting marked the first time in his life that he felt strong opposition to the views of his father. Upon returning to Vienna he criticized the "spirit of absolute passivity" of his father toward the war.[25]

As Europe went to war Friedrich Adler continued to busy himself in his room with books, papers, and stamps for the forthcoming International Socialist Congress, which was scheduled to meet in Vienna. He founded and chaired the Karl Marx Association, an organization of 120 members who opposed Socialist party policy supporting the war and particularly criticized the editorials of the *Arbeiter-Zeitung.* His wife Kathia and his children remained in Zürich. Fritz and Kathia were fully estranged. The couple kept up a public front by saying she stayed in Zürich for her health, and her mother lived with her. Fritz had several affairs with young girls in Zürich beginning in 1908 or 1909. Due to what he termed a "lofty commitment to the truth" Fritz described all of the sexual affairs to his wife. This caused scenes between them that depressed him and alienated the couple from each other. Fritz realized that his work no longer retained its former importance to her. According to the report of the Austrian court psychiatrists:

In July 1911 Fritz entered a relationship with a prostitute in Vienna. He wished to rescue her from her milieu and guide her back to honest work. He secured a work permit for her and sought to keep her from

sexual relations with others. Later he discovered that she had de-
ceived him and had not reformed herself. He was very disappointed
and called this the biggest stupidity of his life.[26]

Fritz had a fantasy of rescuing the prostitute, which in the unconscious
means rescuing the mother—the spiritually innocent and faithful woman
who consorts with other men. This is one of the most classic and familiar
fantasies of men. The mother does not really love the other man, the father.
She loves one and only one—her son—and will sacrifice herself for his sake.
She was led astray by seduction. She submits to the other man from financial
need, not from love. She is waiting for the son to come to her rescue. The
prostitute may give herself to anyone, but in her soul she remains innocent
and faithful to her son and lover.[27] This fantasy suggests Friedrich Adler's
unresolved attachment to his mother and his unconscious bondage to her.
His belief in the genuine innocence of the prostitute waiting to be saved from
brutish wealthy old men by himself as a gallant knight demonstrates his
childish fixation on his mother as the sacrificing woman who is waiting for
him to save her from abuse by the old man.

In Vienna during the war Fritz took his meals with his parents, at which
"there were painful scenes and confrontations with his father at the family
table."[28]

Emma Adler sympathized and identified with her son in his politically
isolated struggle against the Socialist pro-war policy. She gives Karl
Kautsky an account of a confrontation between Fritz and the party cadres
in October 1914:

It is a pity that you were not here for the meeting two weeks ago.
. . . F[ritz] spoke like a god! He has developed quite exceptionally in
the last two years. Even his voice is more pleasant. I was so sorry
for him. Nine-tenths of those present were hostily disposed toward
him, and what was especially painful for me was that such a selfless
and genuine person was misunderstood. People are always so foolish
—they do not forget for one instant whose son he is and they make
comparisons—as if there could not be different people, each of whom
can be virtuous in their own way. On the same evening Willy Ro-
thaar [Wilhelm Ellenbogen] from the podium presumed to be the
experienced superior and treated the 35-year-old man as a youngster
whose nose he was wiping. . . . As Fritz stood amidst the hostile
excited crowd, I went up to him, congratulated him on his speech,
and declared myself in full agreement with him on all issues.[29]

In February or March 1915, Fritz was drafted into the Austrian Army.
He was released after thirteen days because of a heart problem. Fritz suffered

from myocarditis (an inflammation of the muscular tissue of the heart) that was diagnosed in 1911. However, his physician, Dr. Ludwig Braun, told him that his myocarditis was psychologically initiated. Fritz said at his trial that he vowed to himself at the time: "I will not shoot in war." Yet, being out of the big war, he prepared for his private war. Within a brief time of his release from the Austrian Army he took a decisive step in preparation to kill. On Easter, which in 1915 fell on April 4, Fritz, who had never used a weapon, bought a Browning automatic pistol. He said that he bought it in Zürich because handguns were forbidden in Austria and "since he just was in Zürich and happened to have the opportunity."[30] He tried three or four practice shots on a target in the store. He smuggled the pistol back into Austria and hid it behind his washstand.

Fritz's isolation mounted in the face of what he perceived as a "wall of indifference and cynicism" on the part of the party to the ever-increasing autocracy and injustice at home. The Prime Minister had prorogued the Parliament in March 1914 and never reconvened it. The irrationality of wartime censorship of the press was a daily aggravation to Fritz, the radical editor. His newspaper *Das Volk* was regularly confiscated. One issue of *Kampf* had twenty-five blank pages "courtesy of the censor."[31] The abrogation of the due process of law resulted in many judicial outrages and miscarriages of justice.

Fritz was offered two opportunities to escape Vienna and party conflict. At the time of his Easter 1915 trip to Zürich he was invited back to be chief editor of the *Volksrecht*. Karl Kautsky also asked him to assume the editorship of the *Neue Zeit* in Berlin. As Kautsky pointed out to him in his offer, Germany would give him a much larger field of action. Fritz admitted at his trial that he "could not tear myself loose from Austria, by this I mean *my* Austria, I could not break loose from the party I have loved since my childhood. . . . The tragedy in whose center I here stand is grounded in the fact *that I could not tear myself away from Austrian Social Democracy.*"[32] He could not leave Vienna, for the neurotic battle with himself had to be fought out on the territory of his father.

Fritz came to the conclusion that "a revolution in Austria could only be achieved against the Party Executive. The Party Executive was an agent inhibiting revolutionary movements." "It is only possible to achieve real revolutionary change in Austria *against* the Party Executive and in disregard of it to turn to the use of force to move against the government which rules by conditions of force."[33] Austria was disgraced by the lack of constitutional government and his party failed to use the right means to do anything about it.

Much of the hatred for his father was displaced in vehement attacks on Karl Renner, the leader of the moderate wing of the Socialist party, who was in many ways the spokesman for Victor Adler's parliamentary tactics. Fritz called Renner the representative of the spirit of "ingenuous lying" in the Social Democratic party. He was nothing more than "a Lueger of Social Democracy, who has brought into our party the spirit of unprincipledness and deception that one must be ashamed to be identified with." "Dr. Renner," said Fritz, "is a demagogue, but naturally a big demagogue, a very gifted demagogue, who knows how to present what he wants in a very clever form."[34]

Fritz's increasing rage and impatience were manifested at a Party Central Committee meeting on Thursday, October 19, 1916. Fritz and his father had a public confrontation which ended with Victor shouting at him: "You are so provocative, you obviously want to be thrown out!" On the next morning, Friday, October 20, it was announced that a forthcoming Sunday meeting of university professors of the law faculty arranged by Ludo Hartmann to call for a convocation of the Parliament had been banned by the Prime Minister. It was this event, by his own account, that resolved Fritz to kill Count Stürgkh the next day. His self-created isolation within the party came to a head during the meeting of the Party Executive on Friday night, October 20. Here again there was a sharp, acrimonious confrontation in which Fritz made personal charges against a number of party journalists and editors. He was called a "party destroyer [*Parteiverderber*]."* Although Fritz explicitly denied that this charge affected him, he also said at his trial that he was "extraordinarily excited" that night. He went home and worked a few hours, destroying letters he did not wish read by the police and arranging his papers. He recalled thinking: "This will be the last time that you sleep." The next morning Karl Seitz ran into him at party headquarters and said, "What you did was absolutely crazy." Fritz answered, "We'll talk about that yet."[35] From that conversation he went to kill Count Stürgkh.

Fritz chose Saturday, October 21, 1916, for the murder because, as he said, it would then make the Sunday newspapers on the twenty-second. He inquired where the Prime Minister took his lunch and found that "the whole city knew" that he always ate in the Hotel Meissl-Schadn. Fritz went to his office to clear up his work, then entered the hotel dining room at 1:30 p.m. He walked through the room, chose a table near Count Stürgkh, and ordered a large meal in order to calm his nerves. He noted a woman sitting at a table behind the Prime Minister and feared that if he missed his target he might hit her, so he waited seventy-five minutes until she left. After the Prime Minister had been served his post-prandial liqueur, Fritz walked over to the unprotected Count Stürgkh, aimed at his head, and fatally shot him three

*This is according to Karl Seitz; see *Friedrich Adler vor dem Ausnahmegericht, 18 und 19 Mai 1917*, ed. J. W. Brügel (Vienna, 1967), p. 288. Fritz recalled it as "Parteischädling"; see pp. 236–7.

times, shouting, "Down with Absolutism! We want Peace." A fourth shot went wild, slightly injuring two bystanders, who wrestled with him. Fritz feared that one of the German officers who were in the restaurant would run him through with a sword. When he was seized by his collar, had his glasses torn off, and saw a raised sword over him, he said, "I am Dr. Adler, I demand a court trial."[36] And he received one.

The historical setting and the attitude toward personal violence in wartime Austria of 1916 are so at variance with our contemporary world that the difference merits serious consideration. The possession of handguns without license was forbidden in Austria-Hungary. Friedrich Adler had to buy a revolver in Zürich and smuggle it over the Austrian border. When he sought his target, Adler had no difficulty because everyone in the capital knew that the Prime Minister took his midday meal in a well-known restaurant. He was unprotected and available for assassination because the murder of statesmen was not conceived as a realistic possibility. We have come far, and not necessarily for the better, in our "modern" expectations of civil and political murder in the intervening seven decades.

On learning of the assassination, Victor immediately organized an insanity defense. Father and son had their first encounter on the evening after the shooting at the Vienna city jail. Victor stared at his son and said, "What you have committed is vulgar assassination [*gemeiner Meuchelmord*]."[37]

A week after the assassination Fritz wrote Kathia from jail that he felt unexpectedly well in every way. Physically he was in a good state, had the heartiest appetite, and slept as in the best of times. He was in no way nervous or anxious; on the contrary, he was emotionally more contented and at peace than at any time since the war began. He was reading philosophy.

Fritz was brought to trial in May 1917. His father and the Socialist party attorneys presented the insanity defense they had prepared. The court-appointed university psychiatrists found Fritz in a state of mild manic excitability in jail. They pronounced him sane and responsible for his acts, which were explained by his psychopathic heredity, his personality, and the external circumstances. Fritz opened his speech before the tribunal saying that he felt the need to defend himself on two fronts—one against the state, the second against his own counsel, who would plead his non-accountability due to mental instability. He told the court that he knew he was going to his death. He had committed a carefully premeditated murder. "I carried out this deed in the full, clear consciousness that I was thereby ending my life. . . . I am convinced that no other verdict may be delivered than death by hanging."[38]

Fritz told the court of his identification with his father as a hero-lawbreaker in two contiguous associations. He noted that the last political trial before a special tribunal in Vienna was the trial of his father in 1889 when he was *exactly as old as Fritz* now was (age thirty-seven). Fritz was explicitly telling the world that this was for him an anniversary of great personal significance. Anniversaries have unconscious meanings of identification, immortality, and undoing, all of which were present in Fritz's case.* His age-specific comparison with his father shows his immediate view of himself—ever the boy, always comparing, repeating, emulating—and yet in his own mind never quite living up to the ideal. As if to confirm these feelings of identification and comparison, Fritz's next association in his trial statement is: "I came to know this building very well at that time and *now exercise in the same jail yard where my father walked*" (emphasis in original).[39] For Fritz, to be before a court on this anniversary in the name of the proletarian cause was fulfilling a personal time-specific destiny of living up to his internal ideal of what it meant to be a man, a hero, a success, and an Adler. Invoking the memory of his father as a defendant in the same courtroom was now also a source of strength and reparation for the time when he was a ten-year-old boy and so hostile to, and rivalrous with, his father that he wished for him to be incarcerated for twenty years. Now Fritz is affirming: I am no longer the bad boy who wishes to displace his father. At last I am a success in my own eyes. I have done what he has done, and have topped him. I have acted out murderous impulses that he only fantasied and repressed, and I have gotten his backing in my defense.

Fritz was found guilty and sentenced to death on May 19, 1917. His sentence was later commuted to eighteen years of fortress imprisonment. He was freed by Kaiser Karl on November 1, 1918, as the Habsburg monarchy was in dissolution. Victor Adler died on November 10 just as the war ended and the Provisional National Assembly had named him the first Social Democratic Foreign Minister in Austrian history.

Fritz emerged from captivity a hero to both Bolsheviks and Socialists. He had met the father-tyrant, slain him, and come back to tell of it. The *Arbeiter-Zeitung* greeted him on his release as a "Hero and Martyr." He was invited to head a new Austrian Communist party in the expectation that he would lead a Bolshevik revolution in Austria, which he refused to do. In January 1919, Lenin and Trotsky invited him to be Honorary Secretary of the Third International, which he also declined. His historic role in Austria was to keep the Communists in check and hold off a workers revolution. He

*There is a rich psychoanalytical literature on the power of anniversary phenomena. See George Pollock, "Temporal Anniversary Manifestations: Hour, Day, Holiday," *Psychoanalytic Quarterly*, 40 (1971): 123–31; "On Time, Death, and Immortality," *Psychoanalytic Quarterly*, 40 (1971), 435–46; "On Time and Anniversaries," in *The Unconscious Today: Essays in Honor of Max Schur*, ed. Mark Kanzer (New York, 1972), pp. 233–57; George L. Engel, "The Death of a Twin: Mourning and Anniversary Reactions. Fragments of 10 Years of Self-Analysis," *International Journal of Psycho-Analysis*, 56 (1975): 23–40. The assassination of Robert F. Kennedy by Sirhan Sirhan was a homicide on the anniversary of the Six-Day War.

took a middle position, favoring the unity of the left and reunion of the Second and Third Internationals. This made him a minority in the Second International in an unsuccessful fight against the purging of the Bolsheviks. In 1920 Adler resigned from the Second International and in 1921 tried to organize an International "2 1/2" to bridge the two working-class positions. When this failed he returned to the Second International, which elected him its secretary in 1923 and which he guided until its demise in 1940.

With the foregoing life history the reader would be justified in expecting Fritz to have ended his career in further impulsive and self-destructive behavior. This, however, was not the case. After his release he functioned as an integrated personality in the most stressful and responsible situations. He was not impulsive, he was not violent or visibly acting out unconscious conflict. He guided the Second International in the 1920's and 1930's as Secretary of the International Bureau in Brussels, which in the 1920's meant coordinating conferences, conducting correspondence between the parties, traveling to meetings, discussions, and forums. It was a tedious, menial, frustrating, thankless, and inglorious series of tasks. Yet he performed well, was judicious in his proposals, and took an accurate measure of the possible.

His work in the 1930's included aid and rescue activities on behalf of German and Austrian socialist leaders. The workers movement was in defeat and dissolution. These were the darkest days in the history of Social Democracy. He failed to get Robert Danneberg out of the concentration camp at Dachau; he did not manage to get Käthe Leichter out of Ravensbrück. His appeals for intercessions went to the British Home Office and various dignitaries and refugee relief committees in the free world, such as the Austrian Solidarity Committee and the Relief Committee for Victims of German fascism. His appeals to English aristocrats for aid in rescuing Austrian socialist intellectuals make heart rending reading.[40]

Adler moved out of Brussels one jump ahead of the German armies in 1940. In southern France he was issued an American "danger visa" through the good offices of the American Federation of Labor. He and Kathia arrived in New York on October 26, 1940. He founded and chaired the Labor Aid Project, which was endowed with $70,000 by the AF of L and the CIO to engage in refugee rescue work. He secured additional funds from the Jewish Labor Committee and the International Refugee and Rescue Committee to further his work in New York during the war. In 1946 he returned to Europe to settle in Zürich.

Fritz devoted the last years of his life to editing his father's letters. In 1954 he published the major correspondence with Bebel and Kautsky. This was viewed as a preparation for a biography of his father that was never completed. The attraction to his remote father was as strong as ever, but emotional obstacles to finishing were too great. He wrote to Ellenbogen: "I

realized more and more how much I do not know that is absolutely necessary in order to give an accurate but not too diffuse a picture."[41]

What explanation can we offer for the integration of his personality and
the apparent resolution of major conflicts? Acting out murderous fantasies
does not usually contribute to an adaptive resolution of life's problems. In
this case the killing of the symbolic bad father was cathartic and curative
because Fritz for a short time successfully displaced intrafamilial aggression
to a political figure with the highest moral rationalizations—namely, peace,
democracy, and socialism. In his trial he was able to attack both Austrian
autocracy and his father's political tactics. His act of assassination was the
"successful" neurotic compromise formation par excellence: he chose the
mode most abhorrent to his father's politics—terror—to try to achieve his
father's professed life aims: international solidarity and an end to the war.
Fritz's resort to violence acted out what Victor had painfully expunged from
himself and his party. We see in Fritz becoming a murderer the return of
the repressed in the next generation. The father's ambivalence toward violence, as for instance manifested by having almost shot his wife, was communicated to the son and carried as a secret unarticulated unconscious
message that an alternative course to politics is the personally violent resolution of conflict. Adelaide M. Johnson has delineated how children may act
out the forbidden antisocial and repressed impulses of their parents, including murder. She sees this as the result of a superego defect or "lacuna" in
the parent which is passed to the child by conscious and unconscious messages and behavior indicating that unsanctioned behavior is an attractive
forbidden alternative in the parent's mind. The hidden suggestion is a cue
and a provocation which may lead to acting it out by the child. The child's
delinquency gives vicarious gratification to the parent as well as providing
a scapegoat for the parent's own antisocial impulses.[42]

The ability to be apparently anxiety-free after the assassination indicates
what an axial experience of destruction and resolution Fritz had undergone.
Now he had become a man in his own right by acting against one of the most
powerful men in Austria. The only way for Fritz to gain autonomy and
independence was to kill the father figure. In doing so, for the first time in
his life, he took the initiative in the relationship with his father. Now Fritz
was the leader and Victor was compelled to come to his aid, albeit angrily,
rather than be his accuser or jailer. For a brief moment he surpassed his
father's eminence and occupied center stage in the affairs of the world. His
father had discouraged him from taking initiatives to test himself. Now he
drew his father in his wake along a course he charted and was able to
repudiate both his father's politics and his proffered legal defense.

Fritz literally lived out death and rebirth in courting a capital verdict,
being sentenced to die, and emerging as a hero in a new world. He was

historically proven "right" and the old Empire and its war were "wrong." He unconsciously designed his persecution, martyrdom, symbolic death, and resurrection. His bloody attack against the Prime Minister was a suicidal search for persecution. He sought it and provoked it, so that he could glory in what the late D. W. Winnicott called the "delicious simplification of a persecutory position."[43]

Fritz was able to view himself as both victim and hero and to feel exonerated by the disastrous course of the war for Austria-Hungary as 1916 turned into 1917 and the Habsburg Empire literally fell to pieces. By 1918 he was validated by mass public opinion which opposed the war and Empire and which gave him and his position moral and political support.

After his father died things went well for Fritz. He had passed the crisis of autonomy and independence that should be weathered in adolescence. Instead of meeting that crisis in late adolescence, he remained dependent and rebellious. Winnicott's thoughts are relevant:

> If, in the fantasy of early growth, there is contained *death,* then at adolescence there is contained *murder.* Even when growth at the period of puberty goes ahead without major crises, one may need to deal with acute problems of management because growing up means taking the parent's place. *It really does.* In the unconscious fantasy, growing up is inherently an aggressive act. And the child is now no longer child-size. . . . If the child is to become adult, then this move is achieved over the dead body of an adult. . . . In the total unconscious fantasy belonging to growth at puberty and adolescence, there is the *death of someone.* [Emphasis in the original.][44]

For Fritz the dependency of adolescence was so great and the fantasied aggression against his father so awesome that it was not faced until his mid-thirties—then it came with the lethal violence of murder, not in fantasy, but in deadly actuality in conjuncture with the political and moral stress of the Socialist movement and the violence of World War I.

Until the end of his life Fritz was in thrall to his father. At age sixty-nine he still protested his absolute fealty to Victor:

> My entire youth consisted in an absolute *identification* with the politics of my father, and that only changed when the World War sharpened the contradictions. But even there—and this only by the way—the contradictions rose not from an "Oedipus complex," as the armchair psychoanalyst fancies, rather the contrary, the hardest thing in this period was that I had to defend my position *also* against my father, with whom I always felt absolute solidarity. [Emphasis in the original.][45]

Fritz was of course correct about his identification with his father. The proof of his lifelong immature dependency and underlying rebellion lies in his pathetic need, at the end of his life, to proclaim total loyalty to his father —lest the murderous rage again break through—as it did one wartime day in 1916.

Notes

1. Robert Michels, *Political Parties: A Sociological Study of the Oligarchical Tendencies of Modern Democracy* (1911), trans. Eden and Cedar Paul (New York, 1915); Carl E. Schorske, *German Social Democracy, 1905–1917: The Development of the Great Schism* (Cambridge, Mass., 1955); Susanne Miller, *Burgfrieden und Klassenkampf: Die deutsche Sozialdemokratie im ersten Weltkrieg* (Düsseldorf, 1974); Herbert Steiner, "Am Beispiel Otto Bauers–die Oktoberrevolution und der Austromarxismus," *Weg und Ziel* (July 1967), Sondernummer, 21: 3–22; *Käthe Leichter: Leben und Werk,* ed. Herbert Steiner (Vienna, 1973); Felix Kreissler, *Von der Revolution zur Annexion: Österreich 1918 bis 1938* (Vienna, 1970); Ernst Fischer, *Erinnerungen und Reflexionen* (Hamburg, 1969); Anson Rabinbach, "Ernst Fischer and the Left Opposition in Austrian Social Democracy: The Crisis of Austrian Socialism, 1927–1934" (unpublished Ph.D. dissertation, University of Wisconsin, 1973); Joseph Buttinger, *In the Twilight of Socialism: A History of the Revolutionary Socialists of Austria* (New York, 1953); Karl Renner, *An der Wende zweier Zeiten: Lebenserinnerungen* (Vienna, 1946); Adam Wandruszka, "Das sozialistische Lager," in *Geschichte der Republik Österreich,* ed. Heinrich Benedikt, (Vienna, 1954), pp. 422–79; Eric C. Kollman, *Theodor Körner: Militär und Politik* (Vienna, 1973); Norbert Leser, *Zwischen Reformismus und Bolschewismus: Der Austromarxismus als Theorie und Praxis* (Vienna, 1968).

2. Julius Braunthal, *Victor und Friedrich Adler: Zwei Generationen Arbeiterbewegung* (Vienna, 1965), p. 90.

3. Ronald P. Florence, "Victor Adler: The Making of a Socialist" (unpublished Ph.D. dissertation, Harvard University, 1968), pp. 15–16.

4. Adler to Pernerstorfer, April 4, 1971, as quoted in William J. McGrath, "The Telyn Society," in *Dionysian Art and Populist Politics in Austria* (New Haven, 1974), p. 25.

5. Sigmund Freud, "The Interpretation of Dreams" (1900), *Standard Edition of the Complete Psychological Works,* trans. and ed. James Strachey et al. (London, 1953–1974), 4: 212–13.

6. Freud to Julie Braun-Vogelstein, Oct. 30, 1927, in "A Letter by Sigmund Freud with Recollections of His Adolescence," ed. Martin Grotjahn and Suzanne C. Bernfeld, *Journal of the American Psychoanalytic Association,* 4 (1956): 645.

7. Emma Adler, "Biographie Victor Adlers," unpublished manuscript (1930), Archive of the Swedish Worker's Movement, Stockholm, p. 183; Victor Adler to Karl Kautsky, Aug. 21, 1886, in *Victor Adler Briefwechsel mit August Bebel und Karl Kautsky,* ed. Friedrich Adler (Vienna, 1954), p. 13.

8. Hans Mommsen, *Die Sozialdemokratie und die Nationalitätenfrage im habsburgischen Vielvolkerstaat* (Vienna, 1963), pp. 128–54. See also "Victor Adlers Weg zum Sozialismus," in Mommsen, *Arbeiterbewegung und Nationale Frage: Ausgewählte Aufsätze* (Göttingen, 1979), pp. 180–94.

9. Braunthal, p. 47.

10. Emma Adler, "Biographie," p. 164.

11. Victor Adler at his trial, Nov. 12, 1895, in *Aufsätze, Reden und Briefe,* ed. Gustav Pollatscher (Vienna, 1922–29), 2: 219.

12. Emma Adler, "Biographie," p. 168, Braunthal, p. 182.

13. *Friedrich Adler vor dem Ausnahmegericht, 18 und 19 Mai 1917,* ed. J. W. Brügel (Vienna, 1967), pp. 162–3, 176.

14. Braunthal, pp. 182–3.

15. *Ibid.*, pp. 183, 185.

16. *Ibid.*, pp. 184–5.

17. *Ibid.*, p. 187.

18. *Ibid.*, p. 193. For an Eriksonian interpretation of this phase of his life, see Rudolf G. Ardelt, "Friedrich Adler: Probleme der Identitäsbildung," in *Bewegung und Klasse: Studien zur Österreichischen Arbeitergeschichte,* ed. G. Botz, H. Hautmann, H. Konrad, and J. Weidenholzer (Vienna, 1978), pp. 63–87.

19. Braunthal, p. 187.

20. Friedrich Adler to the Zürich Board of Education as quoted in Ronald W. Clark, *Einstein: The Life and Times* (New York, 1971), p. 127.

21. Kathia to Victor Adler, June 23, 1910, *ibid.*, pp. 135–6.

22. Friedrich to Victor Adler, Sept. 23, 1910, *ibid.*, p. 136.

23. Victor Adler, "Die Partei: und die Internationale" (1914), *Aufsätze,* 9: 165. See also Hans Mommsen, "Viktor Adler und die Politik der Österreichischen Sozialdemokratie im Ersten Weltkrieg," in *Politik und Gesellschaft im Alten und Neuen Österreich,* ed. Isabella Ackerl et al. (Vienna, 1981), pp. 378–408.

24. Leon Trotsky, *My Life: An Attempt at an Autobiography* (New York, 1970), p. 235. For Victor Adler as a German nationalist, see McGrath, *Dionysian Art,* pp. 165–72, 208–10; Robert S. Wistrich, *Revolutionary Jews from Marx to Trotsky* (London, 1976), pp. 98–114.

25. Victor Adler, "Um den 4 August" (1914), *Aufsätze,* 9: 106, 107; *Friedrich Adler vor dem Ausnahmegericht,* p. 170; Braunthal, p. 214.

26. Psychiatric report of Drs. Hövel and Bischoff, Nov. 20, 1916, Vienna, S.D. Parteistellan, Inventor 81, Karton 10, Adler Prozess, Vr. xxxiv 6441 / 16, Österreichisches Staatsarchiv, Allgemeines Verwaltungsarchiv, Vienna, p. 35. Courtesy of Douglas D. Alder.

27. See Freud, "A Special Type of Choice of Object Made by Men" (1910), *Standard Edition,* 11: 163–75.

28. Emma Adler, "Biographie," p. 206.

29. Emma Adler to Karl Kautsky, Oct. 27, 1914, *Kautsky Nachlass,* K D I, no. 62, International Institute for Social History, Amsterdam. Due to wartime censorship, Emma did not use proper names.

30. Dr. Ludwig Braun as cited in Mark E. Blum, "The 'Austro-Marxists' Karl Renner, Otto Bauer, Max Adler, and Friedrich Adler and 'Austro-Marxism' in Austria, 1890 to 1918: A Study of the Politics of Metaphor" (unpublished Ph.D. dissertation, University of Pennsylvania, 1970), p. 419, n. 73; *Friedrich Adler vor dem Ausnahmegericht,* pp. 167, 214.

31. *Ibid.*, pp. 136–7, 181.

32. *Ibid.*, pp. 268–9.

33. *Ibid.*, pp. 24, 128.

34. *Ibid.*, pp. 96, 126.

35. *Ibid.*, pp. 181–2, 228, 233.

36. *Ibid.*, pp. 104, 167, 217–18.

37. Emma Adler, "Biographie," p. 203.

38. "Das Gutachten der medizinischen Fakultät," *Friedrich Adler vor dem Ausnahmegericht,* pp. 66–7. See also Douglas D. Alder, "Assassination as Political Efficiency: Two Case Studies from World War I," *East European Quarterly,* 12 (1978): 209–31; "Friedrich Adler: Evaluation of a Revolutionary," *German Studies Review* (October, 1978): 260–84.

39. *Friedrich Adler vor dem Ausnahmegericht,* p. 163.

40. See, for example, the International Department, Labour Party Archives, Transport House, London, concerning Käthe Leichter; Otto Bauer to Friedrich Adler, July 3, 1937, Auslandsbüro österreiche Sozialisten (ALÖS), International Institute for Social History, Amsterdam.

41. Braunthal, p. 322.

42. Adelaide M. Johnson, "Sanctions for Superego Lacunae of Adolescents," in *Searchlights on Delinquency,* ed. K. R. Eissler (New York, 1949, 1963), pp. 225–45.

43. D. W. Winnicott, "Contemporary Concepts of Adolescent Development and Their Implications for Higher Education" (1968), in *Playing and Reality* (London, 1974), p. 174.

44. *Ibid.*, pp. 169–70.

45. Friedrich Adler to Benedikt Kautsky, March 10, 1948, as quoted in Braunthal, pp. 188–9.

Austro-Marxism and Revolution

*Otto Bauer, Freud's "Dora" Case,
and the Crises of the First Austrian Republic*

Movements, like individuals, are not always conscious of what they are really doing or what they truly want. As with individuals, the actions of groups, including the kinds of leaders they choose and support, are a clearer indication of group intentions than the pious words of manifestos and party declarations. What people and groups do tells us more of what they are about than does what they profess to want. Movements tend to choose leaders whose character is compatible with their organizational and ideological goals. This phenomenon has been analyzed by Erik Erikson, who interprets it from the psychodynamic perspective, W. R. Bion from group dynamic observation, and Robert Michels from an institutional viewpoint with particular relevance to socialism.[1]

In the case of Austrian Social Democracy the words were of violence, revolution, and a new world, but the reality was of accommodation and use of the parliamentary system and integration into bourgeois social values and cultural norms. Otto Bauer (1881–1938), the parliamentary leader and major Austro-Marxist theorist of the First Austrian Republic, was the personification of the ambivalence of Social Democracy in the 1920's and 1930's. Bauer's personality was syntonic with the political strategy of militant ideology and meliorist tactics that was the tradition of Austrian socialism.

Bauer's political strategy provided comfort and consolation for the working class rather than mobilization for struggle. We need to ask what psychological function such an ideological position filled and what role it played in Bauer's emotional life. And why did the Austro-Marxist movement choose as a leader such a highly ambivalent obsessional as Otto Bauer? The answer, clearly, does not lie in leadership studies alone. Ambivalence on the issues of revolutionary action is an integral part of the modern Social Democratic heritage. Ambivalent movements tend to choose ambivalent leaders who act out the party's conflict. Otto Bauer's behavior and his process of decision making in specific crises tells us much about the personified ambivalence of the group who chose and supported him as party leader, for Bauer led his movement during all four—1918/19, 1927, 1933, and 1934—crises of the First Austrian Republic. No figure typifies the struggles —the dilemmas, the inconsistencies, and the tragedies—of embattled Austro-Marxism better than Bauer.

In the case of Otto Bauer we also have the unique advantage of an excellent clinical study and family history of the interpersonal dynamics of his childhood and youth by none other than Sigmund Freud. Bauer's sister, Ida (1882–1945), achieved anonymous fame as Freud's "Dora," making this the only case on record in which a political career can be related to the clinical data from a psychoanalysis.* Bauer's father, Philipp, was a prosperous

---

*The first scholarly identification of "Dora" was by Mark E. Blum, "The 'Austro-Marxists' Karl Renner, Otto Bauer, Max Adler, and Friedrich Adler and 'Austro-Marxism' in Austria, 1890 to 1918: A Study of the Politics of Metaphor" (unpublished Ph.D. dissertation, University of Pennsylvania, 1970) p. 208 n. 23. Blum, however, cites no documentation or source other than the Ernest Jones biography of Freud, which identifies "Dora" as "the sister of [a] Socialist leader," but "cannot disclose her name." *The Life and Work of Sigmund Freud,* vol. 1 (New York, 1953) p. 362 n. h. Just how successful the psychological incognito was is demonstrated by John Murray Cuddihy's erroneous identification of "Dora" as the daughter of Victor Adler. *The Ordeal of Civility: Freud, Marx, Lévi-Strauss and the Jewish Struggle with Modernity* (New York, 1974), pp. 45–6 n. "Dora's" identity as Ida Bauer was hinted at in clues in the psychoanalytic literature. Freud presents rich biographical data: The brother is one and a half years older; the father is a "large manufacturer in very comfortable circumstances," who had tuberculosis necessitating residence "in one of our southern provinces," and who "had to go through a course of treatment in a darkened room on account of a detached retina"; the mother is a compulsive house cleaner. "Fragment of an Analysis of a Case of Hysteria" (1905), *Standard Edition of the Complete Psychological Works,* ed. and trans. James Strachey et al. (London, 1953–1974), 7: 18–20. Felix Deutsch, in the report on his 1922 clinical follow-up of the "Dora" case, describes "her brother who had become the leader of a political party," was "also a 'chain smoker,' " and "died much later from coronary disease in Paris where he had escaped under the most adventurous circumstances. He was buried there with the highest honors." "A Footnote to Freud's 'Fragment of an Analysis of a Case of Hysteria,' " *Psychoanalytic Quarterly,* 26 (1957): 161, 167. The document conclusively establishing "Dora's" identity as Ida Bauer appeared in Los Angeles, in a letter by Kurt Eissler to Hannah Fenichel, July 8, 1952, now in the

factory owner with textile mills in Náchod and Warnsdorf in northern Bohemia, and his mother, née Käthe Gerber, also came from Bohemia. Their only other child was Ida, who, like her father, became Freud's patient. The Bauer family lived in Freud's immediate neighborhood in Vienna's Ninth District, literally just around the corner from the Berggasse, at Liechtensteinstrasse 32. Otto and Ida grew up in Königinhof in Bohemia, in Vienna, and in Merano in the Austrian Tyrol, where the father went for a tubercular cure. Otto graduated from the *Gymnasium* in Reichenberg as first of his class *(Primus)*. He studied law, became a Marxist while still a student, and soon became the secretary to the founder and leader of the Austrian Social Democratic Worker's party, Victor Adler.

Both of his parents spoke Czech as a second mother tongue and Otto learned it at home. The family was Jewish. It is significant for Otto Bauer's Jewish identity that he never formally disaffiliated from the Jewish religion even though to be "non-confessional" was a standard expectation of all socialist functionaries and leaders.* Ernst Fischer relates that when he asked Bauer about his continued affiliation with the Jewish community, Bauer replied: "You cannot understand that, since no one ever muttered 'dirty Jew' behind your back."[2]

No issue was more central to Social Democracy and more critical to the life of the Habsburg state before World War I than the issue of nationality. The House of Habsburg postulated a dynastic loyalty which was prenational and which could not compete with the ascendant new nationalisms of the Czechs, Croats, Slovenes, Slovaks, Serbs, Jews, Ruthenians, Rumanians, Italians, Germans, and Poles. These modern nationalisms eventually tore the Austro-Hungarian state apart. The issue of nationalism was the leading concern of Austro-Marxist theorists and one of the grounds on which they were challenged by the Bolsheviks of the Marxist left.

---

possession of the Sigmund Freud Archives, Library of Congress. I am indebted to Dr. Alfred Goldberg for sharing this essential document with me prior to committing it to the archives. "Dora's" identity was independently confirmed in interviews with Professor Marie Jahoda (Brighton, Sussex), July 27, 1972; Dr. Hilde Hannak (Vienna), Sept. 22, 1973; and Professor Paul Lazarsfeld (New York), May 23, 1975.

*Otto Bauer was in the Voting Register of the Vienna Jewish Community for the elections of 1920 and 1924, which proves that he paid his Jewish communal taxes. He did not exercise his franchise. In his voting district, the Sixth District of Vienna, 657 persons voted of 1,179 eligible voters. In 1920 Bauer was listed as *"Nationalrat-Redakteur,"* in 1924 his occupation was *"Industrieller-Nationalrat."* In both registrations his address was Kasernengasse 2; for 1920, for 1924, Fifth Ward, p. 5. *Steueramt Israelitische Kultusgemeinde Wien,* Jewish Historical General Archive, Ohaleh Josef Depository, Jerusalem. I am indebted to archivist Dr. Absalom Hodik for aid in making these documents accessible to me. The police record of the search of Bauer's apartment on Feb. 14, 1934, lists him as "non-confessional." *Dokumentationsarchiv des Österreichischen Widerstandes,* Vienna. However, this was not information volunteered by Bauer. It was recorded by the police after his escape. Otto Leichter, *Otto Bauer: Tragödie oder Triumph* (Vienna, 1970).

The formal Austrian Social Democratic position on nationalities enunciated at Brünn in 1899 called for a democratic federation of nationalities with autonomous self-administration of national affairs by legislative chambers elected by equal and direct franchise. The first Social Democrat to systematically analyze the nationalities question and to propose a comprehensive legal solution was Karl Renner (1870–1950). Renner's works on the nationalities question had to be published under pseudonyms because he was the librarian of the Austrian Parliament, i.e., a government official. As early as 1899 he wrote *Zur österreichischen Nationalitätenfrage* and *Staat und Nation*. His work of 1902, *Der Kampf der österreichischen Nationen um den Staat*, offered a supraregional personal definition of nationalism which was not bound to any territory. He envisioned a dual nationality for each person, one the general state administration and the other a "national" administration of cultural affairs based on personal choice analogous to a religious confession. Belonging to a "nation" should be a matter of free choice which would, under Renner's plan, be declared and enrolled in a nationality register. Thus each nation might constitute a majority in one area and a minority in others. He wrote in 1906:

> We must organize the country according to two principles. We must put a double network on the map, an economic and an ethnic one. We must cut across the functions of the state. We must separate national and political affairs, we must organize the population twice, once nationally and once according to administrative requirements. In either case the territorial units will be different.[3]

Whereas Renner's approach was to the political and legal issues of nationality, Bauer's focus was social and cultural. Bauer's book of 1907, *Die Nationalitätenfrage und die Sozialdemokratie*, was his most original contribution to socialist thought and the most lastingly significant of his writings. This book first made Bauer famous at age twenty-six. He elaborated on Renner's nationalities program, but his definition of a nation was modern even by late-twentieth-century standards. To Bauer, the nation was a community of fate (*"Schicksalsgemeinschaft"*), which he defined as "the collective experience of the same fate [*gemeinsames Erleben desselben Schicksals*]." This common fate, in turn, shapes a commonality of character, and frequent intercourse demands a common language. Said Bauer: "Among people with whom I share a language, I also share intimacy." To Bauer, the most important variable was a common history. It is this, he said, which determines all the other elements of a nation, such as territory, race, language, customs, religion, and finally the character of a people itself. A nation is the totality of the persons bound by a community of fate to a common character.[4]

In his chapter "The National Autonomy of the Jews," Bauer comes to grips with Jewish nationalism and his own Jewish identity. He places the social-economic position of the Jews in the context of a growing money economy in an eastern European peasant society. The Jews are in the process of assimilation to the languages, mores, and culture of the peoples among whom they live; they are no longer a nation. The bourgeoisie and intelligentsia are the classes that are most assimilated among the Jews. The Jews are *"a people without a history,"* for they no longer possess the culture-bearing classes.[5] Because of this their culture is stultified, the Jewish language is lost, there is no national literature. The nineteenth century has brought all the peoples hitherto without a history to new life. Will, Bauer asks, the twentieth century give the Jewish nation the possibility of a new, autonomous cultural development? His answer is no, it will not! In this context of the Habsburg nationalities question, Bauer takes his clearest position on a Jewish identity, anti-Semitism, and Zionism. Here we find his explicit answer to the Jewish nationalism of Theodor Herzl. He in fact cites the Zionist newspaper, *Die Welt,* of August 10, 1906, to prove how assimilated the Jews of Vilna were at the time. He also devoted attention to the national movement of the Jews, Zionism, which he noted had stimulated feelings of pride and personal worth among the lower classes in contrast to previous inferiority feelings among Jewish workers.

Bauer always used the perspective of comparison with the Czech nation as his standard when writing about the Jewish national question. He believed that the geographically contiguous territory and density of the mass of the Czech population made their national revival possible. Here, according to Bauer, lay the critical variable distinguishing the Czechs from the Jews: the Jews possessed no self-contained territory of settlement which could serve as a base, a homeland to demographically and culturally maintain their communities elsewhere. It might seem that this line of reasoning should lead Bauer to a Zionist conclusion. However, his conclusion was that Europe's Jews were moving into ever closer contact with surrounding peoples and the dynamic of capitalist development would not let them become a nation. Economics tied the Jews and Gentiles within a given land closer to each other than it did Jews of various areas. A Jewish (Yiddish) culture and an independent school system would be counter to the interests of the Jewish worker, as he needed free mobility more than anyone. To this end the Jewish worker ought to change his speech, appearance, and dress so as not to be offensive to his Christian class comrades. Bauer depreciates Jewish culture as irrelevant to the modern world. Jews have the culture of "a nation without a history [*einer geschichtslosen Nation*]" and "the psychology of a dead economic system [*Psychologie einer toten Wirtschaftsverfassung*]." A prescription Bauer looked forward to was intermarriage, "a mixing of Jewish blood with the bloods of the other nations." "The courtship of young men and the choices of young women will decide this last of all Jewish questions," he said. "Only then will the special Jewish misery disappear, and there will be only common proletarian misery, which the Jew will fight and conquer in common struggle, shoulder to shoulder with his Aryan colleagues." Robert Wistrich astutely criticizes Bauer for "an element of emotional prejudice, perhaps even anti-Semitism," in his denial to Jews "of elementary rights which he conceded to other national minorities." He also sees Bauer as imbued with racial categories of thought (such as repeated polarization of "Aryan" and "Jew") which were common in the early-twentieth-century popular consciousness.[6]

Bauer's ideas on nationality were the target of a critique by V. I. Lenin in 1913. Lenin, who objected to Bauer's "psychological theses" on nationalism, perceived and exploited the paradox of Bauer denying the Jews national autonomy when, by his own criterion of a commonality of fate, Jews should qualify as a nation. Lenin pointed out that while Bauer devoted a whole chapter of his book to prove that his program of cultural national autonomy "cannot possibly be proposed for the Jews," this is in fact exactly what the Jewish Bundists were proposing in Russia. "What does this go to show?" asked Lenin. "It goes to show that history, through the political practice of another state, has exposed the absurdity of Bauer's invention. . . ."[7]

There was a more intensive and detailed attack on Bauer from a protégé of Lenin's. In February 1912, Lenin wrote to Maxim Gorky of "a wonderful Georgian who has undertaken to write a long article for *Prosveshchenie* after gathering all Austrian and other materials." Lenin's "wonderful Georgian" was, of course, Josef Stalin ("Koba"), who spent six weeks in Cracow and Vienna in 1913, the longest stay abroad of his entire life. Stalin's attack highlighted the inconsistencies of Bauer's position on the Jews, which included definitions of a nation as a "community of character" and a "community of fate," while excluding territory, language, or economic life as criteria of nationhood. Stalin accused Bauer of the capital offense of idealism: "What then distinguishes Bauer's nation from the mystical and self-contained 'national spirit' of the spiritualists? . . . Bauer is obviously confusing *nation,* which is a historical category, with *tribe,* which is an ethnographical category. . . . Bauer wanted to prove that the Jewish workers cannot demand national autonomy, but he thereby inadvertently refuted his own theory." Stalin noted the irrationality of Bauer's argument and exploited it relentlessly. Stalin pointed out that in the beginning of his book Bauer called the Jews a nation, only to deny it later; in one place he said territory is not a prerequisite of nationhood, then he enumerated a closed territory of settlement as a condition of nationality; early in Bauer's arguments language is irrelevant, while in the end no nation is possible without a common language. As Stalin said with characteristic bluntness: "Bauer . . . inadvertently proved something he did not mean to prove, namely the groundlessness of his own theory of nations. . . . this theory, stitched together by idealistic threads, refutes itself."[8]

Bauer's analysis of the problems of nationalism was weak in its treatment of the Jewish question, but was not deserving of such wholesale castigation as it received from the Bolsheviks. Bauer's work was more comprehensive and subtle than any previous approach to the subject. It was most modern in its sensitivity to issues of community of character (*"Charaktergemein-schaft"*) and a national identity shaped by shared historical traumas which he termed a common fate (*"Schicksalsgemeinschaft"*). He offered a complex and inclusive treatment that, much to the discomfort of vulgar Marxists, included such psychological variables as shared experiences and shared childhood socialization. It is when he applied these principles to the Jews that he suddenly became insensitive and inconsistent, thus betraying that it was on the issue of his own national identity that he experienced ambivalence and conflict.

Bauer was called up as an officer of the reserve the day after Austria declared war against Serbia in 1914; he fought well and served the Habsburg Empire loyally. Like the majority of socialists in Central Europe, he feared that a Russian victory would bring a Tsarist autocracy many times worse than the autocracy of Austria. Although he was only a lieutenant, he was named company commander of the 9th Company, 75th Austrian Infantry Regiment, on the Eastern Front. He wrote to Karl Seitz: "I have four officers under me and three times as many men as a captain commands in peacetime." Soon he was promoted to first lieutenant. On November 23, 1914, his troops fled and he found himself with only four men being stormed by thirty Russians. "Since we did not wish to die pointlessly," he wrote to his wife, "we surrendered."[9] He was decorated with the Golden Cross of Merit by the Austrian Empire.

Bauer was interned in a prisoner-of-war camp at Troizkosavsk, near the Mongolian border. He kept busy by studying mathematics. After the outbreak of the February 1917 revolution in Russia, Victor Adler made efforts through the Swedish Socialist leader, Hjalmar Branting, to have Bauer exchanged. In July 1917 these appeals were successful and he was released. Bauer spent several weeks in St. Petersburg observing the revolution, and in September 1917 he was returned to Vienna.

A few weeks after his arrival in Vienna, Bauer, under the name Heinrich Weber,* penned a justification for socialist participation in the war in the

---

Weber means weaver. Since a choice of name is never random, we may ask whether in Bauer's case this was an identification with Gerhart Hauptmann's play of social protest, *Die Weber* (1892), which describes the plight of Silesian weavers who revolted in 1844. It was also, of course, a more immediate identification with the exploited weavers in Bauer's father's factories.

context of urging international proletarian support for the current Russian government of Kerensky. His point was that in 1914 support of the war was reasonable, but in October 1917 Russia was already a model for Europe in proletarian solidarity, in land distribution, and in instituting the eight-hour workday. "As the war broke out in the year 1914, workers of all lands rushed to the front to defend their fatherland. With weapons in their hands they protected their fatherland against invasion of the foreign foe, their economies against the danger that defeat in war could inflict on them. This was . . . to our mind the right and the duty of the workers of all lands."[10] With Adler's death in 1918, Bauer became a major leader of the party together with Karl Seitz and Robert Danneberg. In the new Austrian Republic's first coalition government, Bauer was Foreign Minister under the Social Democratic Chancellor, Karl Renner.

The three chief characteristics of Bauer's political style were indecisiveness in action, brilliance in theory, and the capacity to inspire a devoted following among both the socialist youth, who were often of bourgeois origin, and the workers. There was always a discordance between his words and his actions. His pattern of behavior is virtually exactly described in Freud's phenomenology of the obsessional neurotic:

> *Doubt* makes itself felt in the intellectual field and little by little it begins to gnaw even at what is usually most certain. The whole position ends up in an ever-increasing degree of indecision, loss of energy and restriction of freedom. At the same time, the obsessional neurotic starts off with a very energetic disposition, he is often extraordinarily self-willed and as a rule he has intellectual gifts above the average. He has usually reached a satisfactorily high level of ethical development; he exhibits over-conscientiousness, and is more than ordinarily correct in his behavior.[11]

Bauer's formal thought was revolutionary, his operational tactics avoided violence at all cost. Bauer's strategy of revolutionary theory and tactical political inactivity in day-to-day politics was, of course, within a historical tradition of European socialism. It was consistent with the antirevolutionary policies of his political mentor Victor Adler. And, more important, Bauer was an intellectual heir of the great synthesizer of Central European socialist theory, Karl Kautsky.

The period 1918 to 1919 was a revolutionary moment in the life of Austria. The lost war, the collapse of the Habsburg Empire, the bitterness of the workers, the disappointment of the peasants, the disillusionment of the returning soldiers, and the success of the two Russian revolutions of 1917, all contributed to an expectation that the founding of the new republic would lead to profound social changes.

On the first day of the life of the new republic Otto Bauer became Foreign Minister of Austria in a Social Democratic–Christian Social coalition government. Bauer's self-assigned role was to act as a brake on the revolutionary forces of the time. The defeated troops hated their officers. Peasant representatives demanded the punishment of war profiteers. Thus the Socialists had a significant opportunity to gain the cooperation of the peasantry who had never supported them in peacetime. Bauer feared the outbreak of a bloody civil war and Allied intervention. It is doubtful, however, whether the forces of conservatism in Austria were in a position to engage in civil war in the winter of 1918/19. They were decisively broken by the war and collapse. Only later did they consolidate their forces to combat social reform.

The spring of 1919 saw the proclamation of soviet republics in neighboring Hungary on March 22 and Bavaria on April 7. At that time even the conservative economist Joseph Schumpeter wrote: "Everybody speaks of socialization." Socialization became coalition policy and the Constituent National Assembly created a socialization commission on March 14. Bauer was named chairman of the commission, his vice-chairman was the Christian Social leader and priest Ignaz Seipel. Although Bauer had explicitly written about the need for and feasibility of the communal ownership of factories, banks, and large estates, and although the Christian Social position looked with pride to an anti-capitalist tradition (which included the municipal socialization program of Lord Mayor Karl Lueger) and viewed socialization as an ethical proposition that reaffirmed Christian values, in practice nothing was done to move toward socialization by either the commission or the government.[12]

Bauer, a staunch advocate of socialism in his writings and speeches, now feared the seizure of power by the workers. He declared that a new society could only be achieved after many years and pointed to the preliminary statutory and administrative work necessary to implement socialization: "the political revolution was the work of a few hours; the social revolution will have to be the achievement of bold, but also extraordinary, labors of many years."[13]

There were, however, two laws passed at this time which pointed in the direction of, even if they did not institute, socialization. Laws were passed establishing the legal procedures for the nationalization of industries, but they remained nothing more than procedural laws without any practical effect. Because of changes in the international situation, especially the collapse of the Bavarian and Hungarian soviet republics and the counterrevolutionary solidification, the Christian Socials and the German Nationals resisted any moves toward alteration of the economic structure. Thus, plans for the nationalization of the coal and electrical sectors of the economy were not realized; the same was true for plans to redistribute the large landed estates. In 1919 the Social Democrats' demand for the nationalization of Austria's largest industrial concern, the Österreichische Alpine Montangesellschaft, met a similar defeat. The failure to carry the last-named socialization through had fateful consequences for the First Republic. For precisely this industrial complex was to become the center of support for the rightist paramilitary Heimwehr, which was dedicated to the overthrow of the Republic.

Despite legislation in 1919 for labor-management codetermination of industry, which was enacted predominantly in light industry (shoemaking, leather tanning, laundries, and clothiers), the moves toward socialization remained little more than brave plans and fragmentary beginnings. They had no permanent or penetrating influence on the social structure or economic life of interwar Austria.

Bauer believed the Austrian Republic was not politically or economically viable. He threw his energies into *Anschluss*—union with Germany— because, as he said, "we are too small to be free alone." He went so far as to declare that *Anschluss* should take precedence over domestic social reform in Austria: "The battle for socialism here in the country must henceforth be conducted as a battle for union with Germany." Bauer resigned his office, however, on July 25, 1919, when the Allies stood in the way of *Anschluss,* while Renner, who was prepared to accept the decision, became Foreign Minister as well as Chancellor. This is one example of an ideologically uncompromising position taken by Bauer, which in fact reduced his influence. As Stanley Suval has said, he was "a one-issue minister; the failure of the *Anschluss* movement made him no longer useful to the cabinet."[14]

Though Otto Bauer rejected the politics and life style of his industrialist father, he found a suitable father substitute in the Marxist theoretician Karl Kautsky (1854–1938). Born in Prague, Kautsky maintained ties with Bauer and with Austrian Social Democracy all his life. Kautsky's *Der Weg zur Macht* (1909) presented a strategy of keeping alive the proletarian faith that revolution was close at hand, but he denied that it could be planned. It was impossible, he said, to "know the form and character of the revolution." Thus he passively awaited the inevitable, in contrast to V. I. Lenin, who not only asserted that a revolution must be conspiratorially planned by an elite vanguard of dedicated fighters but also carried his theory out in political action, and Rosa Luxemburg, who saw revolution coming in the form of spontaneous mass strikes. Kautsky held that socialists had no way of knowing whether decisive revolutionary changes in society would be achieved through violence or whether they would be "fought exclusively by means of economic, legislative and moral pressures." The revolution, said Kautsky, is inevitable, but its coming cannot be prepared or stimulated by the socialists. Kautsky favored a pure oppositional attitude within strictly legal methods. The socialists were not to participate in any "ministerialism" or budget voting. They should, however, participate in elections and avoid revolutionary adventurism and premature trials of strength. In effect Kautsky argued for a reformist tactic and a revolutionary theory. As Schorske has characterized him:

> Kautsky . . . tended to harness revolutionary theory into the service of reformist practice. . . . His analysis of the future revolutionary process was remarkable for the passive role which he assigned to the working class and its party. While pointing to an intensification of class struggle as characteristic of the era, he assigned only two clear functions to the proletarian party: agitation and organization. Even if the revolution should be violent, which Kautsky left uncertain, the dynamic element in it would be the ruling class which, through its inner contradictions, corruption, and loss of self-assurance, would hurtle the existing order to destruction. The proletariat would be the passive beneficiary of the process thanks to having maintained its oppositional integrity.[15]

Kautsky's theory of a passive revolution in Germany held the two conflicting wings of the socialist movement—the revolutionary radicals and the trade unionists and revisionists—in the same party until World War I. In the Austrian First Republic, Bauer made this theory of inaction the socialist policy. One of its historical strengths has been that, as a result, the Austrian Communist party has always been a negligible factor in Austrian politics. But the contradictions of this policy became apparent in the crises of Austrian democracy between 1918 and 1934 and led not only to the destruction of the party but to the demise of the First Republic as well.

Bauer's relationship with the older statesman of socialism, who was twenty-seven years his senior, had many aspects of a paternal displacement. Bauer began the relationship by initiating a correspondence which was to last as long as both men were alive. His initial letter enclosed "a modest first work" on Marx's theory of economic crises for publication in *Neue Zeit,* which Kautsky edited. From this point their relationship was one between the grand old man of Central European Social Democracy and his admiring, respectful pupil. To Kautsky, Bauer reported his success in the university examinations and his achievement of the doctorate and shared his concern about the illness of his father, whom he took to Italy to recuperate, and elation over his election to the post of Secretary of the Social Democratic Worker's party's parliamentary *Fraktion.* In September 1913, Bauer's father died, and within a year he changed his form of salutation to Kautsky: Now for the first time he discontinued his customary *"Sehr geehrter Genosse*

Kautsky!" and in October 1914 replaced it with *"Sehr geehrter Freund!"* By this time Bauer was an officer in the Austrian Army serving on the Eastern Front. After his capture in November 1914, his next message comes from Siberia on a "Reply Card of a Prisoner of War." After the war, when Bauer became Foreign Minister of the new Austrian Republic, Kautsky made a bid to be appointed an ambassador by the Austrian government. Thus the relationship between the men was reversed. The elder statesman of Social Democracy, who could never have power while Central European Socialists were ostracized from government, now sought patronage from the younger disciple who had achieved control of a ministry of state. The phenomenon articulated by Michels and Schorske, which is that structural conservatism is compelled by the political situation when revolutionary socialists come near to power, can be seen in Bauer's reply: the post of ambassador to an Allied capital such as Paris or London, he told Kautsky, required a business-man or high bureaucrat conversant with commercial matters who would inspire confidence in government and financial circles; support from Social-ists in a foreign country, he assured Kautsky, would be a liability in a diplomatic post. Instead Bauer offered the senior socialist scholar a job as librarian of the Menger Library.[16]

Sometimes the researcher will find the most personally revealing letters in a context where he least expects it. Otto Bauer's personal life and child-hood memories are matters about which remarkably little is known. States-men are not inclined to make a display of them as do ethical and spiritual figures such as Augustine and Rousseau. In Bauer's case the dissimulation was intentional. Although Bauer wished, as do many politicians, to maintain his privacy and to frustrate biographers, he revealed something of himself and his childhood in a letter to Kautsky, who was ill at the time. The "most impressive experience" of his childhood, he related, from approximately age eleven, was how his father, who was believed to be blind, recovered the sight of a hitherto dysfunctional eye:

> I still remember the evil time out of my childhood, when my father had a detached retina, he had to lie in a darkened room for weeks at a time, and could not read for months. His case was complicated in that he had vision in only one eye and it was just this eye which suffered the detached retina; the other eye was weak from birth and had not functioned at all up to then, so that it was considered blind. But then came the miracle: As the functioning eye was incapacitated by the detachment of the retina, the other eye . . . adapted to the service demanded of it. After about three months he could read and write and my father remained fully competent to carry on his work for twenty years, until the end of his life![17]

Sigmund Freud's account of the same incident, as Bauer's sister "Dora" had perceived it twenty-two years earlier, confirms the facts of the illness, but not the father's "miraculous" compensatory recovery: "When the girl was about ten years old, her father had to go through a course of treatment in a darkened room on account of a detached retina. As a result of this misfortune his vision was permanently impaired."[18] Apparently, a feeling of awe at the power of nature and the power of father so impressed the eleven-year-old Otto that he recalled it vividly three decades later. Just when he was sure his father was blind and when the son's guilt, anxiety, and remorse were at their peak, the father proved to have a new and miraculous (*"wunderbare"*) potency—he could see and be competent and powerful after all! Otto's unconscious hostility and hatred had not destroyed his father as he had feared. He communicated the unconscious fantasy—and it may be the most important governing fantasy of Bauer's politics and his relation to conflict in his entire political life—to Kautsky: If I wait long enough, a miracle will indeed happen! In his relation to conflict and aggression, he repeatedly expressed this fantasy of passive magical thinking: If we wait and do nothing, salvation or resolution of the problem will come to us.

The high-water mark of Socialist electoral power during the First Republic was reached in the elections of April 24, 1927. The degree of Seipel's concern and his "moral" priorities are indicated by the election alliance the Christian Socials negotiated with the Austrian National Socialists. Despite this opposition electoral alliance with the anti-Semites, the Social Democrats gained three seats in the Nationalrat, leaving them just two seats short of the Christian Socials, who had lost nine.* Chancellor Seipel was able to maintain the Christian Socials in government only by forming a coalition with the agrarian Landbund and the Pan Germans. The apparent Socialist ascendancy contributed both to their later confidence of popular support and to Seipel's determination to break them. These twin factors constitute the political background for the most serious crisis in the history of the First Austrian Republic: the confrontation of July 1927.

The immediate cause of the crisis was political violence by the right on January 30, 1927, in the village of Schattendorf in the Burgenland, where paramilitary *Frontkämpfer* shot into a socialist crowd, killing a child and an invalid and wounding five others. On July 15, two accused *Frontkämpfer* were acquitted in a jury trial, which was a judicial reform the Socialists had fought for. Otto Bauer fled the party headquarters building in order to avoid a delegation of municipal electric workers who wished to strike but came

*The Christian Socials dropped from 82 to 73 seats, the Social Democrats increased from 68 to 71, the Pan Germans from 10 to 12, and the agrarian Landbund from 5 to 9.

to ask for instructions from the party leadership on how to respond to the crisis. Bauer jumped into the descending elevator so he would miss the workers' delegation in the ascending elevator. Friedrich Austerlitz, in the *Arbeiter-Zeitung,* in an editorial on July 15 expressed outrage: "The bourgeois world constantly warns against civil war. But is not this straight-out provocational acquittal of men who killed workers, because they killed workers, already civil war? We warn them all, for from the sowing of injustice such as occurred yesterday only grave disaster can result."[19] A crowd gathered outside the Palace of Justice on the Schmerlingplatz in Vienna and set fire to it. The fire brigade had difficulty getting through and only did so when Socialist leaders cleared the way. Police were called and given orders to shoot. Eighty-nine persons in the crowd were killed.

The myths of Bauer's policy were exposed: The Socialist Schutzbund had proved ineffective, and the myth that the electoral power of Social Democracy as a mass party would inhibit the use of force by the government was punctured. The belief that the socialist Viennese police force would not shoot upon workers was belied. The Social Democratic Worker's party responded with a one-day general strike and a transport strike which followed. Both failed miserably. The government under Seipel offered no negotiations and no amnesty. The clerical Chancellor emerged triumphant and pushed his advantage to the hilt. Now he allied openly with the fascist Heimwehr and pressed repressive legislation.

Bauer's response to the events of July 15 in the ensuing parliamentary debate reveals his ambivalence. He opened his statement to the Nationalrat with a confession of shared guilt! He upbraided himself and his party for not planning their own demonstration on July 15 to defuse mass discontent; he rebuked himself and the party leadership for failure to mobilize the Socialist Schutzbund to prevent a riot; and he indicted himself and the Socialists for not calling out the party's Ordnerdienst, which usually supervised demonstrations but was not called out that day.*

This very important speech in which Bauer stood before his followers and the nation as the spokesman for Austrian socialism is indicative of his character and, in particular, of his psychological handling of aggression.

*Paul Federn observed at the time that this point "can only be explained by psychoanalysis. The social democratic leaders are at heart revolutionary, but they did not wish this demonstration. They realized that revolution in little Austria today would be suicidal, and, therefore, at a given moment called out the republican guard with orders to interfere and prevent violence. The guard arrived much too late.

"Why did not the leaders send out the guard at 6 a.m. when they knew the demonstration was beginning? They say they 'forgot.' This is a flagrant example of unconscious forgetfulness. The socialists forgot to take the only step which could have prevented something which they consciously disapproved, but unconsciously desired." Interview with Edgar Ansel Mowrer, Chicago *Daily News,* July 20, 1927, in Harold D. Lasswell, *Psychopathology and Politics* (New York, 1960), p. 181.

The tone is not one of anger, outrage, or indignation; rather, the tone is that of moral superiority and the carping accusation of ethical insensitivity. In speaking of the fifty-seven coffins of victims of July 15 which he saw at the Vienna Central Cemetery, Bauer's self-accusations and his manner of handling opposition through ethical deprecation, as shown in the parliamentary record, are revealing:

> Dr. Bauer: You will see that it is my wish, before I deliver a single word of accusation against others, to declare quite openly in front of this House and before the entire German Austrian people, what the conclusion of our testing of conscience is, openly to confess, wherein we find ourselves guilty. . . . I will confess: Yes, in all these days that have passed since Friday the 15th, there was no day and no night in which I and each of us did not consider, did not examine his conscience, and say to himself repeatedly: Whatever guilt the others bear—and I will also speak of this guilt—let us first examine ourselves and confess to ourselves quite openly, whether we have not done some things, and failed to do others, which must tell us: Yes, this is something needless and frightful which happened. (Shouts and interruptions—stormy shouting.)
>
> President (repeatedly sounding the bell): I ask for silence!
>
> Dr. Bauer: I urgently ask my friends not to allow themselves to be provoked by people who do not understand a moral issue. (Vigorous acclamation, applause.)
>
> I will, gentlemen, not utter a word of indictment here, until I have here before the entire public acknowledged where according to my examination of conscience our guilt and—I confess to it, where I participated in the decisions—my guilt, lies.[20]

Bauer spoke as though he needed to confess to a crime he did not in fact commit. He described how he and the leadership had held the workers from taking up weapons by directing them on the path of bloodless demonstration, namely the transport strike. Bauer sought moral credit for having diverted a civil war and channeled protest into non-violent economic lines. The strike, however, failed disastrously. Chancellor Seipel categorically refused to negotiate until the strike had ended and the workers had capitulated. Yet Bauer's presentation of these events took the lofty high ground; according to Bauer, the Socialists thus prevented a civil war:

> At that time we stood before the following choice: One of us must sacrifice prestige if we are to protect the country from a civil war: either the government or us. The government has not sacrificed, we have sacrificed. I confess that I advised my friends to make this

sacrifice, and I am proud of it. And let me say this, gentlemen: I would not wish to be that man who would permit his country to be pushed into the greatest catastrophe rather than sacrifice his prestige. No, I would not like to be such a man, I leave that role to the Chancellor. . . .

In the hour of greatest danger, we called upon our comrades to end the strike. We did this without regard to petty issues of prestige which are not issues for him who has a conscience.[21]

Bauer closed this important speech on behalf of Austrian Social Democracy by calling for an independent investigation commission, an amnesty for those who were arrested on the night of July 15/16, and compensation for the injured and the survivors of those killed. These motions were to no avail. Seipel refused to make the slightest concession, thus demonstrating Social Democratic impotence. The events of July 1927 are generally regarded as the beginning of the end of Austrian democracy. As Seipel's biographer Klemens von Klemperer has stated, "Starting in the autumn of 1927, the search for alternatives to parliamentary democracy commanded more and more attention."[22]

Bauer's general passivity was underscored when Friedrich Adler, who was administering the Second International from Brussels, inquired about political prisoners in Austria and suggested that something could be done on their behalf by putting international pressure on the Austrian government. Bauer rejected the suggestion and assured Adler:

The people who were arrested due to the events of July were unquestionably not treated badly by the courts. They all complained about the first hours at the police, but unanimously praised their treatment at court. The only complaint was the length of imprisonment during the judicial inquiry, but even this appears cleared up, since the overwhelming majority are already back on the street. Above all, however, I would not like to aggravate the judges now, as long as we do not yet know how they will decide. If there should be a vengeful justice, as in 1911, then we would of course have to use all measures; but I still hope that it will not get that bad since the jurors are now present everywhere.[23]

Friedrich Adler had also suggested that it was time the Second International initiated a rapprochement toward the Third International, and that the occasion of the tenth anniversary of the October Revolution would be an appropriate time to address greetings to Moscow which might be a first step toward a cessation of strife in the socialist camp. To this Otto Bauer responded again with his characteristic passivity that he was "sympathetic in principle to the suggestion that the Executive of the International Socialist Bureau issue a proclamation on the occasion of the tenth anniversary of the Soviet Republic." But, he continued, he was "convinced that one could not obtain such a proclamation, or if one could, it would be drafted with such an anti-Russian tone that it would do more harm than good."[24]

Bauer did not base his lack of any action that might lead to a reconciliation with the Third International on any anti-totalitarian convictions; he had, in fact, opposed any intensified anti-Bolshevik policy by the Socialist International. Rather, his analysis of history led him to believe that events would eventually force the Bolsheviks to move toward the Socialists. Thus Bauer consistently followed a strategy of passivity, of waiting—a stance of expectant and intellectually elaborated receptivity in the assurance that, like the class enemy in Austrian national politics, the Bolshevik threat would sooner or later be removed by circumstance. Four months earlier Bauer had expressed this same position as a reason for taking no initiative:

> It is probable, although not yet certain, that the great hopes of Moscow for China will end in a terrible disappointment. In the same terms I hold it probable, although not yet certain, that the German economy and at a slower pace the English economy will recover to the degree that in a few years Europe will have a period of prosperity and the war-created crisis will then be overcome. This process of recovery could at the most only be slowed by an economic crisis in America, and could only be deterred by serious political disturbances such as war. Should developments in China and in Europe follow this course, the entire ideology of Bolshevism will in a few years become so untenable that Moscow will finally be compelled to change. Thus, I hold it entirely possible that in two, three, or four years we will be able to talk with Moscow, and I believe that the policy of the Socialist International should be geared to this possibility.[25]

We should not, with the benefit of hindsight, blame Bauer because his predictions on the future course of the world's economy and of Bolshevism were wrong. But passivity here is characteristic of both his personality and his political style. Successful statesmen, whether revolutionary like Lenin or conservative like Bismarck, use opportunities that others do not see and mold events by decisive intervention. Successful party leadership and diplomacy demand generative activity; history may be shaped only by sensing and invoking latent potentials. If creative initiative is not taken, then the dynamic possibilities of situations and events will be left to other protagonists who will use them for their own ends.

After his work on nationalism, Otto Bauer's special contributions to the theory of Austro-Marxism were four: (1) the theory of "balance of class forces" of 1921; (2) a particular variant of the "dictatorship of the proletariat" of 1926, dependent on the theory of a 51 percent majority of 1914; (3) the theory of the "pause" of 1928; and (4) the theory of "obstruction" of 1930. In all of these formulations we see the intimate relationship of the man and his intellectual product. Bauer is the cautious, balancing, obsessional theoretician who uses his superior intellect to avoid decision. His conclusion in each case is that the optimal and "correct" current position for Austrian Marxists is to wait and do nothing until the constellation of forces naturally moves in their direction and conflict will be resolved without danger or confrontation.

Bauer's theory of the "balance of classes" was presented to the Social Democratic *Parteitag* in 1921. He took the phrase from Friedrich Engels and applied it to the political situation of the First Republic. He held that the result of the Austrian revolution was that "the conflicting classes held each other in equilibrium."[26] The "balance" was in the power between the industrial areas of Vienna, Lower Austria, and Upper Styria, which could not be governed against the will of the workers, and the agrarian areas, which could not be governed against the peasants. This inherent ideological economic and political conflict between the socialist state (*Land*) of Vienna and the conservative central government of Austria was one of the tragic structural dilemmas of the First Republic.

Bauer also developed other "balances," both positive and negative: the disparity between the power of the proletariat in the Austrian nation and the total powerlessness of the nation itself beyond its boundaries. After 1920, he saw a balance between the government and parliamentary majority, who were bourgeois, and the extra-parliamentary power position of Social Democracy. This he termed a balance between the "parliamentary democracy" of the bourgeoisie and the "functional democracy" which made the government dependent upon the cooperation of proletarian organizations in its most important decisions. Even in the new Austrian Army, he presumed that the command of the bourgeois officers was limited by the socialist consciousness and organization of the men and the Soldier's Councils. Bauer saw the balance between the middle-class paramilitary formations and the proletarian order-keeping force as "holding each other in check." The republic was a "compromise between the classes, a result of the balance of class powers [*Gleichgewicht der Klassenkräfte*]." It was a republic in which "no class was strong enough to rule the other classes, and therefore all classes had to share the power of state with each other."[27]

As early as the spring of 1914, Bauer looked forward to the class-conscious proletariat becoming a majority of the population and a parliamentary majority. Then the ruling classes would have to choose between permitting peaceful reforms in the ownership of the means of production and staging a counterrevolution, which would in turn instigate a proletarian revolution, which would be indomitable as soon as the class-conscious workers constituted a majority of the population.

Bauer incorporated his special theory of the "dictatorship of the proletariat" in the famous Linz Program adopted at the *Parteitag* in November 1926. The formulation and language were Bauer's. Although its immediate purpose was to divert the attempts of the extreme left, led by Max Adler, to promote an endorsement of the tactics of violence, Bauer's phrasing is a tour de force in the adroit expression of ambivalence. He ingeniously managed to present both the acquisition of power through either majority rule or civil war and dictatorship of the proletariat in one statement:

> The Social Democratic Worker's party must . . . maintain for the working class the possibility of destroying the class rule of the bourgeoisie by democratic methods. If, however, despite all these efforts of the Social Democratic Worker's party, a counterrevolution of the bourgeoisie should succeed in shattering democracy, then the working class could only conquer the power of the state by civil war. . . . If, however, the bourgeoisie should resist the social revolutionary change, which will be the task of the state power of the working class, by planned constriction of economic life, by violent uprising, by conspiracy with foreign counterrevolutionary powers, then the working class would be compelled to break the resistance of the bourgeoisie by means of dictatorship.[28]

Bauer's special theory of the "dictatorship of the proletariat" was so hemmed in by qualifications—it would only take place *after* the democratic election of a Socialist government and only if the bourgeois forces engaged in a "violent uprising, by conspiracy with foreign counterrevolutionary powers"—that it would never take place. In fact, it claimed nothing more than the right of a government to defend itself against sabotage, violence, and insurrection. Yet the language was inflammatory and was perceived as threatening by the middle class, so that they remained largely alienated from Social Democracy in the First Republic.

At the party congress in 1917, Bauer's first upon returning from Russian captivity, he was the spokesman for the left-wing opposition which fought against Socialist participation in a bourgeois government: "We reject any lasting alliance with bourgeois parties, any formation of blocs; we reject unconditionally any approval of the budget of the class state, any approval of war credits, any participation in a bourgeois government. We hold firm to the old principle: Not one man, not one penny to the capitalist state."[29] Yet within eighteen months Bauer became a member of a coalition government of the First Austrian Republic. The Social Democratic party spent two years in coalition governments and carried through some labor legislation.

By 1921 Bauer had completely shifted his position in theory as well. Against the Communists, who unconditionally opposed any participation in coalition government with bourgeois parties, he argued that "if in a time in which the sole rule of the working class is impossible, we refuse every coalition government, then we are voluntarily submitting to the sole rule of the bourgeoisie." In the crisis of 1927, however, when Karl Renner advocated coalition, saying, "This theory of pauses is a desolate, enervating conception of socialism" and "A general socialization is a general nonsense,"[30] Bauer steadfastly opposed a coalition, holding that it would only disappoint the workers and strengthen the Communists.

In 1928, events having made his earlier theory untenable, Bauer was ready to reevaluate his theory of "balance" and to redefine the revolution of 1918. He did this with the theory of "the pause" (*"die Pause"*), that period between the former and the next revolution. Whereas in the early 1920's he viewed the Austrian Republic as a compromise between a balance of class forces, now, in the light of the shattering defeat of July 1927, Bauer saw what had happened in 1918 as a triumph of the entire bourgeoisie over the privileged feudal forces of monarchy, dynasty, and the industrial aristocracy. But the present was a phase in the stabilization of capitalism. Therefore, no Social Democrat should serve as minister in a coalition government, for whatever he achieved would be at the expense of the broad mass of the proletariat.[31]

By 1930 Bauer defined the party's "weapon" as that of "obstruction" (*"das Kampfmittel der Obstruktion"*), by which he meant that the Socialist minority should obstruct the bourgeois majority in Parliament; the middle-class parties would not dare to break the obstruction and enforce their will upon the Socialists because they feared a rising of the working masses outside of the Parliament. After 1927 Bauer conceded that the bourgeoisie no longer dreaded proletarian recourse to the streets, for they had superiority there as well as in government. In 1930 he turned to the Parliament as the hope for political equilibrium. Again, as earlier, Bauer's emotional stance was one of passive waiting. He said if the Socialists could strengthen their parliamentary position, their opponents would "be forced to come to us and to share the power of state."[32] Further, since the issue is no longer whether Austria was to be a bourgeois republic—that issue was settled and the republic was stabilized—now the bourgeois political alliances among middle class and peasants would fall apart to the benefit of the working class. Will, Bauer asked, the triumphant bourgeoisie which had then achieved power turn against democracy? He answered in the negative. No land, he claimed, presented less attractive prospects for a violent resolution of class conflict than Austria. Civil war would result in a famine, destruction of foreign credit, and industrial standstill. He was convinced the bourgeoisie would decide to share power, not with fascism against democracy, but with the Socialists to defend the democratic Republic.

The Austrian historian Adam Wandruszka concludes that Bauer always avoided ultimate decisions and resolute action. This is what the psychoanalyst calls obsessing. According to Wandruszka's interpretation of Bauer's psychology, the Austro-Marxist leader viewed his own reluctance to use violence and revolutionary acts as weakness, perhaps a heritage of his bourgeois background, for which he compensated by hard expressions, by radical phrases, by threats of class war and civil war, and by flirting with the concept of a "dictatorship of the proletariat." Bauer had a

> deep personal fright of the decision to act . . . he and the Social Democrats repeatedly let the right point in time slip by. . . . Bauer's inflexible, doctrinaire posture, his maintenance of a once adopted position—not out of strength, since under the pressure of an apparent "historical law of development" he would in the end retreat, rather because he missed the optimal moment to pull back due to theoretical considerations and discussions—in most cases substantially contributed to the defeats of Social Democracy.[33]

Wandruszka attributed Bauer's theorizing and inability to act to the rigidity of Marxist determinism and its laws of historical development. Further, which is more to the point, he has unerringly placed his finger on Bauer's pattern of obsessing and intellectualizing to avoid decision. For we know that Marxists are fully capable of being decisive. *Theory is no explanation for failure, but a neurotic tendency to theorize is.*

Bauer's obsessing was itself the important symptom. Marxist ideology has not held other leaders from taking resolute steps to ensure the survival or success of themselves or their movements in critical junctures. But Bauer exhibited constant ambivalence and doubt. He used intellectual twisting and turning to avoid conflict; he always needed to place events in an explicable, albeit retrospective, Marxist theoretical pattern. It is as though, through such reformulation, he could control the world. He had a strong belief in the power of his own thought to structure and influence events.

Bauer's emphasis on sobriety and abstinence was entirely consonant with the prevailing moral righteousness of the Social Democratic cultural organizations and youth movement. What in another land and context would be called his "puritanism" was an integral part of the Central European Socialist vision of personal purity and moral uplift—in Otto Bauer's words, "to become another person, also in one's private life, in one's relation to one's wife and to one's children, in relation to one's fellow human beings."[34] What is most revealing about Bauer's particular position toward alcohol is the way he related it to a fear of the workers succumbing to the attractions of the petit bourgeoisie, rather than a life of sacrifice. A beer or a glass of wine was dangerous because it made workers less class-conscious, more comfortable and contented, and inclined to become common, vulgar, petit bourgeois *"Kleinbürger," "Spiesser."*

Bauer's writings of the mid-1920's frequently used the backdrop of a past heroic socialist age of conflict as the starting point for a contrast with the relative comfort, social acceptance, and political success of the present. There was a time, he said, when the working class lived in barbarism, in a subhuman, uncultured existence as wage slaves. Then a daily glass of beer would not make one a bourgeois, for those were times of war, against the police, employers, one's wife, brother, and colleagues. The danger of being seduced to becoming bourgeois was then minimal. Today, he wrote in 1926, by contrast, we are too great and powerful to be pushed around, we have won the fruits of our battles. The present danger, now that the period of struggle is over, is that the worker will become a narrow petit bourgeois: "The glass of beer or quarter liter of wine . . . is the agent that will maintain his petit bourgeois thinking, even if he believes himself to be a Social Democrat; [alcohol] is the great tool of petit bourgeois consciousness, which makes it so difficult for the party member to become a real Social Democrat." Socialism, he preached, "not only presumes the overthrow of enemy powers, but changes in the proletariat itself. To this task there is no greater obstacle than the apparently so harmless glass of beer." Whereas the proletariat learned the greatness of passion in the war, "we have also seen," says Bauer, "what a dangerous counselor passions are under some circumstances."[35]

Bauer made it a point to drink water among party comrades as a protest against the petit bourgeois morality which reigned among them. Even at meetings of the International Socialist Executive or the International Socialist Bureau, the two Austrian representatives found themselves alone with water glasses among the many beer and wine glasses at lunch or dinner. The success of the workers abstinence movement, said Bauer, is that it has taken drinking, about which one formerly boasted, and now made it a disgrace to be apologized for. "To have made drinking into something that even those who still drink are ashamed of, and thereby to have built an inhibition against trying alcohol, against vulgarization by alcohol, that is our real success."[36]

Two years later, in March 1928, Bauer directly related alcoholism to what he believed to be its primary material cause: inadequate, crowded housing. In making this case he was defending the model tenant's protection law and the subsidized workers housing program of the Vienna municipality against those who were now pressing to reverse them. He empathically outlines the life cycle of a working-class family in the housing of pre-Socialist Vienna. In the early years of the marriage the apartment was full of children and a bed tenant (*"Bettgeher"*). The tiny apartments, usually one room and a kitchen, with a communal toilet and water tap in the hall, offered not a moment of privacy, rest, or a chance to relax. "The children scream, laundry is being washed, a stranger is in the apartment, the exhausted worker can stand it no longer—he goes to the tavern! The tavern is a necessary adjunct to the sleeping areas called apartments." Bauer presents his ideal of the kind of living conditions Socialists should strive for:

> By apartment I understand something more than merely a protective roof under which one goes to bed. By apartment I understand a space where I can live, which means: where I can comfortably make myself at home, where I can feel good. I mean a space where I can also sometimes be alone, where for example I could read a book in peace. It is no exaggeration to say that 90 percent of Viennese workers have never yet had an apartment in this sense.

Bauer tells of his envy of the municipal housing of Amsterdam because of the number of rooms built in each apartment, which may be as many as five. This is due, not only to the higher wages in Holland, but to the customs of the people. The Dutch like to have many rooms, even if they be small, while the Viennese housewife would not move into such an apartment, would say it would not hold her heavy furniture and sideboard. Bauer affirms his belief in many rooms, no matter how small, in preference to fewer large rooms, because he believes in "the enormous cultural importance of separate bedrooms, so that children do not sleep with their parents, and that above all a person can be alone somewhere in his apartment."[37]

We may well ask whether there are particular reasons why Otto Bauer should be so specifically sensitive to issues of privacy. We know from Freud's case history that Bauer's mother was highly intrusive and controlling. His stringent need to repress the easy pleasures of alcohol and the tavern and his defense of the need for personal privacy by adults and children were founded on the objective conditions of the Viennese working class. But they were also overdetermined.* Their very vehemence was

---

*Many Marxists as well as non-Marxist liberals favored housing reform on progressive and humanitarian grounds. Yet in Otto Bauer's case we can demonstrate from the psychoanalysis of his sister that he had personal reasons in his childhood for passionately embracing the cause of privacy in the home. Obviously, the fact that he had an intrusive and controlling mother does not necessarily mean that others who shared his political position had the same childhood experiences. Identical results in behavior do not demonstrate like causes. Few concepts in the psychohistorical armamentarium have encountered as much incomprehension as "overdetermination," sometimes also called "multidetermination." Clinically, "overdetermination" means that every symptom and symbol has

grounded in his own home life as a child, which lacked privacy. He was arguing for a better life for poorly housed workers and for space for himself as a child.

We can also infer from Freud's treatment of Bauer's sister that separate bedrooms played a very important role in Otto's childhood. In what was definitely not a working-class home, his mother locked the dining-room door each night. This became an issue of dispute between mother and father, as "Dora" told Freud, because Otto's room had "no separate entrance, but can only be reached through the dining room. Father does not want my brother to be locked in like that at night. He says it will not do: something might happen in the night so that it might be necessary to leave the room." The Bauer apartment had a number of locked rooms to which only the mother had a key. She locked the *Herrenzimmer,* or salon, at all times so that it would remain clean. As Otto Leichter puts it, "Philipp Bauer, who kept his cigars in this room, could only get them if the mother, who alone possessed the key, unlocked the holy room. All apparently had to reconcile themselves to this situation. It is understandable that a wife and mother who was dominated by this compulsion was never in a position to give her husband and children joy or even warmth."[38]

As events moved toward the demise of Austrian democracy the "responsibility to mothers" was a repeated favorite symbol used to rationalize inaction in Bauer's rhetoric. At the 1929 Socialist *Parteitag* he said:

> We will continue our policy of prudence and consciousness of responsibility, however the Fascists jeer at it; this we simply owe to the mothers of this land, and this we also owe to the requirements of the working class itself, which must be protected from falling into traps set for it by fascism.[39]

The anticipated crisis came to a head in March 1933 as an Austrian refraction of the Nazi seizure of power in Germany. On March 8, Bauer responded to the first attempt by the Dollfuss government to end Austrian democracy in a speech to 1,500 members of the Socialist party, which, behind its superficial tone of militance, already signaled despair and defeat:

---

many layers of meaning from the present and the psychodynamic past. Functionally, for the psychohistorian, it means that when a person strongly and passionately takes a position, there are invariably private (rational and irrational) reasons as well as the reasons of public discourse for the intensity of the commitment. Jacques Lacan notes: "Freud insists on the minimum of overdetermination constituted by a double meaning (symptom of a conflict long dead apart from its function in a *no less symbolic* present conflict)." "The Function of Language in Psychoanalysis," in *The Language of the Self,* trans. Anthony Wilden (New York, 1968), p. 32. See also Michael Sherwood, *The Logic of Explanation in Psychoanalysis* (New York, 1969), pp. 179–84.

One thing I want to say, without wishing to sound pathetic, in this difficult time there is only one thing which still makes this sad life bearable: the sole fact that in our country we can at least still get together to promote our thoughts, ideas, and ideals. At least we can still fight for another, better, greater future. The bourgeoisie shall know this and from it understand our determination. If they also take this from us, then life would be worthless for us.[40]

The ultimate issues are posed in the idioms of internalized romantic German idealism, merely one step removed from insisting on the right to hold thoughts, ideas, and ideals in the mind. It is reminiscent of the "inner emigration" of some Germans of the 1930's. In all emotional aspects, this speech was a concession of defeat before the battle.

Two days later he surveyed the international scene for the party assemblage in terms of a hopeless encirclement by fascism: in the south Fascist Italy; a military dictatorship in Yugoslavia; a Fascist "Hungary of the Hangmen" to the east; and now Hitler Germany on the western border:

In this situation in which we are surrounded, it will be the great, difficult, but therefore all the more glorious task of the Austrian working class to maintain Austria as an island of democracy, an island of freedom, in the midst of this Fascist sea.

Bauer then prophesied that if fascism did triumph in Austria, it would be inescapably bound to the Fascist alliance, and this would sooner or later mean that we "would be sent to the slaughter bench for the glory of Messrs. Hitler, Mussolini, and Horthy." Again he spoke of the "responsibility to the mothers of the land [*Verantwortung vor den Müttern des Landes*]."[41]

On March 15 Chancellor Dollfuss forcibly prevented the convening of the Parliament, in which his government had a majority of one vote. Thus, Austrian democracy ended in a coup d'état which all observers, including Bauer and the Socialists, had anticipated. This was the moment in the history of the First Republic at which the Social Democrats stood before the decision to fight. The working class was in a stronger position to do battle in March 1933 than it was to be in February 1934. Later, Bauer said the Socialists should have responded with a general strike and their own offensive. When Bauer analyzed these events from exile eleven months later, he took personal responsibility, writing as if to say, I was blind and can now see clearly:

The working masses awaited the signal to fight. At that time the railway workers were not yet as battered as they were twelve months later. The military organization of the government was then much weaker than it was in February 1934. We might have been able to win at that time. But we shrank back before the fight at that time. We still believed we could come to a peaceful solution through negotiations. . . . We were then still stupid enough to trust Dollfuss's promise. We backed out of the fight because we wished to spare the country the catastrophe of a bloody civil war. The civil war broke out eleven months later anyway, but under what were for us essentially more unfavorable conditions. It was an error, the most fatal of our errors.[42]

No action was taken in March 1933. It is doubtful that any would have been successful, even at that date.

The Social Democratic Worker's party convened an extraordinary *Parteitag* in October 1933 to make policy for what was viewed as a critical situation. The Socialists formulated "four points" which were the absolute limits whose breach would cause them to fight: (1) the suspension of the rights of the City of Vienna and the imposition of a government commissioner; (2) attacks on the trade unions; (3) dissolution of the party; (4) the imposition of a Fascist constitution. By the promulgation of these four points or "triggers" to resistance, the Socialists did two disastrous things. They in effect told the government that their other positions of strength, for example the Schutzbund, were vulnerable to attack and would not be defended; and most important, they henceforth left the initiative to the government.

The Schutzbund rising of February 12, 1934, has taken its place as the heroic legend of Austrian Social Democracy's stand against fascism. As such, it has played a role similar to the disastrous July 20, 1944, anti-Hitler putsch attempt in Germany—it served as a moral legacy for the regeneration of a democratic state and political tradition for the postwar Second Austrian Republic. Indeed, the workers who fought the power of the state in 1934 were defending Austrian democracy and the constitutional rights of the Republic. But, as Norbert Leser points out, the fight was at least a year too late. He says: "The 12th of February was a despairing compensatory act of parts of the Schutzbund which did too late, but could no longer repair, what leadership failed to do at the right time."[43]

The incitement to action in 1934 again came from the provinces. In this case the fighting began in Upper Austria when police and army units attacked the Schutzbund headquarters in Linz led by Richard Bernaschek. On receiving the message the night before that conflict was imminent, Bauer sent back a telegram urging a postponement of action by the Schutzbund. Bauer told the emissaries from Linz that all the signs were pointing to an open attack by the government on the Socialists within a few days. He cautioned that as soon as the Heimwehr strikes at the municipal government of Vienna, it will itself thereby have given the indispensable rousing signal for a successful defensive fight. This is precisely when no Socialist leader should lose his head. Bernaschek must retract the order to fight which he distributed to his cadres and subordinates in Upper Austria.[44]

Here again, Bauer is passively waiting for the opposition to give the signal which will lead to an initiative by the masses. In the meantime the enemy chooses the time and place at which it will provoke the rising. Undoubtedly Leser is on the mark when he poses the question whether the party leadership ever was determined earnestly to invoke the threatened sanctions. "Did it," he asks, "really involve a choice of the optimal time, or was the point in question not to find grounds for inaction at every critical juncture? The issue was apparently much more never to arrive at a binding decision at any point in time, rather than being a matter of finding the correct moment."[45]

The initiative by February 1934 was out of the hands of the party leadership. Fighting was focused in workers housing projects such as the George-Washington-Hof, Haydn-Hof, Karl-Marx-Hof, and Goethe-Hof on the outskirts of Vienna and in some mining districts of Styria and Upper Austria. In three days of fighting, the Schutzbund suffered over 1,000 casualties and over 4,000 arrests; on the government side, 280 people were killed and 758 were wounded. The armed workers were no match for the organized power of the state with its police, military, and paramilitary formations. As the Schutzbund general Theodor Körner had pointed out to the Party Executive as early as 1928, irregulars stand no chance in street fighting against organized regular forces. He reevaluated the situation even more pessimistically on February 11, 1934, and warned Bauer against allowing a confrontation to occur because: "My opinion is that any use of force is without prospect of success." Recently the Austrian archivist-historian Rudolf Neck stated: "The heroes of February deserved better leadership."[46]

The result of the rising was that the Social Democratic party and its affiliates were outlawed, its leaders were all in hiding or in prison. Bauer fled incognito across the Czechoslovakian border to Bratislava on February 13.[47] The Social Democrats set up a headquarters in exile in Brünn, Czechoslovakia, where Bauer worked until 1938. In May 1938, a few weeks after Hitler's *Anschluss,* which incorporated Austria into the Third Reich on March 13, Bauer moved to France, crossing Germany by air.

In Paris, Bauer took a peculiar and rigid position on the German *Anschluss* of Austria, a position that reflected the way in which exiles quickly lose touch with their homeland. He wrote of the coming of an all-German revolution which would overthrow fascism. Bauer foresaw the outbreak of a proletarian revolution in Germany to accompany Germany's defeat. Therefore, he contended, to talk now of Austrian independence would be tantamount to separatism and would throw away the historic opportunity of realizing the ideas of the 1848 Revolution. In 1938 he wrote: "The future of the Austrian working class is the future of the German revolution."[48] This is, of course, a throwback to his fantasies of *Anschluss* in 1918 and 1919 when he believed the Austrian Socialist movement would derive strength and power from union with the larger and more influential German Social Democratic party as a consequence of political and economic union of the two German-speaking countries. It is also a manifest fantasy of drawing strength from the stronger, more powerful body and of omnipotent regression to the fantasy: "Time is with us, we need only wait."

Bauer died of a coronary infarction in Paris on July 4, 1938. He died alone in exile in a small hotel room; his wife and friends had great difficulty in getting a doctor. His funeral was an occasion appropriate to one of the great figures of international socialism. Representatives of all the Socialist parties of Europe followed his casket. Dignitaries such as Léon Blum and Friedrich Adler spoke. Bauer's urn was interred at the Père-Lachaise Cemetery on a hill opposite the monument to the fighters of the 1871 Paris Commune. His ashes were returned by his party in 1948 to the Vienna Central Cemetery, where they rest beside those of Victor and Friedrich Adler, Karl Seitz, and Engelbert Pernerstorfer.

Today, the Renner position of moderation and coalition is triumphant within an Austrian socialism which, like its German counterpart, has dropped all vestiges of revolutionary rhetoric or ideology. In the past decade Bauer's thought has been the subject of renewed interest on the part of those young scholarly Social Democratic leaders in Austria who are calling for a return to theoretical consciousness their movement.

We may now make some psychodynamic interpretations relating Otto Bauer's political behavior to his personality. We will utilize the singular data base of Freud's "Dora" case, which provides an excellent family history of the interpersonal dynamics of Bauer's childhood and youth. We will connect the thought and behavior of Bauer the political figure to their psychodynamic origins in his family. The suggestion that Freud was insensitive to social factors will not stand up to a scrutiny of his case histories. The "Dora" case in particular has a richness of insight into the patient's social, family, and interpersonal environment which is a great aid to the historian of her family. We can see Otto's political role as his analogue to "Dora's" hysteria —it was his way of handling the family constellation in which he grew up.

The "Dora" case is one of the classic case reports in the psychiatric literature. This was the first of Freud's great case histories and the first case of adolescent psychoanalysis. It has important aspects of family therapy—

Freud also treated the father and an aunt. It was in the postscript to this case that Freud made his monumental first conceptualization of the cardinal psychotherapeutic tool: the transference.* Freud first saw "Dora" as a sixteen-year-old girl in 1898. In the fall of 1900, at age eighteen, she entered analysis with him for three months. He wrote the case history in January 1901 and withheld it from publication for four years because of the anticipated opprobrium over his discussing sexual material with an adolescent girl.[49]

Bauer's father, a wealthy textile manufacturer, was a philanderer and a syphilitic for whom Freud "prescribed an energetic course of anti-luetic treatment." The family constellation was one in which father Bauer, employing moral justifications, used his daughter in erotic exchange for his own purposes. Philipp Bauer had an affair of many years with Frau K., the wife of a friend. The two couples shared houses during holidays and timed their stays in Vienna to coincide. "Dora," who was fourteen, was courted by Herr K. with, as Freud said, "behaviour that was characteristic of lovemaking." He sent her flowers every day for a whole year, took every opportunity to give her valuable presents, and spent all his spare time in her company. "Dora" felt "she had been handed over to Herr K. as the price of his tolerating relations between her father and his wife; and her rage at her father's making such a use of her was visible behind her affection for him." She said she was "treated as an object for barter." She criticized her father as "insincere, he had a strain of falseness in his character, he only thought of his own enjoyment, and he had a gift for seeing things in the light which suited him best."[50]

While "Dora" had no difficulty in criticizing their father, Otto was unwilling to take a stand against him. "Dora" says:

> I know my brother says we children have no right to criticize this behaviour of Father's. He declares that we ought not to trouble ourselves about it, and ought even to be glad, perhaps, that he has found a woman he can love, since Mother understands him so little. I can quite see that, and I should like to think the same as my brother, but I can't. I can't forgive him for it.[51]

Otto's inhibition in aggression against authorities, fathers, and father surrogates, which we have seen in his political life, was already present when they were adolescents and "Dora" was in treatment with Freud. Otto Bauer's

---

*Steven Marcus views the "Dora Case" in terms of the unanalyzed transference and countertransference and as a new form of literature conceived by Freud—a creative narrative that includes its own analysis and interpretation. "Freud and Dora: Story, History, Case History," *Partisan Review*, 41 (1974): 12–23, 89–108, reprinted in *Representations: Essays on Literature and Society* (New York, 1976), pp. 247–310.

mother had what Freud termed a "housewife's psychosis." Freud felt that she had no understanding of her children's more active interests, and was occupied all day long in cleaning the house with its furniture and utensils and in keeping them clean—to such an extent as to make it almost impossible to use or enjoy them.

In adulthood "Dora" complained of "her unhappy childhood because of her mother's exaggerated cleanliness, her annoying washing compulsions, and her lack of affection for her. Mother's only concern had been her own constipation. . . . She worked herself to death by her never-ending, daily cleaning compulsion—a task which nobody else could fulfil to her satisfaction."[52]

We have from Freud, Deutsch, and Otto Bauer's biographers a picture of a strict, anti-libidinal, complaining, and guilt-inducing mother, "whose peculiarities made the house unbearable for everyone." As Bauer's father told Freud: "You know already that I get nothing out of my own wife." It was Otto Bauer's identification with his controlling and aggressive mother, who made him feel guilty and powerless, that shaped the dynamics of his later politics. It is especially significant that on the nature of his mother's character there is an independent convergence of sources. The Bauer biographies written by his socialist admirers fully corroborate Freud's clinical data. Käthe Bauer dedicated herself to cleaning the apartment and the condition of her bowels. Shoes were to be taken off upon entering the apartment, a habit her son kept all his life. Otto continued to live with his parents while he studied at the university. Even in midwinter, Bauer's mother would open all windows to air out the house. Once a cousin who found Otto sitting in his room reading with an overcoat, hat, and gloves on asked him why he did not ask that the windows be closed. His response was: "But, after all, it's not so bad [*Aber das ist doch nicht so arg*]."[53] This was to be his response to political provocation in adulthood. In childhood he learned to wait—for Mother to be in a good mood. Otto was the good child. He did not make trouble like his sister. He was the passive little boy who waited. He identified with his mother's moralizing and tried to be for the mother exactly what his father was not—an idealistic man. The price he paid for this identification is that he could not be active in conflict situations.

Friday, the day of thorough cleaning, all the occupants avoided the apartment. Whereas Otto's father and "Dora" did not take the restrictions seriously, often causing the mother to despair, Otto surrendered. He conducted himself impeccably so as not to aggravate his mother. All the members of the family had to reconcile themselves to what one of Bauer's biographers, Otto Leichter, calls her "emotional pressure."

Both mother and father manipulated their children by provoking guilt and using moral argument. Philipp Bauer said he could not break off relations with the K.'s because:

> I am bound to Frau K. by ties of honourable friendship and I do not wish to cause her pain. The poor woman is most unhappy with her husband, of whom, by the by, I have no very high opinion. She herself has suffered a great deal with her nerves, and I am her only support. With my state of health I need scarcely assure you that there is nothing wrong in our relations. We are just two poor wretches who give one another what comfort we can by an exchange of friendly sympathy.

Father Bauer tried to make "Dora" feel guilty about her hostility to Frau K., habitually "saying that he could not understand her hostility and that, on the contrary, his children had every reason for being grateful to Frau K."[54] Otto Bauer learned in his own home his political technique of sharing the guilt with his enemies, of reproaching himself while remaining morally superior, as he did in 1927 and 1934. His constant political tone of moral superiority, or what the Austrians call *Überlegenheit,* the attempted use of guilt to get his way, is a reflection of how discipline functioned in his home. This is how he was controlled, by both father and mother, and how he learned to control. His public position was always to take the highest moral ground, to talk down to the opposition from an elevated moral posture.

While Bauer identified with his mother in some respects, in others he rebelled. In adulthood, Bauer was indifferent to his personal appearance and clothing. This suggests that his carelessness in personal matters was a reaction formation to his mother's compulsive neatness and an identification with his cigar-smoking, "dirty," syphilitic father. It appears that Otto's hard-working, abstentious moralism was a reaction to the licentiousness and opulence of his father's life style. He would be the ideal father, the husband that he thought his mother wanted. He was the ascetic sharer of the values and ideology of his father's factory employees and their leader in political struggle against capitalist entrepreneurs like his father. Here we have the inception of his inhibition of political aggression. For Otto Bauer one of the obvious implications of achieving his revolutionary goals would have been the dispossession and humiliation of men like his father. If a man both loves and hates his father, and has not worked that conflict through, he will be unable to identify with the fathers of society and will be inhibited in expressing aggression against authority, even if that combat is displaced to social-political grounds.

Within the family dynamic, Otto, who was one and a half years older than "Dora," "used to try so far as he could to keep out of the family disputes; but when he was obliged to take sides he would support his mother. So that the usual sexual attraction had drawn together the father and daughter on the one side and the mother and son on the other." Otto's passivity and intense closeness to his sister is also demonstrated in the case history. "Dora" told Freud an early memory:

> Dora herself had a clear picture of a scene from her early childhood in which she was sitting on the floor in a corner sucking her left thumb and at the same time tugging with her right hand at the lobe of her brother's ear as he sat quietly beside her.

It is striking and unusual that an older brother passively allows his younger sister to manipulate him. There are other indications of almost twin-like closeness. For brother and sister gratified each other, as Freud inferred:

> Dora's brother must have been concerned in some way with her having acquired the habit of masturbation; for in this connection she told me, with all the emphasis which betrays the presence of a 'screen memory', that her brother used regularly to pass on all his infectious illnesses to her, and that while he used to have them lightly she used, on the contrary, to have them severely. In the dream her brother as well as she was saved from 'destruction'; he, too, had been subject to bed-wetting, but had got over the habit before his sister. Her declaration that she had been able to keep abreast with her brother up to the time of her first illness, but after that she had fallen behind him in her studies, was in a certain sense also a 'screen memory'.[55]

"Dora" told Freud that Otto suffered from enuresis both at night and during the day until his sixth or seventh year. Wetting in the daytime until six or seven is unusual and could well have led to experiences of being shamed by adults and other children. Although enuresis is multidetermined, it is frequently an indication of hostility and passive aggression.

The extreme closeness and unity between brother and sister extended into their adult life. Otto always had a large picture of his sister in his room. It was prominent and had the place of honor.[56] In 1922, when Otto was forty-one and "Dora" was forty, Felix Deutsch reports:

> She recalled with great feeling how close she had always been to her brother who had become the leader of a political party and who still visited whenever she needed him—in contrast to her father who had been unfaithful even to her mother. . . . She finally spoke with pride about her brother's career, but she had little hope that her son would follow in his footsteps. . . . Her brother called

several times shortly after my contact with his sister, expressing his satisfaction with her speedy recovery. He was greatly concerned about her continual suffering and her discord with both her husband and their mother. He admitted it was difficult to get along with her because she distrusted people and attempted to turn them against each other. He wanted to see me at my office, but I declined in view of Dora's improvement.[57]

Otto was the ego ideal held up for "Dora's" son. What the mother herself had not achieved, she wished for her son—to equal the accomplishments of her brother.

As Erik Erikson has pointed out, for "Dora" the central concern in her analysis was fidelity. "Dora" was brought in for treatment with Freud as a sixteen-year-old girl with the request to "please try and bring her to reason." Freud was expected to make "Dora" drop the subject of attempted seduction by Herr K. "Dora" felt she was the victim of her father's manipulation and now she anticipated that Freud would join the conspiracy. The family issue was integrity and this also became "Dora's" therapeutic issue. "She was almost beside herself at the idea of its being supposed that she had merely fancied something" on the occasion of Herr K.'s attempted seduction. Freud said to her: "You will agree that nothing makes you so angry as having it thought that you merely fancied the scene by the lake." Father Bauer had not reckoned with the quality of insight and total honesty of the therapist he chose for his daughter. In fact, Freud "came to the conclusion that Dora's story must correspond to the facts in every respect." She "kept anxiously trying to make sure whether I was being quite straightforward with her." This was a "transference" phenomenon because "Dora" lived in a world of deception and lies. It was, in her words, her father who "always preferred secrecy and roundabout ways," and in Freud's words: "Dora's father was never entirely straightforward." His "words did not always quite tally with" each other. "He was one of those men who know how to evade a dilemma by falsifying their judgement." Freud said: "I could not in general dispute Dora's characterization of her father; and there was one particular respect in which it was easy to see that her reproaches were justified. . . . the idea that she had been handed over to Herr K. as the price of his tolerating the relations between her father and his wife."[58]

The Bauer family had what in contemporary marital therapy would be a family "secret" or "myth" that held relationships in neurotic homeostasis.[59] The parents pretended nothing was going on while the father was having an affair with Frau K. and Herr K. was courting "Dora." Otto colluded in this denial for the sake of surface harmony and to avoid conflict.

"Dora's" refusal to go along with the family myth or blindness, her "impossible behaviour" in confronting the others and bringing them to account, made her conduct extremely uncomfortable for all concerned. She destroyed the homeostasis and precipitated her own therapy by exposing the family conspiracy. What Otto learned from the family constellation was avoidance of perceiving the real events, morally rationalizing and intellectualizing his denial, and an alternative identity. He would not be the deceiving dishonest father—he would be the father of integrity and morality, to the limited and surrogate extent that he was able to be a father at all.

Otto's primary identification was with his obsessional, rage-inducing, aggressive mother, who in Freud's opinion had obsessional symptoms of such severity as to be nearly psychotic. Otto's own obsessional neurosis was marked by his tendency to worry and speculate, overcautious behavior focused on avoiding all conflict, omnipotence in his thought, obsessive confessing as if he had committed the crimes of others, elaborate intellectual doubting when it came to action, a low level of genital activity, much energy, and a high level of intelligence. The underlying dynamics were strong repressed rage against his mother, who, we may infer, ruled the nursery with an iron hand. This anger and defiance, which he learned to fear and from which he had to protect himself, was defended against by reaction formations of high ethical standards, the martyr psychology of duty, and obedience to the imperatives of conscience.

Bauer not only never resolved the oedipal conflict, much of his behavior was as though he had never reached it. An oedipal character would have acted in a conflict situation—either so that he would win or so that he would be defeated and would destroy himself. Bauer did not act at all. He retreated from competition and confrontation in the political sphere and, psychodynamically, from the oedipal phase. In his sexual life he acted out his oedipal conflict by marrying a mother surrogate and having a mistress, but he never resolved the conflict.

From 1912 to 1913 Bauer lost both his parents within a year. After the death of his mother in August 1912, he wrote Karl Kautsky:

> Personally things have gone badly for me in the last weeks, since my father, who has turned to me more since the death of my mother, has been seriously ill for two months. Thus my ability to work is also reduced.

After his father's death nine months later, Bauer complained of being "burdened with many unpleasant and time-consuming business matters following my father's death."[60] The death of his parents freed him emotionally to marry.

In 1914 Bauer, then in his thirty-third year, was married for the first and only time. The woman he chose to re-create his family was ten years older than he and had three children. She was Helene Landau (née Gumplowicz), whom he had known for the past decade as the wife of a Polish socialist lawyer, Max Landau, who lived in Vienna. Helene had married Landau in 1895. She was intellectually powerful, having written a number of books and essays on economics, labor, and commerce in both Polish and German. She is pictured as lively, critical, and strong-minded. She had a salon—a circle of socialist youth who studied at her home. She was a member of the Vienna municipal school board, taught at the workers school, and wrote articles in *Der Kampf,* the theoretical journal of Austro-Marxism. Her relationship to Bauer is variously described as lacking emotional warmth and as very dependent on Bauer's part. The difference in their ages, her three children, and the independence of Helene Bauer suggest that in some important ways Bauer married a woman to whom he could relate as he had to his mother.

He always worked hard and was a heavy smoker, as was his father. After a full day of parliamentary and party business, he went to the offices of the *Arbeiter-Zeitung* late at night, dictated the next day's editorial, and engaged in long discussions with the editor, Friedrich Austerlitz. He was compulsively rigid about his daily routine, as was his mother. When, for example, someone was sitting at his customary table in the coffeehouse, Bauer would pace back and forth on the street outside until the table was free rather than sit elsewhere. His first question on coming home in the afternoon was: "Is the lady of the house in?" If she was not there, he called at her coffeehouse and asked her to come home.

After twelve years of marriage, in 1926, at age forty-five, Bauer developed an extramarital relationship with Hilda Schiller-Marmorek, a beautiful married woman ten years younger than he. She was active in the socialist movement and admired him as a great leader. The relationship began as a walking companionship on Sundays. After two years the couple saw each other privately and on one occasion took a weekend trip together. This relationship sustained Bauer in the last decade of his life, which was a time of frustration and defeat. Hilda Marmorek was to be a courier for Bauer, in the period that the party was illegal, when he was in Brünn.* At some points the couple talked of divorce and remarriage to each other. While Hilda Marmorek says she was willing to do so, Bauer was unwilling to leave Helene. It is suggestive of his father identification

*This information is based on an interview with Dr. Hilda Hannak (Vienna), Sept. 22, 1973. Two other admirable women who served him and the party as illegal couriers across the border between Brünn and Vienna were Professor Marie Jahoda (interview, Brighton, Sussex, July 27, 1972) and Dr. Muriel Gardiner, who was getting her psychoanalytic training in Vienna at the time (interview, New York, Dec. 14, 1973).

that Bauer developed an extramarital liaison just as his father had a mistress in Frau K. On some level of introjection, it may have meant to him that to be a man was to have an unsatisfying marriage and a mistress, like his father.

Otto Bauer showed frequent and specific inhibitions of aggressiveness in his political life. His oedipal aggression had been repressed and defended due to anxiety and guilt feelings. He withdrew politically and emotionally from confrontations with the opposition because to him the world was filled with dangerous murder which he would either have to deal out or have to suffer at the hands of the enemy. When the actual political situation demanded sharp and immediate measures to defend Austrian democracy and the Social Democratic movement, Bauer was unable to call upon enough anger to mobilize his combative skills and take action. The overall impression gained by a close examination of Bauer's behavior and speeches during periods of crisis is his avoidance of rage. His behavior is conspicuous for its apathy, lack of initiative, and reaction-formative moralizing and ethical preaching.

We must ask why this man chose to enter the rough and dangerous world of Austrian politics where aggression and annihilation of the enemy were the latent issues behind political conflict. It is reported that Bauer once discussed his career choice with Sigmund Freud, who advised him not to enter politics, but rather to be a teacher because it was more suited to his temperament. Freud is said to have warned Bauer: "Do not try to make men happy, they do not wish happiness."[61] Freud sensed the creative and adaptive aspects of Bauer's personality—his ability to empathize with and to inspire youth, his moral idealism and humanitarian vision. These were his character strengths and the source of his charisma.

Bauer's stance of moral superiority had political advantages, earning him the steadfast allegiance of dedicated socialist youth. They honored, idealized, and adored him. His appeal was precisely on the level of his purity of motive and humaneness in action. Many former young socialists have stressed what an inspiring figure Bauer was to them. The youth sat at his feet, listened, and learned. Professor Marie Jahoda recalls going to him for the first time in her capacity as the leader of the Austrian socialist high school students. She wished Social Democratic party support for the Communists in Rumania. He lectured her for an hour, explaining Bolshevik history and why the Austro-Marxists could not ally with Bolshevism. She accepted, understood, and became his disciple. The same was true of other youth leaders. Bauer, for example, made the research suggestion to Marie Jahoda, Paul S. Lazarsfeld, and Hans Zeisel that resulted in the first social-psychological study of an unemployed community.[62]

The memoirs of the working-class leader Julius Braunthal are especially candid and unembarrassed at describing the adoration accorded Bauer by one leader of socialist youth. He recalls Bauer as "the strongest spiritual experience I had in the socialist movement." Braunthal relates how he attended a lecture by Bauer in 1905 when the latter was twenty-four years old:

> When I listened to him for the first time—in awe and admiration, of course—I felt at once that from now on my life was bound to his and that there was no escape for me from the domination of his genius. . . . I, of course, longed ardently to enter somehow into personal relations with the man whom I admired so much.

Braunthal approached Bauer after a lecture and was invited to his parents' home, where Bauer lived. Bauer took the young worker to his room, lectured him on Marxism, provided him with a reading list, and won a personal follower. Joseph Buttinger, who as a young leader of the Carinthian Schutzbund worked with Bauer in the underground from 1933 to 1938, confirms Bauer's ability to inspire dedicated following among socialist youth because of his purity, idealism, and lofty moral qualities. Of Bauer, Buttinger said, "He was the Pope and we were the priests." Adam Wandruszka says that, for the leadership cadres he trained, "his word was the Gospel." Buttinger also points to the simple uneducated worker's admiration of the intellectuals who could apparently comprehend and explain the world. What he said applies to Bauer, including the special appeal for the Jew of acceptance by Gentiles:

> The Austrian workers' awe of mental achievement gave to many intellectual Jews the first and deepest happiness of their lives. This was their real escape from the loathsome ghetto. The charismatic idea of socialism superseded the faith of their fathers. The party placed them in the center of great social, political, and cultural processes. The labor movement gave them a chance to satisfy their mental and moral needs together with their material ones.[63]

For his part, Bauer showed the greatest admiration—indeed sometimes it was adulation—for the workers. His arrogance was targeted on the petit bourgeoisie. An example from 1930 reads:

> We are governed by the petit bourgeoisie of the towns of the Alpine provinces and the people of rank from the villages. They are not a cultured, worldly bourgeoisie accustomed to rule; rather they are an ignorant, provincial, clerical, small-minded shopkeeper class filled

with resentment against all that is metropolitan, new, or European
in scope.

Another example of his sarcasm toward the opposition was when, in defending the "dictatorship of the proletariat" concept of the Linz Program, he
said that in discussing democracy and dictatorship he was thinking of German Socialism, English Labor, Russian Bolshevism, the struggle between
Socialists and Communists in the whole world, Victor Adler and Lenin,
"but strangely, in both of my speeches at Linz, not for a single instant did
any of the members of the Austrian government come to my mind. We were
speaking of a world problem of socialism. And they believed we were speaking in order to threaten them."[64]

Bauer's nephew tells of an experience from the period when Bauer was
Foreign Minister which illustrates his rigid sense of personal integrity and
honesty. The nephew was on an outing with a group of boys. The going
got to be too much for a crippled boy, so the nephew telephoned his uncle
at the Foreign Ministry and asked him to send an official car for the boy.
Bauer did so, but later sternly lectured his young nephew never again to
compromise him by calling on his official prerogatives for a personal matter.[65]

Bauer's appeal to youth and his linear, and in that sense quite non-
Marxist, view of history are visible in an editorial he wrote for the *Arbeiter-
Zeitung* in April 1926. He entitled it "The Problem of Our Youth," in which
he said that the time of heroism for socialist youth was past. The dangerous
time of bloody sacrifice and confrontation with police was now merely a
socialist legend from the past. The party had become powerful and cautious
and youth wished to fight. Now even the obvious comfortable targets were
no longer there. Formerly employers were brutal, teachers ruled with the
rod, and fathers beat their children. Now the Social Democrats control
education, the employer may be a party member, and even fathers were
Social Democrats. The fight today, said Bauer, was "against ourselves, it is
a battle against bourgeois customs and prejudices."[66] The significant generational association of Bauer is that he assumed his generation were fighting
their fathers while the present generation were not. He was telling his
readers that, at least to him, joining Social Democracy was a defiance of his
father and paternal values. The irony of Bauer's statement is that the party
and its youth whom he was addressing were on the eve of the bloody
confrontations of 1927 to be followed by the long-embattled retreat to the
fascism of 1934 and illegal operations calling for sacrifice and heroism in a
measure no one anticipated. Those, like Bauer, who used the Habsburg
standards of autocracy as their basis for future judgments were not equipped

to handle the new meanings and personal costs of twentieth-century totalitarian terror.

We have explored two time-specific adaptations, from the same family, to the problem of developing an adult psychosexual and vocational identity. The task of adolescence is to break family libidinal ties, to find non-incestuous sexual relationships, independence, and a socially validated adult identity. "Dora" was held back from these necessary developments of adolescence because she was the victim of a pathological family interaction of half-truths in which she was thrown together with an older married man whose wife was also a mother substitute for her. Otto, the son, on the other hand, developed intellectual and political modes of mastery that were culture-specific "masculine" alternatives available for the displacement and sublimation of the family conflict. "Dora" somatized her conflicts into hysterical conversion symptoms and acted out the family problem in adolescence and then in an unhappy adult life. Politics and intellectualization were not identity alternatives for a girl of her time, class, and culture—they were the "male" solutions of her brother. We may say more—she dealt with the problem directly but ineffectively. Otto was equally ineffective but he displaced much more—into denial, reaction formation, intellectualization, and the sublimations of an ambivalent politics of Marxist non-revolution.

Otto Bauer was reacting against his father's hypocrisy. His identity resolution was to substitute the party and the high ethical principles of humanitarian socialism for the shattered ideal of his father. He would be the ideal father to party youth seeking to escape their family truths. Those who were looking for ideal fathers found him. Otto Bauer became the talking father who teaches his children purity, espouses intellection and morality. He postulated standards that his children could be proud of rather than the hypocrisy he received at home. The tragedy for Austrian socialism is that in reality Bauer was a weak father, inept, impotent, and castrated. As Wandruszka says, his story was "a Hamlet tragedy, the tragedy of a totally spiritual man, governed by theory, which in the end had to shatter in practical politics."[67]

The instrumental aspect of Bauer's characteristic stance in a crisis, of taking the high moral ground and lecturing his opponents, was that it did not work. He talked down to them, delivered sermons, was cutting and sarcastic, and attempted to induce guilt in his political counter-players. The problem with this tactic was twofold: the first was that it was a defensive projection of his own guilt and inability to act; secondly, Bauer's opponents had their own moral values and projective systems—their consciences were not particularly troubled by Bauer's accusations, at least not enough to inhibit action. The clerical Chancellor Seipel and his allies had their own fantasies about civil war and the Marxist danger. Seipel called July 15, 1927, a "revolution" on a scale such as Vienna had not experienced since the year 1848. He was a soldier in the army of the Lord fighting the Antichrist: "If men divide into the army camp of Christ and the army camp of the enemies of Christ, there will be a fight." He proposed to "carry Christ the Lord into the people," and in his diary viewed his "task after the first ten years in politics: Counter-Reformation in view of all the events and tendencies of the time, etc., leading away from religion and the church."[68] The First Austrian Republic had no liberal consensus of tolerance and goodwill toward the opposition. To the Social Democrats, the "Blacks" were the class enemy to be destroyed; to the Christian Socials the "Reds" were the dangerous revolutionary menace to be eradicated.

When we look at Bauer's actions as a political figure, and consider that political power itself is often a primary motive for leaders, we must remember that it may also be a defense against internal conflict. Added to the obvious narcissistic rewards of affection and prestige which public office and leadership of a mass movement offered Bauer, it also gave him reassurance against unconscious fears of passive-receptive and dependent needs. "In general," said Otto Fenichel, "it can be stated that those who strive passionately for power or prestige are unconsciously frightened persons trying to overcome and to deny their anxiety. . . . External power is sought as a means against an internal dependence."[69]

For Bauer, politics fulfilled many functions: By his violence in theory and his passivity in tactics he could attack the person and values of his father, as well as protect the enemy fathers from the fury of his aggression. In socialism he found an idealized cause symbolic of the defense of his mother. He could identify with the young and rebellious, gain their approval, and come into touch with his own unresolved rebellious self. For a period he could cope with his internal conflicts by projecting a politics of moral guilt, violent rhetoric, and paralyzed initiatives, until in the end his followers were discouraged, disheartened, and defeated. Bauer's personal conflict fitted the tragic ambivalence of Austro-Marxism.

Notes

1. Erik H. Erikson, *Childhood and Society,* rev. 2nd ed. (New York, 1963), pp. 326–58; W. R. Bion, *Experiences in Groups and Other Papers* (New York, 1959), pp. 67, 121–2; Robert Michels, *Political Parties,* trans. Eden and Cedar Paul (New York, 1915).

2. Ernst Fischer, *Erinnerungen und Reflexionen* (Hamburg, 1969), p. 152.

3. "Synopticus" [Karl Renner], *Zur österreichischen Nationalitätenfrage* (Vienna, 1899); *Staat und Nation* (Vienna, 1899); Rudolf Springer [Karl Renner], *Der Kampf der österreichischen Nationen um den Staat* (Vienna, 1902); *Grundlagen und Entwicklungsziele der österreichisch-ungarischen Monarchie* (Vienna, 1906), p. 208, as quoted in Robert A. Kann, *The Multinational Empire*, vol. 2. (New York, 1950), p. 159.

4. Otto Bauer, *Die Nationalitätenfrage und die Sozialdemokratie* (Vienna, 1907), in Bauer, *Werkausgabe* (Vienna, 1975), 1: 172, 174, 189. See also Karl W. Deutsch, *Nationalism and Social Communications: An Inquiry into the Foundations of Nationality* (Cambridge, Mass., 1953), for a modern expression of this principle, influenced by Bauer.

5. Bauer, *Werkausgabe*, 1: 421. Emphasis in the original 1907 edition.

6. *Ibid.*, pp. 432, 434, 435. Robert S. Wistrich, *Revolutionary Jews from Marx to Trotsky* (London, 1976), pp. 119–20.

7. V. I. Lenin, "Critical Remarks on the National Question," *Collected Works* (London and Moscow, 1964), 20: 38.

8. Robert C. Tucker, *Stalin as Revolutionary, 1879–1929: A Study in History and Personality* (New York, 1973), p. 152; Joseph Stalin, *Marxism and the National Question* (New York, 1942), pp. 15–17. On the authorship of this essay see Isaac Deutscher, *Stalin: A Political Biography*, rev. ed. (London, 1966), p. 126, and Bertram D. Wolfe, *Three Who Made a Revolution: A Biographical History* (Boston, 1948), pp. 581–3. Deutscher, Wolfe, and Trotsky hold that Stalin merely recorded Lenin's ideas. Tucker, on the other hand, after reviewing the literature and considering the style and language, argues convincingly that the work was primarily Stalin's own, pp. 155–6.

9. Bauer to Karl Seitz, in *Otto Bauer: Eine Auswahl aus seinem Lebenswerk*, ed. Julius Braunthal (Vienna, 1961), p. 24; Bauer to Helene Bauer, *ibid.*, p. 25.

10. Heinrich Weber [Otto Bauer], "Die russische Revolution und das europäanische Proletariat" (Oct. 1917), *Werkausgabe*, 2: 85–6.

11. Sigmund Freud, "Introductory Lectures on Psycho-Analysis" (1916–1917), *Standard Edition of the Complete Psychological Works*, trans. and ed. James Strachey et al. (London, 1953–1974), 16: 259–60. See also Sandor Rado, "Obsessive Behavior: So-called Obsessive-Compulsive Neurosis," Chapter 17 in *American Handbook of Psychiatry*, ed. Silvano Arieti (New York, 1959), 1: 324–44.

12. Joseph Schumpeter, "Sozialistische Möglichkeiten von heute," *Archiv für Sozialwissenschaft und Sozialpolitik*, 48 (1920–1921): 307. For Seipel's position of socialization, see "Die Christlichsoziale Partei und Sozialisierung," *Reichspost*, April 10, 1919. For the official Christian Social position see the *Neue Freie Presse*, Feb. 28, 1919, morning edition.

13. Bauer, "Der Weg zum Sozialismus" (1919), *Werkausgabe*, 2: 95.

14. Braunthal, ed., *Otto Bauer*, p. 33; Bauer, "Der Weg zum Sozialismus," p. 131; Stanley Suval, *The Anschluss Question in the Weimar Era: A Study of Nationalism in Germany and Austria, 1918–1932* (Baltimore, 1974), p. 20.

15. Karl Kautsky, *The Road to Power*, trans. A. M. Simons (Chicago, 1909), pp. 10, 50; Carl E. Schorske, *German Social Democracy, 1905–1917* (Cambridge, Mass., 1955), pp. 114–15.

16. Bauer to Karl Kautsky, May 15, 1904, *Kautsky Nachlass*, KD II, no. 463, International Institute for Social History, Amsterdam; Bauer to Kautsky, Oct. 23, 1914, *ibid.*, no. 490.

17. Bauer to Kautsky, June 20, 1922, *ibid.* no. 521.

18. Freud, "Fragment of an Analysis of a Case of Hysteria" (1905), *Standard Edition,* 7: 19.

19. Heinz Fischer, ed., *Zum Wort gemeldet: Otto Bauer* (Vienna, 1968), pp. 189–95. On Bauer's flight see Ernst Fischer, *An Opposing Man,* trans. Peter and Betty Ross (London, 1974), p. 150. Fischer was an eyewitness. The accuracy of his account was confirmed in an interview with another eyewitness, Professor Hans Zeisel, University of Chicago, March 26, 1974. See also Gerhard Botz, "Die Sozialdemokratische Partei und die Ursachen des '15 Juli 1927,' " *Aktion fur Kultur und Politik,* No. 2 (June–July 1967): 5.

20. Fischer, *Zum Wort gemeldet,* pp. 207–8.

21. *Ibid.*, pp. 236–7.

22. Klemens von Klemperer, *Seipel: Christian Statesman in a Time of Crisis* (Princeton, N.J., 1972), p. 274.

23. Bauer to Adler, Aug. 30, 1927, *Nachlass Friedrich Adler,* International Institute of Social History, Amsterdam, no. 132.

24. *Ibid.*

25. Bauer to Adler, May 13, 1927, *ibid,* no. 113.

26. Bauer, speech to the Social Democratic *Parteitag,* 1921, in "Die österreichische Revolution," *Werkausgabe,* 2: 803.

27. *Ibid.,* pp. 804, 806.

28. *Protokoll des sozialdemokratischen Parteitages 1926* (Vienna, 1926), p. 248.

29. Charles A. Gulick, *Austria from Habsburg to Hitler* (Berkeley and Los Angeles, 1948), 2: 1372.

30. Bauer, "Die österreichische Revolution," *Werkausgabe,* 2: 860; Gulick, 2: 1394.

31. Bauer, "Hoppla, wir leben," *Der Kampf,* 21, no. 1 (Jan. 1928): 1–4.

32. Bauer, "Die Bourgeois-Republik in Österreich," *Der Kampf,* 23, no. 5 (May 1930): 195–202.

33. Adam Wandruszka, "Das socialistische Lager," in *Geschichte der Republik Österreich,* ed. Heinrich Benedikt (Vienna, 1954), p. 450.

34. Bauer, "Idealismus und Nüchternheit," speech to the Twentieth Anniversary Celebration of the Worker's Abstinence League in Austria, Jan. 17, 1926. In Julius Braunthal, p. 333.

35. *Ibid.,* p. 334.

36. *Ibid.,* p. 336.

37. Gulick 1: 407–504 ("Municipal Housing and Tenants' Protection"); Bauer, *Mieterschutz, Volkskultur und Alkoholismus,* speech delivered to a meeting of the Vienna membership of the Workers Abstinence League, March 20, 1928 (Vienna, 1929), pp. 8, 9, 10.

38. Freud, "Fragment of an Analysis," *Standard Edition,* 7: 65; Otto Leichter, *Otto Bauer: Tragödie oder Triumph* (Vienna, 1970), p. 363 n. 6.

39. *Protokoll des sozialdemokratischen Parteitages 1929* (Vienna, 1929).

40. *Arbeiter-Zeitung,* March 8, 1933, in Braunthal, p. 85.

41. Braunthal, pp. 84, 85; Leichter, p. 29.

42. Bauer, "Der Aufstand der österreichischen Arbeiter" (1934), *Werkausgabe,* 3: 189.

43. Norbert Leser, *Zwischen Reformismus und Bolschewismus: Der Austromarxismus als Theorie und Praxis* (Vienna, 1968), p. 470.

44. Inez Kykal and Karl R. Stadler, *Richard Bernaschek: Odyssee eines Rebellen* (Vienna, 1976), pp. 90–5; Record of the Linz Court Hearing of Bernaschek, March 8,

1934, *ibid.,* pp. 290–1. See also Joseph Buttinger, *In the Twilight of Socialism: A History of the Revolutionary Socialists of Austria* (New York, 1953), p. 6.

45. Leser, p. 480.

46. Eric C. Kollman, *Theodor Körner: Militär und Politik* (Vienna, 1973), p. 220; Rudolf Neck, "Thesen zum Februar: Ursprunge, Verlauf und Folgen," in *Das Jahr 1934,* ed. Jedlicka and Neck, p. 24. See also the essay by Norbert Leser, "12 Thesen zum 12 Februar 1934," *ibid.,* pp. 58–64.

47. Interview with Professor Marie Jahoda (Brighton, Sussex), July 27, 1972.

48. *Der Kampf* (April 1938), as quoted in Herbert Steiner, "Am Beispiel Otto Bauers—die Oktober Revolution und der Austromarxismus," *Weg und Ziel* (Vienna, July 1967), p. 20; Leichter, p. 15.

49. Freud, "Fragment of an Analysis," *Standard Edition,* 7:9.

50. *Ibid.,* pp. 19, 34–5.

51. *Ibid.,* p. 54.

52. Felix Deutsch, "A Footnote to Freud's 'Fragment of an Analysis of a Case of Hysteria,' " *Psychoanalytic Quarterly,* 26 (1957): 163, 167.

53. Freud, "Fragment of an Analysis," *Standard Edition,* 7: 26; Leichter, p. 23.

54. Freud, "Fragment of an Analysis," *Standard Edition* 7: 26, 33.

55. *Ibid.,* pp. 21, 51, 82 n. 1. "Screen memories are childhood memories characterized by unusual sharpness and by their apparent insignificance of content. They are displacements from repressed sexual experiences or fantasies." See Freud, "Screen Memories" (1899), *Standard Edition,* 3: 299–322.

56. Interview with Dr. Wanda Lanzer (Vienna), Sept. 6, 1972.

57. Deutsch, "A Footnote to Freud," pp. 161, 163.

58. Freud, "Fragment of an Analysis," *Standard Edition,* 7: 26, 34, 46, 108, 118, 109. See also Erik H. Erikson, "Reality and Actuality," *Journal of the American Psychoanalytic Association,* 10: 451–74. For other interpretations of the "Dora Case," see Karl Kay Lewin, "Dora Revisited," *Psychoanalytic Review,* 60; no. 4 (Winter 1973/74): 519–32; Jules Glenn, "Freud's Adolescent Patients: Katherina, Dora, and the 'Homosexual Woman,' " in *Freud and His Patients,* ed. Mark Kanzer and Jules Glenn (New York, 1980), pp. 23–47; Hyman Muslin and Merton Gill, "Transference in the Dora Case," *Journal of the American Psychoanalytic Association,* 26: 2 (1978) 311–28; Arnold A. Rogow, "A Further Footnote to Freud's 'Fragment of a Case of Hysteria,' " *ibid.,* 331–56; "Dora's Brother," *International Review of Psycho-Analysis,* 6: 2 (1979), 239–59; Hannah S. Decker, "Freud and Dora: Constraints on Medical Progress," *Journal of Social History,* 14 (1981), 445–64; "The Choice of a Name: "Dora" and Freud's Relationship with Breuer," *Journal of the American Psychoanalytic Association,* 30 (1982), 113–36.

59. See, for example, how family myth is interpreted in Paul Watzlawick, Janet Helmick Beavin, and Don D. Jackson, *Pragmatics of Human Communication:* *A Study of Interactional Patterns, Pathologies, and Paradoxes* (New York, 1967), pp. 172–8.

60. Bauer to Kautsky, *Kautsky Nachlass,* Jan. 3, 1913, no. 493; Bauer to Kautsky, *ibid.,* Sept. 25, 1913, no. 496.

61. Leichter, p. 371 n. 13, and interview (Vienna), Sept. 6, 1972.

62. Interview with Professor Marie Jahoda (Brighton, Sussex), July 27, 1972; Marie Jahoda, Paul S. Lazarsfeld, and Hans Zeisel, *Die Arbeitslosen von Marienthal* (Leipzig, 1933), trans. by the authors with John Reginall and Thomas Elsaesser as *Marienthal: The*

Sociography of an Unemployed Community (Chicago, 1971). Lazarsfeld and Zeisel were also admiring Bauer disciples: interview with Lazarsfeld (Los Angeles), May 23, 1975; interview Zeisel (Chicago), March 26, 1974.

63. Braunthal, *Auf der Suche nach dem Millennium* (Nuremberg, 1948), p. 418, trans. as *In Search of the Millennium* (London, 1945), pp. 15, 73; interview with Dr. Joseph Buttinger, New York, Dec. 14, 1973; Wandruszka, "Das sozialistische Lager," p. 444; Buttinger, *In the Twilight of Socialism,* p. 81.

64. Bauer, "Die Bourgeois-Republik in Österreich," *Der Kampf,* 23, no. 5 (May 1930): 197; Wandruska, "Das sozialistische Lager," p. 449.

65. Interview with "Dora's" son, June 20, 1972.

66. Bauer, "Das Problem Unserer Jungen," *Arbeiter-Zeitung,* April 11, 1926, in Braunthal, pp. 325–7.

67. Wandruszka, "Das socialistische Lager," p. 452.

68. Klemperer, *Seipel,* pp. 263, n. 158.

69. Otto Fenichel, *The Psychoanalytic Theory of Neurosis* (New York, 1945), pp. 479, 482–8.

PART IV

The German Case

Leaders, Followers, and Group Process

Psychodynamic analysis and interpretation has from the beginning taken a leading place in the continuing effort to understand the Nazi movement and its leaders. The enterprise has been only partially successful, as have the researches of social scientists and historians, in explaining the primal passions acted out on a world scale in the Third Reich. Nor have the attempts of theologians, philosophers, and novelists been more satisfactory or definitive in capturing and making comprehensible the radical human evil, aggression, and destructiveness that was Nazism. Interpretive efforts in history will always be *post hoc* reconstructions, rather than replications of *wie es eigentlich gewesen ist*. While we may crave total explanations and definitive syntheses, partial insights and new integrations must suffice, for they are all we have or ever will have in history and in the present.

The following two essays look at both the individual and group phenomena of Nazism. The study of Himmler is an exploration, based on unusually complete childhood and adolescent data, of the character of a murderous leader from the top echelon of Nazis, that cadre of Hitler disciples who as bureaucrats operated his death industry and kept the Third Reich functioning for twelve years.

A historian working on the likes of Himmler must be aware of his feelings of repugnance as they intrude on his vision of the past. My aversion was handled by using psychodynamic formulations as a defense, which need not necessarily invalidate the "truth" value of the insights. Six years after publication I received a letter from Bradley Smith affirming my views of Himmler's latent homosexuality from new evidence he had found in Himmler's speeches. He wrote: "I thought it was awfully important to the whole man, and it also showed you were right and my doubts were wrong." It takes a fine man to make a concession validating a method in which he does not believe. Can any historian ask for more generosity from a colleague or greater candor from a critic?

Both of my parents were children in Germany during World War I. Their tales of hunger and deprivation recounted amidst a bountiful American childhood made a lasting impression on me. As a Fulbright student in Berlin in 1961/62, "the year of the Wall," I witnessed and understood the fear of shortages and the food panic of the population. These two direct personal experiences determined the conviction and research behind the Nazi youth cohort essay. The project of moving from individual case studies to historical group phenomena is currently the cutting edge of psychohistorical research, as is the interpretation of symbolic and cultural artifacts such as literature. This essay is conceived as a contribution to these two "next assignments."

The Unsuccessful
Adolescence of Heinrich Himmler

The personality of Heinrich Himmler (1900–1945), the Reichsführer SS, has been an enigma to students of the Third Reich. The German historian Helmut Heiber poses the paradoxes confronting the scholar who would understand the man:

> Who was the true Heinrich Himmler? The petty schoolmaster who distributes report cards to his students? Or the writing-desk murderer whose total balance is just short of ten million people? Or the man of honor who controls millions of marks yet deducts 150 marks for a wristwatch from his salary? Is he the subordinate who can only quakingly stand before his Führer? Or the commander who tries to move his men to hold out until the end with smart orders of the day? The administrator who in rational terms built up an uncannily effective apparatus? Or the believer in occult and magic who accepted counsel and advice from seers? The moralist who is speechless at the sight of smut literature on an SS leader's desk? Or a possessed man whose self-created "mission" drove him beyond the pale of human-

kind? Perhaps a vegetable gardener who seeks to return to the natural life? The leader of knights who always has his men close to his heart?[1]

Heiber thus invokes apparent inconsistencies and contradictions in personality and behavior to suggest what he terms "the especially many faces" of Himmler, which cannot be integrated.

Two American historians, Werner T. Angress and Bradley F. Smith, have collaborated in studying Himmler's early years. They find that there were two distinct Himmlers: an early, "normal" one and a later psychopath. The early Himmler "was to all appearances a normal human being." "It is," they write, "bewildering to discover how genuinely kind, considerate, and at times downright compassionate he was as a youth." This statement suggests that these historians were looking for a psychopath, or at least for a pervert and sadist, a youth who tortured children and animals. "None of the existing passages" from his diary, they say, "convey the impression that the diarist was inherently cruel and inhumane." We may accept their *Problemstellung:* "The real problem posed by the diaries is the image which they give of their author's personality, an image difficult to reconcile with the sinister role played by the same man only a little over a decade later."[2] A modern bureaucratic mass murderer, however, is not necessarily a psychopath. The conclusions of Angress and Smith were based largely on Himmler's adolescent diaries. The diary, a unique and extensive documentary resource that is substantial but incomplete, gives a highly personal view into the life and character formation of Himmler between the ages of fourteen and twenty-four.*

Using the adolescent diary as a source, I shall attempt to show that

---

*The background of these manuscripts dates from 1945 when an American soldier was searching for souvenirs in Himmler's villa at Gmünd on Bavaria's Tegernsee. He found six cheap, soft-covered notebooks of varying sizes that contained sections of Himmler's youthful diaries from Aug. 23, 1914, to Feb. 25, 1924. The inclusive dates covered by the diaries are Aug. 23, 1914, to Sept. 26, 1915; Jan. 1 to June 14, 1916; Aug. 1, 1919, to Feb. 2, 1920; Nov. 1, 1921, to Dec. 12, 1921; Jan. 12, 1922, to March 28, 1922; May 26, 1922, to July 6, 1922; and Feb. 11, 1924, to Feb. 25, 1924. The notebooks were secured by an American intelligence officer as his private possession and in 1957 were turned over to the Hoover Institution on War, Revolution and Peace at Stanford University, where they were authenticated and are now deposited in the vault. I am indebted to Professor Bradley F. Smith for sharing with me his conclusion that Himmler was taught to keep this diary by his father, who supervised its writing and checked it for the first three days it was written. This confirms the thesis that the diary was obsessive in nature even at its genesis. It was for Himmler an act of compliance with his father. Professor Smith also has investigated the content of Himmler's book list of over 280 titles, which is included in his book *Heinrich Himmler: A Nazi in the Making, 1900–1926* (Stanford, 1971), pp. 173–9. Smith sees the concept of *Treue* as the central axis of Himmler's personality (pp. 142, 171–2). Psychodynamically, *Treue* is a superego phenomenon denoting loyalty, duty, obedience, "keeping the faith," and being "good." *Meine Ehre heisst Treue!* was, of course, to be the motto of the SS.

psychoanalytic theory and clinical insight can be utilized to demonstrate an emotional coherence and internal consistency of personality between the adolescent and the adult Himmler. His character could be interpreted as normal in a culture that places a high value on self-control, discipline, order, cleanliness, and punctuality in its childhood socialization. He had a set of behavioral norms that conformed with the demands of his middle-class south German environment. He also had the facets of reactive pity, conscientiousness, and precision that are prototypical of character "armor" against underlying aggression.

The tone and content of Himmler's diary differ markedly from the emotional turmoil typical of adolescence. Peter Blos says of adolescent diaries:

> Daydreams, events, and emotions which cannot be shared with real people are confessed with relief to the diary. . . . The diary stands between daydream and object world, between make-believe and reality, and its content and form change with the times; for material that once was kept as an anxiously guarded secret today is openly expressed. . . . The diary . . . serves the . . . psychological purpose [of] . . . filling the emotional void felt when the novel instinctual drives of puberty can no longer be articulated on old objects and cannot yet be articulated on new objects, so that fantasy life assumes a most important and essential function.[3]

Anna Freud describes the diaries and jottings of adolescents in a similar way:

> We are not only amazed at the wide and unfettered sweep of their thought but impressed by the degree of empathy and understanding manifested, by their apparent superiority to more mature thinkers and sometimes even by the wisdom which they display in their handling of the most difficult problems.[4]

In contrast to the typical adolescent diary, Himmler's diary is flat, virtually emotionless, and colorless. His superego structure was primitive; it was personified by his father, later by the Pope, and finally by Hitler. Women were seen as dangerous creatures. His mother is mentioned only twice in the diary, as though she hardly existed. The diary acted as a tranquilizer used by Himmler to hang on to reality.

The youthful Himmler was addicted to detail. He made a written accounting of the mundane details of his life—showers, shaves, baths, mealtimes, and the totaling of his expenses at the end of the day. A historian encountering these diaries must regret the lack of substantive intellectual content and emotional response. Himmler relates, for example, that he read the newspaper but does not tell how he felt about the events of the time. And when he writes that he talked politics, sex, and religion he gives no indication of his ideas or feelings on these subjects. Angress and Smith ascribe this absence to the fact that

> Himmler, the collector of trivia, thought it too difficult to render the content of a conversation, but easy enough to immortalize the fact that on June 28, 1922, he picked up his eyeglasses from the optician, or that on November 23, 1921, a distant relative gave him a bar of candy before going home. Moreover, Himmler was not always up-to-date on his diary and would write entries for several days at one time. This may account in part for his recollection of routine duties and minor events rather than of the content of conversations which he either forgot or, at best, remembered only superficially.[5]

To explain the flat, colorless descriptions of the diary as arising from Himmler's difficulty in rendering content and his lack of memory for it is a singular denial by excellent historians of the message communicated by the very form of this diary: the diary itself was an obsessional object whose purpose was to guard against feelings. The proposition that dreary details of life are easier to recall after a few days than either the feeling of experience or the content of conversation seems highly questionable; rather the contrary would appear to be normal. What the diary reveals is that its author was a rigid, repressed character who experienced only weak and limited feelings. The prim detail is in itself a manifestation of Himmler's character structure that demands interpretation.

There is another point of view, more widespread and ahistorical, concerning Himmler and the atrocities of National Socialism. This attitude holds that the men who guided the Third Reich are essentially incomprehensible to normal people. Their minds are considered so bizarre, so far removed from anything we know, as to constitute "a different world from the one we have known for the last six or seven centuries. . . . Its [National Socialism's] initiators no longer had any intellectual, moral or spiritual affinities with ourselves in any basic sense; and despite external resemblances, they were as remote from us as the Australian aborigines." This view abjures all critical judgment and comprehension by denying the possibility of empathy and identification with every other human being who has lived and acted in history. Rather than treating Nazi leadership as a human phenomenon whose study may reward us with a better understanding of ourselves and our western and northern European culture, this view regards Himmler as of another universe or at least "another planet." "He did not inhabit the same world [as we do]; he belonged to an entirely different order of things, with a different mentality,"[6] say these seers who wish to consider only the joyful and transcendent aspects of man and who, therefore, mistakenly would try to obviate the powerful aggressive and destructive forces that also reside in him.

But the purveyors of happiness cannot do so, for the powers of aggression will not be denied if we mean to live in this world. Indeed, to deny the forces of aggression and destruction and split them off by saying that they exist elsewhere but not in us and our civilization is the certain way to repress them and to ensure their emergence in all their destructive fury. Nazi Germany, and its Holocaust, was a human phenomenon refracting the forces of sublimation, compulsivity, repression, and regression of our time and our culture, and only by seeing it as such can we come to terms with it. We must recognize and accept that the Nazi Holocaust touches the deepest emotional wellsprings of all who presume to study it and all whose lives have been affected by it, as does psychoanalysis, and as should history itself.

Himmler's adolescent diary, taken as a whole, shows him to have been a schizoid personality who was systematic, rigid, controlled, and restricted in emotional expression in a pattern that is consistent with what psychoanalysis defines as the obsessive-compulsive character.* Freud called the obsessional neurotic "unquestionably the most interesting and repaying subject of analytic research."[7] The psychodynamics of an obsessional character are those of a person whose object relations† are intact and whose character has

---

*The functional meaning of the schizoid personality and the obsessive-compulsive character will be elaborated in context and operational detail in the course of this essay. Briefly, schizoid describes an attempt to withdraw emotionally from the external world and to live in a repressed, internal psychic world of inner objects. An obsessive-compulsive character is one who uses the rituals and routines of daily life to avoid an active, living, experiencing, loving contact with his full inner feelings and with the outer world. Major features of this character are magical thinking, rumination, doubting, and a rigid and destructive conscience. The clinical picture results from a regression to the anal-sadistic phase of development. The character defenses include the mechanisms of isolation (splitting off of ideas from the feelings originally associated with them), reaction formation (replacement of a painful idea or feeling by its opposite), and undoing (symbolically expressing a wish and its reversal); all are designed to bolster and ensure the maintenance of repression. See Sigmund Freud, "Inhibitions, Symptoms and Anxiety" (1926), *Standard Edition*, 20: 77–175. The fascination of this complex is its constant formation of new symptoms because the conflicts of ambivalence are never resolved: "A ceaseless struggle is being waged against the repressed, in which the repressing forces steadily lose ground" (p. 113); an obsessional neurosis "spreads over into a general disposition of the ego" (p. 158); and "the ego and the super-ego have a specially large share in the formation of symptoms" (p. 113); "the ego is the scene of action of symptom formation in obsessional neurosis" (p. 119). The obsessive-compulsive character is particularly fertile ground for research because the symptoms are in the conscious ego and related to reality, "and indeed . . . the very process of thinking becomes hypercathected and erotised" (p. 119). The implications of this suggestion for intellectual history have yet to be fully explored.

†Object relations refers to the individual's relation to infantile internal images of the parents or parent surrogates, primarily the mother or the mothering figure. Object relations are of special interest and value to the historian because they include relations where libidinal and aggressive gratifications are sublimated, as in friendships and love between parent and child. Thus an evaluation can be made of the individual's capacity to love, which may be stunted or immature because

regressed to the anal mode. But Himmler's object relations indicate few mature introjects.* He identified and his identifications were total. Identification is the original and most infantile form of relation to, and dependence upon, objects. Himmler could be as loving or as aggressive as the person with whom he was identifying. Beneath the identification with his cultural environment, which was expressed by his compulsivity, there was an empty inner core to his personality; he lacked emotional structure. His expressions of feeling were transient identifications and imitations rather than genuine emotions. They had the rubber-stamp quality of one who sees and feels what he is expected to see and feel. His emotional life was barren and impoverished, and his expressions were artificial, lacking real relationship. He was, however, precisely what one should expect of the subordinate of a dictator and the head of a vast police network. If historians look at character structure they will indeed find a consistency in Himmler's adolescent and adult emotional attitudes and behavior. Even as an adolescent he showed the severe withdrawal from the object world that he exhibited at the height of his power.

It should be of interest to the historian that the eminent British clinician and theorist of object relations Harry Guntrip uses Heinrich Himmler as his prime example in his description of the schizoid personality. He

---

the personality has been distorted or arrested in its development. The consequences of primitive object relations in contrast to the more mature forms of object love have been developed by Ernest Jones in terms that directly apply to Himmler and the SS personality ideal: "An apparently soft and yielding nature is by no means necessarily the mark of a loving nature. It may simply mean that the unconscious sadism has been retained in its primitive state, needing the energy of reaction formations to keep it there, instead of being transformed into the valuable character traits of firmness and strength with which to meet the difficulties of life or, if necessary, to resist the will of one's adversaries. On the other hand it is equally certain that much of what passes as 'strength' of 'character' is an illusion. Such traits as obstinacy, pugnacity, extreme 'individualism,' cynicism, hardness of heart, insensitiveness to the feelings of other human beings, however useful they may on occasion be to their owner, are often little more than defenses against love of which the person is too afraid—or, more strictly, of possible consequences of this love. A matter-of-fact attitude of being 'superior to sentiment' is often a buttressing of the personality, a self-justification in the presence of deep-seated fear. We thus see that the degree of friendliness and affection is to be estimated by the *internal freedom* of such feelings rather than by the quantity of them that may be manifest. It will then be found that this freedom is accompanied by a slowness of response to hostility or even to opposition. The assimilation and control of the unconscious sadism, the same thing that allows love and friendliness to flow easily, begets an inner confidence and security that enable the person to endure opposition calmly and to be so unintimidated by hostility as to render aggressive opposition on his part unnecessary except in extreme and urgent situations." "The Concept of a Normal Mind" (1931), *Papers on Psycho-Analysis* (Boston, 1961), p. 210.

*An introject is that part of the parent or parent substitute that the child takes into himself as if it were his own, so that he acts in the same way whether or not the object (parent) is present. The child does not copy the parent as in the case of identification; he treats the parent's demands, directions, and admonitions as if they were his own. The difference is this: the child who does what the parent does is responding to an identification, but the child who acts in accordance with the forbidding, regulating, and rewarding aspects of the parent is responding to a parent introject.

writes that "the cold and inscrutable Himmler showed all the marks of a deeply schizoid personality."[8] While this judgment may be based on the adult Himmler, it invites an examination of his adolescence for schizoid symptoms.

The schizoid person is introverted—cut off from the world of outer reality in an emotional sense, withdrawn, and narcissistic. He is emotionally self-sufficient and feels superior to other people because he does not need them, because they are dispensable. He presents a picture lacking in affect, excluding feeling from relationships with other people. The poverty of external relationships results in loneliness that shows itself in an intense longing for friendship and love in the abstract. A schizoid personality often has feelings of depersonalization, of loss of identity and individuality. He flees inward and backward from the external world in states of regression. He is emotionally inaccessible, apathetic, cut off. The schizoid does not experience suffering, excitement or enthusiasm, anger or affection. He builds up a repressed, robot-like, mechanized personality. He does the "correct and necessary thing" without any feeling entering into the action. As Guntrip puts it, "Duty rather than affection becomes the key word." He goes on to cite as indications of the schizoid's repression of feeling and retreat from emotional relationships such obsessional symptomatology as list-making, the routinizing of a whole life, "doing things in order," hard work, and efficient organization. "He keeps detached from human relations in varying degrees while keeping his frightened sense of utter isolation repressed and unconscious." A marked schizoid factor in the personality, according to Ronald Fairbairn, is the *"repression of affect* and an attitude of detachment which leads others to regard them [schizoid personalities] as remote—and, in more extreme cases, even as inhuman." Himmler grossly displayed what Fairbairn calls "the schizoid tendency to treat other people as less than persons with an inherent value of their own." Sometimes, Fairbairn notes, the schizoid treats other people as if they are lower animals rather than persons.[9]

Himmler's family background was typically Bavarian petit bourgeois and white-collar in its values, behavioral norms, and expectations. His father, Gebhard Himmler, a pedantic and conscientious schoolteacher, had been a royal tutor to the Bavarian House of Wittelsbach. After 1913 he was the headmaster of a school, which his sons attended, in Landshut, a provincial town fifty miles northeast of Munich. His wife, Anna, the daughter of a moderately well-to-do tradesman, had brought some money into the marriage. Little is known about her. Unlike Gebhard Himmler, she scarcely receives mention in her son's diary. Heinrich, born in 1900, was the second of the three Himmler boys. Gebhard was two years his senior, and Ernst was five years younger.

The Himmler home was secure, conventional, and highly aware of a social status derived from affiliation with the House of Wittelsbach. Ernst Hanfstaengl, who was a student of Gebhard Himmler, describes him as "a terrible snob, favoring the young titled members of his class and bearing down contemptuously on the commoners." Prince Heinrich of Bavaria was asked to be the godfather and namesake of his former tutor's second son. Heinrich Himmler always maintained a high awareness of rank and titles. He meticulously referred to the correct title and social status of anyone mentioned in his diary.[10]

Himmler was obsessed by time schedules. He filled his diary with the precise minutiae of daily routine, the arrival and departure times of trains, as well as the exact amount of time he was late or delayed. An illustrative entry of a trip to Munich on a June day in 1922, when he was twenty-one, reads:

> 8:00 got up. Ran errands. Newspaper.
> 9:00 to Lorwitz. . . .
> 11:45 ate at Lorwitz.
> 12:20 I was to meet Father at the train station, but I only got there
> at 12:30. . . . Joined Father in a parlor car in Dachau.
> 3:00 arrived in Ingolstadt.
> 4:00 into the center of the city. Mother and Gebhard met us.
> Drank coffee.[11]

Himmler's exaggerated interest in timetables suggests that as long as they function as regulators of his activities he cannot commit the sins that he unconsciously fears. His life is systematized by timetables, and thus he is protected against dangerous instinctual demands. As long as he knows beforehand what he will do next, Himmler need not fear that, in his excitement, he may sin. For him the timetable becomes a protection against the menace of dangerous spontaneity. The prearranged plan is insurance that nothing will go wrong, that objectionable impulses will remain excluded. Time thus became for him the arena in which conflicts between impulse and control were fought out.

The awareness of the flow of time is unconsciously rooted deep in oral and anal erotism. As Otto Fenichel has pointed out, "Anal experiences are of importance for the measurement of time and for the development of schedules as a means of mastering reality." "How often defecation has to take place, at what intervals it has to be done, how long the process itself should take, how long it may successfully be postponed, and so on, are the situations in which the child acquires the ideas of order and disorder regarding time, and of measurement of time in general."[12] Time has important oral qualities as well, with connotations related to feeding and strictly regulated gratification.

The adolescent Himmler wished to be strong. On the eve of his fifteenth birthday he wrote: "I work out with dumbbells every day now to get more strength."[13] But as adolescence developed, his perception of strength became an inner one. Strength was to him a function of inner control, of self-discipline over his emotions. This is essentially an anal-retentive mode of acquiring strength. Strength is to be ensured by holding in feelings and by the repression of self-expression.

Five years later Himmler vows that he will seize "like iron the bit of self-control in my mouth [*ich will mich eisern an die Kandare nehmen*]." "I can only," he writes, "be a friend to my friends, do my duty, work, struggle with myself and never concede the loss of control over myself." On the next day he assures himself that he "never allows his gloomy thoughts and struggles of the soul to be noticed."[14] This self-control, which he must never lose, the feelings he must not show, are the character "armor" of the dissociation of his affects from his ideas. This controlled and restricted affect shows in Himmler's outwardly lukewarm reactions to inner pleasure or rage. His appearance of restraint masked and defended against his undeveloped emotions and the inner unconscious sadism that he harbored and did not allow direct expression.

The "iron" sexual self-control that the nineteen-year-old Himmler strove for was probably the manifestation of the struggle to control his impulse to masturbation and its associated aggressive and libidinous fantasies. He seems to have remained a virgin for the next seven years. His struggle for control reached a peak of intensity during the end of October and early November 1919. It is upon this period that I shall concentrate.

The contrasting images of masculine and feminine in Himmler's consciousness come to the fore when he witnesses a conflict between a girl and her father over the girl's desire for private dance lessons. He describes the father as "unyielding and stiff-necked like a tyrant." According to his own account, Himmler interposed himself and helped the young lady a great deal. "The poor little girl wept tears," he writes. "I truly pitied her. But she had no idea how pretty she was in her tears." Himmler's interpretation of the emotional constellation suggests that he might have viewed this scene previously in his life. Was it a reenactment of something exciting and familiar? Could it be that he had witnessed such scenes at home and that his father had treated his mother in this way? For here we see that, to him, men and fathers were hard, women and mothers were soft and permitted to cry.

When he dealt with a woman he was determined to "show her that I am a man."[15] He views himself as a chivalrous knight fighting for a defenseless girl who is persecuted by an overbearing father. But he has also indicated an identification with those who are dominated and exploited by the fathers.

The one instance recorded in the diary where Himmler appears to show real compassion occurs two years later, when he has contact with a poor old lady who has scarcely enough to eat and who is almost too weak to go out of the house. He is sorry for her. "People are as hard and uncharitable as they can be," he writes. "The princess visits her and does not see her plight. . . . I fetched rolls for her and added a small cake, which I laid down without her noticing it. If only I could do more, but we are poor devils ourselves."[16]

Here his feeling for the deprived woman is an identification with her as a suffering person. Apart from this he had no emotional relationship to her. What he experienced was an identification with the poor old woman who had received no love and little food, whom the princess treated coldly, and who aroused anxiety and pity for himself. He is feeding and empathizing with his own desolated and injured inner objects.

During this period of his life Himmler placed his relations with girls in the context of an aim-inhibited familial relationship. After a long talk about religion with a friend named Maia (Maria) he writes in his diary, "I have now found a sister." But she had a boyfriend, of whom Heinrich says, "I believe he doesn't understand her, his golden girl." They all enjoyed musical evenings together. He describes those group relationships as: "Some in love, others [himself] in the friendship of brothers and sisters." Three days later Heinrich "sees" the bad character of his rival and feels sorry for him and for the girl.[17]

Aggression and hostility became erotized in Himmler under the color of the postwar German nationalism that was particularly strong among young war veterans.* He felt a joy in 1919 over future battles in which he would again wear the King's uniform. To be effective he must maintain control, he must never let himself go: "I do not want to become weak, I never want to lose rein over myself. I may be in a war or battle in a few years and I am joyful over the War of Liberation and will pull an oar if I can then still move a limb." In this case the need for self-control and strength is rationalized by a nationalist purpose. But the homoerotic appeal of the manly companionship of the trenches was not lost on Himmler. He told his brother

---

*Himmler joined the 11th Bavarian Infantry Regiment toward the end of 1917 as a conscript. He completed a course for officer cadets in the summer of 1918 and another as a machine gunner in September. He was released from the Army on Dec. 18, 1918, without having obtained a commission. Roger Manvell and Heinrich Fraenkel, *Heinrich Himmler* (London,1965), p. 4; Angress and Smith, "Diaries of Heinrich Himmler's Early Years," p. 208.

and his friend "how nice it would have been if we had stayed in the military and gone to the front together, etc."[18]

The years 1919 to 1922 were a period of acute identity diffusion* for Himmler. He experienced this typical crisis of adolescence about three or four years later than is normal. His sexual, ethnic, social, vocational, and religious identities were in flux. We may observe the day-by-day oscillation of the components of his identity as he confronts the internal and outer demands of genital sexuality, relations with girls, his self-definition as a man and the counter-definition of females as women, the difficult choice of what to do for life and where to live, the impact of contemporary political and racial agitation, and his struggle with the requirements of Roman Catholicism that were in conflict with his impulses. He had a feeling of inner emptiness and an intense desire to start life anew. Sometimes he regressed to the pleasures of earlier modes of handling tension. He felt hunger fears that he dealt with by consuming great quantities of food. He was frequently a castigating, critical self-observer who tolerated no lapses. Always there was a desperate struggle for control of his impulses, of his surroundings, of time and money, of words, and of anger.

The most pressing decision that Himmler faced at this time was his choice of a life's work. He early decided to become a farmer, as he liked working with animals. The German *Mittelstand,* to which the Himmlers belonged, however, was highly sensitive to downward social mobility in the years immediately after World War I and the vocational choice of farm work represented a distinct loss of social status for the son of a middle-class schoolmaster. Himmler's interest in animal husbandry suggests an erotic displacement onto caring for and fondling beasts and an attempt to get closer to the organic life processes. Individuals who have impoverished object relations often displace their object relations onto lower animals. Later, as Reichsführer SS, Himmler would develop an intense preoccupation with the breeding of a new Nazi race.† In early September 1919, em-

---

*Erik H. Erikson defines identity diffusion as "a split of self-images . . . a loss of centrality, a sense of dispersion and confusion, and a fear of dissolution." "A state of acute identity diffusion usually becomes manifest at a time when the young individual finds himself exposed to a combination of experiences which demand his simultaneous commitment to *physical intimacy* (not by any means always overtly sexual), to decisive *occupational choice,* to *energetic competition,* and to *psycho-social self-definition.* " "During lovemaking or in sexual fantasies, a loosening of *sexual identity* threatens: it even becomes unclear whether sexual excitement is experienced by the individual or by his partner, and this in either heterosexual or homosexual encounters." "The Problem of Ego Identity," in *Identity and the Life Cycle: Selected Papers, Psychological Issues,* vol. 1, no. 1, monograph 1 (New York, 1959), pp. 122 n. 7, 123, 125.

†As Reichsführer SS, Himmler personally screened the racial purity and physical type of the women his SS leaders married. One of his pet ideas was a plan for choosing women for racial breeding with SS men, just as one would breed a strain of animals or plants. Felix Kersten, *Memoirs 1940–1945,* trans. Constantine Fitzgibbon and James Oliver (New York, 1957), pp. 78–9.

ployed on a farm near Ingolstadt, he contracted typhoid fever. Because of an enlarged heart he chose to take a year out from farm work to study.

Within seven weeks he had plans to emigrate to the East that were fused with the ideology of Germany's historic eastward expansion, his own idealized sexual aspirations, and his compulsive controls through work: "I work because it is my duty, because I find peace in work, and I work for my German ideal of womanhood with whom I one day will live my life as a German and fight my battles in the East, far from my beloved Germany."[19] We note that the nationalism of *Drang nach Osten* is here associated with work and self-discipline, which serve to control anxiety and to fulfill his ideal of Germanic feminine purity. Using the tritest clichés of his culture, he fuses sexuality with aggression in the name of German womanhood. Being married and staying in Germany was impossible. It is as though the beloved homeland were an incestuous sexual object where sexual thoughts and feelings are tabooed. He could not be sexual and be in Germany. To have a sexual relationship with a woman near to home would remind him too much of his mother.

Looking forward to emigration, he began to study Russian. These plans show a substantial lack of reality testing—a Russia torn in a civil war between Reds and Whites was the last place where a bourgeois German farmer would be welcome. This plan of emigration was a fantasy he nourished throughout the years of his identity crisis. In November 1921 he considered emigration to Turkey, eastern Europe, and Peru. Two months later his goal was Georgia and the Caucasus. In 1924 he again thought of emigration to the Caucasus or Turkey. In actuality, for the first twenty-two years of his life he never left a radius of fifty miles from his birthplace. His first trip was to a fraternity (*Verbindung*) conference in Nuremberg in 1922. For his first twenty-four years he was very much tied to home and family. All his plans for leaving were indications of the need to run away from himself.

Himmler's busy "doing" was like the superstructure of a building with no foundation to rest upon. He lacked the basic capacity to feel with, and then to feel for, the capacity to feel himself as in relationship with another. He had what Guntrip calls "the most characteristic behavioral expression of the schizoid conflict," the "in and out programme, always breaking away from what one is at the same time holding on to,"[20] as illustrated by fantasies of going far away from home.

For Himmler a masculine identity meant fighting, wearing a uniform and being in the military, carrying Germany's mission to the East, dueling, and restraining one's expression of feelings of pain and anger as well as of joy and pleasure. To him a man must be strong and powerful, stoic, and calm, like his father the schoolmaster. Himmler's attitude toward power comes to the fore in his admiration of an "imposing fortress that testifies to the princely and clerical medieval power. One could hardly create something like this with today's workers and wages," he commented.[21] His identification with great princely power, with the strength of medieval institutions, can be seen here. He identifies with power in the hope of winning love and avoiding danger. He searches for what he interprets as masculinity through identification, which was the only way he could be a man.

Social aspiration and status consciousness are revealed when Himmler writes, "It will be a long time until I have the distinguished sureness of manner that I desire."[22] His strong desire for power was to be gratified through self-control. He berated and experimented with himself in order to increase it. He diminished the spontaneity of sensual pleasure to the point of experiencing it only in predetermined and distinct doses, according to plan, and in contexts that had been carefully prepared in time and space, such as the beer-drinking socials of his fraternity or the festive holiday meals. The gratification of impulse was only permitted if it was in a controlled, isolated manner, and when he could identify with its source.

We see here how Himmler's quest for sexual self-control led to displacement onto ideas of war and romantic conquest. The issues of sexuality and aggression became fused in fantasies of Germanic territorial aggrandizement. His heterosexual strivings met with resistance from the tyranny of the generation of the fathers and became sublimated into brotherly friendship with girls, while his homosexual genitality was sublimated in fantasies he shared with his friends of masculine comradeship in the front-line trenches during war. Strong conflicts between masculine and feminine identifications are manifested by the pseudo-masculine acting out and the feminine image of weakness and tears. Men don't cry, women do.

To Himmler "feminine" implied weakness and "masculine" signified aggressive pseudo-strength. His mind functioned in polarities of personality: manly muscle, toughness, and forced activity, set against womanly softness, gentleness, timidity, and passivity, regardless of which sex actually displayed these qualities. Sexual differences appeared to him as mutually exclusive opposites and as roles to be played rather than as genuine and basic qualities of personality. These elements of personality are, however, mutually necessary and complementary in human development. In Himmler's pathological form the pseudo-male sex role developed into sadism and destructiveness. The forced quality of his values of strenuousness, hardness, and compulsive overactivity indicate that their motivation was reactive and defensive to feelings of passivity, weakness, and non-being. They expressed his empty, disassociated sense of not being a whole person.

This affectless image of pseudo-masculine strength becomes apparent in Himmler's confrontation with a hypnotist at a social evening. He was terrified by the threat: "I defended myself with all of my powers of resistance; naturally, he did not break me down." But the "dear good" Maia did succumb. He was filled with pity on seeing her so helpless. "I could have strangled the dog in cold blood." The idea of submission to a man was so threatening that Heinrich could under no circumstances participate. Even the sight of a girl willingly surrendering her conscious volition to a man was enough to arouse in him a murderous rage against the man and a compassion for the apparently helpless girl. He had to deny his desire to submit to a man and a dangerous instinctual spontaneity. As long as everything was under conscious control, nothing could go wrong. The control was a protection against his homosexual panic. Himmler identified himself with the girl and fantasied submitting to the man. The fear of powerlessness and loss of control that would allow the underlying homosexual impulse expression caused a reinforcement of his compulsive defenses and a desire to kill the threatening man. His arousal on seeing the girl helpless—"I pitied her as I saw her so"—is the breakthrough of his underlying hate, aggression, sadism, and his masochistic identification with the passive female.[23] There is the quality of a primal scene to his description of the girl's submission to the hypnotist that suggests that he had a fantasy of a defenseless mother being overwhelmed and subjugated by a powerful father.

The next month of Himmler's diary, from late December 1919 through January 1920, is marked by a sudden and close attention to food. He was rapturous about the pleasures of coming back home where he could delight in sweet things and regress to childhood. "I drank hot chocolate at home. It is indeed nice to be back at home, one can be a child again and can let oneself go a little." At home, in the world of the kind mother, he regressed to the oral pleasures of the bounteous breast, the gratification of being given, of being indulged, of taking in the mouth. His intense appetite for food extended to the kinds of diary entries he made after social engagements. Reflections on food, not the ideas or substance of conversations or emotional moods, are what he considered noteworthy. "Drank coffee and ate a wonderful cake," he writes after a visit with a friend. "Ate sandwiches and goodies." Some time later he comments, "As long as I visited I had to eat: dumpling soup, filet, veal, potato salad and noodles, with this a beer. We talked of everything imaginable. He is such a decent, conservative man, fully out of the old mold. . . . Thilde, the good soul, accompanied me to the Harras. She gave me yet more cake, goodies, and an apple to take along. I was up to my old form of talking a great deal about everything."[24]

Himmler's close attention to food might reasonably be explained as the effects of the wartime food shortage. While such an explanation initially seems plausible, I find it questionable because of the absence in the diaries of any mention of hunger or of a lack of food during or after the war. One would expect such supporting evidence if physical need were the motive. If, however, these entries were not caused by the food shortage, the significant psychological fact is that the pleasure in eating was a pleasure that Himmler permitted himself to write about. Other, more genital erotic pleasures were not allowed; they had to be repressed. But here he granted himself an indulgence in unalloyed delight in food. Only in regard to food does he experience pleasure.

The detailed listing of foods eaten is striking in itself in suggesting another motive, an avaricious immortalizing of food. The food could now never be lost; he could eat it and still enjoy it. It was to be retained forever. In the words of Karl Abraham, "Those traits, which belong to the clinical phenomena of the anal character, are built up on the ruins of an oral erotism."[25] The classic anal characteristics of covetousness and parsimony have their origin in holding fast to food ingested. Himmler feared losing the "goodies" he had eaten and therefore held on to them in his diary.

The frequent self-castigation that Himmler expresses for talking too much is another classic oral characteristic. Its appearance is especially intense at the end of 1921 and in January 1922. He associates garrulousness with softness and, implicitly, with weakness and femininity. His masculine ego ideal was silence and hardness: "I am much too warmhearted and always talk too much." "I told a lot of jokes, talked much, and jeered much. Oh, why can I not stop it!" "When will I learn not to talk so much?" "I still talk too much unnecessary nonsense." "I am a miserable loudmouth [*elender Schwätzer*], I can never keep my mouth shut. Ill-considered and immature. When will I take myself in hand?" "I absolutely cannot keep my big yap [*Maul*] shut." "I always talk too much." "The product of these days: I am a phrase-coiner and babbler [*Sprüchemacher u. Schwätzer*] and without energy, got no work done."[26]

The constant need to exhibit himself orally to other people, the overflowing urge to talk, is a trait traceable to displacement from the oral sphere. He is giving not things, but words. The oral discharge by speech is an act of giving by way of the mouth. This is a function of an oral identification with the mother. So we find that Himmler's mother, who appears to be neglected throughout the diary, does indeed effectively appear in his voracious eating and incessant talking.

Anna Freud draws an important distinction between the usual process of repression and an abnormal phenomenon of instinctual asceticism that must be considered psychotic. "There is sometimes in adolescence," she says, "an antagonism towards the instincts which far surpasses in intensity anything in the way of repression which we are accustomed to see under normal conditions or in more or less severe cases of neurosis. In the mode of its manifestation and the width of its range it is less akin to the symptoms

of pronounced neurotic disease than to the asceticism of religious fanatics."[27]
In Himmler this adolescent asceticism was massive. All sexual and most
aggressive impulses were repudiated. He was on the other hand tolerant
toward oral gratification, the primary phase of infantile development.

Himmler's view of women was split between an image of a pure, virginal
and innocent, maternal being and a dangerous, uncontrolled, sexual, and
aggressive creature who ensnares men with her lust. Sometimes he would
talk with his friend Ludwig, presumably about women, in a vein that was
"downright dirty [*recht dreckig*]." He categorized the romantic woman,
who should "keep her place," as being of three types—a child, an indulgent
helpmeet, and a holy goddess—elaborating as follows:

> A woman is loved by a man on three levels: as a dear child who has
> to be chided, perhaps even punished on account of its unreasonable-
> ness, and who is protected and taken care of because it is delicate and
> weak and because one loves it. Then as wife and as a loyal, under-
> standing comrade who fights through life with one, who stands
> faithfully at one's side without hemming in or fettering the man and
> his spirit. And as a goddess whose feet one must kiss, who gives one
> strength through her feminine wisdom and childlike, pure sanctity
> that does not weaken in the hardest struggles and in the ideal hours
> gives one heavenly peace.

Women are seen as primitive images of the delicate, weak mother who is
brutally attacked by the father and who must be protected; or the wife-
comrade who is a phallic woman, no different from a man; or the goddess
who is the all-powerful mother of early infancy, whom Edmund Bergler has
termed the "giantess of the nursery." A week after the entry in which he
elaborates on the three categories of women he repeats a family saying
handed down from his maternal grandmother: "One should buy the cow
straight out of the stall," meaning, he says, "not young girls who dance
around until they get a man."[28]

Himmler had frequent "rescue fantasies" about girls and women with
whom he came into contact. For example, he noticed a waitress, a "pretty,
well-put-together thing with a lovely face. I felt sorry for her. Every waitress
inevitably sinks into the depths. If I had had money like a rich man, I would
have given her so much that she could marry and would not have to sink
and be lost." Such a desire to "rescue" women under the conviction that
without his "saving" them they will lose all respectability and sink into
depravity has the unconscious meaning of rescuing the mother. This fantasy
is derived from a fixation of infantile feelings of tenderness for the mother.
Himmler is defending these women against the bad father and against his
own sadism. The following day he talked with his friend Ludwig about the

frustrations of the engagement period—a "stagnant time. The fighting and wooing are over, yet one only possesses a part of her spirit and her body not at all." Women, he later observed, have two sides; they can give themselves to lust and sexual love; but they can also show an incomparable noble love. "Talking with a pure woman in a nice milieu [*schönen milieu*]" is what he always liked to do. But women were weak-willed and lacked good judgment. They could not be trusted. The ego controls had to be exercised by men, especially in all sexual matters. Women were wanton, sensuous creatures who would seduce men if given the slightest opening.

> I have experienced it. One lay in couples so closely together, body to body, not human being next to human being. One catches on fire so that one must pull together all one's rationality. The girls are by then so far gone they no longer know what they do. It is the hot unconscious yearning of the whole individual for the gratification of a terribly strong natural drive. That is why it is also so dangerous for the man, and so full of responsibility. One could do as one wills with the helpless girls and yet one has enough to do to struggle with one's self. I am so sorry for the girls.[29]

Attributing the loss of sexual control to the girls is, of course, a projection of Himmler's own sexual impulses. Projection is one of the most ubiquitous and primitive of character defenses. It is the expulsion of prohibited impulses from the person to the outside world rather than integrating the ideas and affects within the self. Projection leads to intolerance of other people and protection against unpleasant self-knowledge. In addition to the projection, this account from Himmler's diary should communicate many things to the psychoanalytically informed historian. Himmler experienced great sexual anxiety. There is a strong suggestion of a mother's hostility here. The woman is the aggressor and temptress. But Himmler is fully aware that the struggle is within himself. He is saying: "Can I control my impulses?" The total reversal of roles is striking. He, not the girl, is responsible for guarding her virginity. The female, not the male, is viewed as having the uncontrollable sexual impulses.

This image of women as "weak" is coupled with an essentially sadistic view as Himmler describes how a friend of his had "evil experiences" with women that had entirely destroyed the friend's wonderful idealism. He tells of another friend's warning against Sopherl, "a girl with a devastating temperament. She teases a man for a year and a half, she embarrasses and confuses him." In reporting this experience he is not only telling what a friend related to him, he is also revealing his own image of women and his perception of his mother's conduct and her hostility. At a costume party he complains again about how "frightfully hot one gets at these affairs, namely

Mariele. She can't help it. But one does have to pity the girls. One cannot be restrained enough."[30] The restraint, the ego controls, had to come from him, the man, because women (of a certain kind) were uninhibited and irresponsible, and, therefore, libidinously dangerous creatures.

One of Himmler's most consistent patterns is the intense compulsivity whereby he manages his rage against his father. The difference in the responses of Heinrich at nineteen and his older brother Gebhard to a provocative letter from his father is significant. Heinrich writes that the letter was outrageous; it could have been put on the wall as a placard. Gebhard became angry, but Heinrich did not. He could not endure any anger or feeling. Instead, he went on errands. His hostility was contained and held in. He did not feel it or discharge it as his brother did. It is this very lack of genuine anger and rage that makes Himmler's personality so flat and colorless.

Erikson has redefined the adolescent process as being "conclusively complete only when the individual has subordinated his childhood identifications to a new kind of identification. . . . With dire urgency [these new identifications] . . . force the young individual into choices and decisions which will, with increasing immediacy, lead to a more final self-definition, to irreversible role pattern, and thus to commitments 'for life.' " Erikson sees six functions of ideology for youth. It offers:

> (1) an overly clear perspective of the future, encompassing all foreseeable time, and thus counteracting individual "time diffusion"; (2) an opportunity for the exhibition of some uniformity of appearance and action counteracting individual identity consciousness; (3) inducement to collective role and work experimentation which can counteract a sense of inhibition and personal guilt; (4) submission to leaders who as "big brothers" escape the ambivalence of the parent-child relation; (5) introduction into the ethos of the prevailing technology, and thus into sanctioned and regulated competition; and (6) a seeming correspondence between the internal world of ideals and evils, on the one hand, and, on the other, the outer world with its organized goals and dangers in real space and time: a geographic-historical framework for the young individual's budding identity.

Sometimes one can find all the themes and manifold identities of a personality in crisis synopsized in one episode of life. On four consecutive days in late May 1922 Himmler presents us with associations that state his fantasies of good and evil identity. We see images of purity and ideal Nordic strength set against the evil identity of ethnic outgroups. He defines what his ego fears most—the lascivious, free, and sensual "negative" identity to which he is attracted but that is viewed by him as threatening and dangerous.[31]

On Friday evening he notes having seen a girl of three jump about naked before going to bed. His reaction was: "I do not believe this to be right at the age of three years when one should be teaching a child modesty."[32] We may speculate that he was unconsciously aroused by sexual fantasies on seeing the child romp freely and sensually. The child, said Freud, is an erotic plaything. If libidinal spontaneity is dangerous and must be inhibited, then so must an erotic girl-child.

On the next day Himmler talks with the young wife of a doctor and tells her that he has never courted a girl. She teases him and calls him a eunuch. Himmler goes on to speculate that there are two sorts of people. One is "the melancholic, stern, among which I include myself," austere types who eventually succumb to sin if they do not get engaged or married early enough, "since the animal in man is too powerful in us." He adds that perhaps the fall, "when it occurs among us, is all the greater for this." This hard, ascetic type Himmler contrasted with the light, gay peoples who are fiery and easygoing, who chase women whether they are married or single, and flirt, kiss, and copulate without thinking about it merely because it is human and fun. Himmler numbers the doctor and his wife as among this second type, but he likes them nevertheless, and they like him. In fact he likes all of this second type of people, among whom he classifies Rhinelanders and Austrians, "who are all easygoing but straight and honest." "However," he writes, "I cannot become like them internally, even when trying to do so strongly tempts me as it does now." Sunday was no exception to the catalogue-like listing of daily routine that characterizes Himmler's diary and perceptions. The entry opens with: "Got up at 7:30. Shaved. Ate breakfast." He also notes that the new teacher chases skirts, despite being married. Himmler's positive ego ideal is personified in a Norwegian engineer and his wife whom he meets later that day. Of them he says: "true Northlanders, still, quiet, large, blond, blue-eyed [*echte Nordländer, still, ruhig, gross, blond, blauäugig*]."[33] With them it is a pleasure for him to identify.

Whereas the diary entries for Saturday and Sunday are couched in characterological and racist idioms, on Monday we can clearly observe the underlying psychodynamics at work. We see how Himmler's most extreme compulsivity coincided with his rage at his father. His feelings of anger toward his father were repressed and defended against by obsessional mechanisms of concentrating on trivia so that the feelings of hostility were never recognized or permitted expression. His father was the only person he was aware of loving. His feelings toward his father oscillated between sentimental affection and a need to describe his father's irascibility, which he denied upset him. The account in the diary is always of his father's bad mood and acrimony; never is there any suggestion of his own rage and resentment, for such feelings depended upon his identifications. A typical description of the relationship between father and son as Heinrich experienced it is: "Arrived in Munich at 6:45. Changed. Suddenly Father came in a great state of excitement and in a terrible mood, accusing me, etc. Ate dinner. My whole good mood was destroyed and smashed: this is the way things may turn out if we are constantly together, a living Hell for us and our parents, and after all, these are trivial things." On the same day he details the items he carried on the train: a gun, egg boxes for Mother, rucksack, two kinds of flowers. He tells how long he had to lay over en route and the exact time of his arrival in Munich.[34]

A week later Himmler describes his father as being in a "frightful, depressing mood, deadly." A few weeks later he is angry at his father, but he defends against this anger by excusing him as the "good" father who takes everything so hard. When he has to go to his father, who is holding his money, to get five hundred marks for books, there is a great excited debate. "I too, unfortunately, was hotheaded," he writes. But when he goes to his father for money seven months later, his resentment is well defended. He says: "Father is so good, if only I did not have to plague him any longer." There is no hostility expressed. Instead the entry is followed by a listing of the routine chores of the day: "went home, drank tea, figured accounts, wrote diary, studied, 7 o'clock Asta meeting."[35] Then he explains that the present young, undisciplined generation is a great danger for Germany. They live by the slogans of freedom and self-determination.

Himmler's response to the culturally pervasive middle-class Bavarian anti-Semitism is of historical and characterological interest. On July 3, 1922, his political and social attitudes toward Jews are expressed in two different contexts that indicate that his anti-Semitism was at that time stereotyped rather than pathological. First he notes: "In the evening the democratic students together with the Republican Reichsbund are staging a meeting against the black-white-red terror at the Munich universities. One of the organizers is Wolfg[ang] Hallgarten, the Jew-boy [*Judenbub*], an officer's candidate in 1918, now a pacifist. Home. Studied. 1:00 p.m. Dinner." Himmler did not go to the meeting, but he records that "Hallgarten, the Jewish rascal [*Judenlauser*], is a big operator. He is said to have been insolent under the protection of the Republican Reichsbund." The same evening Himmler and a friend visited some cabarets. There he had an encounter with a dancer that led to his second series of references to Jews that day:

> The dancer Inge Barco came to us. (A couple of days later I received a picture from her; see mementos.) . . . We then went to the Reich-sadler bar. Pretentious, many Jews there. She is a quiet girl, simple,

not vain or arrogant, values good manners. No one would take her to be a cabaret dancer. She is Viennese, but a Jewess. But she has absolutely nothing Jewish about her, at least as far as one can judge. At first I made a number of comments about the Jews. I thought it inconceivable that she was one. She does, however, have in every way the Austrian woman's manner of talking and giving of herself, harmlessly joking and being good-natured, without ever being offensive. She freely admits that she is no longer innocent. But she has given her body only out of love. She is madly in love [*verschossen*] with Kurt Wetterstein, a student, and is absolutely true to him. She has very poor circumstances at home. She nevertheless sends money home. In a word, a girl who deserves respect, notwithstanding the conceits of bourgeois opinion. We drove her out to the home of her married sister in the Nymphenburger Street, where she lives. 1:00 a.m. home. Bed.[36]

These two passages quoted from the same day's entry show that at the age of twenty-two Himmler possessed all the conventional anti-Semitism of his class and culture, but nothing more. He was able to idealize the Jewish dancer and to write of her with some stereotyped romantic clichés, demonstrating that his anti-Semitism was at this point the product of identification with his social environment. He took it from his surroundings, family, college fraternity associates, and the parochial middle-class world of south Germany.

The virulent and pathological anti-Semitism of Nazism that Himmler was shortly to adopt was also a product of identification. It was borrowed from his new father figure, his new Pope—Adolf Hitler. Himmler's anti-Semitism had all the schizoid flexibility of an ideology by identification. He absorbed it as though apart from it he would have no reality; he swallowed it with his acceptance of the authority who dispensed it. He had no true individuality of his own, and he could not exist as a person apart from his objects of identification. His destiny became bound up with Hitler's in an identification that was his only means of maintaining selfhood.

A study of Himmler invites a consideration of the great scholarship on the variables of personality that tend to anti-Semitism. The prevailing psychodynamic view of the racially prejudiced person is that he has a weak ego. We may single out the classic study by the Adorno group, *The Authoritarian Personality,* which concludes:

Comparison with high scorers [in anti-Semitism and authoritarianism] . . . gave the impression that the low scorers had relatively much stronger egos—that is, they appeared to us to be able to handle their impulses much more successfully due to relatively less extensive repressions and countercathexes and to greater capacity for sublimation and other modifications.[37]

The bigot uses the non-adaptive defenses of displacement and projection and therefore does not meet reality on a rational basis. Adorno's appraisal is comforting but deceptively unrealistic for Himmler's case.

For Himmler, and for others like him, anti-Semitism was ego syntonic and integrative because they found in the Nazi ideology a solution to their problems of aggression and identity. In the *Völkisch* movement Himmler found a sense of belonging and an integration of his various identifications —sexual, occupational, ethnic, and national. He found his identity through National Socialist racial ideology and secured it when he achieved a position as a functionary in the Nazi party. Nazi ideology was permanently necessary to stabilize his ego and his identity; it channeled his asceticism and his need for an absolute hierarchy of values and rigid principles of conduct. It promised him control of the future and eternalization of ancestry; martial discipline creating a band of armed supermen; total inner reform and the sanction to wage a holy race war, without compromise or mercy, against an external enemy.

Himmler experienced an accelerating conflict with his Roman Catholic faith because the Church was opposed to dueling. In December 1919 he wrote: "I believe that I am coming into collision with my religion. Whatever happens, I will always love God, pray to him, and cleave to and defend the Catholic Church, even if I am expelled from her." As he listened to a Christmas Day sermon, he said he had to fight his "inner battles of faith as never before. The business of dueling bothers me again and again. I prayed in the evening; I had more or less overcome it earlier. God will help me in all my doubts."[38]

Dueling remained a major preoccupation for Himmler between the ages of nineteen and twenty-two. He wanted to duel but had difficulty in finding partners. He was repeatedly rejected by his fraternity brothers for club office. He was told that the management of the fencing matches would not be in good hands and that his father's opposition would inhibit his dueling. He displayed no guilt feelings toward his father, however, as an obsessive would have. He felt that his rejection by the fraternity was because he talked too much and because his fraternity brothers were talking against him.

Himmler's feelings of masculine identification were associated with dueling and war. One evening after he and a friend had walked two girls home, he wrote: "One notices how one thirsts for love and yet how hard and responsible it is to bind oneself and to choose. Then one has the thought, if only there were battle again; War; the march to the front. I look forward to my fencing match."[39] This entry reveals the tensions creating his dull, restricted personality. True to the isolation of affect by a compulsive, Himmler uses the indefinite pronoun "one," the third-person form, rather than "I." Love has an oral quality; it is something that is imbibed regardless of its source. Where it comes from is a matter of indifference. He does not want to choose a single object and be responsible to her. If only Germany were at war once more he could unambivalently (so it appears to him) be a man again by going to battle at the front—and in doing so identify with the aggressor. For now, he has his dueling.

He eventually got his dueling match. "I did not get at all excited. I stood very well and technically fought very nicely. My opponent was Mr. Renner of the Alemanians. . . . As it later turned out I received five bloody blows . . . five stitches, one ligature. I truly did not flinch, even once. Distl held my head in old comradeship."[40] Here we see Himmler defining his values of masculinity with unmistakable clarity. To be a man is to bear pain without flinching and then to be comforted by another man in the brotherhood of combat.

Himmler's world has been drastically polarized by his unconscious into categories of "good" and "bad" conduct and feeling, and his system of thought carries unconscious emotional significance. The category of "strength," aggression and violence, and the repression of feelings associated with "hardness" is Himmler's identification with his father. The realm of feelings of spontaneity, sexuality, warmth, and tenderness is associated with weakness and is his identification with his mother. In the patriarchal Himmler household the child Heinrich's view of the behavior and emotional position of his father was that his acts and values were strong, hard, and self-disciplined, while his image of his mother was that she was soft and weak.

Himmler's projection onto Jews, Bolsheviks, homosexuals, and ethnic outgroups of the categories of sexuality, low voluptuousness, and inadmissible feelings of murderous rage that he identified with his mother was a defense against the feared inner danger of yielding to irresistible impulses. This defense is demonstrated in the bull sessions he shared with friends in their rooms. These sessions concerned, as he recorded the topics seriatim, "land reform, degeneration, homosexuality, the Jewish question." One friend loaned him Hans Blüher's book praising the role of homosexuality in social organization. Himmler recorded in his diary only the loan of the book and not his response to it. But in the book list that Himmler kept he commented on Blüher's thesis, noting that "pure physical homosexuality is an error of degenerate individualism that is contrary to nature."[41] Himmler's attitude of opprobrium and moralistic condemnation suggests that homo-sexuality was a very anxiety-inducing subject, one that he vigorously had to defend against.

The single most frequent entry in Himmler's diaries during his years in school was in all probability *"Akten studiert,"* referring to his favorite pastime of working in the files of the student government (ASTA or Allge-meiner Studenten Ausschuss). Here he could be happy in the obsessional world of rules and regulations. Here pleasure was to be had in indexing and registering, filing and checking, scheduling and planning, and in all the compulsive systems of office routine. Himmler was to be a bureaucrat par excellence until the end of his life.

Throughout his life Himmler was plagued by stomachaches, cramps, and colitis. He frequently complained of stomach upsets in adolescence, a physical complaint that is highly significant in terms of underlying emo-tional conflict. Chronic gastrointestinal disturbances have been among the most carefully studied of all psychosomatic symptoms, as the gastrointesti-nal tract is the classic target area for anxiety. Recent research in psychoso-matic medicine has stressed the multiple determinants, somatic and psycho-logical, of organ breakdown. Some organic factor, either genetic or from the life history, is considered necessary for a specific psychosomatic disease to develop. The predetermined target organ is then vulnerable when the person is in conflict or psychological stress, particularly stress of a kind that is related intimately to the organ by development, object-relating, or charac-terological mode of expression, as is the gastrointestinal tract. The studies of George Engel show that "there are patients who at one time or another display headaches, bowel trouble, an obsessive-compulsive character struc-ture, paranoid trends, and depression." Engel found that this cluster or group of patients includes those with ulcerative, mucous, and spastic colitis.[42]

One indication that Himmler's stomach complaint was psychogenic in nature and that its etiology was oral dependent is that he sought and found relief from his pain at the hands of a masseur. According to Felix Kersten, Himmler's Finnish masseur from 1939 to 1945, only his hands could relieve the Reichsführer's intestinal pains. Himmler described Kersten as his "Bud-dha" and his touch as a unique magic that soothed his pain and cured everything. The way in which Kersten was also able to manipulate Himmler on issues of policy indicates a strong transference relationship. Kersten was a parent figure, and the massage resulted in a transference cure of the psychosomatic stomach complaints. The "laying on of the hands" by a male "doctor" and the surrender to passive manual manipulation bear connota-tions of homoerotic and masturbatory indulgence. Here Himmler found the receptive gratification of his unconscious infantile longings for love and help.

In this situation he could be "handled," succored, and cared for as the seductive mother touches, feeds, and cleans the ill or "very good" boy. As a patient being ministered to by his "Buddha," Himmler no longer had to act the role of the aggressive, dynamic, efficient, stoic Nazi chieftain.[43]

Himmler received his diploma in agriculture from the Munich Technische Hochschule in August 1922. He joined the National Socialist German Worker's party a year later, in August 1923. In November 1923 he and his brother Gebhard participated in Hitler's Munich putsch as members of Captain Ernst Röhm's paramilitary Reichskriegsflagge. This unit occupied the War Ministry building in Munich. One surviving photograph shows Himmler as a standard bearer holding the German imperial war flag behind a barbed-wire street barricade. After the failure of the putsch, Himmler, having lost his job as a laboratory assistant in a fertilizer plant, visited Captain Röhm in prison, who, he recorded, "still has his good humor and is ever the good Captain Röhm."[44]

There are few outbursts of direct brutality in the diaries. Himmler admired the "imposing power" represented by the medieval castles of Bavaria. He writes that he is fascinated by fortresses and torture chambers, and then states that he admires the spirit of honor, greatness, and strictness of the Middle Ages, "for which we will always have respect." In June 1922, when the Republican Foreign Minister was assassinated, and the vast majority of Germans condemned the act, Himmler wrote: "Rathenau is murdered. I am glad." Two days later he responded to the national reaction: "The majority condemns the murder. Rathenau is a martyr. Oh, blinded people!"[45]

In the final entry in the diary—February 25, 1924—Himmler tells of his speech on behalf of the *Völkisch* movement in the Bavarian countryside. "I spoke one and a half hours, I think quite well, to the farm folk. . . . At the end a buyer for a Jewish hop dealer came; I think the farmers squeezed him between their fingers later [*den nahmen die Bauern glaube ich hernach zwischen die Finger*]." We can sense Himmler's pleasure at the sadistic fantasy of the philo-Semite man being pinched and crushed by the crowd whipped up by his speech.

At the end of Himmler's adolescence Hitler became a father figure to him. The new religion of National Socialism became his way out of the inner prohibitions presented by father and Church. These he could now give up for a new set of ideals that allowed him to express aggression. His archaic superego was still, however, dependent on identification with his environment. He needed to please Hitler.

Himmler's adolescence manifested all of the ego and superego defects, the lack of object relationships, the defense mechanisms of denial and projection, and the regression to orality of a severely disturbed borderline character. National Socialist ideology offered him a substitute for his Christian superego or conscience. It was to give him a role in life and a future career with a uniform that counteracted his feeling of individuation and aloneness. It gave him a leader to whom he could submit and from whom he received superego sanction to act out his libidinal and aggressive fantasies. As Freud has noted, if enough narcissistic support is available from identification with a leader, then the superego may be completely disregarded. Its functions will be assumed by the leader and membership in a group that shares the leader's ideals.[46]

As the Reichsführer SS, Himmler was able totally to block his own feelings regarding the work of extermination. He praised and, indeed, made a virtue of the repression of feelings of revulsion among SS men. Before dispatching special sections of SS men to Poland for the extermination of Jews, he told them: "I have to expect of you superhuman acts of inhumanity. But it is the Führer's will." Of course, this complete denial of affect included himself. When speaking of the work of liquidating Jews, he said: "The Führer has charged me with carrying out this very difficult task. No one can relieve me of the responsibility. I cannot allow myself the luxury of discussing it."[47] While repressing any feelings, Himmler insisted on the Führer's sanction for all that he did. He was telling his SS audience that because the leader takes upon himself all the responsibility for aggression, you who carry out the commands may do so with no guilt. A little boy has no responsibility.

Himmler used another device to diminish guilt. He always sought a legal façade for his acts. With the high formalism of the compulsive superego and its attribution of magical power to words, he stubbornly pursued the legal legitimation of his activities, although changes in the law that he achieved on July 1, 1941, depriving Jews of any protection of the law were irrelevant as Jews had already been deprived of all enforceable rights of life and property. When speaking of the systematic murder of the Polish upper classes, Himmler said:

> However hideous it may be, it has been necessary for us to do it, and it will be necessary in many other cases. If we lose our nerve now, we shall pass weak nerves on to our sons and our grandsons. . . . We who live in these times, who have been taught by Adolf Hitler, who have the good fortune to live in Adolf Hitler's Reich and to work for Germany under the guidance of Adolf Hitler, have no right to be weak. Inevitably an execution is a grim duty for our men. Nevertheless they must never be soft; they must grit their teeth and do their duty.

We see explicitly how Himmler, speaking for the SS state, rates virtue by the degree of repression involved. Hardness is equated with strength, and softness means weakness. Morality is associated with obedience to duty. Acts of violence and aggression are seen as hard, while feelings of warmth and benevolence are viewed as soft. These values were publicly normative in the Third Reich. In a speech to SS Gruppenführen in Posen on October 4, 1943, Himmler said:

> I would like here to mention a very different chapter in all candid-ness. Among ourselves it shall be discussed in complete frankness, and yet we shall never speak of it in public. Just as little as we hesitated to do our duty and to put comrades who had failed to the wall and shoot them on June 30, 1934, so little did we speak of it then and will we speak of it in the future. It was, thank God, an inborn natural sense of tact that we never discussed it among ourselves, never spoke about it. It caused all of us to shudder, and yet everyone knew that he would do it again next time if it was ordered and was necessary.
>
> I am referring to the evacuation of the Jews, the extermination of the Jewish people. It is among those things that are easy to speak of. "The Jewish people will be exterminated," says every member of the party, "that's clear, it's in the program, we'll do it." . . . Of all those who so speak, none has witnessed, not one has had to bear it. Most of you know what it means when 100 corpses are piled up, when 500 or 1,000 are piled there. To have gone through this and—with exceptions due to human weaknesses—to have remained decent, this is what has made us hard.[48]

The association of "human" (*menschlicher*) with "weakness" (*Schwächen*) on the one hand, and "superhuman" with sadism, cruelty, and the denial of affect on the other, shows how in Himmler's mind the very process of thinking had become aggressivized and libidinized. He repeatedly uses the guilt-alleviating device of verbal indirection: We shall do it, but we shall never speak of it, even among ourselves. This maneuver can only be ex-plained by the great significance attached to words by the compulsive char-acter. Something that is not mentioned does not exist or did not happen. If it is referred to by a euphemism, it may be treated as something different from what it actually is.

This coldness of feeling, this repression of emotions—including the be-trayals involved in the Blood Purge of June 1934, which for Himmler passed under the euphemism of "tact"—is entirely consistent with the adolescent whom we have studied. For the youth as well as the adult Himmler, the qualities of hardness and strength are ascribed not to the acts performed but to the ability to control emotions successfully. This is his definition of a man. Feelings, pleasure, and emotions are ascribed to human weakness and left to women.

Nazi propaganda stressed the themes of racial purity and described Jews as vermin and viruses. Himmler in 1943 also spoke in the idioms of disease and hygiene: "We don't want in the end, just because we have exterminated a germ, to be infected by that germ and die from it. I will not stand by while a slight infection forms. Whenever such an infected spot appears, we will burn it out."[49]

This language of political hygiene, of cleaning and disinfection, is language indicating a regression to the phase of anal sadism, a time when the infant is closest to its mother and soiling is permitted without restraint. As Richard L. Rubenstein has pointed out, the Nazi death camps were the scene of the acting out of the most primitive fantasies of excremental aggression.[50] Here human beings were manipulated and controlled as feces and finally literally turned into feces amid the stench of corpses.

On the other side of the relationship, the side of the inmates, the psychoanalyst Bruno Bettelheim has conceptualized the concentration camp experience as a process of forced regression "to the level they [the prisoners] were at before toilet training was achieved."[51] This regression included forcing prisoners to wet and soil themselves, the public regulation of elimination, and a whole regimen of pointless and demeaning tasks that robbed them of adult identities and mature responses, compelling a reversion to childlike behavior.

When the Nazi state was falling apart in the final days of World War II, Himmler's personality decompensated as in a psychosis. His ability to test reality completely failed; reality became too painful. In the spring of 1945 he thought he would be conducting negotiations with General Eisenhower. This was the megalomania of a man who could not face the reality that his career was finished. As late as May 5, 1945, Himmler planned to establish an SS government in Schleswig-Holstein and to conduct peace negotiations with the Allies. As long as his ideology held up it served Himmler as a defense against identity diffusion. It also answered his doubts about who he was and what his life meant. For Himmler anti-Semitism may have been personally integrative and adaptive because it solved his own problems of aggression and identity. For Germany as a nation it was a cultural regression that led to disaster.

The striking thing about Himmler's adolescence, and in this consists its abnormality, is that it was so flat, depressed, and emotionally colorless. The development of adolescence, virtually by definition, is a stormy, emotionally exaggerated period charged with contradictions, desperation, and wild fantasy. The youth who is seeking to become an individual adult goes through struggle and turmoil that recapitulate all the tensions, frustrations, and gratifications of earlier years. Adolescence contains an infantile admixture that often causes it to appear bizarre and aberrant. The youth in crisis shifts rapidly from melancholic depths of isolation, loneliness, and depression to the exhilarated heaven of megalomanic fantasies.

Instead of the emotional storms of normal adolescence we find in Himmler's adolescent years a coldness, a pure expression of learned emotions, and massive ascetic defenses against all sexual impulses. We do not learn how he subjectively experienced life; nothing "inner" comes to the surface. His experience is in the form of the most conventional clichés. Life consists of stereotyped feelings appropriate to the restricted south German background and norms of expression of Himmler's middle-class origin where "one has to" feel and do this or that in a prescribed way. He is the so-called good, good boy who always did his duty as he was told, who ate everything on his plate, and who never revolted or said no.

The lack of Himmler's emotional engagement is borne out in the coldness of his cruelty as Reichsführer SS. He did not act out of rage or intense hatred. He never personally committed an atrocity; he always ordered others to do it. He had no life of his own; he was the administrator who hid behind the commands of others. In short, Himmler never was an adolescent in the emotional connotation of the word. He did not achieve individuation or any responses other than those he was taught. He never fused love and aggression. There was only aggression.

The reader may ask how the adolescent Himmler is materially different from millions of other boys of his time and culture. Could one have predicted from his adolescence that this youth would grow up to be the greatest mass murderer of all time? Clearly such prediction is beyond the scope of either history or psychoanalysis. The variables are too numerous; as Freud said, psychic life is "overdetermined."[52] History, too, seeks multiple explanations for a single phenomenon and is not engaged in the tasks of replication or meeting the scientific test of predictability. What can be affirmed, however, by concentration on the precise details of Himmler's youth and on inferences from the whole range of his life, is that adolescent patterns can be identified that would lead the adult to be a police bureaucrat who treats human beings as feces. While this consistency does not provide a definitive image of the past, it goes further toward establishing the unity of man in history than do those fantasies of denial that maintain the innocence of youth by insisting on a discontinuity between the child, the adolescent, and the man.

Notes

1. Helmut Heiber, ed., *Reichsführer! Briefe an und von Himmler* (Stuttgart, 1968), p. 8.

2. Werner T. Angress and Bradley F. Smith, "Diaries of Heinrich Himmler's Early Years," *Journal of Modern History,* 31 (1959): 214, 222.

3. Peter Blos, *On Adolescence: A Psychoanalytic Interpretation* (New York, 1962), pp. 94–5.

4. Anna Freud, *The Ego and the Mechanisms of Defense,* trans. Cecil Baines (New York, 1946), p. 175.

5. Angress and Smith, "Diaries of Heinrich Himmler's Early Years," p. 213.

6. Louis Pauwells and Jacques Bergier, *The Morning of the Magicians,* trans. Rollo Myers (New York, 1968), pp. 257–8, 286.

7. Sigmund Freud, "Inhibitions, Symptoms and Anxiety" (1926), *Standard Edition of the Complete Psychological Works,* trans. and ed. James Strachey et al. (London, 1953–1974), 20:113.

8. Harry Guntrip, *Schizoid Phenomena, Object Relations, and the Self* (New York, 1968), p. 47.

9. *Ibid.,* pp. 38, 89; W. Ronald D. Fairbairn, *An Object-Relations Theory of the Personality* (New York, 1952), pp. 12, 15.

10. Ernst Hanfstaengl, *Unheard Witness* (Philadelphia, 1957), p. 23. For family setting and biographical data, see Heiber, *Reichführer!,* p. 9; Roger Manvell and Heinrich Fraenkel, *Heinrich Himmler* (London, 1965), pp. 1–2.

11. Himmler Diaries, Hoover Institution on War, Revolution, and Peace, Stanford University, June 3, 1922.

12. Otto Fenichel, *The Psychoanalytic Theory of Neurosis* (New York, 1945), p. 282.

13. Himmler Diaries, Sept. 27, 1914.

14. *Ibid.,* Oct. 19, Nov. 7, 8, 1919.

15. *Ibid.,* Oct. 20, 1919.

16. *Ibid.,* Nov. 24, 1921.

17. *Ibid.,* Nov. 2, 4, 7, 1919.

18. *Ibid.,* Nov. 4, 14, 1919.

19. *Ibid.,* Nov. 11, 1919.

20. Guntrip, *Schizoid Phenomena,* pp. 36–7.

21. Himmler Diaries, Oct. 7, 1919.

22. *Ibid.* Nov. 18, 1921.

23. *Ibid.,* Nov. 13, 1919.

24. *Ibid.,* Dec. 21, 1919; Jan. 19, 25, 1920; Nov. 1, 1921.

25. Karl Abraham, "The Influence of Oral Erotism on Character-Formation" (1924), *Selected Papers of Karl Abraham,* trans. Douglas Bryan and Alix Strachey (New York, 1953), p. 398.

26. Himmler Diaries, Nov. 4, 13, 18, 24; Dec. 1, 4, 7, 1921; Jan. 28, 1922.

27. A. Freud, *Ego and Mechanisms of Defense,* p. 167.

28. Himmler Diaries, Jan. 22, 1920; Nov. 24, 1921; Edmund Bergler, *Counterfeit-Sex: Homosexuality, Impotence, Frigidity* (New York, 1961), pp. 45–50; Himmler Diaries, Dec. 1, 1921.

29. *Ibid.,* Dec. 5, 6, 1921; Jan. 15, 22, Feb. 5, 1922.

30. Himmler Diaries, Feb. 17, 20, 28, 1922.

31. Erik H. Erikson, "The Problem of Ego Identity," *Identity and the Life Cycle:*

Selected Papers (New York, 1959), pp. 110–11, 146; "Ego Development and Historical Change," *ibid.*, p.30.

32. Himmler Diaries, May 26, 1922.

33. *Ibid.*, May 27, 28, 1922.

34. *Ibid.*, May 29, 1922.

35. *Ibid.*, Jun 6, 26, 1922; Nov. 13, 1921; June 30, 1922.

36. *Ibid.*, June 3, 1922.

37. T. W. Adorno, Else Frenkel-Brunswik, Daniel J. Levinson, R. Nevitt Sanford, et al., *The Authoritarian Personality* (New York, 1950), p. 969. See also Nathan W. Ackerman and Marie Jahoda, *Anti-Semitism and Emotional Disorder: A Psychoanalytic Interpretation* (New York, 1950); Ernst Simmel, ed., *Anti-Semitism: A Social Disease* (New York, 1946); Bruno Bettelheim and Morris Janowitz, *Dynamics of Prejudice* (New York, 1950), reissued in *Social Change and Prejudice* (Glencoe, Ill., 1964).

38. Himmler Diaries, Dec. 15, 26, 1919.

39. *Ibid.*, Feb. 19, 22, 1922.

40. *Ibid.*, June 17, 1922.

41. *Ibid.*, March 4, 1922; Hans Blüher, *Die Rolle der Erotik in der männlichen Gesellschaft* (Geneva, 1917); Bradley F. Smith, *Heinrich Himmler: A Nazi in the Making, 1900–1926* (Stanford, Calif., 1971), p. 115.

42. George L. Engel, "Studies of Ulcerative Colitis," Part 4: "The Significance of Headaches," *Psychosomatic Medicine,* 18 (1956): 342.

43. Felix Kersten, *Memoirs 1940–1945,* trans. Constantine Fitzgibbon and James Oliver (New York, 1957), pp. 10, 157; Count Galeazzo Ciano, *Diaries: 1939–1943,* ed. Hugh Gibson (Garden City, N.Y., 1946), entry for Oct. 7, 1942, p. 527.

44. Himmler Diaries, Feb. 15, 1924.

45. *Ibid.*, Oct. 9, 1919; June 21, 24, 26, 1922.

46. S. Freud, "Group Psychology and the Analysis of the Ego" (1921), *Standard Edition,* 18: 116, 129; Joseph Sandler, "On the Concept of Superego," *Psychoanalytic Study of the Child,* 15 (1960): 156–7.

47. *Trial of the Major War Criminals Before the International Military Tribunal, Nuremberg, 14 November 1945–1 October 1946* (Nuremberg, 1948), vol. 42, affidavit SS–67, Dr. Konrad Morgen, p. 564. Nuremberg document NO626, Himmler to SS Gruppenführer Gottlob Berber, July 28, 1942, in Helmut Krausnick, "The Persecution of the Jews," in *Anatomy of the SS State,* trans. Richard Barry, Marian Jackson, and Dorothy Long (New York, 1968), p. 69.

48. In Hans Buchheim, "Command and Compliance," in *Anatomy of the SS State,* p. 338; *International Military Tribunal,* vol. 28, 1919–PS, p. 145; this speech of Oct. 4, 1943, to an SS group leaders' meeting in Posen, is one of the most candid and revealing of Himmler's innermost feelings toward his task of Reichsführer SS.

49. *International Military Tribunal,* vol. 29, 1919–PS, p. 146.

50. Richard L. Rubenstein, "Religion and the Origins of the Death Camps: A Psychoanalytic Interpretation," in *After Auschwitz: Radical Theology and Contemporary Judaism* (Indianapolis, 1966), pp. 1–44.

51. Bruno Bettelheim, *The Informed Heart: Autonomy in a Mass Age* (Glencoe, Ill., 1960), p. 132.

52. S. Freud, "The Interpretation of Dreams" (1900), *Standard Edition,* 5: 480, 569.

The Psychohistorical Origins
of the Nazi Youth Cohort

The historical relationship between the events of World War I and its catastrophic aftermath in Central Europe and the rise of National Socialism has often been postulated. The causal relationship is usually drawn from the savagery of trench warfare on the Western Front, the bitterness of defeat and revolution, to the spectacular series of National Socialist electoral victories beginning in 1930, as if such a relationship were historically self-evident. The relationship between the period from 1914 to 1920 and the rise and triumph of National Socialism from 1929 to 1935 is specifically generational. The war and postwar experiences of the small children and youth of World War I explicitly conditioned the nature and success of National Socialism. The new adults who became politically effective after 1929 and who filled the ranks of the SA and other paramilitary party organizations, such as the Hitler-Jugend and the Bund-Deutscher-Mädel, were the children socialized in World War I.

This essay examines what happened to the members of this generation in their decisive period of character development—particularly in early childhood—and studies their common experiences in childhood, in psychosexual development, and in political socialization that led to similar fixations and distortions of adult character. The specific factors that conditioned this generation include the prolonged absence of the parents, the return of the father in defeat, extreme hunger and privation, and a national defeat in war, which meant the loss of the prevailing political authority and left no viable replacement with which to identify.

Most explanations for the rise of National Socialism stress elements of continuity in German history. These explanations point to political, intellectual, social, diplomatic, military, and economic factors, all of which are important and none of which should be ignored. The historian and social scientist studying Nazism should be well versed in these categories of explanation. The study of political leadership is also of unquestioned importance for the understanding of the dynamics of totalitarianism, and it should be intensively developed by historians as an approach to that understanding.[1]

This essay, however, will focus not on the leader but on the followers, not on the charismatic figure but rather on the masses who endow him with special superhuman qualities. It will apply psychoanalytic perceptions to the problem of National Socialism in German history in order to consider the issues of change rather than continuity in history, to deal with social groups rather than individual biography, and to focus on the ego-psychological processes of adaptation to the historical, political, and socioeconomic context rather than on the instinctual biological drives that all men share.

The rapid political ascendancy of the Nazi party (NSDAP) in the period from 1928 to 1933 was marked by particularly strong support from youth. Since this generation experienced childhood deprivation in World War I, the argument becomes a psychoanalytical one of taking seriously the developments of infancy and childhood and their effect on behavior in adulthood. I wish to offer an added factor, one to be included as an explanation in addition to, rather than instead of, the other explanatory schemata of history. Both history and psychoanalysis subscribe to overdetermination in causation. It would be a poor historian who sought to attribute a war or a revolution to only a single cause. Similarly, in psychoanalytic theory every symptom and symbol is psychically overdetermined and serves multiple functions. When the subject of study is a modern totalitarian mass movement it requires analysis utilizing all the tools for perceiving and conceptualizing irrational and affective behavior that the twentieth century has to offer, including psychoanalysis and dynamic psychology.*

No genuine historical understanding is possible without the perspective

---

*"Dynamic" in psychology is a descriptive term used to imply activity in contrast to theories that are "static" or "potential." Karl Menninger defines dynamic psychology and psychoanalysis as "theories of personality in which motivation, especially unconscious, is considered basic." *The Vital Balance: The Life Process in Mental Health and Illness* (New York, 1963), p. 467. Henry Murray uses "dynamic" "to designate a psychology which accepts as prevailingly fundamental the goal-

of self-understanding from which the historian can then move forth to deal with historical materials. Likewise there can be no measure of historical understanding if we research what men said and did and fail to understand why they acted. The twentieth century has experienced the gross magnification of political and personal irrationality correlative to the exponential increment in the power of modern technology. No history will speak with relevance or accuracy to the contemporary human condition if it fails to assess realistically the profound capacity of the irrational to move men.

Psychoanalysts are concerned with many things that are relevant to the historical problem of what happens to children in a nation at war. They have studied the effects of separation from parents and have seen the long-term consequences of deprivation, material and emotional. They know the hows and whys of a child's identification with his parents. Above all, psychoanalysis as a clinical technique of investigation demonstrates that only the smallest part of human thought and conduct is rational. The world of disembodied minds acting in an emotional vacuum has no place in a psychoanalytically informed history. Too much of history is still written as though men had no feelings, no childhood, and no bodily senses. What is needed is a new kind of history, a history that tells us how men responded to and felt about the great political and economic events that shaped their lives, a history that gives due place to the irrational, the unconscious, and the emotions not only of men but also of the child in the man.

This new kind of history requires an understanding of the dual and related concepts of fixation and regression. Sigmund Freud, in a demographic metaphor of migration, once compared human development to the progress of a people through new territory. At those points where resistance is greatest and conflict most intense the people will leave behind its strongest detachments and move on. If the advanced parties, now reduced in strength, should suffer defeat or come up against a superior enemy, they will retreat to former stopping places where support stands ready. "But," says Freud, "they will also be in greater danger of being defeated the more of their number they have left behind on their migration." Thus, the greater the strength of early fixations, the greater will be the later need for regression: "The stronger the fixations on its path of development, the more readily will the function evade external difficulties by regressing to the fixations—the more incapable, therefore, does the developed function turn out to be of resisting external obstacles in its course." As in Freud's migration metaphor, when an individual who has passed through the maturational phases of development meets with persistent and intense frustration, one of the means

---

directed (adaptive) character of behavior, and attempts to discover and formulate the internal as well as the external factors which determine it." As quoted in *ibid*.

of coping with the pain and lack of satisfaction is to revert from the more highly developed stages of mental organization to modes of functioning typical of an earlier period. The falling back, or regression, will be to phases of psychosexual development that have left areas of weakness, where the maturational step has been marked by unresolved conflicts and anxieties. Arrests of development or points of fixation occur in sexual-drive organization, ways of relating to people, fears of conscience, persistence of primitive kinds of gratification and of reacting defensively to old, no longer present, dangers. As Freud formulated it in 1913:

> We have become aware that the psychical functions concerned— above all, the sexual function, but various important ego functions too—have to undergo a long and complicated development before reaching the state characteristic of the normal adult. We can assume that these developments are not always so smoothly carried out that the total function passes through this regular progressive modification. Wherever a portion of it clings to a previous stage, what is known as a "point of fixation" results, to which the function may regress if the subject falls ill through some external disturbance.[2]

The concepts of fixation and regression may be best illustrated by an operational example taken from a clinical case. A German lady comes into psychoanalytic treatment because of intense marital discord and an acute telephone phobia that interferes with her work. She cannot speak on the telephone, breaks out into a cold sweat, becomes intensely anxious, and loses her voice. In 1943, when she was three years old, she experienced the bombing of Hamburg. She remembers the air raids, the burning and explosions. She was not evacuated. Her family lived near the city center. Her father was a fireman who was called to duty by a bell that rang on the wall of the house because the family had no telephone. The patient can recall being strafed by an airplane. She has no recollection, however, of any panic, fear, or rage. Her memories are affectless. They are clear but disassociated from any of the powerful emotions that must have been present in the child. Now, in a current marital crisis, her feelings of explosive destructive anger and fears of abandonment by a man who is important to her cause a regression. The symptom of the telephone bell symbolizes an earlier point of fixation when she was traumatized by fears of external disaster and internal loss. She now, as an adult, reexperiences all of the emotions that were buried and repressed after the childhood trauma because the later, adult trauma has mobilized the earlier point of fixation and caused a regression to the feelings of the child.

Returning to the larger historical case of the German children of World War I, it is Germany's Great Depression, with its unemployment, governmental chaos and impotence, and widespread anxiety about the future, that constituted precisely such an "external disturbance" as Freud describes. The early point of fixation was World War I, when the peoples of Central Europe experienced prolonged hunger, war propaganda, the absence of fathers and often both parents, and the bankruptcy of all political values and norms.

The psychological symptoms of regression to phases of ego functioning "fixed" by the traumas of a childhood in war included responding to internal personal stress with externalized violence, projecting all negative antinational or antisocial qualities onto foreign and ethnic individuals and groups, and meeting frustrations that would otherwise be tolerated with patience and rationally approached for solutions with a necessity for immediate gratification. The political expression of weakened egos and superegos that fostered regression was manifest not only in turning to violence but most especially in the longing for a glorified and idealized but distant father who is all-knowing and all-powerful, who preaches the military virtues and permits his sons and daughters to identify with him by wearing a uniform and joining combat in a national cause.

It is time to lay at rest the idea that psychoanalytical explanations are necessarily unicausal or that they are inherently incompatible with quantitative data such as demographic, election, consumption, and health statistics. Indeed, psychoanalysis can give these macrodata new coherence and meaning, thus adding a vital qualitative dimension to history. Psychohistory uses dynamic psychology to integrate political and economic explanations with past experience, patterns of repetition, and the irrationality of conduct in times of anxiety, deprivation, and stress.

Traditional psychological interpretations of both political leadership and the personal dynamics of the adherents of mass totalitarian movements, in their explanatory model of adult political behavior, have stressed origins in childhood emotional traumas and in relations with the parents. This has been a particularly successful approach with biography. A consideration of childhood reveals much about the way people are programmed to respond in adulthood. Yet intensive experiences in later life, if they are of a massive traumatic nature, can supersede both earlier influences and individual predispositions. This means that a major catastrophe will have an impact on all ages who are subject to its blows. It will necessarily affect the very young most because their egos are the most fragile. But it will also affect children in latency and adolescence and even adults, each according to his ego strength—that is, according to his ability to tolerate frustration, anxiety, and deprivation. In other words, if the adult trauma is great enough, for example an economic depression or a lost war, it does not matter who the parents were or how democratic they may have been; the anxiety-inducing social or political situation will bring to the fore feelings of helplessness and political irrationality. One of the foremost students of the authoritarian personality, Else Frenkel-Brunswik, has pointed out that "it seems that external pressures of a traumatic character, be they past or be they presently imposed, are likely not only to bring authoritarian personalities to the fore but to reinforce authoritarian trends in individuals who otherwise would remain democratic minded."[3]

The demographic approach offers new categories of explanation and presents an advantage from the standpoint of evidence. Human motivation and behavior are infinitely complex. Any choice of action by a single individual may be attributed to a multiplicity of unique and idiosyncratic causes that could be clarified only after an extensive psychoanalysis. The appeal of a generational approach is that it deals with probabilities—with the law of averages on a macroscale—thus canceling out any of the many individual variables that determine conduct. Whereas it can always be said that in a particular case there are other variables that have been overlooked, such an objection does not hold when we deal with a demographic scale of events affecting a population. In the latter case we have responses of an entire society to events that, while they may be confirmed in many particular cases, are not limited in their general impact by the idiosyncratic developments of a single life.

The seminal conceptual formulation of the generation as a force acting in history was established by Karl Mannheim in 1927 in his essay "The Sociological Problem of Generations." Here Mannheim speaks of the human mind as "stratified" or layered, with the earliest experiences being the basis, and all subsequent experience building on this primary foundation or reacting against it. The influence of psychoanalytic thought on Mannheim's conceptualization of the problem is apparent.

> The human consciousness, structurally speaking, is characterized by a particular inner "dialectic." It is of considerable importance for the formation of the consciousness which experiences happen to make those all-important "first impressions," "childhood experiences"— and which follow to form the second, third, and other "strata." Conversely, in estimating the biographical significance of a particular experience, it is important to know whether it is undergone by an individual as a decisive childhood experience, or later in life, superimposed upon other basic and early impressions. Early impressions tend to coalesce into a *natural view* of the world. All later experiences then tend to receive their meaning from this original set, whether they appear as that set's verification and fulfilment or as its negation and antithesis. . . . Mental data are of sociological importance not

only because of their actual content, but also because they cause the individuals sharing them to form one group—they have a socializing effect.

Mannheim then structures a further "concrete nexus" of the generation in history as *"participation in the common destiny* of [the] historical and social unit." And such groups he terms "generation units."

> *Youth experiencing the same concrete historical problems may be said to be part of the same actual generation while those groups within the same actual generation which work up the material of their common experiences in different specific ways, constitute generation units.* . . . These are characterized by the fact that they do not merely involve a loose participation by a number of individuals in a pattern of events shared by all alike though interpreted by the different individuals differently, but an identity of responses, a certain affinity in the way in which all move with and are formed by their common experiences.[4]

This means that those of a generation who experienced the same event, such as a world war, may respond to it differently. They were all decisively influenced by it but not in the same way. Some became pacifists, others embraced international Leninism, some longed to return to the prewar, conservative, monarchist social order, and the ones we are concerned with sought personal and national solutions in a violence-oriented movement subservient to the will of a total leader. What was politically significant in the early 1930's was the facility with which individuals of this generation moved from one allegiance to the other. Mannheim's point is that although the units of a generation do not respond to a formative crisis in the same way due to a multiplicity of variables, the overriding fact is their response to that particular event. Because of this they are oriented toward each other for the rest of their lives and constitute a generation.

An organization, such as a youth group, says Mannheim, may serve to mobilize latent opinion in a generation unit. It attracts to itself those individuals who share the formative experiences and impulses of the particular generation location, thus institutionalizing and realizing collectively the potentialities inherent in the historical and social situation.[5]

Following the theoretical work of Mannheim, sociological demographers have developed the highly suggestive concept of the "cohort," a term whose Latin etymology significantly refers to a group of fighting men who made up one of the ten divisions of a legion in the Roman army. In the modern discipline of demography a cohort is the aggregate of individuals within a population who have shared a significant common experience of a personal or historical event at the same time. This is distinguished from the loose term "generation," by which historians usually mean a temporal unit of family kinship structure such as "the founding generation," or, more ambiguously, a broad and often unspecified age span during a particular institutional, political, or cultural epoch, such as "the generation of '48" or "the lost generation." An example of a cohort would be college graduates of the year 1929, who completed their education in prosperity and in their first months on the labor market experienced the onset of the Great Depression. This cohort is distinctively marked by the period-specific stimulus of the economic depression for their entire working years in the labor force, so that they are to be distinguished from other cohorts, even thirty years later, by their common experience of having endured significant events simultaneously. The same may be said for those who served in the armed forces during World Wars I and II, or those who were children during a war.

These are, of course, examples of birth cohorts. But a cohort need not necessarily be born at the same time. A cohort may include people of all ages, even those *in utero,* if the historian seeks to define all of those who were influenced by a single traumatic event. When Robert Jay Lifton, for example, studied the people who were victims of the atomic bombing of Hiroshima, he interviewed a wide range of people—from a boy who was but two years old to a number of elderly men and women—who constitute the cohort of atomic survivors. Likewise, those who have survived a Nazi concentration camp, regardless of age, have been through a traumatic experience that marks them for life. They will never be the same; they are the concentration-camp cohort. As the demographer Norman Ryder says: "The concept [of cohort analysis] can be extended to the identification and surveillance of any group in terms of the time it enters any category of exposure to an event or behavior pattern of interest."[6] Thus each cohort is itself unique; its members are different from all those who have preceded it and all who will follow because they have experienced certain traumatic episodes in their collective life at a common time and a specific historical moment.

In emphasizing what distinguishes one generation from another, Ryder and other generation and cohort theorists naturally tend to understate the equally important bonds of continuity that tie a society together by connecting one generation to another. In the last analysis it is these latter attachments that are most fundamental to society because they provide for the transmission of cultural modes such as language and social norms of behavior from parents to children and thus from one generation to another.*

*The process of the birth of the individual personality is described by Margaret Mahler as follows: "Infants present a large variety of cues—to indicate needs, tension, and pleasure. In a complex manner, the mother responds selectively to only *certain* of these cues. The infant gradually alters his behavior in relation to this selective response; he does so in a characteristic way—the resultant

War has received special attention from cohort theorists as the most dramatic instance of a cohort influenced by external events. Ryder writes

> The Great War weakened a whole cohort in Europe to the extent that normal succession of personnel in roles, including positions of power, was disturbed. Sometimes the old retained power too long; sometimes the young seized power too soon. The most obvious effect of war is the mortality and morbidity of the participants, but war transforms non-combatants as well. . . . Traumatic episodes like war and revolution may become the foci of crystallization of the mentality of a cohort. The dramatic impact may mark indelibly the "naive eyes and virgin senses" of the cohort . . . and change them into . . . a virtual community of thought and action. . . . Solidarity is encouraged by idealized self-definitions, . . . by sharing anxieties concerning imminent and hazardous transitions, and by explicit associations that encourage the development of attitudes unsanctioned by family and community.[7]

The concept of the birth cohort—that is, those born at the same time —implies common characteristics because of common formative experiences that condition later life. Character formation, the direction of primary drives, and the internalization of family and social values are determined in the years of infancy and childhood. Each cohort carries the impress of its specific encounter with history, be it war or revolution, defeat or national disaster, inflation or depression, throughout its life.* Any given political,

---

of his own innate endowment and the mother-child relationship." *On Human Symbiosis and the Vicissitudes of Individuation*, vol. I: *Infantile Psychosis* (New York, 1968), p. 18. This is not only how a child acquires his individual uniqueness; it is also the pattern of transmission and acquisition of the cultural norms of a society. See also Talcott Parsons, "Social Structure and the Development of Personality: Freud's Contribution to the Integration of Psychology and Sociology," in his *Social Structure and Personality* (New York, 1964), pp. 78–III.

*Such cohort analysis, emphasizing the importance of time-specific childhood socialization, has enabled Ronald Inglehart, for example, to explain convincingly why Dutch adults favor European unification to a higher degree than the adults of France, Germany, or Britain. Inglehart attributes this to the fact that, alone among these four countries, the Netherlands was not involved in World War I and the great-power struggles that preceded it, when the age group he tested in 1963 at age fifty-five and over would have been children. He suggests that this difference is due to "a residue from the experiences of childhood and youth" in which the individuals over fifty-five in France, Germany, and Britain "were exposed to the period of intense nationalism which preceded that war, and to the powerful fears and suspicions the war aroused during a relative[ly] impressionable stage of life." Inglehart goes on to postulate that because by the end of the 1970's a majority of the voting population in the Common Market countries will consist of people who entered primary school after World War II, thus having derived an early "sense of positive participation in common activities" and of growing up "with some awareness of common endeavor," the advocates of the movement for European integration will move into positions of leadership within their respective countries. "An End to European Integration?" *American Political Science Review*, 61 (1967): 93 and 94.

social, or economic event affects people of different ages in different ways. The impact of war, hunger, defeat, and revolution on a child will be of an entirely different order of magnitude than the impact on an adult. This commonplace fact suggests that the event specificity of history must be fused with the generational-age specificity of the cohort of sociological demography and the developmental-phase specificity of psychoanalysis and childhood socialization to understand historical change. In this sense history may be the syncretic catalyst of qualitative longitudinal life history and the quantitative data of sociological statistical analysis.

Rather than proceeding with the story of the Nazi youth cohort chronologically and beginning with its origins, this essay will use what Marc Bloch termed the "prudently retrogressive" method of looking at the outcome first, and then tracking down the beginnings or "causes" of the phenomenon.[8] This, of course, corresponds to the clinical method of examining the "presenting complaints" first and then investigating etiology. The outcome of the story in this case is the related and concomitant economic depression, the influx of German youth to the ranks of National Socialism, the political decline of the Weimar Republic, and the Nazi seizure of power.

The Great Depression hit Germany harder than any other country, with the possible exception of the United States. Germany's gross national income, which rose by 25 percent between 1925 and 1928, sank 43 percent from 71 billion RM in 1929 to 41 billion RM in 1932. The production index for industry in 1927/28 was halved by 1932/33. In the critical area of capital goods, production in 1933 was one-third of what it had been five years earlier. The very aspect of Nazi success at the polls in the elections of 1930 accelerated the withdrawal of foreign capital from Germany, thus deepening the financial crisis.

The greatest social impact of the economic crisis was in creating unemployment. By 1932 one of every three Germans in the labor market was without a job. This meant that even those who held jobs were insecure, for there were numerous workers available to take the place of every employee. The young people were, of course, the most vulnerable sector of the labor market. New jobs were nonexistent, and the young had the least seniority and experience with which to compete for employment. To this must be added that the number of apprenticeships was sharply diminishing for working-class youths. For example, apprenticeships in iron, steel, and metalworking declined from 132,000 in 1925 to 19,000 in 1932.[9] University graduates had no better prospects for finding employment. They soon formed an underemployed intellectual proletariat that looked to National Socialism for relief and status.

The electoral ascendancy of the Nazi party in the four years between 1928 and 1932 constitutes one of the most dramatic increments of votes and political power in the history of electoral democracy. In the Reichstag elections of May 20, 1928, the National Socialists received 810,127 votes, constituting 2.6 percent of the total vote and 12 Reichstag seats. In the communal elections of 1929 the Nazis made decisive gains. With this election Germany had its first Nazi minister, in Thuringia in the person of Wilhelm Frick, a putschist of 1923. In the next Reichstag elections of September 14, 1930, the National Socialists obtained 6,379,672 votes, for 18.3 percent of the total and 107 seats. At the election of July 31, 1932, the National Socialists became the largest party in the country and in the Reichstag with 13,765,781 votes, giving them 37.4 percent of the total vote and 230 parliamentary seats.[10]

This extremely rapid growth of Nazi power can be attributed to the participation in politics of previously inactive people and of those who were newly enfranchised because they had reached voting eligibility at twenty years of age. There were 5.7 million new voters in 1930.* The participation of eligible voters in elections increased from 74.6 percent in 1928 to 81.41 percent in 1930, and 83.9 percent in 1932. In the elections of March 5, 1933, there were 2.5 million new voters over the previous year and voting participation rose to 88.04 percent of the electorate.[11]

The German political sociologist Heinrich Streifler makes the point that not only were new, youthful voters added at each election, but there were losses from the voting rolls due to deaths that must be calculated. He shows that 3 million voters died in the period between 1928 and 1933. The increment of first-time, new voters in the same period was 6,500,000.[12]

In the elections of 1928, 3.5 million young voters who were eligible did not participate in the voting. "This," says Streifler, "is a reserve that could be mobilized to a much greater extent than the older non-voters."[13] He goes on to suggest that these young non-voters were more likely to be mobilized by a radical party that appealed to passions and emotions rather than to reason.

The Nazis made a spectacular and highly successful appeal to German youth. An official slogan of the party ran: "National Socialism is the organized will of youth [Nationalsozialismus ist organisierter Jugendwille]." Nazi propagandists like Gregor Strasser skillfully utilized the theme of the battle of the generations. "Step down, you old ones! [Macht Platz, ihr Alten!]," he

*I derived this figure by subtracting the total number of votes cast in 1928 (30,753,300) from the corresponding figure for 1930 (34,970,900), and adding the 1.5 million older voters who died in this period according to Arthur Dix, Die Deutschen Reichstagswahlen 1871–1930 und die Wandlungen der Volksgliederung (Tübingen, 1930), p. 36.

shouted as he invoked the names of the senior political leaders from left to right and associated them with the disappointments of the generation of the fathers and the deprivations of war, defeat, and revolution.

> Whether they are named Scheidemann and Wels, whether Dernburg or Koch, whether Bell and Marx, Stresemann and Riesser, whether Hergt and Westarp—they are the same men we know from the time before the war, when they failed to recognize the essentials of life for the German people; we know them from the war years, when they failed in the will to leadership and victory; we know them from the years of revolution, when they failed in character as well as in ability, in the need of a heroic hour, which, if it had found great men, would have been a great hour for the German people—who, however, became small and mean because its leading men were small and mean.[14]

The Nazis developed a strong following among the students, making headway in the universities in advance of their general electoral successes. National Socialism made its first visible breakthrough into a mass sector of the German people with its conquest of academic youth. The student government (ASTA) elections of 1929 were called a "National Socialist storm of the universities" by the alarmed opposition press. The Nazi Student Organization (Nationalsozialistische Deutsche Studentenbund) received more than half the votes and dominated the student government in 1929 at the universities of Erlangen and Greifswald. In the 1930 student election it also captured absolute majorities in the universities of Breslau, Giessen, Rostock, Jena, Königsberg, and the Berlin Technische Hochschule. Both of these student elections preceded the Reichstag elections of 1930 in which the Nazis made their decisive breakthrough into the center of national political life. Developments toward National Socialism among the university students anticipated by four years the developments in German society at large.[15]

The comparative age structure of the Nazi movement also tells a story of youthful preponderance on the extreme right. According to the Reich's census of 1933, those 18 to 30 constituted 31.1 percent of the German population. The proportion of National Socialist party members of this age group rose from 37.6 percent in 1931 to 42.2 percent a year later, on the eve of power. "The National Socialist party," says the sociologist Hans Gerth, "could truthfully boast of being a 'young party.'" By contrast, the Social Democratic party, second in size and the strongest democratic force in German politics, had only 19.3 percent of its members in the 18-to-30 age group in 1931. In 1930 the Social Democrats reported that less than 8 percent of their membership was under 25, and less than half was under 40.[16]

"National Socialism," says Walter Laqueur, the historian of the German youth movement, "came to power as the party of youth."[17] The Nazi party's ideology and organization coincided with those of the elitist and antidemocratic elements of the German youth movement. The Wandervogel, while essentially non-political, retreated to a rustic life on the moors, heaths, and forests where they cultivated the bonds of group life. The Nazi emphasis on a mystical union of blood and soil, of *Volk,* nation, language, and culture, appealed to the romanticism of German youth *Bünde.*

The Hitler Youth adopted many of the symbols and much of the content of the German youth movement. The Nazis incorporated the uniform, the Führer principle and authoritarian organization (group, tribe, *gau*), the flags and banners, the songs, and the war games of the *Bünde.* The National Socialists were able to take over the youth movement with virtually no opposition. On April 15, 1933, the executive of the Grossdeutsche Jugenbund voted to integrate with the Nazi movement. On June 17, 1933, the Jugenbund was dissolved and Baldur von Schirach was appointed the supreme youth leader by Hitler.

A number of scholars have interpreted the radicalization of newly enfranchised German youth in the years of the rise of National Socialism. The Nazification of the youth has also been variously attributed to the spirit of adventure and idealism, a lust for violence and military discipline, the appeal of an attack on age and established power, and the quest for emotional and material security.[18]

Among the first and most incisive political analysts to focus on the youthful element in the success of National Socialism was the left socialist leader Carl Mierendorff, who has been described by Koppel Pinson as "a flash of genius shining across the Socialist horizon" of the late Weimar years. After the municipal elections of November 1929, in which the Nazis made their first significant gains, Mierendorff called attention to the Nazi achievement of rivaling the Social Democratic party in breadth and scope of party organization to the point where it now presented a challenge to the Socialists in every precinct and township. To explain this Mierendorff pointed to the age structure of the Nazi party. To a great extent National Socialist membership was born in the years between 1905 and 1912, which he termed: "a generation which knows little or nothing of the war." While Mierendorff's observations and data are excellent, the conclusion that children are ignorant of war and that, as a childhood experience, war will not affect them in later life, is a viewpoint that no one conversant with modern concepts of psychology and the childhood socialization process is likely to share. The thesis propounded in this essay is in specific contravention to Mierendorff's Marxist interpretation. By contrast with his emphasis on conscious experience Mierendorff's psychological insight is perceptive when he evaluates the motives for this National Socialist appeal to youth. "It makes no intellectual demands of its followers, instead it expects of them first of all enthusiasm and both personal and intellectual arrogance. It flirts with pseudo-masculine manners and presents itself in a basically aggressive pseudo-heroic posture."[19]

The historical demographer Herbert Moller, on the other hand, stresses the factor of cohort size in creating the preconditions for political turbulence in Germany in the early 1930's. He points out that the proportion of young adults in Germany was very high at this time as a result of the high birth rates twenty to thirty years earlier. "The cohorts of 1900 to 1914," he writes, "more numerous than any earlier ones, had not been decimated by the war." Moller shows that precisely this cohort had its ranks swelled by immigrants from the territories ceded under the Treaty of Versailles and by German nationals from abroad, especially from eastern and southeastern Europe. Close to one and a half million immigrants entered Germany from 1918 to 1925, just when emigration to America was being curtailed by immigration-quota legislation in the United States. By 1930, because of the depression, a reverse movement of reemigration from America back to Germany occurred. As a result of these developments, in 1933 the age group from 20 to 45 was the largest in German history and constituted the highest relative percentage of the German population of any period before or since. In 1890 this age group constituted 34.4 percent of Germany's population. In 1933 it peaked to make up 41.5 percent of all Germans. By 1959 the 20-to-45 age cohorts had dropped to only 33.7 percent of the German people. "From a demographic viewpoint," says Moller, "the economic depression hit Germany at the worst possible time: employment was shrinking precisely at a time when the employable population reached its postwar peak."[20]

There is ample evidence that this generation of German youth was more inclined toward violent and aggressive behavior than previous generations. At this point the explanations offered for this phenomenon are inadequate in their one-dimensionality. To say that the youth craved action or that they sought comfort in the immersion in a sheltering group is to beg the question of what made this generation of German youth different from all previous generations. What unique experiences did this group of people have in their developmental years that could induce regression to infantile attitudes in adulthood? One persuasive answer lies in fusing the knowledge we have of personality functioning from psychoanalysis—the most comprehensive and dynamic theory of personality available to the social and humanistic sciences today—with the cohort theory of generational change from historical demography and with the data on the leadership and structure of the

Nazi party that we have from the researches of political scientists, historians, and sociologists.

In the half century prior to World War I, Germany was transformed from an agricultural to an industrial economy, and her population grew from an agriculturally self-sufficient forty million to sixty-seven million by 1913. This mounting industrial population made her increasingly dependent on the importation of foreign foodstuffs. In the decade preceding World War I, five-sixths of Germany's vegetable fats, more than half of her dairy goods, and one-third of the eggs her people consumed were imported. This inability to be self-sufficient in foodstuffs made the German population particularly susceptible to the weapon of the blockade. The civilian population began to feel the pressure of severe shortages in 1916. The winter of 1916/17 is still known as the infamous "turnip winter," in which hunger and privation became widespread experiences in Germany. Getting something to eat was the foremost concern of most people. The official food rations for the summer of 1917 were 1,000 calories per day, whereas the Health Ministry estimated that 2,280 calories was a subsistence minimum. From 1914 to 1918 three-quarters of a million people died of starvation in Germany.[21]

The armistice of November 11, 1918, did not bring the relief that the weary and hungry Germans anticipated. The ordeal of the previous three years was intensified into famine in the winter of 1918/19. The blockade was continued until the Germans turned over their merchant fleet to the Allies. The armistice blockade was extended by the victorious Allies to include the Baltic Sea, thus cutting off trade with Scandinavia and the Baltic states. Although the Allies undertook responsibility for the German food supply under Article 26 of the Armistice Agreement, the first food shipment was not unloaded in Hamburg until March 26, 1919. On July 11, 1919, the Allied Supreme Economic Council decided to terminate the blockade of Germany as of the next day, July 12. Unrestricted trade between the United States and Germany was resumed three days later, on July 15.[22]

The degree of German suffering under the postwar Allied blockade is a matter on which contemporary opinions differed. Some Allied diplomats and journalists charged that the German government exaggerated the plight of her people in order to increase Allied food deliveries. Today the weight of the historical evidence is that there was widespread extreme hunger and malnutrition in the last three years of the war, which was intensified by the postwar blockade. We may concur with the evaluation of two American historians that "the suffering of the German children, women, and men, with the exception of farmers and rich hoarders, was greater under the continued blockade than prior to the Armistice."[23]

Among the documents that Mathias Erzberger, the chairman of the German Armistice Commission in 1918, requested from the Reichsgesundheitsamt (Reich Public Health Service) was a memorandum discussing the effects of the blockade on the civilian population. The memorandum, entitled "Damage to the Strength of the German People due to the Enemy Blockade Which Contravenes International Law,"* was submitted on December 16, 1918. This document is of special psychological interest because it consists of statistics giving increases in deaths, disease, stillbirths, and loss of strength in the labor force, all of which bear sums indicating monetary losses per individual and to the nation. The most remarkable set of figures are those that conclude that, on the basis of a population of 50 million with an average weight of 114.4 pounds, who have each lost one-fifth of their weight, the German people have lost 520,000 tons of human mass (*Menschenmasse*). The memorandum goes on to estimate that 1,560,000 to 1,768,000 tons of food would be necessary to restore the flesh (*Fleische*) that had been lost according to the previous calculation.[24]

The demographic and statistical data constitute an overwhelming case that the German civilian population, particularly infants and children, suffered widely and intensively during the war and blockade. Public health authorities and medical researchers have compiled population studies indicating damage to health, fertility, and emotions from 1914 to 1920. These are quantifiable indexes of physical deprivation from which the equally damaging but much more difficult to measure facts of emotional deprivation may be inferred.

On the grossest level the figures show a decline in the number of live births from 1,353,714 in 1915 to 926,813 in 1918. The birth rate per 1,000 population, including stillbirths, declined from 28.25 in 1913 to 14.73 in 1918. The number of deaths among the civilian population over one year old rose from 729,000 in 1914 to 1,084,000 in 1918. While there was a decline in deaths from causes related to nutrition and caloric intake, such as diabetes mellitus, alcoholism, obesity, diseases of the gastrointestinal tract, as well as a decrease in suicides, the gross mortality of the German population increased due to malnutrition, lack of heating, and consequent weakened resistance to

*The psychology of this quantification of human flesh is itself a subject requiring psychohistorical analysis. The high degree of isolation of feelings permitted by the use of statistics gives them an attractiveness to social scientists who wish to avoid their own painful emotions. "Statistics do not cry or bleed." This is not to question the undeniable advances in historical understanding that have been achieved by quantitative methods, but it is to suggest that these methods are ego syntonic for personalities who need emotional defenses against experience. It was by this mental process of compulsive depersonalizing and bureaucratic deemotionalizing of experience that the suicidal depression of many Germans in 1918 was converted to the genocidal defense against depression by turning human beings into tons of hair and fertilizer a quarter of a century later. This was the active reexperiencing of a passively endured trauma of starvation and dehumanization.

disease. Specific causes of death that increased sharply during the war were influenza, lung infections and pneumonia, tuberculosis, diseases of the circulatory system, diphtheria, typhus, dysentery, and diseases of the urinary and reproductive organs.[25] All these diseases indicate a population whose biological ability to maintain health and to counter infection had been seriously undermined in the war years.

Upon looking at the comparative statistics for neonates and infants, we find a decline in weight and size at birth, a decline in the ability of mothers to nurse, a higher incidence of disease, particularly rickets and tuberculosis, as well as an increase in neurotic symptoms such as bed-wetting and in the death rate. In the third year of the war the weight of neonates was 50 to 100 grams less at birth than before the war. In one Munich clinic in 1918 the females averaged 50 grams and the males 70 grams less at birth than in peacetime.[26]

During the first year of the war more mothers nursed babies and the period of breast feeding was longer than previously, but by the winter of 1915 a decline in breast feeding had set in that was to continue through 1919. This is attributed to the war work of mothers and the "prolonged malnutrition and the damaged body of the mother due to psychic insult." One chemical analysis done in Berlin found a marked decline in the quantity and quality of mother's milk, resulting in the retarded development of breast-fed children and a delay in their normal weight gain. Infants fed on cow's milk also received milk that was short of nutriments, butterfat, and vitamins because of the lack of feed for the milk cows and the skimming off of cream for butter production.[27] To the shortage and inferior quality of milk must be added the almost total absence of fresh vegetables and fruit, important sources of vitamins, in the diets of children during the war and postwar period.

Not only infants but small children also were materially deprived by malnutrition. By the third year of the war children in the third year of life were up to 2.2 pounds lighter than normal body weight for their age. A study comparing 300 Berlin children in 1919 with figures from 1908 and 1909 showed that the boys were retarded in growth to the level of children 1.5 years younger, and the girls were 1.25 years behind normal.[28]

Like the infants, young children were also particularly afflicted with rickets, tuberculosis, and parasites. A medical examination of 2,154 children between 1914 and 1921 found that 39.1 percent had rickets. Of the children in this group who fell ill between 12 and 18 months of age, 49.2 percent had rickets. Cases of childhood miliary tuberculosis in the state of Baden rose 50 percent after December 1918. A comparative sample of Berlin children aged 3 showed 8.1 percent infected with tuberculosis in 1918; this rose to 29.9 percent in 1919.[29]

The pattern of increased illness and death among infants and small children in Germany carried through to children of school age. Deaths of children between 5 and 15 years of age more than doubled between 1913 and 1918. Using figures for 1913 as a base of 100, the death figures for this age group in 1918 were 189.2 for boys aged 5 to 10 and 215 for boys aged 10 to 15. Among the girls the death rates for these age groups were 207.3 and 239.9, respectively.[30]

Among the leading causes of illness and death in this age group, as with the younger children, were rickets and tuberculosis. Corresponding losses in size and weight relative to age are also recorded. The medical statistics demonstrate an increased incidence among children of gastrointestinal disorders, worms, fleas, and lice. Psychological indications of stress among schoolchildren include an "enormous increase" in bed-wetting, "nervousness," and juvenile delinquency.[31]

The evidence for deprivation is supported from Allied and neutral sources. The British war correspondent Henry W. Nevinson reported from Cologne in March 1919 that tuberculosis had more than doubled among women and children and that the death rate among girls between 6 and 16 years had tripled. Because the children were so weak, school hours were reduced from seven to two hours daily. He wrote: "Although I have seen many horrible things in the world, I have seen nothing so pitiful as these rows of babies feverish from want of food, exhausted by privation to the point that their little limbs were like slender wands, their expression hopeless, and their faces full of pain."[32]

The British medical journal *Lancet* reported comparative figures derived from official German sources showing that the effect of food scarcity on the health of the German population was felt after mid-1916 but was kept hidden by skillful press censorship in wartime Germany. Among children from 1 to 5 years old the mortality was 50 percent greater in 1917 than the norm of 1913. Among the children aged 5 to 15 mortality had risen 75 percent.[33]

A tripartite commission of doctors was appointed by the medical faculties of the Netherlands, Sweden, and Norway to examine health conditions in Germany after the cessation of hostilities. This neutral medical commission found a state so deplorable that John Maynard Keynes was moved in 1920 to ask with prescience: "Who can say how much is endurable, or in what direction men will seek at last to escape from their misfortunes?" The physicians reported on the effects of prolonged hunger and malnutrition.

Tuberculosis, especially in children, is increasing in an appalling way, and, generally speaking, is malignant. In the same way rickets is more serious and widely prevalent. It is impossible to do anything for these diseases; there is no milk for the tuberculosis, and no cod-liver oil for those suffering from rickets. . . . Tuberculosis is assuming almost unprecedented aspects, such as have hitherto only been known in exceptional cases. The whole body is attacked simultaneously, and the illness in this form is practically incurable. . . . Tuberculosis is nearly always fatal now among adults. It is the cause of 90 percent of the hospital cases. Nothing can be done against it owing to lack of foodstuffs. . . . It appears in the most terrible forms, such as glandular tuberculosis, which turns into purulent dissolution.

Contemporary German sources confirm this report. A writer for a prestigious liberal newspaper accompanied the Hoover Commission to the Erzgebirge, where there was severe famine. He wrote:

I visited large country districts where 90 percent of all the children were ricketty and where children of three years are only beginning to walk. . . . Accompany me to a school in the Erzgebirge. You think it is a kindergarten for the little ones. No, these are children of seven and eight years. Tiny faces, with large dull eyes, overshadowed by huge puffed, ricketty foreheads, their small arms just skin and bone, and above the crooked legs with their dislocated joints the swollen, pointed stomachs of the hunger oedema.[34]

World War I was the first total war in history—it involved the labor and the commitment of full energies of its participant peoples as no previous war had. The men were in the armed services, but a modern war requires a major industrial plant and increased production of foodstuffs and supplies to support the armies. Yet the number of men working in industry in Germany dropped 24 percent between 1913 and 1917. In the state of Prussia in 1917 the number of men working in plants employing over ten workers was 2,558,000, including foreigners and prisoners of war, while in 1913 the total of men employed had been 3,387,000.[35]

In Germany this meant a shift of major proportions of women from the home and domestic occupations to war work. In the state of Prussia alone the number of women engaged in industrial labor rose by 76 percent, from 788,100 in 1913 to 1,393,000 in 1917. For Germany as a whole 1.2 million women newly joined the labor force in medium- and large-sized plants during the war. The number of women workers in the armaments industry rose from 113,750 in 1913 to 702,100 in 1917, a gain of 500 percent. The number of women laborers who were covered under compulsory insurance laws on October 1, 1917, was 6,750,000. The increase of adult female workers in Prussia in 1917 was 80.4 percent over 1913. The number of women railroad workers in Prussia rose from 10,000 in 1914 to 100,000 in 1918, an increase of 1,000 percent.[36]

Another new factor in the labor force was the youthful workers. The number of adolescents aged 14 to 16 employed in chemical manufacturing increased 225 percent between 1913 and 1917. For heavy industry the corresponding figure was 97 percent. Many of these were young girls aged 16 to 21. This age group constituted 29 percent of all working women.[37]

German women massively engaged in war work was recognized as resulting in the neglect of Germany's war children and damage to the health of the mothers. Reports came from government offices of increased injuries to children of ages 1 to 5 years due to lack of supervision. S. Rudolf Steinmetz evaluates the demoralization of youth between 1914 and 1918 as an indirect consequence of the war. He ascribes to "the absence of many fathers, the war work of many mothers" the damaged morals and morality of youth.[38]

Many of the war-related phenomena under discussion were not unique to the Central European countries. The factor of a chauvinistic atmosphere of war propaganda was certainly present in all belligerent countries. The absence of the parents in wartime service was also not unique to Germany or Austria. The children of other countries involved in the war too had absent parents and were often orphaned. French and British families undoubtedly experienced the sense of fatherlessness and desertion by the mother as much as did German and Austrian families. Two added factors, however, make the critical difference in the constellation of the child's view of the world: the absence of German and Austrian parents was coupled with extreme and persistent hunger bordering in the cities on starvation, and when the German or Austrian father returned he came in defeat and was unable to protect his family in the postwar period of unemployment and inflation. Not only was the nation defeated, but the whole political-social world was overturned. The Kaiser of Germany had fled, and the Kaiser of Austria had been deposed. Some Germans would say that the Kaiser had deserted his people, to be replaced by an insecure and highly ambivalent republic under equivocating socialist leadership. Much more than an army collapsed—an entire orientation to the state and the conduct of civic life was under assault in 1918–1919. These national factors unique to Central Europe exacerbated the familial crisis of the absence of parents and made of this wartime experience a generational crisis.

Today it is widely recognized that the emotional constellation of the childhood years is decisive for the future psychological health and normality of the adult. Modern war conditions, through the long-term breakup of family life, added in some cases to a lack of essential food and shelter, and a national atmosphere highly charged with unmitigated expressions of patriotism, hatred, and violence must inevitably distort the emotional and mental development of children, for imbalance in the fulfillment of essential psychic and bodily needs in childhood results in lasting psychological malformations.

It may be helpful to review briefly modern theories of phase-specific development and emotional growth from infancy to adulthood in order to point to the areas of greatest potential stress due to family or social trauma. What follows is necessarily no more than a theoretical model of development, an ideal typology of the psychodynamics of personality development that will be useful as a heuristic device against which to test empirical and cultural data. It does not presume to be a precise model of any single individual's development.

More is now known than ever before about the psychological processes and fantasies of children. There is a high level of agreement among child-guidance specialists that maternal deprivation of the child has long-ranging effects on the mental health and emotional strength of the adult. The first relationship a child forms is with his mother. His attitude to the object—in the first case, the mother—is a passive, receptive one; that is, the child is narcissistic and selfish, he wishes to be given pleasure and to have his discomforts removed. A number of British psychoanalysts of what has come to be known as the "English school" have stressed the quality of destructive oral rage that is normally present in all children. This cataclysmic world-destroying rage is, of course, intensified in cases of deprivation.

The late British pediatrician and psychoanalyst D. W. Winnicott described the rages experienced by infants in which they want to destroy their mother's breasts and believe they can do so by feeding from them. Melanie Klein also pictures the world of the infant as a seething cauldron of intense emotions of love and hate in which the baby is dominated by impulses to destroy the very object of all his desires—his mother. When describing the baby's uncontrollable sensations of rage and his experience of threatened destruction from within and without, Joan Riviere writes:

> He becomes aggressive. He automatically explodes, as it were, with hate and aggressive craving. If he feels emptiness and loneliness, an automatic reaction sets in, which may soon become uncontrollable and overwhelming, an aggressive rage which brings pain and explosive, burning, suffocating, choking bodily sensations; and these in turn cause further feelings of lack, pain and apprehension. The baby cannot distinguish between "me" and "not me"; his own sensations are his world, *the* world to him; so when he is cold, hungry or lonely there is no milk, no well-being or pleasure in the world—the valuable things in life have vanished. And when he is tortured with desire or anger, with uncontrollable, suffocating screaming, and painful, burn-

ing evacuations, the whole of his world is one of suffering; it is scalded, torn and racked too.

René Spitz, in his classic studies of hospitalism, has shown that the absence of an emotionally available mother during the child's first year damages his physical development as well as his personality. Spitz compared children who were cared for by their own mothers in a prison nursery with children in an orphanage whose care was in the hands of professionally competent nurses but who had no close personal care or contact with their mothers. Although on admission the children in the orphan home rated much higher in body-mastery, development, and achievement indexes, within four months they deteriorated and continued to sink. They were unable to speak, feed themselves, or acquire habits of cleanliness. The infants in the prison nursery went through a progressive development because they had an intense emotional interchange with their mothers during the first twelve months of life.[39]

A somewhat later and very great threat to a child's security is the trauma of separation. It is considered to be essential for sound personality development that the infant and young child should experience a warm, intimate, and continuous relationship with a mother or permanent mother figure, a relationship in which both infant and mother find gratification and pleasure. John Bowlby observes: "Prolonged breaks [in the mother-child relationship] during the first three years of life leave a characteristic impression on the child's personality. Clinically such children appear emotionally withdrawn and isolated. They fail to develop libidinal ties with other children or with adults and consequently have no friendships worth the name."[40]

For the infant and child the mother is the supreme agent who can give gratification and assuage pain. "The absence of the mother," writes Margaret Mahler, "exposes the normal infant . . . to the danger of helplessness and longing, with consequent anxiety." The danger is particularly threatening to the child not only because of his utter dependence and helplessness but because of his own acute ambivalence. There is a great accumulation of aggression toward love objects during the oral sadistic, anal sadistic, and oedipal phases of child development. The child must struggle with intense fears of loss of love due to his own hostility and aggression. He must preserve his love for the object (mother) despite his rage and fear. If the mother's love and acceptance of the child is not forthcoming, he reacts as if he has been rejected for his badness. There is a deficit in self-esteem.[41] The child views himself as unlovable and worthless, as an evil creature who drives loved ones away. His healthy narcissistic balance is destroyed, and his ego is weakened.

One way of coping with feelings of inner badness is to project these evil, asocial parts of the self out onto others.

Bowlby terms separation from the mother or mothering figure the "primal anxiety" in the life of a young child. The condition of separation causes intense alarm, fright, and distress. Because of the mother's tremendous importance for the child's survival, the response of separation anxiety is permanently ready for activation; it is easily activated and cannot be completely terminated except by the child's preferred mother figure.[42]

Some specialists in the problems of childhood separation and individuation suggest that the desire to merge with a mass movement in adolescence and adulthood expresses the need to regress, while in a state of panic or terror, to the pre-individuation phase. The merging may be a crowd fusing with each other or with an authoritarian regime and its dictatorial leader.[43]

Separation from the mother engenders hostility because it is interpreted as rejection by the loved person; it is experienced as the loss of love. The period when this anxiety and hostility are most active is also the period when patterns of control and of regulating conflict are laid down. Thus, separation anxiety and hostility are provoked by the same experience. The hostility must be repressed because it is directed at the loved person and to express it and risk further loss is far too dangerous. Being repressed, the hostility generates further anxiety. Both the increased need for the mother and the heightened unconscious hostility toward her promote a neurotic, anxiety-prone personality inclined to regress to primal anxiety and rage when confronted with frustration in later life.

Children are traumatized by the horrors of war, by hearing reports and seeing actual pictures of killed and maimed fathers, mothers, and dead children. But it is a fantasy of the innocence of childhood and a misconception of the nature of children to believe that destruction and aggression are unknown to them.

Aggression, of course, does not end in infancy and childhood. What Winnicott, Riviere, Klein, Spitz, Bowlby, and Mahler describe as anger and rage in neonates and infants is observable as destructive behavior in any nursery as the infant becomes a child. Anna Freud and Dorothy T. Burlingham describe their observations of the conflicts with aggression and control that characterize the struggle of bowel training:

> Children between the ages of one and two years, when put together in a playpen will bite each other, pull each other's hair and steal each other's toys without regard for the other child's unhappiness. They are passing through a stage of development where destruction and aggression play one of the leading parts. If we observe young children at play, we notice that they will destroy their toys, pull off the arms

and legs of their dolls or soldiers, puncture their balls, smash whatever is breakable. . . . The more their strength and independence are
growing the more they will have to be watched so as not to create
too much damage, not to hurt each other or those weaker than
themselves.

The authors then add a highly significant sentence: "We often say, half
jokingly, that there is a continual war raging in a nursery."[44]

The young child experiences murderous death wishes toward all people
who have disturbed, offended, or rejected him in fantasy or reality. The
jealous desire to do away with an interfering sibling or rival is a universal
commonplace. One of the most important social aims of education is to
curb the unmitigated aggressiveness of children. At first direct action on
destructive wishes is prohibited by outside authority. Later the child learns
to inhibit these impulses in himself. They are defended against by reaction
formations such as compassion and pity, and compulsive defenses such as
scrupulous care and meticulousness. They may be repressed or sublimated
into competitive and constructive activity. The child learns to criticize and
overcome in himself his hostile, antisocial wishes, which is to say that he
refuses them conscious expression. He accepts that it is bad to hurt, crip-
ple, and kill. He believes that he has no further wish to do any of these
violent and destructive things. He can only maintain this belief, however,
if the outer social world is supportive of his struggle by likewise curbing its
aggression.

When a child who is struggling with his aggressive and destructive
impulses finds himself in a society at war, the hatred and violence around
him in the outer world meet the as yet untamed aggression raging in his
inner world. At the very age when education is beginning to deal with the
impulses in the inner environment the same wishes receive sanction and
validation from a society at war. It is impossible to repress murderous and
destructive wishes when fantasied and actual fighting, maiming, and killing
are the preoccupation of all the people among whom the child lives. Instead
of turning away from the horrors and atrocities of war, he turns toward
them with primitive excitement. The very murderous and destructive impulses that he has been trying to bury in himself are now nourished by the
official ideology and mass media of a country at war.

The power of his aroused inner fantasies of violence is anxiety-producing
for the child. It is as though an inner signal alerts him to beware of the
danger of losing control. When, in addition, the child is not with his family,
he will often develop the symptoms of nervousness, bed-wetting, fecal incon-
tinence, stealing, truancy, and delinquency that Winnicott describes.[45]

Many political scientists and historians have pointed to the function of

National Socialism as a defense against emotional insecurity. Harold Lass-well, in contrast to those who have interpreted Hitler as a father or a son symbol,* develops precisely the theme of Hitler's maternal function for the German people, suggesting that Nazism was a regressive attempt to com-pensate for mothering and family life that had been inadequate. Lasswell stresses the anal-phase in imagery of cleanliness and pollution in Nazi propoganda.

> There is a profound sense in which Hitler himself plays a maternal role for certain classes in German society. His incessant moralizing is that of the anxious mother who is totally preoccupied with the physical, intellectual and ethical development of her children. He discourses in public, as he has written in his autobiography, on all manner of pedagogical problems, from the best form of history teach-ing to the ways of reducing the ravages of social disease. His constant preoccupation with "purity" is consistent with these interests; he alludes constantly to the "purity of the racial stock" and often to the code of personal abstinence or moderation. This master of modern Galahadism uses the language of Protestant puritanism and of Cath-olic reverence for the institution of family life. The conscience for which he stands is full of obsessional doubts, repetitive affirmations, resounding negations and stern compulsions. It is essentially the bundle of "don'ts" of the nursemaid conscience.[46]

Similarly, research indicates that paternal deprivation in childhood, which assumes increasing importance in later years as the child approaches and works through his oedipal conflict, also has a profound impact on the personality and ideas of youth concerning father images, political authority, and sources of power. In a study comparing father-separated and father-at-home elementary school children, George R. Bach found that "father-separated children produce an idealistic fantasy picture of the father" that "seem[s] to indicate the existence of strong drives for paternal affection." In turn, then, "the severely deprivated [sic] drive for paternal affection provides strong instigation for the idealistic, wish-fulfilling fantasies."[47] The absent father is idealized. This is in part a reaction formation—that is, a defense against hatred toward the father by replacing these repressed hostile feelings with their conscious opposite.†

*These interpretations are not necessarily mutually exclusive. Hitler, in accord with the principles of multiple function and overdetermination, may have represented mothering, fathering, and filial roles to the same people at various times and to different groups of people at the same time.
†Bach's research showed that "beyond influencing the child through father-typing, the mother may actually modify the child's personality development in the direction of femininity during the period of father-absence. The father is not available for imitation of or identification with mascu-line social behavior, and there is now more opportunity to imitate feminine attitudes, manners,

Psychoanalytic theory and clinical evidence tell us that prolonged absence of the father results in intensified closeness to the mother. This in turn will heighten oedipal conflict for the son in latency. Stimulated incestuous fantasies will increase the fear of punishment for the forbidden longings. The sharpened castration anxiety of the boy left alone with his mother results in strengthened identification with the absent idealized father and in homosexual longings for him. The homosexual feelings for the distant father are a love for him shared with the mother and a defense against heightened incestuous feelings for her.

The emancipation of women, which was accelerated greatly in World War I by the needs of a total war economy, gave to women what had been traditionally men's vocational roles and familial responsibilities. In such circumstances, in her own eyes and in the eyes of her children, the woman who works in industry and agriculture is now doing "man's" work. Thus the mother who manages the affairs of the family may acquire a "phallic" or masculine image to her children. As she is not accustomed to bearing the full responsibility for the family welfare and discipline, she will tend to become anxious. This anxiety is further exacerbated by her sexual and emotional frustration and concern for her husband. Anxieties of all kinds are immediately and inevitably communicated to children, who then become anxious as well. In her uncertainty a mother will often be more punitive than she would be under normal circumstances, both to ward off her own sexual feelings and because of anxiety about her role as disciplinarian. This heightens the passive masochism and castration anxiety in young boys.

Boys who become homosexuals are often those who were left alone with their mothers and formed an intense attachment to them that was unmediated by the father's presence and protection. The struggle against feminine identification and the regression to narcissistic object choice—that is, choosing someone who is like himself, what he was, or what he would like to be—are all greatly intensified in boys raised without fathers.

If early separation and deprivation damages the frustration tolerance and reality-testing functions of children, we must look at the process of the political socialization and political-fantasy formation of normal children.

---

and values of the mother. The idealistic father-fantasies of *both* the separated boys and the separated girls with their stereotyped, affectionate and non-aggressive themes are very similar to the doll play fantasies *characteristically produced by girls* (in contrast to boys) under ordinary family conditions. This 'feminization' of the father-separated child's fantasy may then be a reflection of the increased potency of the mother as a social stimulus. The idealistic father-fantasies may, therefore, not only be an expression of the child's wish for an affectionate father but may actually also be symptomatic of a personality reorganization produced by exclusive maternal domination." George R. Bach, "Father-Fantasies and Father-Typing in Father-Separated Children," *Child Development,* 17 (1946): 71.

Research in the field of children's concepts of politics, political leadership, and national identity indicates that many of the primary identifications of a lifetime are already formed by the second grade of elementary school, that is, at age eight or nine.* Children in elementary school develop predispositions for a political party, intense nationalistic chauvinism of a "we are good, they are bad" variety, and positive affectual attachment to symbols of patriotism such as the flag or the Statue of Liberty. "Affect," David O. Sears points out, "precedes information. Children express strong positive affect toward leaders, and only later acquire supporting rationalizations." Familiarity with high leaders is practically at adult levels by the second grade. In Fred Greenstein's sample, 96 percent of American children aged nine knew who the President was. In Robert D. Hess's study 95 percent of the children aged seven through nine recognized and correctly identified the President. A similarly high level of recognition was found for the national leaders in studies done in Chile, Japan, and Australia.[48]

Children tend to idealize the President and to personalize the government—that is, they see it in terms of the person of the leader rather than as an institution in which people play roles. The extent to which children exaggerate the personal power and charisma of the leader is impressive. He has God-like qualities in the child's imagery. Eighty-six percent of second-graders see the President of the United States as "running the country"; 76 percent of second-graders think that the President makes the laws. The President is viewed by children as benevolent and protective, powerful and strong. In a study of 366 children in Chicago, 60 percent of the second-graders felt that the President is "the best person in the world."[49]

The mentality of a state of war complements the child's most archaic psychic mechanisms for coping with himself and the world, the devices of splitting and projection. Splitting is what a people at war does by dividing the world into "good" and "bad" countries, those on our side who have only virtues and whom we love, and the enemy who is evil and whom we hate. We are thus enabled to get pleasure by gratifying our aggressive feelings. For the child, too, there are two kinds of men, one "good" and the other "bad." In wartime the absent father-soldier is idealized. He is glorified and any

*Marvin Rintala, a historian, explicitly argues for the years of "late adolescence and early adulthood" as "the formative years during which a distinctive personal outlook on politics emerges, which remains essentially unchanged through old age. The crucial years are regarded as approximately 17 to 25. If these years are in fact formative, neither the years preceding nor the years following them are decisive in the formation of political attitudes." "Political Generations," *International Encyclopedia of the Social Sciences,* 6: 93. This is undoubtedly an overstatement by Rintala. The earlier determinants of the political-socialization process, including the preschool years of infancy and childhood when the identifications that constitute the basic components of identity are formed, may not be discounted or ignored.

hostile feelings toward him are projected onto the evil enemy on the other side.*

Much of recent emphasis in psychoanalytic research and clinical work, particularly in psychoanalytic ego psychology, has been on the importance of the years of adolescence for character formation and identity resolution. These are the years when the basic choices and commitments of a lifetime are made after much painful searching, testing, and doubt. What then happens when children who have been deprived become politically effective? How do they respond as adolescents to the frustrations of reality? There are many theoretical and empirical approaches to adolescent aggression. Albert Bandura and Richard H. Walters offer what is essentially a social-modeling or imitational view of adolescent aggression. Their study is significant because it shows that aggressive boys come from families where they have experienced deprivation of affectional nurturance. The postoedipal child has to repress his sexual and hostile impulses in favor of affectionate attachments to his parents. In adolescence the biological maturation process leads to a temporary revival of the oedipal strivings. But now the incestuous sexual and hostile wishes must be finally relinquished. The adolescent's affectionate ties to his parents must also be sufficiently loosened to guarantee his future freedom of object choice and a sound adjustment to social reality. His practical and emotional dependency on his parents must be definitely and finally abandoned.† This detachment from parental authority is, said Sigmund Freud, "one of the most significant, but also one of the most painful, psychical achievements of the pubertal period."[50]

In discussing the effects of childhood deprivation we have followed the phase-specific psychosexual development of the child. We saw, in order, the traumas of the oral phase, of separation-individuation from the mother, the struggles with aggression and control that constitute the anal phase, the oedipal conflict, the latency years of grade-school political socialization, to

---

*George L. Mosse specifies the function of anti-Semitism as a displacement for the frustrations of the postwar children. He asserts the role of anti-Semitic agitation in the Weimar Republic was to provide "the children with a clearly defined object to vent their frustrations on, an identifiable obstacle to their aspirations which could be blamed for all their failures in later life." *The Crisis of German Ideology: Intellectual Origins of the Third Reich* (New York, 1964), p. 267.

†Erik H. Erikson emphasizes the marked adolescent quality of Hitler's self-created image before the German public. He interprets *Mein Kampf* as a skillful portrayal of a fantasy that would appeal to the psychic needs of many Germans of the postwar generation. It is the fantasy of the adolescent who never gave in and identified with the domineering father. He stubbornly never surrendered. Hitler presented himself as a glorified older brother, "an unbroken adolescent," "a gang leader who kept the boys together by demanding their admiration, by creating terror, and by shrewdly involving them in crimes from which there was no way back. And he was a ruthless exploiter of parental failures." *Childhood and Society*, rev. 2nd ed. (New York, 1963), p. 337.

the crisis of adolescence that precedes adulthood. Each phase has its special stresses and focuses of conflict. Each may become a point of fixation to be returned to at a later date if the turmoil has been too great or the storm too violent to permit the child passage unharmed.

We must seek the widest possible type and range of clinical material, cultural documentation, and quantitative statistical data in our quest for historical evidence. This essay will present three bodies of historical materials, some from each of these categories of data: comparative, qualitative, and quantitative. All varieties of historical evidence have an important and complementary function in generating new hypotheses, contributing new insight, and demarking future areas for exploration.

Psychoanalytical interest was directed at the war generation almost contemporaneously with the events. As early as 1919 Paul Federn interpreted the psychological dimensions of the postwar strikes and the soldiers and workers councils that sprang up throughout Central Europe. He viewed the loss of the national father figure, the Kaiser, who could no longer satisfy infantile fantasies of a father who is omnipotently powerful, wise, and strong, who offers absolute security and protection, as the traumatic psychological event of the war. Now the Kaisers of Germany and Austria were deprived of land, throne, power, and the ability to offer a feeling of security. Thus a fatherless society was created that no longer stood in awe of the state. For some sons of the state, Federn suggested, the disappointment came during the war when their leaders and army officers made irresponsible and sometimes impossible demands that condemned them to death. The soldiers and workers councils were seen as an attempt to establish a non-patriarchal social order, a brotherhood to replace the defeated father. Such a situation is, however, unstable. Federn in March 1919—the date is worth noting, for it was the zenith of republicanism in Europe—predicts the demise of the republic in Central Europe and a turn to dictatorship on the psychological grounds of prevailing family patterns and man's desire to be dominated. The fatherless society will not succeed. "Among those who have now freed themselves of the social father-son relationship, the tendency toward it still remains so strong, that they only wait for a suitable newly appearing personality who embodies their father ideal, in order to again relate as a son to him."[51]

A study such as the present one, which attempts to assess the impact on children of a catastrophe like a war, should use the best clinical observations in comparative historical situations when these are available. If wartime deprivation has profound emotional effects on young children, these effects should not be limited to one time and place in the modern world. The findings in Germany should also be evident in another industrial land and for other twentieth-century wars, such as for England in World War II.

The British experience is especially valuable to the historian who would consider the emotional effect of war on children because many English children were evacuated from their homes and families in London and the other big cities during World War II, and they were helped through this trying experience by the expert guidance of such specialists in the psychology of children as Anna Freud, Dorothy T. Burlingham, and D. W. Winnicott. These psychoanalysts carried out close residential observation of the evacuated children and published detailed studies of the children's responses and adaptations to the breakup of families in wartime. These were "normal" children, they were not hospitalized, nor were they juvenile offenders. They were not so heavily traumatized by their experience that their regressive defenses resisted all modification, as is the case with most of the children who survived concentration camps.[52] The blitzed English children were provided with a homelike environment and encouraged in every way toward normal development.* The fact that they were out of their homes and away from their families provides a degree of objectivity to the observations. The data were not filtered through reports of the parents; they are firsthand observations by trained professionals.

Anna Freud and Dorothy Burlingham found that while a child will accept mother substitutes in the absence of its own mother, "there is . . . no father substitute who can fill the place which is left empty by the child's own father." "The infant's emotional relationship to its father begins later in life than that of its mother," they write, "but certainly from the second year onward it is an integral part of its emotional life and a necessary ingredient in the complex forces which work towards the formation of its character and its personality."[53]

The researchers found that absent parents were greatly idealized. Their letters were carried around and had to be read to the children innumerable times. When the father was away in the armed services he was spoken of by his child in terms of endearment and admiration. Especially children who were in reality rejected or disappointed by their fathers formed passionate, loving, and admiring relationships to them. When a child had never known his father he would invent an idealized fantasy father who sanctioned his forbidden greedy and destructive wishes, who loved him and gave him security.[54]

---

*I am especially impressed by the warmth and empathic quality of D. W. Winnicott's wartime papers and broadcasts on the BBC. See "Children in the War" (1940), "The Deprived Mother" (1939), "The Evacuated Child" (1945), "The Return of the Evacuated Child" (1945), "Home Again" (1945), all in *The Child and the Outside World: Studies in Developing Relationships* (New York, 1957).

When a father came home on leave, however, and thereby encroached on the existing close mother-child relationship, he was met with resentment and hostility by the child. The father was viewed as an intruder who separated the mother and son. One little boy said: "Do write to my Daddy, I don't want him to come here. I don't want to have lunch with him. Somebody else can have my Daddy."[55] But the same son and his father were best of friends when they were left alone without the mother.

When in some cases the ultimate disaster struck, Freud and Burlingham report a complete inability of the children to accept their father's death. All the orphaned children talked about their dead fathers as if they were still alive. They denied the fact of death with fantasies of the father's rebirth and return from heaven.[56]

The most original psychoanalytical approach to National Socialist youth, and the one that I find conceptually most perceptive and useful, is Martin Wangh's excellent analysis of 1964.[57] He structures the psychodynamics of the World War I German children who came to the age of political effectiveness with the rise of Hitler with precision and insight. A preoccupation with guilt, Wangh points out, is also an unrecognized self-reproach for unresolved aggression against the father. Aggression toward the absent father-rival is expressed in gleeful ideas concerning his degradation and defeat. But the hostility is coupled with a longing for the idealized father that exacerbates childish homosexual wishes. These homosexual longings offer a way out of the oedipal conflict that is heightened for sons left alone with their mothers. In these circumstances the woman is often rejected, and the incestuous wish is ascribed to someone else. These mental defenses, Wangh suggests, were renewed in the Nazi movement's deification of the Führer and its infernalization of the Jew. Homosexual tension was relieved through submission to an all-powerful leader, through turning women into "breeders" of children, and by persecuting Jews as "incestuous criminals" and "defilers of the race." The passive-masochistic inclinations that develop when boys are brought up and disciplined by mothers who are anxious and punitive may be defended against by preference for submission to a man, as this is less threatening and less castrating than submission to a woman. Self-humiliation and self-contempt were displaced onto the Jews and other supposedly inferior people, thereby assuaging feelings of unworthiness and masochistic fantasies of rejection. Since the former wartime enemies were for the time being unassailable, the Jew, who was defenseless and available, became by the mechanism of displacement the victim of those who needed a target for regressive action.

This line of research has been carried on to the contemporary problem of the children of World War II. Herman Roskamp, in a clinical study of German university students born during World War II, emphasizes the conflict between the child's perception of the father during the war as a highly idealized fantasy object bearing his ideas of omnipotence and the way in which the father was perceived on his return in defeat.[58] While away the father had been honored and admired; he was the object of extreme hopes and expectations upon his return. It quickly became apparent that he was not what had been longed for. Instead he was a defeated, insecure father breaking into a heretofore fatherless family. Up to this time the mother had represented all aspects of reality. The father, by contrast, was now a demanding rival who left most wishes unfulfilled, who disappointed many hopes, and who set many limits where formerly there had been none.

Among the richest sources for the expression of the experience of young Germans during the war and postwar years is the literature of the period, which more than held its place amid the cultural fecundity of the Weimar epoch. Sometimes literary expression can capture for historians the essence of a generation's experience both graphically and with a depth of emotional subtlety that cannot be conveyed by statistics or quantitative data. Many qualitative affects cannot be statistically comprehended or documented. It is possible to see, identify, and demonstrate father identification and castration anxiety without necessarily being able to computerize them. This is the appeal to the historian of both clinical insight and literary sensibility. Can one measure or compare quantitatively, for example, the degree of suffering, mourning, loss, or rage a subject feels? For this kind of emotional evidence we must rely on that most sensitive of our cultural materials—the subjective word of literature.

When this has been said, it is nevertheless astonishing to experience the great autobiographical pacifist novel *Jahrgang 1902* by Ernst Glaeser (1902–1963), which describes the author's feelings with such intensity and pathos that it often reads more like the free associations of a patient in psychoanalysis than a novel. The critic William Soskin ranked *Jahrgang 1902* with *Sergeant Grisha* and *All Quiet on the Western Front* as one of the most significant works on World War I.[59] This book ran through six German printings during the winter of 1928/29. It sold seventy thousand copies in Germany and was translated into twenty-five languages.

The book takes its title from the year of the author's birth, which also automatically became the year of his military-service class. The class of 1902 was not to experience the war of 1914 to 1918 on the front.* For that they

*For a sardonic expression from among the youngest class that went to war, see Erich Kastner, "The Class of 1899" in his *Bei Durchsicht meiner Bücher* . . . (Zürich, 1946), pp. 97–8. "We took the women to bed, / While the men stood in France. / We had imagined that it would be much more wonderful. / We were merely confirmants. / Then they took us to the army, / For nothing more than cannon fodder. / The benches at school were emptied, / Mother wept at home. / Then we had a bit of revolution / And potato chips came raining down. / Then came the women, just like they used to / And then we caught the clap. / Meanwhile the old man lost his money, / So we became were too young, but as Glaeser pointedly noted, "The war did not establish a moratorium on puberty." The book, he said, deals with "the tragedy of murdered minds and souls and diseased temperaments in the noncombatant social body."[60]

As the war began the fathers left to join their regiments and the twelve-year-old boy observes that "life in our town became quieter." The boys played war games in which the French and Russians were always soundly beaten. The fathers were sorely missed. They were quickly idealized and glorified. Glaeser describes the process of overestimation and identification with the father who is absent at war:

> We thought only of our fathers in these days. Overnight they had become heroes. . . . We loved our fathers with a new sublime love. As ideals. And just as we formerly used to express our admiration for the Homeric heroes or the figures of the Wars of Liberation by token symbols of clothing such as golden helmets of tin foil or Lützow caps, so we now also began, but in far greater measure, to turn ourselves symbolically into the idealized figures of our fathers.

The boys of the village went to the barber to have their hair cut in the close-cropped military style like their fathers.

> We had our hair cut. Bare. Smooth. Three millimeters high. For this is how we had seen it on our fathers as they left for the front. None of them had hair to part now.
>
> One evening late in September a group of fifteen determined boys went to the barber. We stood according to height and let the instrument pass over our heads. As the barber was sweeping up our hair with a broom an hour later, he said: "Now you look like recruits."
>
> We were proud of this distinction and enthusiastically paid 40 pfennigs each.[61]

By the winter of 1916 the privation of the war began to be felt in the daily lives of the boys. They were always hungry. There was never enough to eat. The steady diet of turnip soup became inedible. City folk bribed and

---

night-school students. / By day we worked in an office / And dealt with rates of interest. / Then she almost had a child, / Whether by you or by me—who knows! / A friend of ours scraped it out. / And the next thing you know we will be thirty. / We even passed an examination / And have already forgotten most of it. / Now we are alone day and night / And have nothing decent to eat! / We looked the world straight in the snout, / Instead of playing with dolls / We spit at the rest of the world, / Insofar as we were not killed at Ypres. / They made our bodies or our spirit / A wee bit too weak / They threw us into world history too long, / Too fast, and too much. / The old folks maintained that the time has come / For us to sow and to reap. / But wait a moment. Soon we will be ready./ Just a moment. Soon we will be there! / Then we will show you what we have learned!"

bartered away precious possessions in order to get nourishing food from the farmers. The mother gave Kathinka, the maid, one of her finest blouses so that she would bring back food when she visited her peasant parents. Faithfully Kathinka smuggled butter past the gendarmes in her woolen bloomers. Field gendarmes and controllers appeared on the roads and at the stations to search travelers for contraband foodstuffs. The children developed tactics for deceiving the gendarmes and smuggling forbidden foodstuffs home. One boy would serve as a decoy to draw the gendarme's attention while the other raced home across the fields with a sack of flour or a ham.

This progression within two years from idealism to hunger and the struggle for survival is vividly described by Glaeser.

> The winter remained hard until the end. The war began to burst over the fronts and to strike the people. Hunger destroyed our unity; in the families children stole each other's rations. . . . Soon the women who stood in gray lines in front of the shops talked more about the hunger of their children than of the death of their husbands. The sensations of war had been altered.
>
> A new front existed. It was held by women. The enemies were the entente of field gendarmes and uncompromising guards. Every smuggled pound of butter, every sack of potatoes gleefully secreted by night was celebrated in the families with the same enthusiasm as the victories of the armies two years earlier. . . . It was wonderful and inspiring to outwit the gendarmes and after successfully triumphing to be honored by one's mother as a hero.

Oedipal longings were heightened for the sons left alone with their mothers during years of war. Starvation led to the mobilization of unconscious wishes for a return to the oral comforts of early mother-child units. Occasionally the prolonged hunger was broken by feasting on an illegally slaughtered pig or a smuggled goose that the father sent home from the Eastern Front. Then an orgy of feeding took place. Gluttony reigned and undernourished bellies got sick on the rich food. The windows had to be stuffed to keep the neighbors from smelling the meat. The adolescent boy and his mother consumed almost an entire twelve-pound goose in one night. A stolen drumstick for his girlfriend was to her the convincing symbol of love.* Glaeser

---

*"Strange what part food now plays," noted a Hamburg educator and poet in his diary. "Every conversation turns on food. Whoever has hoarded supplies keeps it secret. Whoever gets anything hides it as if it were a crime. A pound of butter has become the object of a thousand questions and outpourings of envy. From where? from whom? how?" (Nov. 11, 1916). "Formerly, eating was a means to live, now it has become its purpose" (Dec. 18, 1917). Quoted in Ernst L. Loewenberg, "Jakob Loewenberg: Excerpts from His Diaries and Letters," *Leo Baeck Institute Yearbook*, 25 (1970): 192.

writes: "We scarcely spoke of the war any more, we only spoke of hunger. Our mothers were closer to us than our fathers."[62]

The fathers were not present to shield the sons from maternal seduction. One young adolescent in the novel is seduced by a motherly farmer's wife with the promise of a large ham. But, much as the pangs of his stomach and his mother's pleading letters argued for bringing the ham home, he could not do it. The great succulent ham had become an incestuous object. He had earned it from the farm wife by taking her husband's place. Now he was too guilty and too anxious to permit himself and his family to enjoy it. The pangs of guilt were stronger than the pains of hunger. As if he could "undo" his oedipal crime, the boy laid the ham on the farm wife's bed and left. He was tearful and depressed, feelings he rationalized as being due to his injured feelings because he was really only a substitute (*Ersatz*) for the husband. He climbed into bed with his boy comrade. In the stillness of the dawn they embraced, keeping each other warm, and he shared his story of seduction and sexual discovery. In this episode we see fully elaborated the heightened oedipal conflict when the father is absent, the increased guilt and fear of retribution, and finally the rejection of the woman as a sexual object and an exacerbation of adolescent homosexuality arising from the emotional effects of the war.

By the winter of 1917 the fathers had become aliens to their sons. But they were not only unknown men, they were feared and threatening strangers who claimed rights and control over the lives of their sons. They had become distant but powerful figures who could punish and exact a terrible price for disobedience and transgressions. Glaeser recounts his reaction as a fifteen-year-old to a letter from his father on the Russian front in terms of intense castration anxiety. The adolescent boy's oedipal victory in having displaced his father would now be terribly expiated and revenged by a towering, castrating monster of his guilt-laden fantasies. Glaeser attempts to deny that his father has any legitimate claim to control over him at all. But his father would know where to find him and the inevitable retribution would be inexorable.

> We were frightened. That was the voice of the front. That was the voice of those men who formerly were once our fathers, who now, however, removed from us for years, were strangers before us, fearsome, huge, overpowering, casting dark shadows, oppressive as a monument. What did they still know of us? They knew where we lived, but they no longer knew what we looked like and thought.[63]

It is of biographical interest for the thesis of this essay that Glaeser went into emigration from Germany after 1933, living in Prague, Zürich, and Paris. In Zürich in 1939 he wrote a newspaper article condoning Hitler's policies and condemning his fellow émigrés. Within days he received a contract from a Berlin publisher. He returned to Germany and joined the war effort, becoming a war reporter for the Luftwaffe and the editor of the military newspaper *Adler im Suden.* [64]

Thus, as did so many others of his cohort, Glaeser was two decades later to choose to wear a uniform and to identify with his distant and glorified father. The identification with the father who went out to war served to erase the memory of the feared and hated strange father who came home in defeat. By being a patriot and submitting to authority, the ambivalence of the young boy who gleefully observed his father's humiliating defeat and degradation was denied and expiated. Now he would do obeisance to an idealized but remote leader who was deified and untouchable.

Many of the emotions of German middle-class generational conflict in the decade after World War I were profoundly explored by Thomas Mann in his story of 1925, "Disorder and Early Sorrow." The setting is the home of Professor Cornelius, a historian, the time is during the inflation of 1923, and the social climate is filled with anxiety about loss of status, a widening gap between the cultures of youth and adults, and the deepening economic crisis that has caused a deterioration of faith in stable moral norms. Solid bourgeois ladies are now the Corneliuses' house servants, while the brash young man who lives by speculation, drives a car, treats his friends to champagne suppers, and showers the children of the professor with gauche gifts of "barbaric" size and taste represents the postwar generation.

The story opens with the menu of the midday meal in which the main dish is croquettes made of turnip greens. The meatless dinner is a meager contrast to the opulent menus succulently described by Mann in *Budden-brooks* and *The Magic Mountain.* What reader can easily forget the sumptuous repasts in the restaurant of the International Sanatorium Berghof or Mann's descriptions of solid fare on the table of the patrician merchant home in the Hanseatic seaport? In the professorial home of the Weimar era the dessert is a powdered pudding that tastes of almonds and soap—an ersatz concoction symbolizing the current hard times and the decline in standard of living. Many people have had to give up their telephones, but the Corneliuses have so far been able to keep theirs. Repairs cannot be made on the house for lack of materials. The professor washes at a broken basin that cannot be repaired because there is nobody to mend it. Clothing is worn and turned, yet the adolescents of the family do not notice, for they wear a simple belted linen smock and sandals. They are, says Mann, by birth the "villa proletariat [*Villenproletarier*]" who no longer know or care about the correct evening dress of the middle classes or the manners of a gentleman. In fact, the professor cannot, from observing their style of dress or personal bearing, distinguish his son from his working-class Bolshevik household servant. "Both, he thinks, look like young moujiks." His children are products of the disrupted times, specimens of their generation, with a jargon of their own that the adults find incomprehensible. The young enjoy contriving to get the family extra allotments of rationed foods, such as eggs, by deceiving the shopkeepers. They function better than the old folk in a world in which money has lost its value. The generational struggle is underlined by the professor's consistent mental depreciation of his adolescent son when comparing him with other young men: "And here is my poor Bert, who knows nothing and can do nothing and thinks of nothing except playing the clown, without even talent for that!" The younger son, who is but four years old, is subject to the rages of "a howling dervish." He, who is "born and brought up in these desolate, distracted times, . . . has been endowed by them with an unstable and hypersensitive nervous system and suffers greatly under life's disharmonies. He is prone to sudden anger and outbursts of bitter tears, stamping his feet at every trifle."[65]

Thus Mann pictures the dislocation of continuity between the generations of the Weimar Republic. They differ in expectations and methods of dealing with reality. In the decade since 1913, when the professor bought his home, the family has in fact been proletarianized. One of the themes of the story is their varied response, as individuals of different ages, to this fact. The old generation cannot adjust, while their children are born into the new situation and need not make any adaptation of life style. Mann has sketched superbly and for all time the psychological experience of the impoverishment of the German upper middle class and the rebellion against the norms and values of their parents by the children of the war.

The third variety of data I wish to examine is quantitative. It is a series of autobiographical essays collected in 1934 by Theodore Abel, a sociologist at Columbia University, in an essay contest offering cash prizes for "the best personal life history of an adherent of the Hitler movement."*

---

*Abel stressed that style, spelling, or dramatic story value were of no consideration. What was to be considered were "accounts of family life, education, economic conditions, membership in associations, participation in the Hitler movement, and important experiences, thoughts, and feelings about events and ideas of the postwar period." Theodore Abel, *Why Hitler Came into Power: An Answer Based on the Original Life Stories of Six Hundred of His Followers* (New York, 1938), p. 3. Abel had the cooperation of the National Socialist party in gathering his data. His announcement soliciting essays was distributed to all local Nazi party headquarters and was published in the party press. Abel used 600 of the 683 manuscripts contributed to the contest for his study. He did not use those that were too brief and the 48 written by women. Fortunately for historical research the original autobiographical manuscripts were turned over to the Hoover Institution on War, Revolution and Peace in Stanford, Calif. Today 582 of these essays are available for research, the others having been lost. There are factors that should induce caution in drawing generalizations from the Abel autobiographies. The sample is self-selected, not random, suggesting that motives such as the prize money and exhibitionism may have biased it. The sample is geographically weighted toward Berlin (30 percent) and the Rhineland, and in favor of large- and medium-sized cities rather than small towns and the countryside.

In reading the essays one is often struck by their didactic quality. Some writers say outright that they are delighted to write down their experiences for the benefit of American researchers at Columbia University. As the essays were solicited by a bulletin at all local headquarters of the NSDAP and by announcements in the party press, and as the writers were not anonymous, one may infer that the writers suspected that party organs would be informed of any criticism and political or personal deviance in the essays. In some cases one senses that a local party functionary may have encouraged the writers to respond to the essay contest. Some contributions bear the NSDAP *Abteilung Propaganda* stamp. Many tiresomely repeat propaganda slogans about Jewish war profiteering, Red vandalism in the revolution of 1918–1919, and so forth.

All these caveats notwithstanding, these nearly six hundred essays constitute a valuable historical source. In the first place, it is a contemporary source. No set of interviews of ex-Nazis thirty-seven years later could possibly elicit the same material. The Abel autobiographies may be utilized, not as a statistical sample for generalizations, but as bases for theory building. They will serve as a cognitive prism for drawing attention to necessary variables of political behavior rather than as a monolithic statistical sample that can produce conclusive findings for the population of the Nazi party. They can tell us, however, what excited and stimulated the writers, what preoccupied their fantasies and imaginations, how they viewed themselves, their childhoods and homes, and their enemies. These data can then become referents for further theoretical conceptualization and behavioral model building, particularly with respect to emotional connotations that are not censored by the writers because they appear to be apolitical and therefore unimportant.

The most striking emotional affects expressed in the Abel autobiographies are the adult memories of intense hunger and privation from childhood. A party member who was a child of the war years recollects: "Sometimes I had to scurry around eight to ten hours—occasionally at night—to procure a few potatoes or a bit of butter. Carrots and beets, previously considered fit only for cattle, came to be table luxuries." Another man's memory is vivid in its sense of abandonment and isolation expressed in language that makes a feeling of maternal deprivation very clear.

> Hunger was upon us. Bread and potatoes were scarce, while meat and fats were almost non-existent. We were hungry all the time; we had forgotten how it felt to have our stomachs full.
>
> All family life was at an end. None of us really knew what it meant—we were left to our own devices. For women had to take the place of their fighting men. They toiled in factories and in offices, as

ostlers and as commercial travelers, in all fields of activity previously allotted to men—behind the plow as well as on the omnibus. Thus while we never saw our fathers, we had only glimpses of our mothers in the evening. Even then they could not devote themselves to us because, tired as they were, they had to take care of their household, after their strenuous day at work. So we grew up, amid hunger and privation, with no semblance of decent family life.[66]

A study of the Abel autobiographies focused on a sample from the birth cohorts 1911 to 1915, who were small children during the war, indicates the presence of the defensive mechanisms of projection, displacement, low frustration tolerance, and the search for an idealized father. For example, the essays of two sisters born in 1913 and 1915, whose father fell in 1915, clearly demonstrate that Hitler served as an idealized father figure for them. Their earliest memories are of their mother crying a great deal and of all the people wearing black. They relate their excitement at first hearing the Führer speak in person at a rally in Kassel in 1931. The sisters were so exhilarated that neither of them could sleep all night. They prayed for the protection of the Führer, and asked forgiveness for ever having doubted him. The sisters began their Nazi party activities by caring for and feeding SA men.[67]

Some of the men in the Abel Collection who lost their fathers early in life and were separated from their mothers especially valued the comradeship of the SA. One such man wrote, "It was wonderful to belong to the bond of comradeship of the SA. Each one stood up for the other." Massive projection of ego-alien impulses is evident in many of the essays. One man says that bejeweled Jewesses tried to seduce him politically with cake. Many of the SA men who engaged in street brawls and violence blamed others, such as the police and the Communists, for instigating the fighting and for persecuting them. One man displays remarkable projection and displacement of his own murderous feelings toward a younger brother when he relates the death of that brother in an unnecessary operation performed by a Jewish doctor. "Since I especially loved my dead brother," he writes, "a grudge arose in me against the doctor, and this not yet comprehensible hatred increased with age to become an antagonism against everything Jewish." A body of autobiographies such as the Abel Collection invites a variety of research approaches, each suited to its own ends. These include a quantitative computerization done by Peter H. Merkl with the aim of discovering and conceptualizing the phases of political mobilization.[68]

The demographic factors of massive health, nutritional, and material deprivation and parental absence in Central Europe during World War I should lead the historian to apply theoretical and clinical knowledge of the long-term effects of such a deprived childhood on personality. The anticipation of weakened character structure manifested in aggression, defenses of projection and displacement, and inner rage that may be mobilized by a renewed anxiety-inducing trauma in adulthood is validated in the subsequent political conduct of this cohort during the Great Depression when they joined extremist paramilitary and youth organizations and political parties. In view of these two bodies of data, for which a psychoanalytic understanding of personality provides the essential linkage, it is postulated that a direct relationship existed between the deprivation German children experienced in World War I and the response of these children and adolescents to the anxieties aroused by the Great Depression of the early 1930's. This relationship is psychodynamic: The war generation had weakened egos and superegos, meaning that the members of this generation turned readily to programs based on facile solutions and violence when they met new frustrations during the depression. They then reverted to earlier phase-specific fixations in their child development marked by rage, sadism, and the defensive idealization of their absent parents, especially the father. These elements made this age cohort particularly susceptible to the appeal of a mass movement utilizing the crudest devices of projection and displacement in its ideology. Above all, it prepared the young voters of Germany for submission to a total, charismatic leader.

But fantasy is always in the end less satisfying than mundane reality. Ironically, instead of finding the idealized father, they, with Hitler as their leader, plunged Germany and Europe headlong into a series of deprivations many times worse than those of World War I. Thus the repetition was to seek the glory of identification with the absent soldier-father, but like all quests for a fantasied past, it had to fail. Hitler and National Socialism were so much a repetition and fulfillment of the traumatic childhoods of the generation of World War I that the attempt to undo that war and those childhoods was to become a political program. As a result, the regressive illusion of Nazism ended in a repetition of misery at the front and starvation at home made worse by destroyed cities, irremediable guilt, and millions of new orphans.

A return to the past is always unreal. To attempt it is the path of certain disaster. There was no glorified father who went to war and who could be recaptured in Hitler. He existed only in fantasy, and he could never be brought back in reality. There are no ideal mothers and fathers; there are only flawed human parents. Therefore, for a World War I generation seeking restitution of a lost childhood there was to be only bitter reality in the form of a psychotic charlatan who skillfully manipulated human needs and left destruction to Germany and Europe. What the youth cohort wanted was a fantasy of warmth, closeness, security, power, and love. What they re-created was a repetition of their own childhoods. They gave to their children and to Europe in greater measure precisely the traumas they had suffered as children and adolescents a quarter of a century earlier.

Notes

1. There is a growing bibliography of psychodynamic studies of Nazi leaders. See Gertrude M. Kurth, "The Jew and Adolf Hitler," *Psychoanalytic Quarterly,* 16 (1947): 11–32; Robert Waite, *Psychopathic God: Adolf Hitler* (New York, 1977); James H. McRandle, *The Track of the Wolf: Essays on National Socialism and Its Leader, Adolf Hitler* (Evanston, Ill., 1965); Richard McMasters Hunt, "Joseph Goebbels: A Study of the Formation of His National-Socialist Consciousness (unpublished Ph.D. dissertation, Harvard University, 1960); Norbert Bromberg, "Totalitarian Ideology as a Defense Technique," *Psychoanalytic Study of Society,* 1 (1961): 26–38. Sigmund Neumann has treated the Nazi leadership, as distinguished from the mass of party adherents, in terms of the generation born between 1890 and 1900 in *The Future in Perspective* (New York, 1946), pp. 224–5.

2. Sigmund Freud, "Introductory Lectures on Psycho-Analysis" (1916–1917), *Standard Edition of the Complete Psychological Works,* trans. and ed. James Strachey et al. (1953–1974), 16: 341; "The Disposition to Obsessional Neurosis: A Contribution to the Choice of Neurosis" (1913), 12: 317–18.

3. Else Frenkel-Brunswik, "Environmental Controls and the Impoverishment of Thought," in *Totalitarianism,* ed. Carl J. Friedrich (New York, 1964), p. 177.

4. Karl Mannheim, "The Sociological Problem of Generations," in *Essays on the Sociology of Knowledge,* ed. Paul Kecskemeti (London, 1952), pp. 298, 303, 304 (emphasis in original), 306.

5. *Ibid.,* p. 310.

6. Robert Jay Lifton, *Death in Life: Survivors of Hiroshima* (New York, 1967); Norman B. Ryder, "Cohort Analysis," *International Encyclopedia of the Social Sciences,* 2nd ed. (New York, 1968), 2: 549.

7. Ryder, "The Cohort as a Concept in the Study of Social Change," *American Sociological Review,* 30 (1965): 848–9, 851, 855.

8. Marc Bloch, *The Historian's Craft,* trans. Peter Putnam (New York, 1953), pp. 45–6.

9. Dieter Petzina, "Germany and the Great Depression," *Journal of Contemporary History,* 4 (1969): 59–74.

10. Koppel S. Pinson, *Modern Germany: Its History and Civilization,* 2nd ed. (New York, 1966), pp. 603–4. The Nazi vote declined to 11,737,000, or 33.1 percent, in the elections of Nov. 6, 1932. At the last quasi-free election in Germany, on March 5, 1933, five weeks after Hitler's accession to power, the Nazi vote was 17,277,200, or 43.9 percent.

11. *Ibid.*

12. Heinrich Streiffler, *Deutsche Wahlen in Bildern und Zahlen: Eine soziografische Studie über die Reichstagswahlen der Weimarer Republik* (Düsseldorf, 1946), p. 16.

13. *Ibid.,* p. 20.

14. Gregor Strasser, "Macht Platz, Ihr Alten!", speech delivered May 8, 1927, as quoted in Karl Dietrich Bracher, *Die Auflösung der Weimarer Republik: Eine Studie zum Problem des Machtverfalls in der Demokratie,* 3rd ed. (Villingen, Schwarzwald, 1960), p. 116 n. 84.

15. Bracher, *Die deutsche Diktatur: Entstehung, Struktur, Folgen des National-*

sozialismus (Cologne, 1969), pp. 179–83; *Die Auflösung der Weimarer Republik,* pp. 147–9; Wolfgang Zorn, "Student Politics in the Weimar Republic," *Journal of Contemporary History,* 5 (1970): 128–43.

16. Hans H. Gerth, "The Nazi Party: Its Leadership and Composition," *American Journal of Sociology,* 45 (1940): 529; Peter Gay, *Weimar Culture: The Outsider as Insider* (New York, 1968), p. 140.

17. Walter Z. Laqueur, *Young Germany: A History of the German Youth Movement* (London, 1962), p. 191.

18. Reinhard Bendix, "Social Stratification and Political Power," *American Political Science Review,* 46 (1952): 357–75; Bracher, *Die Auflösung der Weimarer Republik,* p. 116; Petzina, "Germany and the Great Depression," p. 73; Arthur Dix, *Die Deutschen Reichstagswahlen 1871–1930 und Die Wandlugen der Volksgliederung* (Tübingen, 1930), pp. 37–43; Alice Hamilton, "The Youth Who Are Hitler's Strength: A Study of the Nazi Followers and the Appeal That Has Aroused Them," *New York Times Magazine,* Oct. 8, 1933, pp. 3, 16; Rudolf Heberle, *From Democracy to Nazism: A Regional Case Study on Political Parties in Germany* (Baton Rouge, La., 1945), pp. 9–10.

19. Pinson, *Modern Germany,* p. 415; Carl Mierendorff, "Gesicht und Charakter der Nationalsozialistischen Bewegung," *Die Gesellschaft* (Berlin, 1930): 497, 498.

20. Herbert Moller, "Youth as a Force in the Modern World," *Comparative Studies in Society and History,* 10 (1968): 243, 244.

21. Karl Dietrich Erdmann, "Die Zeit der Weltkriege," in *Handbuch der Deutschen Geschichte,* ed. Bruno Gebhardt (Stuttgart, 1963), 4: 49, 77.

22. James A. Huston, "The Allied Blockade of Germany 1918–1919," *Journal of Central European Affairs,* 10 (1950): 161–2; Suda Lorena Bane and Ralph Haswell Lutz, eds., *The Blockade of Germany after the Armistice 1918–1919: Selected Documents of the Supreme Economic Council, Superior Blockade Council, American Relief Administration and Other Wartime Organizations* (Stanford, 1942), pp. 558–60.

23. *Ibid.,* pp. 670–1, 796–8.

24. Dr. Rubner, "Notwendigkeit der Wiederauffütterung der durch die Blocade abgehungerten Bevölkerung," in *Das Werk des Untersuchungsausschusses der Verfassunggebenden Deutschen Nationalversammlung und des Deutschen Reichstages 1919–1928,* Reihe 4: *Die Ursachen des Deutschen Zusammenbruches im Jahre 1918,* Abteilung 2: "Der Zusammenbruch," Band 6, ed. Dr.Albrecht Philipp, MDR et al. (Berlin, 1928), pp. 419–42.

25. Dr. Roesle, "Die Begurts und Sterblichkeitsverhältnisse," in *Deutschlands Gesundheitsverhältnisse unter dem Einfluss des Weltkrieges,* ed. Franz Bumm (Stuttgart, 1928), 1: 15, 17, 25, 58.

26. L. Langstein and F. Rott, "Der Gesundheitsstand unter den Säuglingen und Kleinkindern," in *ibid.,* p. 90.

27. *Ibid.,* pp. 91, 92.

28. *Ibid.,* pp. 93, 95.

29. *Ibid.,* pp. 99, 100, 102.

30. Dr. Stephani, "Der Gesundheitsstand unter den Schulkindern," in *ibid.,* p. 117.

31. *Ibid.,* pp. 122–3, 129.

32. Henry W. Nevinson, "Babies 'Withering Away,'" *Daily News* (London and Manchester), March 13, 1919; "Famine in Europe," *Nation* (New York), March 8, 1919 —both quoted in Bane and Lutz, *Blockade of Germany,* pp. 727, 731. See also Nevinson's report carried as "Starving Europe" in *Herald* (London), Jan. 18, 1919, also quoted in *ibid.,* p. 701.

33. "The European Food Situation," *Lancet* (London), March 8, 1919, quoted in *ibid.*, pp. 726–7.

34. John Maynard Keynes, *The Economic Consequences of the Peace* (New York, 1920), p. 251; Swedish press of April 1919, as reported in *ibid.*, p. 250 n; *Vossische Zeitung*, June 5, 1919, as reported and translated in *ibid.*, pp. 250–1 n.

35. Marie-Elizabeth Lüders, *Das Unbekannte Heer: Frauen Kämpfen für Deutschland, 1914–1918* (Berlin, 1937), pp. 85, 85 n. 1.

36. *Ibid.*, pp. 84, 85, 86, 151, 151 n. 1, 153 n. 2.

37. *Ibid.*, pp. 85, 86.

38. *Ibid.*, pp. 91, 128 n. 1; S. Rudolf Steinmetz, *Soziologie des Krieges* (Leipzig, 1929), p. 169.

39. D. W. Winnicott, "Aggression" (1939), in *The Child and the Outside World: Studies in Developing Relationships* (New York, 1957), p. 170; Melanie Klein, "Love, Guilt and Reparation," in *Love, Hate and Reparation* (New York, 1964), p. 58; Joan Riviere, "Hate, Greed and Aggression," in *ibid.*, pp. 8–9; René A. Spitz, "Hospitalism: An Inquiry into the Genesis of Psychiatric Conditions in Early Childhood," *Psychoanalytic Study of the Child*, 1 (1945): 53–74; "Hospitalism: A Follow-up Report on Investigation Described in Volume I, 1945," *ibid.*, 2 (1946): 113–17.

40. John Bowlby et al., *Maternal Care and Mental Health and Deprivation of Maternal Care* (New York, 1966), pp. 11, 32.

41. Margaret S. Mahler, *On Human Symbiosis and the Vicissitudes of Individuation: Infantile Psychosis* (New York, 1968), 1: 234, 222.

42. Bowlby, "Separation Anxiety," *International Journal of Psycho-Analysis*, 41 (1960): 105.

43. Edith Jacobson, *The Self and the Object World* (New York, 1964), p. 41 n. 4.

44. Anna Freud and Dorothy T. Burlingham, *War and Children* (New York, 1943), pp. 21–2.

45. Winnicott, "Residential Management as Treatment for Difficult Children" (1947), in *The Child and the Outside World*, p. 100.

46. Harold D. Lasswell, "The Psychology of Hitlerism as a Response of the Lower Middle Classes to Continuing Insecurity" (1933), in *The Analysis of Political Behavior: An Empirical Approach* (Hamden, Conn., 1966), pp. 240–1.

47. George R. Bach, "Father-Fantasies and Father-Typing in Father-Separated Children," *Child Development*, 17 (1946): 71. See also Lois Meek Stolz et al., *Father Relations of War-Born Children* (Stanford, Calif., 1954), pp. 192–207.

48. David O. Sears, "Political Behavior," *Handbook of Social Psychology*, 2nd ed. (Reading, Mass., 1969), 5: 415, 416; Fred I. Greenstein, *Children and Politics* (New Haven, 1965), p. 32; Robert D. Hess, "The Socialization of Attitudes toward Political Authority: Some Cross-National Comparisons," *International Social Science Journal*, 25 (1963): 555.

49. Robert D. Hess and Judith V. Torney, *The Development of Political Attitudes in Children* (Chicago, 1967), p. 35; David Easton and Jack Dennis, "The Child's Image of the Government," *Annals of the American Academy of Political and Social Sciences*, 361 (1965): 48; Greenstein, *Children and Politics*, pp. 37–42; "The Benevolent Leader: Children's Images of Political Authority," *American Political Science Review*, 54 (1960): 934–43; Robert D. Hess and David Easton, "The Child's Image of the President," *Public Opinion Quarterly*, 24 (1960): 648–54.

50. Albert Bandura and Richard H. Walters, *Adolescent Aggression: A Study of the Influence of Child-Training Practices and Family Inter-relationship* (New York, 1959); S. Freud, "Three Essays on the Theory of Sexuality" (1905), *Standard Edition*, 7: 227.

51. Paul Federn, *Psychologie der Revolution—Die vaterlose Gesellschaft* (Vienna, 1919), p. 28.

52. Gerd Biermann, "Identitätsprobleme jüdischer Kinder und Jugendlicher in Deutschland," *Praxis der Kinderpsychologie und Kinderpsychiatrie,* 13 (1964): 213–21.

53. Freud and Burlingham, *Infants without Families: The Case for and against Residential Nurseries* (New York, 1944), pp. 102, 103.

54. Freud and Burlingham, *War and Children,* pp. 154–5; *Infants without Families,* pp. 108, 110, 113.

55. *Ibid.,* p. 111.

56. *Ibid.,* p. 107.

57. Martin Wangh, "National Socialism and the Genocide of the Jews: A Psycho-Analytic Study of a Historical Event," *International Journal of Psycho-Analysis,* 45 (1964): 386–95; see also "A Psycho-Genetic Factor in the Recurrence of War," *ibid.,* 49 (1968): 319–23.

58. Herman Roskamp, "Über Identitätskonflikte bei im zweiten Weltkrieg ge-bornen Studenten," *Psyche: Zeitschrift für Psychoanalyse und ihre Anwendungen,* 23 (1969): 754–61. See also Alexander Mitscherlich, *Society without the Father: A Contribution to Social Psychology,* trans. Eric Mosbacher (London, 1969).

59. William Soskin, as quoted in *Twentieth Century Authors,* ed. Stanley J. Kunitz and Howard Haycraft (New York, 1942), p. 540.

60. Ernst Glaeser, as quoted in *ibid.,* p. 540.

61. Glaeser, *Jahrhang 1902* (Berlin, 1929), pp. 242, 243.

62. *Ibid.,* pp. 292–3, 314.

63. *Ibid.,* p. 323.

64. Erich Stockhorst, *Fünftausend Köpfe: Wer war was im Dritten Reich* (Bruchsal, Baden, 1967), p. 155.

65. Thomas Mann, "Disorder and Early Sorrow," in *Death in Venice and Seven Other Stories,* trans. H. T. Lowe-Porter (New York, 1959), pp. 182, 183, 185, 188, 196, 204.

66. Theodore Abel, *Why Hitler Came into Power: An Answer Based on the Original Life Stories of Six Hundred of His Followers* (New York, 1938), pp. 14–15.

67. Abel Collection, Hoover Institution on War, Revolution, and Peace, Stanford University, nos. 41, 42.

68. *Ibid.,* nos. 61, 96, 167; Peter H. Merkel, *Political Violence Under the Swastika: 581 Early Nazis* (Princeton, N.J., 1975); *The Making of a Stormtrooper* (Princeton, N.J., 1980).

Index

Abel, Theodore, collector of essays by
Hitler supporters, 276
Abraham, Karl, on anality, 223
academic world
communication problems in, 73–5
emotional problems of students, *see*
graduate students
envy in, 70–1
faculty relations, 74–7
faculty-student relations, *see*
faculty–graduate student relations
hierarchical structure of, 74–5
idealization and disparagement in,
70–1
improving quality of, 56–8, 71–2
rote and imitative learning in, 65
sexist biases in, 45–6
Adams, John Quincy, identity
formation of, 26
Adler, Emma Braun, wife of Victor,
138

depressive episodes of, 138–9
family life and letters of, 141–2, 150
Adler, Friedrich (Fritz), 99, 100, 188
assassination of Count Stürgkh, 138,
143, 151–4; psychoanalytic
significance of, 156–7
and Austro-Marxists, 138, 148, 150–2,
154, 176
and Bauer, 176–7, 188
birth and boyhood, 141–2
conflicts with father, 144–6, 149–53;
resolution of, 155–7
education, 144
humanitarian conditioning of, 141–2
identification with father, 143, 153–4,
157–8
marriage and children, 145, 149
opposition to World War I, 149, 150
relations with mother, 150
relief and rescue work, 1930s and
1940s, 155

285

Adler, Friedrich (*continued*)
  with Second International, 138,
    154–5, 176–7
  sexual affairs of, 149–50
  trial, imprisonment, and release of,
    153–4
Adler, Johanna Herzl, mother of
    Victor, 138
Adler, Katharina (Kathia)
    Germanischkaja, wife of Friedrich,
    147, 153, 155
  background and marriage, 145
  estrangement from husband, 149
Adler, Max, Austrian leftist theorist, 179
Adler, Solomon Marcus, father of
    Victor, 138
  opposition to son's radicalism, 140
Adler, Victor, 99, 100, 188, 198
  Bauer aided by, 167
  birth and parentage, 138
  death of, 154, 168
  education and youth, 139–40
  financial difficulties of, 141
  German nationalism of, 148
  humanitarianism of, 141–3
  letters edited by son, 155–6
  marriage and family, 141
  medical education and practice, 140,
    141
  opposition to terrorism, 141, 156
  political influence of, 148
  as political prisoner, 143
  relationship with father, 140
  relationship with son, 143–5, 149, 152,
    153
  repressed violence in, 141, 142
  with Second International, 148
  Social Democratic Worker's Party
    founded by, 138, 140–1
  views on World War I, 148–9
adolescence
  aggression of, 157, 267
  identity crisis of, 24, 199, 226, 267;
    in Himmler, 219
  recognized as phase of life, 31
Adorno et al., *The Authoritarian
    Personality*, 26, 229–30
aggression
  adolescent, 157, 267

cause-oriented, in Herzl, 126
equated with strength by Nazis,
    234–5
in infants and young children, 260–3
inherent nature of, 213
inhibitions against, in Bauer, 189,
    194, 196
intellectual, of students, 61
passive, of subordinates, 60–1
of post-World War I German youth,
    253
traits used as "armor" against, 211
Alexander the Great, celibate
    propensities of, 110
Alkalai of Semlin, Rabbi, 103
America (U.S.), psychohistorical
    studies of, 31–2
  of contemporary leaders, 29
  of identity formation in adolescents,
    25
  of racial and ethnic relations, 27
American Historical Association, 16,
    63, 81
American Historical Review,
    psychohistory in, 18
Anabaptists, psychological study of, 29
anal erotic syndrome
  character traits of, 21–2, 223
  creative process identified with, 131
  Luther as example of, 25
  and time awareness, 216–17
  utilization by Nazism, 22
anal-sadistic development phase,
    importance of maternal presence
    during, 261
  regression to, under Nazism, 236,
    264
Angress, Werner T., on young
    Himmler, 210
Anschluss (Austrian union with
    Germany)
  Bauer support for, 170
  forced by Nazis, 137, 187, 188
anti-Semitism
  in Austria, of National Socialist
    party, 173; in Vienna, 1890s, 116–17
  Bauer criticized for, 166
  Herzl's reactions to, 107, 111–12,
    116–17, 119

anti-Semitism (*continued*)
   of Himmler, 228–9, 234–6
   Jewish state as solution for, 102
   of Jews, 120–1, 166
   in Nazi Germany, 27, 119, 234–6,
      270, 278; development of, 22–3
   psychodynamic theories on, 229–30
anxiety-arousing conditions
   aggressive impulses as, 263
   in historical data, 5, 12
   intellectualization as defense against,
      73–4, 77
   projection as defense against, 67
arrests of development, *see* fixation
   points of character development
Aryanism, 236, 264
asceticism as psychotic form of
      repression, 224
   of Himmler, 223–7, 237
Austria
   Anschluss, 137, 170, 187, 188
   class struggle in, 177–81
   crisis of July 1927, 174–5
   Dollfuss government, 184
   First Republic, 161, 168, 169, 173, 179,
      180; end of, 185
   Habsburg dynasty, *see* Habsburg,
      House of
   political parties, 170, 173
   Stürgkh assassinated, 151–2
   in World War I, 167
Austrian Social Democratic Worker's
      party, founding of, 138
   See also Austro-Marxists
Austro-Marxists
   Adler family role in, 137–8, 140–1,
      152, 154
   Bauer role in, 161–2, 173–81, 184–7,
      199–200
   influence in Austria, 136, 147–8, 173
   Linz Program of, 179, 198
   outlawing of, 187
   policy on fascism, 186
   position on nationalities, 163–4
   rightist attacks on, 137, 173–4
authoritarian personalities
   in academic world, 71, 74
   emotional traumas as conditioning
      for, 245

obsessive-compulsive traits in, 26
sadomasochistic traits in, 26

Bach, George R., on father-separated
      children, 264
Bates, Gregory, analysis of Nazi
      propaganda films, 31
Bauer, Helene Gumplowicz Landau,
      wife of Otto, 195
Bauer, Ida (Freud's "Dora"), sister of
      Otto, material from Freud's
      psychoanalysis of, 162, 188
   on brother, 192–3
   family conflict somatized into
      hysterical conversion symptoms,
      199
   fidelity as central concern of, 193–4
   on parents, 173, 189–91, 192–3
Bauer, Käthe Gerber, mother of Otto,
      163
   obsessive-compulsive behavior of,
      183, 190, 194
   son's identification with, 190–2, 194
Bauer, Otto, 99, 100
   Anschluss supporter, 170, 187–8
   as Austro-Marxist leader, 161–2,
      173–6, 181
   closeness to sister, 192–3
   death of, 188
   extramarital affairs, 195–6
   family background, 161–3, 194–5; *see
      also* Bauer, Ida
   flight and exile of, 187–8
   as foreign minister of Austrian
      Republic, 168, 169, 172
   guilt-sharing behavior, 191, 194
   identification with father, 191, 195;
      with mother, 190–2
   identity resolutions, 199, 200
   marriage and family, 195
   military service, 167, 172
   moral righteousness of, 181–2, 191,
      194, 196, 198
   as obsessive personality, 181, 194
   oedipal psychodynamics of, 194, 196
   opinions on Jewish identity and
      nationalism, 165–7

Bauer, Otto (*continued*)
  political style, 168, 170–1, 173–7, 181,
    185–7; psychological sources of,
    190–1, 194, 196, 199
  privacy as political cause, 183–4
  relationship with Kautsky, 170–2
  relationship with young socialists,
    196–8
  Russian internment of, 167–8, 172,
    179
Bauer, Philipp (father of Otto and
    Ida), 161–2, 172, 189
  affair of, 189, 191, 193, 196
  son's identification with, 191
Bein, Alex, biography of Herzl, 108
Bernaschek, Richard, in Schutzbund
    rising, 186–7
Bettelheim, Bruno, on concentration
    camp prisoners, 236
Bion, W. R., group dynamics studies,
    28–9, 68, 161
Bismarck, Otto von, 30, 82, 86, 113, 177
Black Death, survivors of, 82
blind spots in analytical and historical
    perception, 6
  and self-ignorance, 72
Bloch, Marc, historical perspective of,
    12, 16, 249
Blood Purge of 1934, 235–6
Blum, Léon, 188
Bolsheviks
  Friedrich Adler made hero by, 154–5
  and Otto Bauer, 167
  psychological studies of, 29
  and Social Democrats, 136
  See also Lenin; Trotsky
bowel training as aggression and
    control struggle, 262
Branting, Hjalmar, Swedish socialist
    leader, 167
Braunthal, Julius, memoirs of, 143
  on Fritz Adler, 143
  on Otto Bauer, 197
Bridenbaugh, Carl, 63
Brown and Ellithorp, study of
    McCarthy's 1968 presidential
    campaign, 29
Burckhardt, Jacob, 12

Burlingham, Dorothy, on father
    substitutes, 262, 269
Bushman, Richard, 26

Carroll, Peter N., psychobiography of
    Samuel Johnson, 32
castration anxiety
  exacerbated by wartime conditions,
    265, 274
  provoked by graduate student exams,
    54
causation, overdetermination in, 241
change in time as historian's subject
    matter, 11–12
character analysis, importance to
    historians of, 20, 21
character structure
  early formation of, 248; *see also*
    identity formation
  indicated by modes of thought, 21
Charcot, Jean Martin, 140, 141
charismatic personality
  celibate propensities of, 109–10
  Herzl as case study of, 102, 109–10,
    112–13
  libidinal displacement of, 110, 130
childhood
  aggressive behavior of, 261–4
  changes in American concept of, 32
  control developed during, 262
  effects of wartime traumas on, *see*
    World War I in Germany, effect
    of, on infants and children; World
    War II, effects of, on British
    children
  exhibitionistic behavior of, 88
  importance of, in character
    formation, 248
  projection of belief systems from, 67
Christian Social party in Austria,
    173–5, 200
class struggle, Otto Bauer theories on,
    177–83
cleaning compulsion, 183, 190
cohort, concept of, 246–7
  concentration camp survivors as, 247

cohort, concept of (*continued*)
  Hiroshima victims as, 28, 247
  wartime contemporaries as, 248
Collingwood, R. G., on communication
  between historical creators and
  perceivers, 5
communication
  in academic world, 73–7
  definition of, 71–2
  and emotional integrity, 72–3
compulsive character traits, 21–2
  See also obsessive-compulsive
  syndrome
conservancy of evidence, 16
control patterns of behavior,
  development of, 262–3
countertransference
  facilitation of communication by, 4
  importance of in historical research, 3
  processes involved in, 4, 6, 12
  as tool of perception, 4
creative process, elements in, 64–5
  as anal activity, 131
  libidinal excitement in, 130
  narcissistic nature of, 113
  as objectification of private illusion,
  121, 132
cultural modes, transmission of, 247
Czech nationalism, pre–World War I,
  163, 165

Danneberg, Robert, Austro-Marxist
  leader, 155, 168
defense mechanisms
  adaptive role of, 22
  intellectualization, *see*
  intellectualization
  obsessive-compulsive syndrome, *see*
  obsessive-compulsive syndrome
  projection, *see* projection
defensive reactions to historical data, 5,
  12
"democratic" personality, difficulty in
  delineation of, 26
demographic approach to explaining
  Nazism, 242

generational aspects of, 245–6
deprivation as World War I trauma of
  German children, 28, 242, 244,
  249, 251, 254–7, 272–9
  effect on political orientation of,
  265–6
detachment as trait of schizoid
  personality, 215
developmental emphasis in
  psychohistory, 15
developmental phases most vulnerable
  to fixation points, 243
Devereux, George, on
  countertransference in research,
  5
diary, psychological purpose of,
  211
"dictatorship of proletariat," Bauer
  concept of, 178–9, 198
disease, psychic response to, 103
Dollfuss government of Austria, 184,
  185
dominance-submission orientation
  in faculty-student relationships,
  50–1
  of psychohistorical subjects, 26,
  30
double-bind messages, 73
Drang nach Osten (eastward
  expansion) ideology of Germany,
  220
dreams, projection in, 68
Dreyfus case, as influence on Herzl,
  103, 112

economic depression as factor in rise of
  Nazism, 243–4, 249, 253
ego psychology, psychohistorian's use
  of, 20, 23
  Erikson contributions to, 24
  interpretation of anti-Semitism, 230
  and libido psychology, 22
  use in psychobiography, 24–6
  See also object relations
Einstein, Albert, 12, 129
  and Fritz Adler, 144–7

Elkins, Stanley, study of American slavery, 27
emotional traumas
   age as factor in impact of, 248
   as conditioning for fixations, 243–5
   of German children in World War I, 28, 241, 244, 249, 251, 254–7, 259, 272–80
   shared by "cohort," 246–9
Engel, George, psychoanalytic studies of, 88, 232
Engels, Friedrich, 178
   and Victor Adler, 142
enuresis, as indication of hostility, 192
Erzberger, Mathias, 255
evaluation of work, and personality of evaluator, 76–7
exhibitionism
   of Adolf Hitler, 87
   shame as defensive reaction against, 87–9

"Fascism" ("F") scale, 26
faculty–graduate student relations
   communication problems of, 73–5
   domination-submission orientation of, 50–2, 55
   evaluative functions, 60
   generational scholastic conflicts, 61
   grants and awards as pawns in, 50, 60
   projection mechanism of teacher, 69–70
   reducing traumas of, 56–8
   sadomasochism in, 56
   transference reactions in, 48–56
Fairbairn, Ronald
   object-relational model applied to Bismarck, 30
   on schizoid personality, 215
family, behavior patterns and character defenses shaped by, 32–3, 89
family background, emphasis on, in psychohistory, 15
fantasies, 128–9
   conscious and unconscious, 128

consideration of, in psychohistory, 15–16
   diary as medium for, 211
   disease-induced, 103
   male, of rescuing prostitutes, 150
   and masturbation, 217
   neurotic and non-neurotic, 128
   objectification of, in creative process, 121, 129, 132
   as projection of feelings, 68
   revelation of character in, 121
   use by Herzl as preparation for action, 129–32
father-child relationship
   development of, in infancy, 269
   psychological impact of father's wartime absence, 266–7, 269–72
Federn, Paul, 1919 prediction of German dictatorship, 268
Fenichel, Otto
   on time factor in German anti-Semitism, 22–3
   on stage fright, 88
Ferenczi, Sandor, "The Ontogenesis of the Interest in Money," 21
Feyerabend, Paul, relativism about "truth" and "reality" of, 65
Fischer, Ernst, on Bauer's Jewish affiliations, 163
fixation points of character development, 240–6
   of post–World War I German youth, 240–1
Forgie, George, study of Lincoln generation of Americans, 28
France, psychohistorical studies
   of family relationships in, 32
   of French Revolution power elite, 29
Franklin, Benjamin, diplomatic skills related to family experiences, 26
Frenkel-Brunswik, Else, on authoritarian personality, 245
Freud, Anna, work in ego psychology, 23
   analysis of Walter Langer, 89
   on infant and child development, 262, 269
   on repression and asceticism, 223–4

Freud, Sigmund
  on adolescent crisis, 267
  on anality and sadism, 21
  on biological-cultural conflict, 33
  career advice to Otto Bauer, 196
  case study of "Dora," *see* Bauer, Ida
  on generational conflict, 61
  migration metaphor of, 242
  on overdetermination of causation,
    16
  on projection, 68
  on psychoanalytical process, 4–6, 16,
    21
  transference first conceptualized by,
    189
  and Victor Adler, 139–40
  Vienna residence of, 138
  works on culture and history, 19–20
Friedländer, Saul, on psychohistory,
  19
frustration, feelings of
  during creative process, 64
  handling of, as concern of
    psychohistory, 30

gambling, psychoanalytical meaning of,
  108
Gandhi, Mahatma, Erikson
    psychobiography of, 25
gastrointestinal disturbances,
    psychogenic causes of, 237
generation unit, common destiny as
    influence on, 246
Germany
  aftermath of World War I in, 254
  eastward expansionary ambitions,
    220
  Great Depression in, 243–4, 249, 253
  immigration to, in 1920s, 253
  Industrial Revolution in, 254
  "inner emigration" in, in 1930s, 185
  Kaiser, symbolic importance of, 268
  leaders, psychohistorical studies of,
    see Bismarck; Himmler; Hitler
  post–World War I youth in, 25,
    252–3; *see also* World War I
  putsch attempt, July 20, 1944, 186

rise of dictatorship predicted 1919,
    268
  seizure of Austria, 137, 187, 188
  values emphasized in childhood, 211
  World War I, *see* World War I
Geyl, Pieter, Dutch historian, 261–3
Glaeser, Ernst, *Jahrgang 1902*, 271–2
Gorky, Maxim, *Mother*, 167
  as image of Russian identity
    formation, 25
graduate students
  academic awards and grants for, 60
  aggressive reactions of, 52–4, 60–1
  attrition of, 50–1
  coping devices of, 63–4
  duration of study, 50, 56
  examinations, 53–4, 56
  identification with authority, 55–6
  infantilization of, 50–1
  psychodynamic education for, 78–9
  relationship with faculty, *see*
    faculty–graduate student relations
  relationship with peers, 53
  separation anxiety in, 55
  transference regression in, 48–52,
    55–6
Grazie, Maria E. delle, on Herzl's
    marital relationship, 110
Greenson, Ralph, "therapeutic
    alliance" of, 19
Greven, Philip, psychohistorical study
    of American Revolution, 32
Group for the Use of Psychology in
    History, The, 18
guilt feelings
  handling of by Nazis, 234–5
  in son of absent father, 270
Guntrip, Harry, on Himmler, 214, 215,
    220

Habsburg, House of
  dissolution of, 154, 168
  Franz Josef, 147
  prenational character of, 163
Hainfeld, Congress of (founding of the
    Austrian Social Democratic
    Worker's Party), 140

Hall, Jenny Waelder, professional
    relationships with Langers, 85
Hallgarten, Wolfgang, Himmler
    reference to, 228
Hansfstaengl, Ernst, on Himmler's
    father, 216
Harrison, G. B., on academic diversity,
    75
Hartmann, Heinz, interest in
    psychohistory, 23, 46
Heiber, Helmut, on paradoxes of
    Himmler, 209–10
Heimwehr rightist party, 170
    Christian Democrat alliance with,
    174
Heinrich, prince of Bavaria, godfather
    of Himmler, 216
Heisenberg, Werner, on experimenter's
    impact on experiment, 12
Herzl, Julie Naschauer, as wife of
    Theodor, 109, 110, 112
Herzl, Theodor
    Altneuland, 109
    and anti-Semitism, 107, 111–12, 116–17,
        119–21, 127
    attitudes toward the powerful and
        toward subordinates, 125–6, 129–31
    cause-oriented nature of
        relationships, 126–7
    commitment to Zionism, 110–21,
        127–33
    death of, 127–8
    death of sister, 103, 124
    Der Judenstaat, 115, 126
    Diaries, 112–13
    gambling episode of, 107–8
    interest in appearances of, 116
    libido model of genetic psychosexual
        development for, 131
    marriage, 109–10
    messianic drives and fantasies, 103–4
        113, 115, 124, 127, 130, 132–3
    moodiness and melancholia, 106–7,
        110
    New Ghetto, The, 111–12, 120
    plan for Christian conversion of
        Jews, 111, 119–20
    relationship with parents, 103, 104,
        108, 109, 125, 131

    respect for technology, 118
    role in changing Jewish character,
        119–31
    and Arthur Schnitzler, 112
    self-revelation in creative writing,
        102–3, 109, 111–13, 120, 122–5
    sexual orientation of, 104–6, 130–1
    theatricality of, 115–17
    use of fantasy, 129–30, 132
    venereal infection, 104–5
    view of politics, 117
    vision of Jewish state and citizens,
        102, 123–4, 129
    Zionist accomplishments of, 128,
        132–3
Hess, Robert D., on children's
    recognition of leaders, 266
Himmler, Gebhard, father of Heinrich,
    215–16, 226
Himmler, Heinrich
    adolescent concerns of, 236–7
    anti-Semitism of, 228–9
    asceticism of, 223–7, 237
    attitudes toward women, 211, 217–18,
        220, 221, 223–5
    bureaucratic talents of, 232
    career interest in animal husbandry,
        219, 233
    concern with detail, 211–12, 216
    diaries of, 210–11; absence of
        expressed feelings in, 211, 212;
        concern with detail reflected in,
        211–12
    dueling of, 230–1
    family background, 215
    food and gastrointestinal functions,
        importance of, 219, 222–3, 232–3
    garrulousness as concern of, 223
    identification with Hitler of, 229,
        233
    identity diffusion crisis of, 219
    latent homosexuality of, 208, 221,
        222, 231–2
    liquidation of Jews, 234–6
    militaristic interests of, 218, 220–1,
        230–1, 233
    nationalistic drives of, 218, 220
    in Nazi party, 233–7
    paradoxes in personality, 209–11

Himmler, Heinrich (*continued*)
personality decompensation in final
days of, 236
"racial" concerns of, 219, 226, 227
relationship with father, 226–8, 231
relationship with mother, 220, 223,
225, 231
religious conflict of, 230, 233
sadomasochistic manifestations of,
222, 224
schizoid manifestations of, 215, 220
sexual tendencies and behavior, 217,
221, 224
social values instilled in childhood, 211
status consciousness of, 216, 221
strength and control as concern of,
217–19, 221, 225–7, 231, 237
superego structure of, 214
timetable obsession of, 216, 228
view of masculinity, 217, 220–1, 223
Hiroshima bombing as group trauma,
28, 247
Hirsch, Baron de, and Herzl, 120
Historian, The, psychohistory in, 18
historians
relativists, 12
self-understanding important for, 242
subjectivity of, 4, 12, 13–15, 19
See also psychohistorians
historical data
anxiety-arousing content in, 5–6
historian's personality as part of, 12
interpretation of, choice of theories
for, 19
perception of unconscious themes in,
3, 15
psychohistorian's approach to, *see*
psychohistorians; psychohistory
selection and distortion of, 6
time factor in, 11–12
historical identity, concept of, 24–5
historical research and psychoanalysis,
shared elements in, 3–7, 16–19
History of Childhood Quarterly, The,
see *Journal of Psychohistory, The*
Hitler, Adolf
assexual propensities of, 110
Himmler identification with, 229,
233–4

idealization of, by Nazi movement,
264, 270, 278, 279
Mein Kampf as source on, 25
studies of, 31, 83, 86, 87
Holocaust of Nazi Germany
effect on Jews of, 119
Himmler's role in, 234–5
as a human phenomenon, 213
homosexuality
latent in Himmler, 208, 221, 222,
232
tendencies toward, intensified by
paternal absence, 265, 270, 274
Hoover Commission, 258
Horowitz, David, psychohistorical
study of American Revolution,
32
housewife's psychosis, 183, 190
Hughes, Judith, psychohistorical study
of Bismarck, 30
hypochondria in
narcissistic-exhibitionistic
personalities, 88, 89

ideal analyst/historian defined by
Freud, 6–7
idealization
of absent parent, 265, 269
of leaders, 266
of projected self-image, 56, 70–1; in
romantic love, 72
identification
with aggressor, 120
as aid to communication, 72
of Fritz Adler with father, 158
of graduate student with instructor,
55–7, 60
Himmler pattern of, 214, 229
identity diffusion
of Himmler, 219, 236
resolution of, by anti-Semitism, 230,
236
identity formation
adolescent crisis of, 24, 226, 267; in
Himmler, 219
Erikson's concept of, 24, 76–7
and persecution, 69

"immersion" approach in historical
  research, 3
inferiority feelings in preparatory
  period for creative work, 64
Inge, William, on psychoanalysis, 77
initiation rite, doctoral examination as,
  54
insight
  in creative process, 64
  psychoanalytical meaning of, 19
intellectualization
  and ambivalence of communication,
    72, 77
  as defense mechanism of academics,
    73–4, 77; of Otto Bauer, 181
intelligence services, psychodynamic
  studies of foreign leaders, 17
irrationality as force in history, 15,
  242
Israel, Herzl's role in founding of,
  101

Jackson, Andrew, Rogin biography of,
  27
Jahoda, Marie, and Otto Bauer, 196
James, Henry, on personalized nature
  of novel, 121
James, William, father identification of,
  26
Jaques, Elliott, uses of projection, 68
Jencks, Christopher, recommendation
  on graduate education, 78
Jesus on asceticism of disciples, 110
Jews
  assimilation proposals, 165–6; by
    Christian conversion, 111, 119–20,
    138
  Bauer views on identity and
    nationalism of, 165–7
  character change in 20th century,
    118–20
  in Nazi death camps, 236
  prejudice against, *see* anti-Semitism
  return to Jerusalem of, 119; *see also*
    Zionism
  self-hatred of, 120–1, 166
  traditional values of, 119

Johnson, Adelaide, on parent-to-child
  transmission of antisocial
  impulses, 156
*Journal of Interdisciplinary History,
  The,* 18
Journal of Modern History,
  psychohistory issue, 18
Journal of Psychohistory, The, 18

Kana, Heinrich, friendship with Herzl,
  104, 126
Karl Marx Association founded by
  Fritz Adler, 149
Kautsky, Karl, 150, 151, 168
  relationship with Bauer, 170–2, 194
  theory of passive socialist revolution,
    170–1
Kerensky government of Russia, Bauer
  support for, 168
Kersten, Felix, on Himmler, 232
Keynes, John Maynard, on post–World
  War I conditions in Germany, 257
Klein, Melanie, 68, 262
Kleinian theory and Tavistock model
  of group dynamics, 28–9
Klemperer, Klemens von, biography of
  Seipel, 176
Kohut, Heinz, on narcissistic
  personality, 88–9
Körner, Theodor, Schutzbund general,
  187
Kreissler, Felix, criticism of Social
  Democrats, 137
Kuhn, Thomas, "paradigm shift"
  theory of scientific revolutions, 65

Labor Aid Project founded by Fritz
  Adler, 155
Landbund agrarian party in Austria, 173
Langer, Susanne K., 85
Langer, Walter
  as analysand of Anna Freud, 89–90
  memoir of 1930s European
    experiences, 89–92
  work on Hitler study for OSS, 83, 85

Langer, William L., 81–8
  advocacy of appeasement, 86, 88
  loss of father, 82–3
  praise of Bismarck, 86
  psychoanalysis of, 85
  relationship with mother, 93–4
  role in development of
    psychohistory, 16, 46, 47, 81, 94
  stage fright of, 84–5, 87
  study of Black Death, 82–3
  work with OSS and CIA, 17, 83,
    92–3
language, use of
  associated with oral psychogenetic
    phase, 131
  in Nazi references to death camps,
    236
  revelation of character in, 121
Laqueur, Walter, on German youth
  movement, 252
Lasswell, Harold
  on development of political man, 26
  on Hitler as mother figure, 264
Lazarsfeld, Paul S., and Otto Bauer, 196
leaders, recognition and idealization of,
  by children, 266
leadership
  cause-oriented in Herzl, 126
  Nazi, treated as unique phenomenon,
    212
  qualities of, that promote
    cooperation, 75
  as reflection of group goals, 161–2
  sought as defense against internal
    conflict, 200
  vacillating style of Bauer, 200
leadership groups, psychohistorical
  studies of, 28–9
Leichter, Käthe
  criticism of Social Democrats, 137
  in Ravensbruck concentration camp,
    155
Leichter, Otto, biography of Bauer,
  190
Lenin, V. I., 126, 154, 166, 170, 177, 198
Leser, Norbert, on Austrian resistance
  to fascism, 186, 187
Lifton, Robert Jay, Hiroshima study,
  247

Lincoln, Abraham, 94
  generational group study of, 28
Linz Program of Austro-Socialists, 179,
  198
Loewald, Hans, on transference and
  resistance, 4
Loewenstein, Rudolph, work in ego
  psychology, 23
love
  divorced from erotic feelings in
    Herzl, 104
  as idealization of self-image, 72
Lueger, Karl, mayor of Vienna, 116–17,
  169
Luther, Martin, Erikson biography of,
  25
Luxemburg, Rosa, 170

McCarthy, Eugene, 1968 presidential
  campaign, 29
McGrath, William, 100
  psychohistorical study of Viennese
    culture, 32
Mahler, Margaret, on infant-mother
  relation, 261, 262
Mann, Thomas, "Disorder and Early
  Sorrow," 275
Mannheim, Karl, "The Sociological
  Problem of Generations," 245–6
Marmorek, Hilda, affair with Otto
  Bauer, 195–6
masochistic inclinations in
  mother-reared sons, 265, 270
mass movements, desire to merge in,
  262, 279
masturbation
  Bauer concern with, 191
  Himmler concern with, 217
  massage as related gratification, 232
Merkl, Peter H., on political
  mobilization, 278
Meyer, Donald, on psychoanalytic
  biography, 29
Meynert, Theodor, and Adler, 140
Michels, Robert, study of European
  Marxist parties, 137, 161, 172
Mierendorff, Carl, on Nazi youth, 252

Miller, Susanne, study of German Social Democratic party, 137
Moller, Herbert, on Nazi youth, 253
Money-Kyrle, R. E., 68
mother-child relationship, basic role of in child's personality development, 260–2
  in absence of father, 265, 270
mothering, inadequate, Nazism as compensation for, 264
murderous impulses
  defenses against, 263
  as displacement of familial aggression, 156–7
  in young children, 263
Mussolini, Benito, 185
Musto, David, work in psychohistory, 26, 29

narcissistic personalities, 88–9
  charisma as trait of, 113
  creativity as trait of, 113
  teachers and scholars as, 92, 54, 56
nationalism as Austrian problem, 163–4
nationalistic chauvinism, childhood development of, 266
nationalization of Austrian industry, Bauer policy on, 169–70
National Socialism, *see* Nazi movement
Nazi concentration camps as group trauma, 247
Nazi movement
  anti-Semitism of, 22–3, 27, 119, 234–6, 270, 278
  appeal to German youth, 250–1; traumatic conditioning of, 264, 270, 278–80
  compulsive personality traits compatible with, 22
  electoral ascendancy of, 250
  Himmler in, *see* Himmler
  leadership caste, psychoanalytical study of, 29
  mass phenomena of, 82

  paramilitary party organizations of, 240
  political personality studies of, 26
  psychological function of, 264
  racial purity obsession of, 219
  seizure of power by, 184
Neck, Rudolf, on Schutzbund uprising, 187
Nelson, Rowena Morse, marriage to William Langer, 85–6
Nevinson, Henry W., on effects of World War I in Germany, 257
nomenclature variations in psychodynamic therapies, 19

object relations
  definition of, 30
  displacement to animals, 219
  as framework for analyzing academia, 46
  and gastrointestinal disturbances, 232
  of Himmler, 214
  theory versus libido theory, 22, 30, 46
obsessive-compulsive syndrome, 22, 147, 148
  and authoritarian ideologies, 26
  of Bauer, 181
  Freud description of, 168, 213
  gastrointestinal disturbances related to, 232
  of Himmler, 213
  and Nazism, 22, 213
oedipal psychodynamics
  aggression toward love object, 261
  of Bauer, 194, 196
  of Herzl, 108
  intensified by paternal absence, 265, 270, 273, 274
oral erotic syndrome, 234
  time as concern of, 217
oral rage of infant, 261
oral sadistic development phase, 261
Osterreichische Alpine Montangesellschaft, role of, in

Osterreichische (*continued*)
  Austrian Republic's overthrow,
    170
overdetermination in causation of
  historical events, 16, 241

Pan German political party, 173
"paradigm shift" theory of scientific
  revolution, 65
parental absence, effects of
  on British children in World War II,
    269–70
  on German youth of World War I,
    240, 241, 259, 265–7, 269–70, 278;
    compensatory role of Nazism, 264,
    270, 278
parenting modes, linkage with group
  behavior, 33
Parsons, Talcott, object-relations
  model, 34
Pernerstorfer, Engelbert, and Adler,
  138, 188
personal identity, Erikson definition of,
  24
Pflanze, Otto, psychohistory of
  Bismarck, 30
phase specificity concepts applied in
  history, 28
Pinson, Koppel, on Carl Mierendorff,
  252
Pirenne, Henri, Belgian historian, 61–3
political concepts, childhood formation
  of, 265–6
political man, Lasswell formula for
  development of, 26
Potter, David, study of American
  national character, 33
power elite, psychoanalytic studies of,
  28–9
preconscious mind as source of
  creativity, 64
"primal anxiety" of young child, 262
privacy as issue in Bauer's life and
  theories, 183–4
projection
  defensive use of, 67–8

and anti-Semitism, 229–30, 244
as block to understanding, 68
by children, in wartime, 266
defined, 30
in dreams, 68
of good qualities, 69–71
by Himmler, 225, 234
intellectual, *see* intellectualization
of negative qualities, 69, 71; onto
  outside groups, 244
propaganda, German, World War II
  studies of, 31
Protestantism as psychological force,
  22, 32
psychoanalysis
  analogues with historical research,
    3–5
  clinical data produced by, 7;
    synthesis of, 21
  in graduate education, 56, 78–9
  nonmedical researchers trained in, 17
  timeless quality of, 22
  transference phenomenon in, 49–50
psychoanalytic situation, 4
psychobiography, leaders as subjects of,
  25, 29–30
  use of tools of literary criticism for,
    121
psychodynamic theories, schools of, 19
psychohistorians
  academic locus of, 46–7
  graduate education of, *see* graduate
    students, psychodynamic
    education for
  relativism of, 45
  self-analysis by, 7, 45
  subjectivity of, 46
psychohistory
  countertransference phenomenon in,
    3–5, 14–15
  Freud's work as basis of, 19–20
  objection of critics to, 18–19
  object relations model of social
    internalization applied to, 34
  proposed by William Langer, 81
  static versus variable elements in,
    46
  unconscious themes in, 3, 14

psychohistory (*continued*)
  universities offering doctoral degrees
    in, 18
  value-neutral nature of, 33
  Psychohistory Review, The, 18
psycholinguistic studies of Nazi press
    and radio, 31
psychosocial identity, 24
  of national groups, 25
publications on psychohistory, 18
Puritanism, American, psychohistorical
    studies of childhood, 32
puritanism, aspects of, in Nazism, 264

racial prejudice in America, 27
racial purity as Nazi theme, 236, 264
Rathenau, Walter, assassination, 233
reaction formation, 213
  idealization of absent father as, 264
  used as defense against impulses, 263
reality testing
  in academic environment, 75–6, 78
  damaged by wartime conditions, 265
  failure of, in Himmler, 236
  of Zionist cause by Herzl, 132
regression, 213
  of graduate students, 49–55
  of Himmler, 214, 215
  and Nazism, 213
  to points of fixation, 242–3
  in service of the ego, 64; by Herzl,
    131–3
Reich, Wilhelm
  compulsive character delineated by,
    21
  psychodynamic model of, applied to
    Bismarck, 30
Reik, Theodor, on third ear, 6
relativism
  and creativity, 65
  of psychohistorians, 45
Renner, Karl
  as Austrian chancellor, 168, 170
  Fritz Adler attacks on, 151–2
  plan for Austro-Hungarian
    nationalities, 164
  policies of, 188

repression
  as force in Nazi movement, 213, 234–5
  psychotically manifested in
    asceticism, 223–4, 227
  of schizoid personality, 215
Riesman, David, on graduate
    education, 78
Riviere, Joan, on infant rage, 260, 262
Rogin, Michael Paul, biography of
    Andrew Jackson, 27
Röhm, Ernst, and Himmler, 233
Rorschach test, race prejudice as
    cultural version of, 26
Russian adolescent, identity formation
    of, 25
Russian Revolution, Kerensky
    government of, 167–8
Ryder, Norman, on cohort analysis,
    247–8

Sachs, Hanns, analysis of Langer, 85
sadism
  associated with anal erotic
    syndrome, 21–2
  associated with pseudo-male sex role,
    221
  masked in young Himmler, 217
sadomasochism
  and authoritarian ideologies, 26
  in graduate student–faculty
    relationship, 56
  manifested in Himmler, 222
Salem witch trials, psychohistorical
    studies of, 32
Schirach, Baldur von, 252
schizoid personality, 213, 215
  double-bind message in development
    of, 73
  Himmler as, 213, 215, 220
Schnitzler, Arthur, and Herzl, 112
Schorske, Carl E., 100, 172
  historical studies of German social
    democracy, 137; of Viennese
    culture, 32
  on William Langer, 85
Schumpeter, Joseph, 169
Schutzbund 1934 rising, 186–7

Sears, David O., on affect and
information, 266
Seipel, Ignaz
as Austrian chancellor, 173–6, 200
on socialization commission, 169
Seitz, Karl, party chairman of Austrian
Social Democrats, 148, 152, 167,
168, 188
Sempell, Charlotte, psychohistorical
study of Bismarck, 30
separation anxiety of graduate
students, 55
separation and individuation phase in
child's personality development,
262
sexual attitudes
of Herzl, 103–5
of Himmler, 217, 220–2
psychohistorical interest in, 15–16, 30
sexual drive organization, fixations in,
243
sexualization of graduate student
exams, 54
sexual viewpoint in academic training,
45–6
shame reactions of
narcissistic-exhibitionistic
personalities, 87–9, 92
Smith, Bradley F., study of Himmler,
208, 209, 210
Social Democratic parties of Europe
Austrian party, *see* Austro-Marxists
on eve of World War I, 7, 148
Fritz Adler's work with, 155
German party, 251
rightist and leftist criticisms of, 137
Second International, 148
social internalization, Parson's
psychoanalytic model of, 34
social legislation
Victor Adler as advocate of, 142–3
in Vienna of 1920s, 136
Spitz, René, studies of hospitalism, 261,
262
splitting of "good" and "bad" by
wartime children, 266
stage fright of William Langer, 84–5,
87, 88
Stalin, Josef, 26, 166

Steiner, Herbert, criticism of Social
Democrats, 137
Stekel, Wilhelm, on analytic blind
spots, 6
Strasser, Gregor, 250–1
Streifler, Heinrich, on Nazi political
ascendancy, 250
Strout, Cushing, biography of William
James, 26
Stürgkh, Count Karl, assassination of,
152–3
subconscious mind as source of
creativity, 64
subjectivity of historians, 4, 12–15, 19
sublimation
of family conflict by Otto Bauer, 199
as force in Nazi movement, 213
superego, weakness of
in Himmler, 233–4
political manifestations of:
authoritarianism, 245; nationalism,
244; violence, 244
as result of emotional traumas, 244
Suval, Stanley, on Bauer as foreign
minister, 170
symbols, emotional meaning of, 16

Tarn, W. W., on Alexander the Great,
110
Tavistock model of group dynamics,
28–9
therapeutic alliance, 19
"third ear" of Theodor Reik, 6
thought modes and character structure,
21
time awareness in oral and anal
eroticism, 216–17
time factor in history, 11, 12, 22–4
transference
cure of Himmler's stomach pains, 232
first conceptualized by Freud, 189, 193
regression of graduate student, 48–56
resolution of, in psychoanalysis, 4
role of, in psychoanalysis, 49–50
susceptibility of historians to, 5
Treitschke, Heinrich von, anti-Semitic
essay of, 120

Trotsky, Leon, Adlers' association
with, 147, 148, 154
Tucker, Robert, psychobiography of
Stalin, 26

unconscious
memory, importance to analyst of,
4–6
themes in psychohistory, 3, 14, 15
U.S. Office of Strategic Services (OSS),
psychodynamic studies by, 17, 31

Vienna
Adler family residence, 138
as Austro-Marxist social model, 136
Bauer family residence, 138, 163
Freud family residence, 138
Volksrecht (Zurich), 146, 151

Waite, R. G. L., psychobiography of
Hitler, 31
Wandruszka, Adam, on Bauer, 181, 197,
199
Wangh, Martin, on Nazi youth, 270
wartime contemporaries as cohort,
248
Weber, Max, 61
on charismatic personalities, 109–10
on Protestant capitalist culture,
22
Wheelis, Allen, on stage fright, 88
Wilson, Woodrow, personality study
of, 21
Winnicott, D. W., 157, 262, 263, 269

Wistrich, Robert, on Bauer's racial
categorizations, 166
Wohl, Robert, on Langer, 81
women
attitudes toward, of Herzl, 103–5; of
Himmler, 211, 217–18, 220–1, 223–5;
of Nazis, 270
wartime role of, impact on sons,
265, 270
World War I in
Austria and Hungary, 167, 169:
Adler family views on, 148–9;
Bauer service in, 167
Germany: birth and death rates in,
255–6; blockade of, 254; effect of,
on infants and children, 28, 241,
244, 249, 251, 254–7, 59; as
emotional conditioning for
Nazism, 240–4; famine, 254–6;
industrial production and
employment, 258–9
Russia, 167
World War II, effects of, on British
children, 269
World Zionist Organization created by
Herzl, 128

Zangwill, Israel, Zionist writer, 110
Zeisel, Hans, and Otto Bauer, 196
Zionism developed by Herzl, 101,
112–21, 128
Altneuland as vision for, 123–4
Balfour Declaration, 128
banner designed for, 116
Bauer views on, 165
first Zionist Congress, 116
institutional structures created for,
128

A NOTE ABOUT THE AUTHOR

Peter Loewenberg is a professor of history at the University of California, Los Angeles, and a member of the faculty of the Southern California Psychoanalytic Institute and the Los Angeles Psychoanalytic Society and Institute. Born in Hamburg in 1933, he attended the University of California at Santa Barbara, did graduate work at the Free University in Berlin, and received his Ph.D. in 1965 from the University of California at Berkeley. Dr. Loewenberg integrates the careers of university historian and research psychoanalyst with a clinical practice. He has served on the editorial boards of the *Journal of the American Psychoanalytic Association, The Historian,* and *The Psychohistory Review*; holds the Franz Alexander Prize in Psychoanalysis; and is a member of the Center for Advanced Psychoanalytic Study at Princeton. He has published and lectured widely in America, Europe, and Israel; his writings are on modern German and Austrian history, European cultural and intellectual history, psychohistory, and racism and anti-Semitism. He is the recipient of fellowships and awards from the John Simon Guggenheim Memorial Foundation, National Endowment for the Humanities, Austrian Institute, Ford Foundation, Rockefeller Foundation, American Council of Learned Societies, Social Science Research Council, and German Fulbright Commission.

A NOTE ON THE TYPE

The text of this book was set via computer-driven cathode-ray tube in a face
called Times Roman, designed by Stanley Morison for The Times (London),
and first introduced by that newspaper in 1932.

Among typographers and designers of the twentieth century, Stanley
Morison has been a strong forming influence, as typographical advisor to the
English Monotype Corporation, as a director of two distinguished English
publishing houses, and as a writer of sensibility, erudition, and keen practical
sense.

Composed, printed, and bound by The Haddon Craftsmen, Inc.,
Scranton, Pennsylvania

Typography by Joe Marc Freedman